FROM ENLIGHTENMENT TO REVOLUTION

Eric Voegelin

FROM ENLIGHTENMENT
TO REVOLUTION

Edited by John H. Hallowell

Duke University Press   Durham, North Carolina   1975

© 1975, Duke University Press

L.C.C. card no. 74–81864

I.S.B.N. 0–8223–0326–4

PRINTED IN THE UNITED STATES
OF AMERICA BY KINGSPORT PRESS

CONTENTS

EDITOR'S PREFACE

The present volume consists of a portion of an unpublished history of political ideas which Eric Voegelin wrote in the nineteen forties and early fifties. His reluctance to publish the history at the time it was written stemmed in part from a growing conviction that such a history, however well-conceived and executed, could not penetrate the depths of consciousness from which such a history emerges. Too often the history of political ideas is presented as an on-going argument about commonly perceived problems of social order; it thus assumes a continuity of argument and a universal community of discourse which in fact does not exist. The sentiments, passions and experiences of which ideas are the crystallization tend to be ignored and arguments are generated about the validity of ideas as though the ideas had a life and a reality of their own. It is the experiences which give rise to ideas which should engage our attention if we want to understand both the human promise and the human predicament.

Accordingly Professor Voegelin put aside the history of political ideas and embarked upon a much more ambitious undertaking. He became more and more convinced that it was societies and not ideas that were the real entities and that societies express themselves in history through a variety of complex symbols. More and more he has turned his attention to the role of myth in history and to the relationships between myth, philosophy and revelation. He was invited to give the Walgreen Lectures at the University of Chicago in 1951 and these lectures were published the following year under the title *The New Science of Politics*. He examined in these lectures the Christian symbolism by means of which the Western world sought to understand itself and focused attention upon the distortion of this symbolism in various forms of Gnosticism—religious, intellectual and political. He showed how the Christian promise of salvation beyond history became in its Gnostic derailment the promise of perfection both of man and of society in history.[1]

1. He elaborated upon the phenomenon of Gnosticism in *Wissenschaft, Politik und Gnosis* (Munich, 1959). This work has been published in English under the title *Science, Politics and Gnosticism* (Chicago, Henry Regnery Co., 1968). The temptation to transmute the Christian promise of salvation beyond history into the promise of perfection upon earth in time is not, he shows here, peculiar to the Christian experience and faith but the same phenomenon can be found in Jewish, Islamic and Hellenic cultures. "The temptation to fall from a spiritual height that brings the element of uncertainty into final clarity down into the more solid certainty of world-immanent, sensible fulfillment . . . seems to be a general human problem" (Op. cit., p. 114).

In abbreviated form *The New Science of Politics* anticipated the present work in which he is engaged and a portion of which has already appeared in three volumes, namely *Order and History*. The first volume *Israel and Revelation* appeared in 1956, followed in 1957 by two additional volumes, *The World of the Polis* and *Plato and Aristotle*. Two more volumes will appear under the titles *In Search of Order* and *The Ecumenic Age*. This remarkable intellectual achievement, which may well become a landmark of twentieth-century scholarship, invites by its broad scope and profound insights comparison with the work of such men as Hegel, Spengler and Toynbee. While it shares with these works an attempt to elucidate a philosophy of history, it respects the ultimate mystery of human existence and claims to have found but one constant in history, "the constancy of a process that leaves a trail of equivalent symbols in time and space."[2] Professor Voegelin's philosophy is, perhaps, best summarized in the Platonic experience of tension. He explains it by saying:

> Existence has the structure of the In-Between, of the Platonic *metaxy*, and if anything is constant in the history of mankind it is the language of tension between life and death, immortality and mortality, perfection and imperfection, time and timelessness, between order and disorder, truth and untruth, sense and senselessness of existence; between *amor Dei* and *amor sui*, *l'âme ouverte* and *l'âme close;* between the virtues of openness toward the ground of being such as faith, hope and love and the vices of infolding closure such as hybris and revolt; between the moods of joy and despair; and between alienation in its double meaning of alienation from the world and alienation from God. If we split these pairs of symbols, and hypostatize the poles of the tension as independent entities, we destroy the reality of existence as it has been experienced by the creators of the tensional symbolisms; we lose consciousness and intellect; we deform our humanity and reduce ourselves to a state of quiet despair or activist conformity to the "age", of drug addiction or television watching, of hedonistic stupor or murderous possession of truth, of suffering from the absurdity of existence or indulgence in any divertissement (in Pascal's sense) that promises to substitute as a "value" for reality lost. In the language of Heraclitus and Plato: Dream life usurps the place of wake life.[3]

2. "Equivalences of Experience and Symbolization in History," unpublished ms., p. 23.

3. Ibid., p. 7. For an introduction to Professor Voegelin, the man and the scholar, the reader is referred to William C. Havard, "The Changing Pattern of

Although these words represent Professor Voegelin's most recent expression of the experience of tension in existence the same insight, if not the same words, is to be found in the detailed analysis of the ideas of the men whom we shall encounter in the pages of this book. Dream life usurping the place of wake life is the theme of this volume when reason torn loose from its moorings in the ground of being seeks to create man-made constructions of reality in place of the mysterious reality of God's creation. It is for some, perhaps, a comforting but nevertheless dangerous illusion of the modern world that man can create a reality more to his liking and a human "nature" unflawed by the defects which an earlier tradition assumed it was necessary to live with. With increasing emphasis upon the self, and what some have praised as the "liberation" of selfish passions and desires from noetic control and restraint, the self-proclaimed autonomy of reason ends in the enslavement of reason to passion. What starts out in the so-called Age of Enlightenment as nothing more formidable than a dream, even an absurd dream, turns out in the twentieth century to be a living nightmare. Professor Voegelin in the pages which follow traces step by step through a detailed analysis of the works of a number of representative thinkers of the modern age how this eighteenth-century dream of immanent progress turns into the Gnostic political mass movements of contemporary times. What many regard as the political crisis of our times is shown to be a deeply rooted spiritual crisis that challenges the very substance of our humanity. With faithful attention to the texts themselves Professor Voegelin uncovers sentiments that previous analysts of the same texts have sometimes overlooked. He rejects the conventional interpretations of these thinkers when those interpretations are simply not borne out by a careful reading of their own work. He refuses, quite rightly, to assume that the ideas to be found in these works have some kind of existence or authenticity apart from the sentiments and experiences which generated them.

It was the editor's hope in persuading Professor Voegelin to release these manuscripts for publication that they would be helpful not only in shedding new light on some well-known thinkers of the modern age but helpful to the reader who wants better to understand the path which Professor Voegelin has followed to his present undertaking.

JOHN H. HALLOWELL

Voegelin's Conception of History and Consciousness," *The Southern Review*, 7 no. 1 (January, 1971), 49–67. See also Ellis Sandoz, "The Foundations of Voegelin's Political Theory," *The Political Science Reviewer*, 1 (Fall, 1971), 30–73.

FROM ENLIGHTENMENT TO REVOLUTION

I. THE EMERGENCE OF SECULARIZED HISTORY: BOSSUET AND VOLTAIRE

The eighteenth century has been variously characterized as the century of Enlightenment and Revolution or alternatively as the Age of Reason. Whatever the merit of these designations, they embody a denial of cognitive value to spiritual experiences, attest to the atrophy of Christian transcendental experiences and seek to enthrone the Newtonian method of science as the only valid method of arriving at truth. The apostatic revolt, for such it was, released a movement of ideas which would shape decisively the political structure of the West. With the formal abolition of Christianity as the authoritatively unifying spiritual substance of mankind, the particular community substances could move into the vacuum. The mystical bodies of the nations which had been growing ever since the high Middle Ages had achieved by the eighteenth century a considerable coherence and articulation and now they could begin to substitute with increasing effectiveness for the mystical body of Christ.

Increasingly in the eighteenth century the sentiment grows that one age has come to its close and that a new age of Western civilization is about to be born. We might well characterize this sentiment as a new consciousness of epoch. The consciousness of epoch itself, however, is not a new phenomenon in Western history—it does not suddenly make itself felt after 1700. We encounter it for the first time at the height of imperial Christianity in the thirteenth century, notably in the writings of Joachim of Flora. The consciousness of epoch was vivid enough in Joachim to crystallize in the idea of a Third Realm of the Spirit that would follow the Realms of the Father and the Son. This idea repudiated the Augustinian conception of the saeculum as a time of waiting for the second coming of Christ and envisaged a new era of meaning in sacred history. The idea was strong enough to engender among the Franciscans the belief in a *corpus mysticum Francisci* but ultimately it remained ineffectual and did not break through to the level of a mass movement.

While the eighteenth-century's consciousness of epoch is a continuation of the movement that started in the thirteenth century, it is distinguished from the earlier phases of this process by its increased intensity, by a comprehensiveness which embraces all aspects of human existence, above all, by its broad social effectiveness which results in the final disruption of the medieval sentiments of the Western com-

munity and paves the way for new types of schismatic political movements. After 1300 the new intramundane forces revealed their strength
in a multitude of minor sectarian movements, in the English and Bo-
hemian pre-Reformation, in the movement of German mysticism, in the
reorganization of the Church and in the trend towards the sovereign,
absolute state. A world of sentiments, institutions and ideas was growing and hollowing out the structure of imperial Christianity, but the
shell of Church and Empire did not break for another two centuries.
The break did occur only in the sixteenth and seventeenth centuries,
when the Church split under the impact of the Reformation and when,
after the Thirty Years War, the constitution of the Empire became an
appendix to an international treaty.

The time from Joachim of Flora to Luther we may characterize as a
period of social incubation. The actual disruption of medieval institutions, which occurred with the Reformation, created the new social
facts of a plurality of churches as well as of a plurality of sovereign
states. These new social facts became the material with which the
movement of ideas had to cope. The institutional unity of Christian
mankind had broken down irrevocably and the plurality of parochial
institutions which express the diversified field of intramundane social
forces had become an established fact. With the Peace of Utrecht of
1713, the balance of power is accepted as the political constitution of
Western mankind; with the renunciation by Habsburg and France of
the effort to dominate Europe by dominating Spain, the medieval tension between the Empire and the states separating from it is brought
to an end.

The elimination of Church and Empire as public powers was accompanied by a growth of new community substances which, functionally, tended to substitute for the dissolving substance of Christian
mankind. Within the sovereign national states, the intensity of national
consciousness was noticeably increasing. The English Revolution of
the seventeenth century revealed for the first time the strength of the
new demonic parochialism; it revealed the faith in the nation as the
chosen people as well as the universalist claim that the parochial civilization represents Civilization written large. On the international scale
a variety of ideas tried to cope with the new situation: an idea of
mankind which assumed a nature of man equal for all; an idea of the
Christianitas as the Western civilizational unit, in opposition to non-
Western civilizations; ideas concerning the relations between Christian
republics; and ideas concerning intercivilizational relations. And,
finally, the search for a nature of man beyond the strife of the confessions expressed itself in the attempt to use the Stoic idea of nature

as the basis for speculations on natural law, in the influence of the idea
of nature that was developed in the mathematized sciences of the external world on the interpretation of man, and in the use of the new
psychology of passions for determining the generic nature of man.

The trend towards a new order of substances, thus, has a considerable breadth and momentum. Nevertheless we do not find before
1700 a comprehensive interpretation of man in society and history
that would take into account the constituent factors of the new situation, that is: the breakdown of the Church as the universal institution
of Christian mankind, the plurality of sovereign states as ultimate political units, the discovery of the New World and the more intimate acquaintance with Asiatic civilizations, the idea of a non-Christian nature
of man as the foundation for speculation on law and ethics, the demonism of the parochial, national communities and the idea of the passions
as motivating forces of man. Only after 1700 does the cumulative
effect of these various factors make itself felt in the acute consciousness
that, in the aggregate, an epoch has come to an end and that the new
situation requires a gigantic effort of interpretation in order to recover
for the existence of man in society and history a meaning which could
substitute for the lost meaning of Christian existence.

This problem is, indeed, of such a magnitude that even today it is
not realized in all its dimensions. But in the eighteenth century we find
at least the first clear consciousness of its outlines and the first efforts
at its formulation. We can approach it perhaps best by studying the
reasons which induced Voltaire to write his *Essai sur les moeurs* for
his hostess and friend, the Marquise du Châtelet-Lorraine.

The Marquise du Châtelet was a woman whose charms were equalled
by her intellectual powers. She had enjoyed the pleasures of life under
the Regency, and was now, in her riper years, participating actively in
the development of mathematics and of the sciences of her age. This
Venus Newtonia, as Frederick the Great named her, experienced the
urge to enlarge her horizon beyond the arts and the natural sciences into
the field of history, and for that purpose she studied Bossuet's *Discours
sur l'histoire universelle*. The illustrious lady was not amused by the
Discours. Voltaire reports two of her marginal notes. On a page of
Bossuet's chapter on Israel she wrote: "One may talk much of this
people in theology, but it merits little space in history." And in the
section on the Roman Empire she wrote: "Why does the author say
that Rome engulfed all the empires of the universe? Russia alone is
bigger than all the Roman Empire."

The two notes touch the crucial problems of the *Discours*. Bossuet's
treatise consists of a chronological survey of events from Adam to

Charlemagne (part 1), followed by the two discursive parts on the unfolding of religion and on the empires. The conception of history and the organization of materials is still that of St. Augustine. The unfolding of religion, presented in part 2, corresponds to the sacred history of St. Augustine's *Civitas Dei*, the revolution of the empires, presented in part 3, to the profane history of Orosius. For Bossuet in the seventeenth, as for St. Augustine in the fifth century, the universality of history lies in the providential guidance of mankind toward the true religion. The history of Israel, the appearance of Christ, and the history of the Church are the meaningful history of mankind, while profane history with its revolutions of empire has only the function of providing the educative tribulations for Israel and the Church preparatory to the ultimate triumph.[1] The *Discours*, published in 1681, shows that at this late date a universal interpretation of history had still to use the patristic pattern, although the monographic profane history had developed richly following the example of the humanists of the sixteenth century. In spite of the inroads of profane history on the traditional historical accounts, however, no historian would have dared to challenge the Christian idea of universality in the face of the reawakened religious sentiments of Reformation and Counter-Reformation.[2]

Secularized history

The notes of the Marquise du Châtelet frankly challenge the Christian universality by the appeal to a profane principle of universality. The note on the relative importance of Israel opposes history to theology. "History" is in this remark a realm independent of the providential plan; its meaning and order, if any, cannot be derived from the drama of fall and salvation. The people of Israel may have a unique importance in the sacred drama, but they have little importance in a field whose structure is determined by the rise and fall of political powers. This aspect of the note, however, would not yet be so very revolution-

1. See particularly pt. 3: "Ainsi tous les grands empires que nous avons vu sur la terre ont concourru par divers moyens au bien de la religion et à la gloire de Dieu, comme Dieu même l'a déclaré par ses prophètes" (Bossuet, *Textes Choisis et Commentes par H. Bremond* [Paris, 1913], 2, p. 58).

2. The only major attempt at a world history before 1700, from a humanistic point of view, is the *Enneades* (1498–1504) of Sabellicus. An incipient humanistic universalism makes itself felt, however, only in the extension of Bruni's methods to a subject matter that usually was dealt with in sacred history. Otherwise no constructive ideas are introduced. See on this question Eduard Fueter, *Geschichte der neueren Historiographie*, 3rd ed. (Muenchen, Berlin, 1936), pp. 33ff. on the *Enneades*, and pp. 288f. on the absence of any nontheological approach to the problem of universal history before the eighteenth century.

ary; Bossuet might even agree with the Marquise on this point and insist that precisely for this reason he had dealt with Israel in the *Suite de la religion* and not in the part on the empires. The note becomes revolutionary by its implication that the sacred history, the "theology," is unimportant and that profane history has the monopoly of determining the relevance of peoples and events. The center of universality is shifted from the sacred to the profane level, and this shift implies the turning of the tables: that the construction of history will, in the future, not be subordinated to the spiritual drama of humanity, but that Christianity will be understood as an event in history. Through this shift of the center of interpretation the dualism of sacred and profane history disappears. The profane history is profane only as long as sacred history is accepted as the absolute frame of reference and when this position is abandoned, the two histories merge on the level of secularized history. By secularization we mean the attitude in which history, including the Christian religious phenomena, is conceived as an innerworldly chain of human events, while, at the same time, there is retained the Christian belief in a universal, meaningful order of human history.

The second note, on the relative importance of Russia and Rome, is quite as revolutionary as the first, for it introduces the category of quantity as a standard and attacks thereby the function of Rome as a constituent factor of Western universality. The relevance of Rome is not a question of her bigness. Western civilization, as it emerges from the Middle Ages, rests on the unique and precarious balance between the elements of ancient civilizations that were merged in it: Hellenic rationalism, Israelite spiritualism, and the Roman jurisdictional order governing the private wills and public offices. The *koine* of Hellenistic civilization, the universality of the Roman *imperium* and the catholicity of the Church are continued, on a new ethnical basis, in the Christian imperial merger of the Middle Ages. The myth of the universality of the Empire can dominate the sentiments so long as the plurality of other worlds does not intrude itself too strongly. In the Roman period the sentiment of universality apparently could be maintained by a magnificent forgetfulness about the Sassanian Empire and still more about the remoter parts of the Eurasian continent and Africa. Throughout the Middle Ages the sentiment could be held against Islam by the crusading expansiveness which put the Mohammedans into the position of a temporary infidel nuisance that would be ultimately overcome. With the Turkish and Mongol advances, however, with the discovery of America, the increased knowledge of China and India, and the emergence of Russia, an uneasiness would have inevitably to beset the sentiment of medieval universality. If the existence of mankind in history had a universal meaning at all, it would have to rest on something different from the myth provided by the dissolving institutions of Church and Empire. The remark of the Marquise du Châtelet, of course, did not start a revolution, it rather pronounced a revolution which had in fact already taken place. An intelligent woman could state with the innocence of the child who saw the emperor without clothes what the foremost thinkers of the seventeenth century would still have shuddered to admit.

Voltaire was receptive to the criticisms of the Marquise. She complained that in his universal history Bossuet had forgotten nothing less than the universe, and Voltaire undertook in his *Essai* to supplement the missing parts. He recognized the value of Bossuet's *Discours* for the history of antiquity, though not without severe strictures for inaccuracies and the favoritism shown to Israel, and restricted his task to the addition of studies on China, India, Persia and the Islam, and to a continuation of the *Discours* from the time of Charlemagne to Louis XIII. This supplementary character of the *Essai* implies the idea that universality in historiography can be achieved by completeness, and insofar as the *Essai* implies this identification it rather opens than solves the problem of universality. By completeness one can achieve an encyclopedia, but not automatically a unity of meaning. It is true that Voltaire's *Essai* in its final form has the distinction of being the first universal history[3] in the sense that it embraces the whole of mankind, as it was known at the time in historical literature. But it is also true that it reveals the weakness of all universal histories since Voltaire: the impossibility of finding a meaning that could substitute, on the larger scene, for the providential meaning of Western history under the Christian interpretation. The meaning, of course, cannot be found, since a meaningful construction of history from a secular, intramundane position presupposes that history is known as a whole. Since history is

3. On the history of publication, extending from 1745 to 1753, and on the relations of the *Essai sur les moeurs et l'esprit des nations, et sur les principaux faits de l'histoire, depuis Charlemagne jusqu'à Louis XIII*, to the other historical works of Voltaire, the *Siècle de Louis XIV* and the *Siècle de Louis XV*, see the bibliographical note in Fueter's *Geschichte der neueren Historiographie*, pp. 349ff. The *Essai* was published in 1753 under the title of *Abrégé de l'Histoire universelle*. The edition used is that of *Oeuvres Complètes de Voltaire* (1785), vols. 16–21. For the motivation of Voltaire and the criticisms of the Marquise du Châtelet see the *Remarques pour servir de Supplement à l'Essai, Oeuvres*, vol. 21, particularly the *Première Remarque*. On Voltaire's view of Bossuet see furthermore the *Avant-Propos* to the *Essai, Oeuvres*, 16, pp. 300f.; and *Le Pyrrhonisme de l'Histoire*, ch. 2, *Oeuvres*, 31, pp. 13ff. Voltaire lived at Cirey, as the guest of the Marquise du Châtelet, from 1734 to 1749.

known only for the past, all secular meaning must be derived from the present perspective of the author. Even a limited perspectivist construction, however, would presuppose the empirical existence of a recognizable structure of human history, though in fact no such structure, comprising the major civilizations of mankind beyond the Western, is recognizable. The Christian construction of the Augustinian type can be truly universal because it embraces the "whole" of history in the anticipation of the second coming of Christ as the end of history. When this transcendental universalism disintegrates under the impact of profane materials which cannot be related, however tenuously, to the course of sacred history, the universality of meaning has to degenerate into the ideal of empirical completeness.

The ideal of empirical completeness, however, cannot be more than a transitory position in the movement of ideas. As soon as the question is raised why one should know with any degree of completeness whatever has happened in the existence of mankind in time, the curiosity shop is revealed as senseless. Encyclopedic knowledge, collected in handbooks, has to be moved into the functional position of a collection of materials which ultimately might become of importance for a *relevant* interpretation of history. And when historians do not entertain the idea of such ultimate use of their inquiries, historical research develops into a practice of vocational asceticism—it ceases to have a meaning for history, altogether, and becomes a discipline for the life of the historian.

The "esprit humain" as the object of history

The ideal of completeness is, indeed, no more than an incidental factor in the *Essai sur les moeurs*. Voltaire embarks on a reconstruction of historical meaning and the pattern resulting from his efforts has become the standard of secularist reconstruction for more than a century. The object of the *Essai* is "the history of the human spirit and not the detail of facts which are usually distorted anyway"; there is no sense in exploring the family history of some medieval feudatory who made war against the king of France; "we rather have to see by what steps we have advanced from the barbarian rusticity of his time to the politeness of ours."[4] The struggle between the spiritual and temporal powers is the guiding principle for the understanding of Western Christian history. But these powers are powers of "opinion." When the "opinions" are purified, that is when people cease to believe in the

4. *Remarques de l'Essai, II, Oeuvres*, 21, p. 264.

claims of popes and emperors, we enter a new period of increasing truth
and reason. The evolution of "opinion" is the principle that enables the
historian to order and select the events which are illustrative of this
meaningful development. What is the cause of this fortunate change of
opinion? On this point the argument is somewhat hazy, as so frequently
with Voltaire when a serious question has to be answered. When history, says Voltaire, is conceived in the terms just indicated, we can
observe the spectacle of errors and prejudices following each other and
defeating truth and reason. In time men will enlighten themselves by
this record of their misfortunes and stupidities, societies will rectify
their ideas and man will begin to think. Obviously Voltaire is begging
the question. The picture of errors and prejudices is the picture that he
is painting in the *Essai* for the first time; the enlightening, however,
must have begun at some earlier time for now we are already well on
the way of progress; we are on this way, to be precise, since the time
of Henry IV. With Voltaire, we have to glide gracefully over this
century and a half with its problem of causation in order to arrive at
the conclusion that now, in the *Essai*, the purpose is not to assemble a
mass of facts but to make a selection that will enable the reader to
judge "the extinction, the renaissance and the progress of the human
spirit (*l'esprit humain*)." For this is the only method appropriate for a
general history.[5]

These remarks of Voltaire touch on the principal categories that
have to be used in the secularistic construction of history and they contain by implication the rules which have to be observed for their successful use. The *esprit humain* and its changes have become the object
of general history. The transcendental pneuma of Christ is replaced by
the intramundane spirit of man, and the change of heart by the change
of opinion. The *corpus mysticum Christi* has given way to the *corpus
mysticum humanitatis*. The meaning of history on this intramundane
level is constructed as an analogue to the Christian meaning so closely
that we can trace the parallelism step by step. In any construction of a
meaningful universal history, in the first place the object that shows a
meaningful structure has to be constituted as a whole. In the Christian
system, the whole is constituted through the idea of creation and the
descent of mankind from Adam; in the secularistic construction, the
whole is evoked as a totality of empirical knowledge. The ideal of
empirical completeness which appeared as a degenerative substitute for
Christian universality, of no more than transitory importance, becomes
the secularistic analogue of the divine creation of mankind if it is
coupled with a new construction of historical meaning.

5. *Remarques, III*, ibid., pp. 266ff.

Since human history has no recognizable structure of meaning, the historian has to resort to an ingenuous device, for which Voltaire has set the model: the historian selects a partial structure of meaning, declares it to be the total, and arranges the rest of the historical materials more or less elegantly around this preferred center of meaning. The construction is a repetition of the Christian division into sacred and profane history, with the difference, however, that the new sacred history has no transcendental implications; the partial history selected as sacred gains its preferential status because it serves as the expression of a new intraworldly religiousness. The operation is rationally untenable and the constructions are shortlived because they have to follow closely the rapidly changing intraworldly sentiments of the eighteenth and nineteenth centuries. Nevertheless, they are of decisive importance in the history of political ideas because they are genuine evocations of new communities which tend to replace the Christian *corpus mysticum*.

In the analysis of the construction we have to distinguish between the categories of meaning and the historical materials to which they are applied. The categories of meaning are again Christian analogues. Voltaire speaks of the extinction, renaissance and progress of the human spirit. The extinction corresponds to the Fall, the renaissance to the Redemption, the progress to a Third Realm of spiritual perfection. The materials entering into the system are the Middle Ages (extinction), the era of beginning toleration since Henry IV (renaissance) and Voltaire's own age (progress). The categorization is not analogous to the Augustinian with its *saeculum senescens* but rather to the trinitarian of Joachim of Flora. Voltaire resumes the rearticulation of history at the point where the thinkers of the thirteenth century had to abandon it in face of the orthodox resistance—with the fundamental change of substance, however, that the spirit of the Third Realm is not the spirit of the autonomous Christian personality but the spirit of the autonomous intellectual. While the construction is not thoroughly elaborated, it clearly foreshadows the later construction of Saint-Simon and Comte with its "law" of the three phases: the religious, the metaphysical and the positive-scientific. Since the content which enters the categories is an independent variable, it foreshadows, furthermore, the possibility that new materials may enter the categorical pattern, as has actually happened in the Marxist and National-Socialist constructions.

The structure of intramundane history

The insight into the type of secularistic construction created by Voltaire permits the formulation of a few rules for the interpretation of the historico-political conceptions that have arisen in its wake. A historical conception like the Voltairian, Comtian, or Marxian is unacceptable at its face value. Its claim to offer a valid interpretation of universal history or, in the nineteenth century, of a sociological "law," is untenable. In our analysis of these conceptions we shall have to distinguish between the following levels of construction. First, they contain a "thesis of generality": that the sequence of evolutionary phases, selected as "sacred history," is the general pattern of the history of mankind into which all empirical materials can be fitted in a satisfactory manner. While this "thesis of generality" inevitably is false for the reasons given above, it still has its importance as a clue to the particular "model" that has been "generalized." The particular "model" marks the second level in the construction to which we have to penetrate. Comte's law of the three phases is no more a law of universal history than the Marxian scientific conception of an evolution tending toward ultimate communism or Voltaire's three phases of enlightenment. But the general thesis is based on a particular meaningful structure of history which may have been observed correctly. Voltaire has correctly seen the struggle between the spiritual and temporal powers as decisive for the Middle Ages, and Comte's analysis of the Middle Ages is a great achievement in his time; moreover, both thinkers have seen correctly that with the rise of the autonomous critical intellect an epoch is marked in Western history. Hence the model construction can rank very high as an empirical analysis of a particular phase of history in spite of the fact that the model is used as a secularistic "sacred history." Thirdly and finally, we have to penetrate beyond the model into the sentiments which cause its imaginative transformation into a general pattern of history. On this level we have to observe the shift from the transcendental faith in the spirit of Christ to Voltaire's intramundane faith in the *esprit humain* and furthermore the shifts of intramundane faith from Voltaire's *esprit* to Comte's faith in the organizing and engineering intellect, to the Marxian faith in the proletarian as the true man and the proletariat as the chosen people, and further on to the various beliefs in chosen nations and chosen races. Of the various strata of the historical construction, the upper levels which contain the "model" and the "thesis of generality" are no more than an ephemeral dogmatic surface over the basic movement of intramundane religious sentiments which descends from the deification of reason and intellect to the deification of the animal basis of existence. If we may use Schelling's term somewhat freely, we may designate this basic movement of religious sentiments as the theogonic process.

The trinitarian conception of secularistic history is closely related to the Joachitic. This relation, however, has hardly ever become overtly conscious because the creators of the various secularistic, historical constructions have in most instances interpreted their own ideas as constituting a break with Christianity. They supposed that the continuity was interrupted and that a new beginning was made when Reason and Science (capitalized) defeated the dogmatism of the Churches. The preceding analysis has shown, however, that the trinitarian pattern of the secular construction evolves in close analogy with the Christian trinitarian pattern of history. The selected "models" of Voltaire's and Comte's histories have, by virtue of the "thesis of generality," the same function in the secularistic context as the "sacred history" in the Christian conception. We have now to show that the parallelism is not accidental but that a continuity of problems leads from the earlier conception to the later, and we have to inquire particularly into the intellectual operations and the changes of sentiment which result in the "break" of continuity.

A key to the problem of continuity is offered by the development of secularistic history after Voltaire. Below the surface of dogmatic symbols we observed the movement of intramundane religious sentiments, pressing the interpretation of history and politics downward from the spirit to the animal basis of existence. Neither the "model" of the secular "sacred history," nor the dogmatic symbols on the level of the "thesis of generality" remain constant; they change continuously in accordance with the stratum of human nature that commands the attention of the time and becomes the object of the process of deification. The rapid descent from reason, through technical and planning intellect, to the economic, psychological and biological levels of human nature, as the dominants in the image of man, is a strong contrast to the imposing stability of the Christian anthropology through eighteen centuries. Once the transcendental anchorage is surrendered, the descent from the rational to the animal nature, so it seems, is inevitable. The instability of the intramundane "sacred histories" is the characteristic trait of the new age: the great dogmatisms after Voltaire hardly outlast the generation in which they were created. Where does this curious instability of sentiment originate? What are the antecedents of the religious disorientation which expresses itself in the frantic creation of new gods?

Bossuet's Histoire des variations des églises protestantes

The answers to these questions were given by Bossuet. The instability of the secularistic historical constructions continues an instability that begins with the schisms of the Reformation in the sixteenth century. Bossuet observed the phenomenon of religious disorientation and of the consequent instability of sentiment and dogma at the time when the rapid variation still took place within the general framework of Christian doctrine. In the *Histoire des variations des églises protestantes* (1688), he surveyed the Protestant variations of Lutheranism, Zwinglianism and Calvinism and in the preface to the *Histoire* he furnished some suggestions concerning the dynamics of heresies. The succession of Protestant variations seemed to him comparable to the succession of heresies in the early Christian period and he based, therefore, his own view of the problem on a remark by Tertullian concerning the early variations: "The heretics, says Tertullian, change their rules, that is their *confessions of faith;* everyone of them believes himself entitled to change and modify the tradition by his own light (*esprit*), for it is by his own light that the author of the sect has formed the tradition; heresy remains true to its nature if it does not cease to innovate, and its progress is similar to its origin. What is permitted to Valentinus, is permitted to the Valentinians; the Marcionites have the same right as Marcion; and the authors of a sect have no more right to innovate than their sectarian followers."[6] The instability, thus, is the consequence of the initial break; once the authority of the tradition is broken by the individual innovator, the style of individual innovation determines the further course of variations. In the words of Chrysostom: "Avoid the novelties in your discourse, for matters will not rest there: one novelty produces another; and we deviate without end, once we have begun to deviate."[7]

Bossuet's own attitude is that of the ecclesiastical statesman. The unstable course of heresies, and their tendency to beget new heresies, is caused by the nature of the *esprit humain*, which cannot cease to crave for the sweetness of novelty once it has tasted of it. And it is, furthermore, caused by the difference between a perfect truth revealed by God and the weak production of the human mind. This second argument, however, has a peculiar sociological flavor in Bossuet's context, for Bossuet does not rely so much on the contrast between the truth of faith and the falsehood of heresy, but rather on the circumstance that the truth of faith is to be found in the collective wisdom of the Church and of the Fathers, while the innovation is a source of falsehood because it is the product of an individual. The individual will not be capable of anticipating clearly all the implications of an innovation, and the inconveniences appearing on second thought will compel correc-

6. Bossuet, *Histoire des variations des églises protestantes*, "Préface," p. iii.
7. Quoted in ibid., p. vi.

tions and thereby further deviation from the truth. The intellectual powers of the individual cannot substitute for the accumulated wisdom of the collectivity.[8] In these reflections Bossuet has touched upon a fundamental problem of the function of ideas in modern history: the impossibility of creating a spiritual substance and an intellectual style for a community under the condition of free competition between individual intellectuals. The problem appeared to him still under the special form of the tension between the authority of the Church and the individualism of the reformers. This special form, however, is the first instance of the general phenomenon: that established community substances, or incipient communities, are continuously dissolved and broken by the competition of new foundations until the chaotic multiplicity of sects, schools, parties, factions, movements, groupings, associations, communes, is reached which characterized the European social situation before the outbreak of violence in our time.[9] The continuity of the problem will appear more clearly if we compare Bossuet's remarks with a passage from a modern ecclesiastical statesman who had to deal with the problem of heresy; he found the following features characteristic of the heretics: "a disdainful attitude toward theory and an inclination toward eclecticism; disrespect for the tradition of their own organization; anxiety for personal 'independence' at the expense of anxiety for objective truth; nervousness instead of consistency; readiness to jump from one position to another; lack of understanding of revolutionary centralism and hostility toward it; and finally, inclination to substitute clique ties and personal relationships for party discipline."[10]

It has been said of Bossuet that he was a Gallican in order to be a Catholic, and a Catholic in order to be a Christian.[11] Christianity outside the one, visible Church was inconceivable to him. This attitude would not be noteworthy if it were simply a manifestation of Catholic adherence to the Symbolon and the dogma. It is of importance here because it expresses Bossuet's concern about Christianity as a historical phenomenon. The Church preserves and develops the Christian tradition; if the authority of the Church is questioned, the living continuity

8. Bossuet, ibid., p. vii. For modern formulations of this problem, see the volume on *Foi et "mystiques" humaines*, *Etudes Carmélitaines*, 22e Année, vol. 1 (Paris: April, 1937); see in this volume particularly Etienne de Greeff, "Le drame humain et la psychologie des 'mystiques' humaines," pp. 105–155.

9. For this question see Karl Mannheim, *Man and Society in an Age of Reconstruction* (New York, 1960), particularly pt. 2 on "Social Causes of the Contemporary Crisis in Culture."

10. Leon Trotsky, *A Petty-Bourgeois Opposition in the Socialist Workers Party*, December 15, 1939; reprinted in Leon Trotsky, *In Defense of Marxism* (New York, 1942), p. 43.

11. G. Lanson, *Bossuet* (Paris, 1891), p. 365.

of Christianity is broken. One must not question the tradition at any point for such questioning inevitably will lead to the ultimate questioning of Christianity as a whole: what guarantee do we have of the sacredness of Scripture unless we receive it on the authority of the Church—this is Bossuet's decisive argument. His concern was not the content of heresies but the fact of schism and its origin in the *libre examen*. The critical enquiry into tradition and Scripture must lead to the disintegration of Christianity. That the Christian sources can be interpreted in more than one way, Bossuet does not deny; on the contrary, he stresses the point in order to show where the variations of interpretation have led the Protestant reform. Hence he is inclined to accentuate the claims of the majority against the rebellious individual. "What pride is it to believe that one can understand the word of God better than the rest of the Church; in that event there will be as many religions as there are heads."[12] He has a clear conception of the consequences of independence and the authority of critical reason. He is not so much afraid of Protestantism as a new religion as of the principle of historical critique introduced by the reversion to an original meaning of Christianity. The Catholic historians of his time, Dupin and Simon, who organized critical editions of, and commentaries to, the Patristic literature, the Old and New Testaments, also induce him to controversies and countermeasures. Worse than a Protestant heresy, which at least takes Christianity seriously, is the indifference of historical and philological investigation, for Christianity as a divine evocation in history is exposed to atrophy and destruction if it is submitted to rational critique and psychological investigation as a myth. "Under the pretext that we should admit only what we can understand clearly—a proposition that is very true within certain limits—everybody grants himself the freedom to say: I understand this, and I don't understand that; and on this basis he approves or rejects whatever he wants . . . . Under this pretext a freedom of judgment is introduced which encourages one to advance whatever one thinks, without regard to tradition."[13] In Protestantism and historical critique Bossuet did not see primarily a danger to the Catholic Church but a danger to Christianity. In the free judgment and independent interpretation he anticipated the rational dissolution of the Christian mystery through the eighteenth-century movement toward deism and atheism.[14]

12. Bossuet, *Récit de la conférence avec M. Claude*, Bremond, 2, p. 252.
13. Bossuet, *Letters*, 27, p. 221.
14. See on this question Lanson, *Bossuet*, ch. 7, particularly pp. 353–378.

Bossuet's Conférence avec M. Claude

The decisive point of transition from schismatic Protestantism to the historization of Christianity was touched upon by Bossuet incidentally in his religious colloquy with M. Claude, the Huguenot minister of Charenton.[15] Bossuet pressed the question of the authority of the Church and Claude maintained the necessity of independent judgment. Finally, Claude introduced the instance of the Synagogue who condemned Christ and declared that He was not the Messiah promised by the prophets. Would Bossuet maintain in this case that the individual that followed Christ against the decision of the Synagogue had acted wrongly? In this case obviously the individual, acting independently, had done rightly what Bossuet wished to deny Christians in the future. Bossuet rose to the occasion. He pointed out to his opponent that he denied by implication that God had no other external means (*moyen extérieur*) to dissipate the doubts of the ignorant but the authority of the Church. In order to support this argument, one would have to assume that at the time no authority existed on which the faithful could rely. "But, sir, when Jesus Christ Himself was on earth, when the Truth itself appeared visibly among mankind, who would have said that?" His authority certainly was contested, as is the authority of the Church today; still His authority was infallible.[16]

According to Bossuet's account, Claude was at a loss for an answer. On the level of this argument, he obviously was faced by a dilemma: either he would have to deny the convincingly visible presence of the Truth in Christ or he would have to attribute to the founders of the reformed Churches a visible presence of the Truth. The first assumption would have made of the Incarnation a historical human opinion about the nature of Christ with which other men might disagree. The second assumption would have perverted the meaning of the Reform and elevated the Reformers into paracletical figures. Claude was not willing to make either one of these assumptions. He remained in the peculiar suspense of early Protestantism: of interpreting a step, which like every historical step is a step forward, as a step backward to the origins. The forward character of the step, as sensed by Bossuet, reveals

15. Bossuet, *Récit de la conférence avec M. Claude, Ministre de Charenton, sur la matière de l'eglise.* The occasion for the Conference was furnished by the desire of Mlle de Durras, the niece of Turenne, to have herself informed on the Catholic and Protestant positions, preparatory to her conversion to Catholicism. The Conference took place in Paris in 1678.

16. Bossuet, *Conférence, Bremond,* 2, pp. 254ff.

itself fully only in the following centuries when, under the pressure of historical critique and liberal theology, Protestantism evolves forms which are "progressive" to the point that Christianity is thinned out to a code of social ethics and Christ has become one of the great teachers of mankind together with Confucius, and others of similar stature. The active religious forces, on the other hand, proceed to the evocation of the new realms and their leaders. We observed the hesitation of Voltaire in this respect: he was an advocate of Enlightenment but he did not declare himself the Light. Comte and Marx were less restrained in this respect and the later mass movements have evolved into new *corpora mystica*—a fact that is veiled only thinly by their heritage of antireligious ideology.[17]

The dynamics of secularization

The preceding analysis has shown the continuity of the process in which Christianity becomes historized and history secularized. We have a sufficient foundation now for a few general remarks concerning the dynamics of the process. The eighteenth century has to be characterized as the age in which the dissociation of the three European universalisms reaches the stage of critical consciousness. The harmonious balance of spirit, reason and imperium could be maintained only as long as the actual dissociation did not surpass a certain degree. The first of the three component factors to break loose from the combination was the imperium. With the fragmentation and particularization of the imperium through the national realms a substitute order had to be found for the world of Western political units, and we see it in formation with the rise of international law by the time of Grotius. The establishment of a secularized, autonomous sphere of politics outside the spiritual-temporal unity of Christian mankind has moved the spiritual order into the position of the Church in the modern sense, of the religious organization as distinguished from the autonomous political organization of the state. The second component factor to move away from the combina-

17. I have analysed the conflict of, and the continuity between Christian and intraworldly problems in the context of French development because in France the conflict between Catholicism on the one side, Protestantism and Enlightenment on the other, compelled a clearer consciousness of the issues than the parallel development in England where the Catholic position had practically no function in the movement of ideas. The transition from Protestant rationalism to secular deism in England is gradual and compromising; neither the Christian nor the secular positions had protagonists like Bossuet and Voltaire. For the English history see Sir Leslie Stephen, *History of English Thought in the Eighteenth Century* (1876), 3rd ed. (London, 1902); see particularly vol. 1, ch. 2 on "The Starting-Point of Deism."

tion was reason. The tendency became noticeable in the nominalism and Averroism of the Middle Ages. It received its social support from the increasing numbers of lawyers, royal administrators, philosophers and scientists outside the ecclesiastical order, and it reached the stage of autonomous secular reason in the natural science and natural law of the seventeenth century.

The derelictions obviously faced the Church with the problem of its own spirituality. The ascendency of the spiritual power in the Middle Ages was not dependent on its spirituality alone, but to an equal degree on its strength as the superior civilizing force of Christian mankind. It could exert this civilizing function by virtue of the inheritance which it had acquired through the compromise with Roman-Hellenistic civilization. Both the civilizing function and the inheritance which made its exertion possible become by the twelfth century the sources of the frictions which accompany the process of dissociation. When, firstly, the civilizing work of the Church had been successful to the point that the growing Western communities in the cities and the realms could continue it with their own forces, this new situation would have required a voluntary withdrawal of the Church from its material position as the greatest economic power, which could be justified earlier by the actual civilizing performance. The Church, however, did not liquidate its economic and political position voluntarily. When, secondly, an independent, secular civilization began to grow, a conflict between the contents of this new civilization and the ecclesiastic inheritance from antiquity was bound to ensue. This new situation would have required a voluntary surrender on the part of the Church of those of its ancient civilization elements which proved incompatible with the new Western civilization, and would have made necessary a new civilizational compromise similar to that which the early Church concluded with Roman-Hellenistic civilization. Again the Church proved hesitant in adjusting adequately and in time.

These necessities and failures of adjustment are the causes of frictions in the process of dissociation. Its principal phases, determined by the character of the predominant friction, are roughly three, making allowances for overlapping. The first phase extends from 1300 to 1500. It is the time in which the dissociation of the imperium reaches its acute stage. The refusal of the Church to reduce its economic and financial power position in the emerging nation-states leads to the Anglicanism of the fourteenth and the Gallicanism of the fifteenth centuries, and finally to the Reformation with its vast confiscations of Church property. As far as hypothetical propositions can be entertained in history at all, those scholars are probably right who believe that the schism of the

Reformation could have been avoided by the Church if it had judiciously reduced the property holdings which it lost by force. The second phase extends from 1500 to 1700. Astronomy and physics develop, and the heliocentric conception clashes with the Babylonian cosmology of the Old Testament; it is the time of the *causes célèbres*, of Giordano Bruno and of Galilei. The aftermath of this type of friction reaches into the nineteenth century with the conflict over evolution. The third phase extends from 1700 to the present. It is the age of historical science and of the higher criticism with its clash between a critical treatment of sacred texts, of Church history and history of the dogma, and the ecclesiastic interpretation of the truth of faith.

The sequence of these frictions, which invariably culminate in the victory of the civilizational forces dissociating from the medieval compound, has left deep scars in the spiritual and intellectual structure of the West. The adventures of imperial and rational autonomy have not left simply a spiritual Church as the residue. The frictions and maladjustments have worked a profound spiritual destruction in the autonomous secular sphere and have severely impaired the civilizational position of the Church. The first type of frictions resulted in a far-reaching expropriation of the Church, but the confiscation of Church property alone would not have endangered the spiritual substance of the Church. The decisive consequence of the struggle between the spiritual and temporal powers over this question, going as far back as the Investiture Struggle, was the political tension between the Church and the state in the course of which the spiritual institution was finally relegated to the private sphere, while the autonomous political institutions achieved the monopoly of publicity. This privatization of the spirit left the field open for a respiritualization of the public sphere from other sources, in the forms of nationalism, humanitarianism, economism both liberal and socialist, biologism, and psychologism. The growth of a plurality of counter spirits and counter churches to the traditional spiritual institutions is the most fateful consequence of the failure of the Church to find a compromise with the new pluralistic world of politics.

The tension originating in the problems of the first phase was aggravated by the frictions caused by the advancement of science. This second failure of adjustment left the Church with the stigma of obscurantism, and the stigma of a force which opposes the freedom of scientific inquiry attaches to it in popular opinion even today, after the Church has made its peace with science. Again, the clash did not simply drive science into an autonomous development. Such a development would not have constituted a danger to the spiritual substance of Christianity. More fateful was the spiritual devastation wrought by the wide-spread conviction that the rational-scientific approach could be a substitute for the spiritual integration of personality. The effect of the scientistic creed is, very similar to the effect of autonomy in the political sphere, the openness of the individual to respiritualization from non-Christian sources. On the side of the Church thereby a problem comes more clearly into view than was present even in the first phase and will dominate more seriously the third phase: the problem that the Church is losing its leadership, not only the leadership of the civilizational process itself, but the leadership of the spirit. The futile opposition to the civilization process engenders an increasing opposition among its bearers against the claim of the Church to be the institution that preserves authoritatively the Western spiritual tradition. Hence the inadequacy and belatedness of the civilizational compromise becomes of growing importance as a cause of de-Christianization and non-Christian respiritualization.

The gravest problem for the spiritual substance of Christianity arises, in the third phase, from the conflict between Christian symbolism and its rational, historical critique. The symbolic language in which the truth of Christianity is expressed stems from Hebrew and Hellenistic sources. The mythical language was, at the time of its original employment, the precise instrument for expressing the irruption of transcendental reality, its incarnation and its operation in man. In the age of Christ and the centuries of early Christianity, this language was not a "myth" but the exact terminology for the designation of religious phenomena. It has become a "myth" as a consequence of the penetration of our world by a rationalism which destroys the transcendental meanings of symbols taken from the world of the senses. In the course of this "de-divinization" (*Entgötterung*) of the world, sensual symbols have lost their transparency for transcendental reality; they have become opaque and are no longer revelatory of the immersion of the finite world in the transcendent. Christianity has become historized in the sense that a universe of symbols that belongs to the age of the myth is seen in the perspective of categories which belong to an age of rationalism. In this perspective only, when symbols and dogmas are seen in a "literal," disenchanted opaqueness from the outside, do they acquire the "irrationality" which brings them into conflict with logic, with biology, history, etc. For a modern man who has grown up outside Christian traditions and institutions, it is extremely difficult to regain the original meaning of ancient symbolisms, be they Hellenic or Christian, but he can gain an understanding of the problem when he observes the symbolisms of modern spiritual perversions which are quite as far beyond the sphere of rational critique as are the ancient symbolisms.

Anybody who has ever tried to explain to a convinced Marxist that the idea of a communist stateless society is a derivative eschatology and that Marxism is not a "scientific" socialism, or who has tried to explain to a fanatic of world organization that terms like world peace, peace-loving nations, aggressors, etc., are not concepts of empirical politics, but symbols of an intramundane eschatology, can guage by the reaction he encounters how senseless it must have appeared to an early Christian if somebody had argued against the Incarnation with biological reasons.

In this historical situation the Church has shown admirable wisdom as far as the defensive attitude is concerned. It has resisted until recently all tampering with the symbols through modernistic, rational interpretations which would reduce the mystery of the spiritual drama to a psychology of intraworldly human experiences. Nothing could have been gained by concessions and the spiritual substance preserved in the symbols would have been endangered. Less admirable is the helplessness in dealing actively with the problem. A problem undeniably exists and it cannot be solved, like the problems of the first and second phases, by a belated acceptance of the new situation. It is not for us to offer a solution, but certainly a part of it would have to be a new Christian philosophy of history and of mythical symbols that would make intelligible, firstly, the new dimension of meaning which has accrued to the historical existence of Christianity through the fact that the Church has survived two civilizations; and that would make intelligible, secondly, the myth as an objective language for the expression of a transcendental irruption, more adequate and exact as an instrument of expression than any rational system of symbols, not to be misunderstood in a literalism which results from opacity nor reduced to an experiential level of psychology. Obviously it is a task that would require a new Thomas rather than a neo-Thomist. The master stroke of ecclesiastical statesmanship, St. Paul's identification of the three community forces of his time (the Pagan, the Hebrew, and the Christian) with the three laws (natural law, Hebrew external law, Christian law of the heart), has not been duplicated in our time. The Pauline translation of the triad of forces into progressively higher levels of spirituality made the historical situation for his contemporaries meaningful and intelligible. If we formulate the deepest sentiment that causes the spiritual tensions of the West since the Middle Ages somewhat drastically, we might say: that the bearers of Western civilization do not want to be a senseless appendix to the history of antiquity; they want to understand their civilizational existence as meaningful. If the Church is not able to see the hand of God in the history of mankind, men will not remain satisfied but will go out in search of gods who take some interest in their civilizational efforts. The Church has abandoned its spiritual leadership insofar as it has left postmedieval man without guidance in his endeavors to find meaning in a complex civilization which differs profoundly in its horizons of reason, nature and history from the ancient that was absorbed and penetrated by the early Church. In the face of this abandonment of the *magisterium* it is futile when Christian thinkers accuse the *superbia* of modern man who will not submit to the authority of the Church. There is always enough *superbia* in man to bolster the accusation plausibly, but the complaint dodges the real issue: that man in search of authority cannot find it in the Church, through no fault of his own. From the dissatisfaction of being engaged in a civilizational process without meaning there are engendered attempts, beginning with Voltaire, at a reconstruction of meaning through the evocation of a new "sacred history." And with Voltaire begins also the concerted attack on Christian symbols and the attempt at evoking an image of man in the cosmos under the guidance of intraworldly reason. We have to turn now to this highly effective attack, which advanced the apostatic movement within a generation from the deism of Descartes and Locke to the atheism of Holbach and La Mettrie.

Voltaire's attack

Voltaire was not a systematic thinker. He did not elaborate a system of concepts and axioms that would have served as the basis for his attack on Christian symbols and particularly on the concepts of a Christian anthropology. His attack took the form of pamphlets on persecution affairs, of aphoristic articles, aperçus, malicious witticisms, sallies à propos, sarcasms and satires. The principles of the attack are implied in the critical and publicistic work and they have to be disengaged from a wealth of literary pieces. A comprehensive presentation of Voltaire's position would have to take into account practically the whole of his production. In spite of interesting variations and nuances, a good deal of this work, however, is repetitious. For most of the questions relevant in our context one can penetrate to the core of his position by means of the articles in the *Dictionnaire Philosophique*.

The form of the attack is intimately related to its content. A systematic elaboration of problems is unnecessary for Voltaire because he is sufficiently equipped with convictions. He inaugurates the type of man who is at the height of an age that conceives of itself as being at the height of human civilization. He surveys the horizon of mankind not only historically and geographically; he possesses as well a surprisingly solid smattering of knowledge with regard to physics, philosophy, public affairs and even religious questions. He has developed his intellectual and moral faculties to the point where they can become the standard for others: if Voltaire does not understand Leibniz, the philosopher obviously has written something that he did not understand himself. From the apex of his reason and humanity he can see the evil in the world that is caused by obscurantism and malice; with the fire of tolerance he will attack superstition and persecution, frequently with great courage and at a personal risk. The full consciousness of his superiority does not impair, however, his humility: faced with the mysteries of religion he will frankly admit that he does not understand them and that, therefore, they have to be eliminated from the public scene. The light of reason should fall into every corner of the human mind, and if it falls on a substance that is solid enough not to be dissolved by its rays, the obstacle should be destroyed because it is a scandal to enlightened man.

The Elemens de Philosophie de Newton

What is reason? and when is man enlightened?—the answer to these questions cannot be simple. The reason of Voltaire is not a philosophical idea like the reason of Kant's *Critique*. It is a complex of sentiments and knowledge that has been collected from widely different sources and we can understand it only by surveying the constituent factors. One of the most important factors for our problem is the identification of a rational view of the world with the philosophy of Newton. During his residence in England, Voltaire was profoundly impressed by the philosophy of Locke and the physics of Newton. He studied the Leibniz-Clarke controversy with great care and he wrote later, after his return to France, a presentation of the Newtonian system for the general reader.[18] The *Elemens de Philosophie de Newton* is not as detailed in the attack as the articles of the *Dictionnaire Philosophique* and of the *Questions sur l'Encyclopédie*, but it makes the foundations of the attack more clearly visible than the later works. Hence an analysis of the *Elemens* will be the best introduction to Voltaire's position.

The problem raised by the *Elemens* can be formulated briefly as follows: The Christian doctrinal symbols concerning the human soul, the transcendental reality and the relations between them are not a body of empirically verifiable propositions to be accepted as true after due examination. They receive their meaning as expressions of the spiritual process in which the soul responds with *caritas* to the super-

18. Voltaire, *Elemens de Philosophie de Newton* (1738), *Oeuvres*, vols. 38, 39 (1785).

natural aid of the *gratia;* in this response is constituted the *fides caritate formata* which opens the possibilities of reaching out understandingly into the supernatural; it develops the faculties of the *cognitio fidei*, the cognition by faith, concerning matters which are not accessible to natural reason.[19] Without the actuality of this spiritual process the theologoumena and the anthropology become empty shells. The professional theological occupation with them will tend to degenerate, if the substance is lost, in the dubious controversies of the seventeenth century, both Catholic and Protestant, which have made scholasticism a byword. When not only the substance is lost, but when also the active center of intellectual life has shifted to the plane of our knowledge of the external world, the symbols expressive of Christian spiritual life acquire the opaqueness which we discussed above. The symbols will either be abandoned entirely because they have become irrelevant or, when the sentiments of tradition are still strong, they will be submitted to rational simplification, psychological interpretation and utilitarian justification. That last position, the combination of opaqueness of the symbols with traditional reverence for them, is the position of Newton and Voltaire.

When we now turn to the *Elemens* itself, we have to observe that the spiritual life of the soul in the Christian sense has disappeared and with it the *cognitio fidei*. The knowledge of the external world, particularly in astronomy and physics, sets the standard for what can be considered as knowledge. Hence the discussion concerning Christian symbols cannot open with the analysis of a spiritual process; rather it has to open with a formula indicating the acceptance of God as a biographical fact in the life of Newton: "Newton was intimately persuaded of the existence of a God." The source of the persuasion remains for the moment obscure and the next step is a definition: "He understood by this word not only an infinite, omnipotent being, eternal and creator, but a master Who has established a relation between Himself and His creatures." The definition then is followed by the "reason" for the assumption that a personal relation exists between God and His creature: "Without that relation the knowledge of a God is a sterile idea inviting to crime by the hope of impunity, for every *raisonneur* is born perverse."[20] These opening sentences of the *Elemens* set the style for the new attitude towards Christian symbols. The existence of God has become a human persuasion which has to be filled with a certain content in order to make it useful. The personal relationship between God and His creatures has to be postulated be-

19. See St. Thomas Aquinas, *Summa contra Gentiles*, pt. 3, chs. 151, 152.
20. *Elemens, Oeuvres*, 38, p. 25.

cause otherwise the trespasser would not be deterred by fear of punishment. The line is indicated which leads from fire-and-brimstone Christianity to the utilitarian pleasure-pain calculus. And the concluding
remark offers one of the occasional profundities of Voltaire: that the
man who reasons (the *raisonneur*) is perverse and needs the fear of
punishment because his life is no longer transcendentally oriented by
grace and love.

Once these principles are established, the treatment of the sub-
problems is logically more or less compulsory. The "persuasion" of the
existence of God is due to a reasoning which draws from the order of
the universe, as revealed in physics, the conclusion that it ought to be
due to an artificer who created it. The Christian *credo ut intelligam*,
which presupposes the substance of faith, is reversed into an *intelligo
ut credam*. The existence of God is the object of an hypothesis with a
high degree of probability. There has disappeared, furthermore, the
basis of Christian theology, the *analogia entis*, and with it the possibility of speculation on the attributes of God. "Philosophy can prove that
there is a God; but it is incapable of teaching what He is, what He
does."[21] The article on "God" in the *Dictionnaire Philosophique* sup-
plements this position by pragmatic arguments concerning the uselessness of metaphysical speculation: if I know that God is a Spirit,
"would I be more just? would I be a better husband, father, master,
citizen?" "I do not want to be a philosopher, I want to be a man."[22]

The soul has to share the fate of God. The spiritual process, that
is the experiential reality which is designated by the symbol "soul,"
has ceased to exist. For Voltaire there exists no Augustinian *anima
animi* from which man reaches out in the *intentio* into the transcendent,
the human personality has lost the integrating spiritual center with its
phenomena of love, faith, hope, contrition, penitence, renovation and
acquiescence. The only human faculty that is left is thought (*le
penser*)—and do we have to assume a soul in order to explain the
function of thought? Would it not be possible that thought is a function
of matter like gravitation? "Can reason alone give you sufficient light
to conclude, without supernatural aid, that you have a soul?"[23] We
cannot experience a soul, and if we had one we could not penetrate

21. *Elemens*, pt. 1, ch. 1.
22. Article *Dieu* in *Dictionnaire Philosophique*. The edition used is the Flam-
marion reprint of the first edition of 1764. The volumes bearing the title *Dictionnaire Philosophique* in the *Oeuvres* of 1785 contain the original *Dictionnaire*
edited and fused with the articles of the *Encyclopédie*, the *Lettres Anglaises* and
other, minor pieces. The editors have mutilated the text frequently at their discretion.
23. Article *Âme* in *Dictionnaire Philosophique*.

to its essence, for "God has given you understanding in order that you can conduct yourself well, but not in order to penetrate the essence of the things which He has created."[24] The freedom of the soul is disposed of in the same manner. Whether the soul is free to will or not, we do not know and it does not matter. In practice we act *as if* we were free;[25] beyond that point speculation is senseless, whatever we think: "the wheels which move the machine of the universe are always the same."[26]

The foundation of ethics

The spiritual obscurantism of Voltaire makes it impossible for him to center a philosophy of morals in the idea of the spiritually integrated personality. The problems of ethics are dealt with under the title of "natural religion": "I understand by natural religion the principles of morals which are common to the human species."[27] Such common rules are supposed to exist because they have their source in the biological structure of man and serve the purpose of making possible life in society. The fundamental rule is, therefore, a collectivized version of the Golden Rule: that you should act towards others as you would wish them to act toward you. The rule is not founded on the assumption of a spiritual person or of the recognition of the spiritual person in fellowman; rather it is founded on the utility for society of a conduct in accordance with the rule. "In every society one calls by the name of virtue that which is useful to society."[28] Voltaire denies expressly the legitimacy of a personalistic ethics. "What does it mean to me that you are temperate? It is a rule of health which you observe; you will fare better with it and I wish you well. You have faith and hope and I wish you well still more: they will secure for you the eternal life. Your theological virtues are gifts from heaven; your cardinal virtues are excellent qualities which help you in your conduct; but they are not virtues with regard to your neighbors. The prudent will do good to himself, the virtuous to other men." The saint is neither good nor bad; he is nothing to us. "Virtue among men is a commerce of good deeds; who has no part in this commerce should not be counted."[29] These passages grant perhaps the clearest insight into the intraworldly

24. Loc. cit.; see also *Elemens*, pt. 1, ch. 7, on Newton's ideas.
25. *Elemens*, pt. 1, ch. 4, *in fine*.
26. Ibid., pt. 1, ch. 5, sec 15; see also article *Liberté* in *Dictionnaire Philosophique*.
27. *Elemens*, pt. 1, ch. 6.
28. Ibid., p. 63.
29. Article *Vertu* in *Dictionnaire Philosophique*.

religious sentiment as well as into the ideas of man and morality determined by it. The transcendental constitution of mankind through the
pneuma of Christ is replaced by faith in the intraworldly constitution
of mankind through "compassion." On this point Voltaire follows Newton closely. "Newton thought that the disposition which we have to
live in society is the foundation of natural law." The disposition of
compassion in man is as general as his other instincts. "Newton has
cultivated this sentiment of humanity and he extended it even to the
animals." "This compassion which he had for animals turned into
true charity with regard to man. Indeed, without humanity, the virtue
which comprises all virtues, a man hardly merits the name of philosopher."[30] Elements of Stoicism and Averroism obviously have entered
the belief in humanity as a rarefied biological instinct which serves the
existence of the animal tribe. The chattering discourse of Voltaire,
furthermore, betrays more openly than the more carefully considered
formulations of later thinkers the relations between humanitarian
tribalism and certain other phenomena. The attack on the saint as a
prudent person who takes care of himself and forgets the neighbor is
on principle already the Communist and National Socialist attack on
the freedom and the achievements of the spirit, as well as on the
spiritual formation of personality, as socially useless and perhaps even
dangerous private concerns. The sphere of the socially valuable is
restricted to the procurement of animal comforts and to scientific discoveries which may serve this purpose.[31] Behind the phrase that a man
who is not socially useful in this restricted sense does not count looms
the virtuous *terreur* of Robespierre and the massacres by the later
humanitarians whose hearts are filled with compassion to the point
that they are willing to slaughter one half of mankind in order to make
the other half happy. The complacent assumption that charitable compassion is a general disposition of man abandons the healthy Christian

30. *Elemens*, pt. 1, ch. 6.
31. See the praise of the Royal Society, founded in 1660, for its "useful and
admirable inventions" in *Lettres Anglaises* (1734), Lettre XXIV, "Sur les
académies." See particularly the following passage in this letter: "Je suis bien
loin d'inférer de là qu'il faille s'en tenir seulement à une pratique aveugle; mais
il serait heureux que les physiciens et les géomètres joignissent, autant qu'il est
possible, la pratique à la spéculation. Faut-il que ce qui fait de plus d'honneur à
l'esprit humain soit souvent ce qui est le moins utile? Un homme, avec les quatre
règles d'arithmétique, et du bon sens, devient un Jacques Coeur, un Delmet, un
Bernard; tandis qu'un pauvre algébriste passe sa vie à chercher dans les nombres
des rapports et des propriétés étonnantes, mais sans usage, et qui ne lui ap-
prendront pas ce que c'est que le change. Tous les arts sont à peu près dans ce
cas: il y a un point passé lequel les recherches ne sont plus que pour la curiosité.
Ces vérités ingénieuses et inutiles ressemblent à des étoiles, qui, placées trop loin
de nous, ne nous donnent point de clarté."

cynicism which is aware of the precarious ascendancy of the spirit over the passions and takes its precautions. The identification of the good with the socially useful foreshadows the compulsory goodness of the social planner as well as the idea of revolutionary justice, with its assumption that right is what serves the proletariat, the nation or the chosen race.

The meaning of reason

We must not fall into the mistake, however, of laying the evils of the future at the doorstep of Voltaire. Man can bend any religion, transcendental no less than intraworldly, to the purpose of war and persecution, and Voltaire would have raised his voice against intraworldly religious persecutions probably quite as vehemently as against the Christian of his age. We have to return to the more immediate problems of Voltaire. Reason, as used by Voltaire, is a symbol designating a complex of sentiments and ideas. The fundamental sentiment is the intraworldly faith in a society which finds its coherence through compassion and humanity. Humanity is a general disposition in man arising out of his biological structure. Negatively, the reasonable attitude is characterized by the absence of immediate spiritual experiences. As a consequence of this deficiency, the symbolic expressions of spiritual experiences become opaque and are misunderstood as depending for their validity on their resistance to rational critique. The monopoly of legitimate orientation in the world is arrogated, on principle, to the methods of natural science. The remnants of Christian orientation towards the transcendent have to be justified, like the existence of God, in terms of a hypothesis based on the order of nature as revealed in physics, or like the belief in supernatural punishment, on its pragmatic usefulness. The spiritual orientation and integration of personality is ignored as a problem, the principles of ethics are severed from their spiritual roots, and the rules of conduct are determined by the standard of social utility.

The implications of this complex designated by the name of Reason cannot be fully understood, however, unless one takes into account Voltaire's opinion concerning its social function. In spite of the fact that Voltaire was a professional publicist, he seems to have been convinced that his ideas were relevant only to a comparatively small social circle and that they would not, and perhaps should not, penetrate into the consciousness of the masses. Voltaire's attitude bears some resemblance to that of Averroes and the Latin Averroists: the cultivation of Reason should be confined to a sect of intellectuals, while society at large, the people as well as the rulers, should remain in the orthodox faith.[32] He deviated, however, in his conduct from the Averroist counsel of abstinence insofar as he intervened with intense aggressiveness in public affairs involving the orthodox faith. His intervention in the persecution affairs gave to his work a public resonance which he disclaimed for it on principle. This peculiar tension between an esoteric sentiment and aggressive intervention pervades the whole work of Voltaire and makes it frequently difficult to judge whether a particular declaration in favor of revealed religion is a political device to protect himself against unpleasant consequences or a sincere protestation of his respect for a religious sphere which he considers necessary for the orderly functioning of society. Public effectiveness on the European scale has become the predominant characteristic of Voltaire's work but the esotericism as an undercurrent, and perhaps the original sentiment, must not be lost sight of. The problem deserves some attention, for in Voltaire's tension we have to recognize the late phase in the evolution of intraworldly intellectualism of which the early phase is represented by the Averroist sectarianism of the thirteenth and fourteenth centuries. In the *Lettres Anglaises* of 1734 Voltaire still expressed the opinion that no philosophical sentiment would ever hurt the religion of a country. The objects of Reason and Faith are different, and no Christian will cease to respect the mysteries of his religion because they are in conflict with reason. "The philosophers will never become a religious sect."[33] Why? Because they don't write for the people and because they have no enthusiasm. The number of men who know the name of a Locke is small, only very few of them read at all, and those who read prefer novels to philosophical studies. "The number of those who think is excessively small; and they have no intention of bothering the world."[34] Nevertheless, he was clear about the sectarian character of the new philosophical movement. In the Letter on Socinianism he speaks of the small English sect, consisting of a few clergymen and savants, who do not call themselves Arians or Socinians but who do not at all agree with the Athanasian creed and who place the Father higher than the Son. Whatever one calls them, there is a distinct revival of Arianism in England, Holland and Poland. Newton expressed him-

32. See particularly the revealing *Troisième Entretien* of the *Catechisme Chinois* in the *Dictionnaire Philosophique;* see also the conclusion of sec. 3 of the article *Âme* in the *Dictionnaire Philosophique* in the *Oeuvres*, vol. 47, of 1785.
33. One should read this passage rather as "a successful religious sect." That Voltaire considered the philosophers, indeed, to be a sect will appear presently in the text.
34. *Lettres Anglaises*, no. XIII, "Sur Locke,"

self favorably on it; "and the firmest advocate of Arian doctrine is the illustrious Clarke." The admiring characterization of Clarke seems to reflect Voltaire's own preferences: "This man is of a rigid virtue and a sweet character, more enamored with his beliefs than impassioned to make proselytes, exclusively occupied with calculations and demonstrations, blind and deaf for everything else, a veritable reasoning machine." The Arian revival, however, has chosen its time badly for the age is preoccupied with sectarian disputes. The new sect is too small to obtain the freedom of public assembly, but it will obtain it if it ever becomes more numerous. Still, this is not the age "to succeed with a new or a revived religion." "Is it not a nice state of things that Luther, Calvin and Zwingli, all writers whom one cannot read, have founded sects who divide Europe among them, that the ignorant Mohammed has given a religion to Asia and Africa, and that Newton, Clarke, Locke, Leclerc, the greatest philosophers and best pens of their time, have hardly been able to collect a small troupe of followers."[35]

These passages illustrate the ambiguity of Voltaire's attitude. On the one hand, the philosophers are a small group and they do not want to bother the public; on the other hand, he hopes that they will have public meetings when their sect becomes more numerous, and the comparison with the Reformers and Mohammed leaves hardly a doubt that he looks with some envy on the mass success of other religious movements. His remarks also betray the sources of the ambiguity: Voltaire's understanding of his own position was limited. He saw in the philosophers' ideas a deviation from orthodox Christianity and he classified it in dogmatic terms as a unitarian heresy, but he did not recognize the new intraworldly religiousness as the force behind the dogmatic innovation. He even denied the enthusiasm without which the movement would be inexplicable. The old faith was lost and the new faith had not yet reached the level of a conscious, responsible will to order the world of man and society anew. We have observed earlier a haziness in Voltaire's reconstruction of the historical pattern: the *esprit humain* advanced somehow from medieval darkness to modern enlightenment, while the motive force of the advancement remained obscure. Voltaire did not see himself as the spiritual substance by means of which history advances; he was not a revolutionary spiritual founder, rather he remained in suspense before the revolution.

The state of prerevolutionary suspense is perhaps the most intimate Voltarian sentiment. From this center we can gain an understanding of the connection between personality traits which otherwise would ap-

35. Ibid., no. VII, "Sur les sociniens, ou ariens, ou anti-trinitaires."

pear confusingly unrelated. We have to beware in the case of Voltaire of falling into the extremes of partisan judgments. Voltaire was neither superficial nor was he a great positive or negative force. One can make a long list of his more reprehensible qualities. He was deficient in spiritual substance and he was vulgarly irreverent. His surprising range of solid knowledge was coupled with an equally surprising ignorance concerning the more intricate questions of philosophy and religion; as a result his judgment was frequently superficial, though delivered with authority. He has set the style for brilliantly precise misinformation, as well as for the second-rater's smart detraction of the better man. He was ever ready to sacrifice intellectual solidity to a clever witticism. He introduced to the European scene the unhappy persuasion that a good writer can talk about everything, that every unsound utterance has to be considered an opinion, and that irresponsibility of thought is synonymous with freedom of thought. In short: he has done more than anybody else to make the darkness of enlightened reason descend on the Western world. But all this does not add up to a demonic force of evil. If we subtract Voltaire's vitality, literary qualities and intellectual temperament, there become visible in the distance rather the Homard of Flaubert's *Madame Bovary* or the exasperating Bouvard and Pecuchet who have to try their hands at everything. On the positive side we are in a similar difficulty. There we find the achievements of the poet, the historian, the essayist, the correspondent, the reporter on England, the excellent popularizer of Newtonian physics and the effective publicist. They certainly make Voltaire one of the greatest men of letters, but the range and quality of the performance can never quite anaesthetize the awareness of the ultimate defect of substance.

Still, Voltaire is not superficial. There is in him a quality which is praised in such terms as his spirit of tolerance, his common sense, his indignation at scholastic obscurantism and at bigotry, his hatred of oppression and persecution, his advocacy of freedom of speech and thought. The praise is merited, indeed. Voltaire's strength lies in this twilight zone of procedural virtues which are peculiar to a man who has lost the old faith sufficiently to see its shortcomings as an outsider and to attack them without compunction, and who has not enough substance of the new faith to create its law as the master but enough to fight with skill and courage for its establishment. This intermediate position is the soil for the style of critique and attack, of proselytizing and defense, sarcasm and satire, which Voltaire has developed to perfection. It is a realm not of the spirit, but between the spirits, where man can live for a moment in the illusion that he can, by discarding the old spirit, free himself of the evil which inevitably arises from the life of the spirit in the world, and that the new one will create a world without evil. The protest against the world and the cry for the light are futile if we expect to find the light in the world, but even this futility and illusion are still ennobled by the *contemptus mundi*, by a glimpse of the light and a sincere desire for deliverance from the evil. The child-of-the-world's dream of a terrestrial paradise of compassion and humanity is only a shadow of the heavenly city, but still it is a shadow cast by the eternal light.

The paradise of compassion

And, finally, we have to consider that Voltaire could dream of a paradise of compassion and humanity because he experienced these qualities as active in his person. However dubious his anthropology may appear as a systematic achievement, there can be no doubt that his compassion with the suffering creature was sincere. The religious wars of the sixteenth and seventeenth centuries, the innumerable individual persecutions perpetrated by the Catholic as well as the Protestant churches of all persuasions, were a stark reality. "Only the ignorant will scoff at the sacred and pious ring which the words: Natural Religion, Enlightenment, Tolerance and Humanity had for the men of those days. They express a sigh of relief in a world that was on the point of succumbing to the oppression of the confessions."[36] The human situation will appear perhaps more clearly if we relate a simple case. In 1596, a poor artisan was tried in Amsterdam because his struggle with the Bible, in the two original languages, had led him to the belief that Jesus was a man only. Peter van Hooft, the Mayor of Amsterdam, said in his defense speech: "I hear that he has been excommunicated because of his opinions. The Church should content itself with the excommunication and proceed not further against the poor man. It is certain that a man who frequently visited his house, saw his wife and his children on their knees in prayer before the meals. And that proves that he has brought them up in the fear of the Lord according to his

36. Wilhelm Dilthey, *Das natürliche System der Geisteswissenschaften im 17. Jahrhundert*, in *Gesammelte Schriften* (Leipzig, Berlin, 1914), 2, p. 95. On the problem and the history of persecutions see W. E. H. Lecky, *History of the Rise and Influence of the Spirit of Rationalism in Europe*, rev. ed. (New York, 1882), ch. 4, pt. 1, "The Antecedents of Persecution," pt. 2, "The History of Persecution." "Indeed, even at the close of the seventeenth century, Bossuet was able to maintain that the right of the civil magistrate to punish religious error was one of the points on which both churches agreed; and he added that he knew only two bodies of Christians who denied it. They were the Socinians and the Anabaptists" (Lecky, p. 60).

lights. I believe that the life of a man should not depend on the sub-
tleties of scholars."[37] The elements of the situation have not changed
by the time of Voltaire; as far as the dogmatic question is concerned,
a Newton or Clarke might stand in the place of the artisan. There we
see on the one side a poor fellow in his spiritual troubles, exerting himself to the extent of studying Greek and Hebrew, and finally arriving
at a heretical christological view. On the other side: the institutional
machinery of church and state with its threats of excommunication
and death penalty. And then the reaction of compassion: it cannot be
the purpose of Christianity to persecute such a man, to kill him and
to inflict infinite misery on his wife and children. The ecclesiastics who
are responsible for the persecution appear no longer as defenders of
the spirit but as intellectuals who bring human sacrifices to dogmatic
subleties which should be of secondary importance as compared with
the substance of the faith. The inability of the Churches to cope with
the problems of postmedieval history which we discussed earlier
reaches the breaking point when compassion turns against them and
threatens to throw the spirit overboard together with the degenerative
excrescences. The compassion with the suffering creature which is
trampled underfoot by historical forces beyond its understanding and
control is the great positive quality in Voltaire. And if his compassion
had been less passionate and more spiritual, one might almost recognize
a Franciscan in him. In the thirteenth century the mute creation had
to be discovered and to be drawn into the orbit of spiritual sympathy;
in the eighteenth century, man in society and history had to be recognized as part of the God-willed creation and to be accepted in compassion. It may be considered unfortunate that the institutions of the spirit
had sunk so low at the time that a Voltaire had to devote himself to
the task and to act with authority as the defender of man in historical
society, but one cannot deny that he acted with grandeur the role of a
defensor humanitatis against the professionals of the faith.

37. Dilthey, p. 101; the original source is G. Brandt, *History of the Reformation in the Low-Countries*, 4 vols. (London, 1720–23), vol. 1,

II. HELVÉTIUS AND THE GENEALOGY OF PASSIONS

It is difficult, if not impossible, even today to achieve a balanced view of the person and work of Helvétius. There is more than one reason for this difficulty. Helvétius (1715–1771) lived in the age of Montesquieu and Voltaire, of Hume and Rousseau. His figure, though quite respectable, does not measure up to the stature of these dominating figures of the Age of Enlightenment and as a consequence his work has never received the same careful, detailed attention as the work of his greater contemporaries. Moreover, his work is expressive of the movement of enlightenment to such a degree that its typical features were seen more clearly than its far more important and peculiarly personal ones. Helvétius belonged intimately to the circle of the *encyclopédistes* though he himself never contributed to the *Encyclopédie*. One may say of his first great work, *De l'Esprit* (1758), that it focussed in the form of a systematic treatise the political views which, in the articles of the *Encyclopédie*, appear in the form of a wide spectrum of divergent opinions of several authors. This relation of the *Esprit* to the *Encyclopédie* was strongly sensed at the time when the treatise appeared. The *Parlement de Paris*, in 1759, when it ordered the burning of the *Esprit*, ordered at the same time an inquiry into the orthodoxy of the *Encyclopédie*. As a consequence, the permission for the publication of the *Encyclopédie*, of which seven volumes had appeared between 1751 and 1757, was withdrawn and publication could be resumed only in 1765. Quite as much as by a too close association with the *Encyclopédie*, the personal achievement of Helvétius has been obscured by its being related too closely to the evolution of English utilitarianism. What is perhaps best known today about Helvétius is his dependence upon Locke and his influence on Bentham. One may say, indeed, that Helvétius did what Locke failed to do, that is to apply the principles of the *Essay concerning Human Understanding* to the problems of politics, and there is no doubt that certain formulations of the *Esprit* suggested the principle of the greatest happiness of the greatest number both to Beccaria and Bentham. This historical function of Helvétius as the transmittor from Locke to Bentham should by no means be slighted; nevertheless, there was more substance to the French thinker than can be absorbed by this view. It was this substance that Nietzsche had in mind when he described the work of Helvétius as "the last great event in morals."[1]

The heritage of Locke

There does exist, indeed, a relation between Helvétius's method and the ideas of Locke's *Essay*. Helvétius insists on the point with pride.[2] Nevertheless, the relationship does not have the simple form of an adoption of certain ideas of Locke. Locke's *Essay* had appeared in 1690; sixty-five years later, at the time when Helvétius was writing his *Esprit*, conventional assumptions had developed concerning what Locke's ideas were, and these assumptions moved sometimes at a considerable distance from the original meaning of Locke's *Essay*. This latitude of interpretation was inevitably caused by the fact that Locke's theory of morals itself was an agglomeration of assumptions, hardly consistent with each other. The attack on innate ideas in the field of morals resulted in the assumption that a desire for happiness and an aversion to misery are the fundamental appetites determining human conduct. "Good and evil are nothing but pleasure and pain, or that which occasions or procures pleasure or pain to us."[3] For every moral rule offered to us we have to demand proof of its reasonableness, and the appeal lies ultimately to this principle. This crude formula, if taken seriously, could lead to interesting results; some of them can be seen in Mandeville's *Fable of the Bees* (1723). Locke himself would not have accepted this malicious and delightful play with virtues and vices. To him right and wrong were beyond doubt and morality was "capable of demonstration as well as mathematics."[4] But where do we find the operating rules for this mathematics of morality? Bentham's later answer was the principle of the greatest happiness of the greatest number. For Locke, the ultimate standard is the "law of God," extending the pleasure-pain principle into the beyond, for virtuous or sinful conduct will procure for man "happiness or misery from the hands of

1. Nietzsche, *Unveröffentlichtes aus der Umwerthungszeit*, no. 248 (*Werke*, 13, p. 107). See also *Menschliches, Allzumenschlisches*, no. 216 (*Werke*, 3, p. 316).

2. See *De l'Homme*, "Conclusion Générale," the first chapter, on "L'analogie de mes opinions avec celles de Locke," *Oeuvres* (Paris, 1795), 4, p. 413ff. See, furthermore, the passage on Locke in the poem "Bonheur," *Chant Second*, *Oeuvres* (Paris, 1795), 5, p. 26; another version of the same passage in *Oeuvres* (London, 1776), 2, p. 126.

3. Locke, *Essay*, bk. 2, ch. 28, sec. 5; see also bk. 2, ch. 20, sec. 2, and bk. 2, ch. 21, sec. 42.

4. Ibid., bk. 4, ch. 12, sec. 8; see also bk. 4, ch. 3, secs. 18–20, and ch. 4, sec. 7.

the Almighty."[5] But how can we be assured of this "only true touchstone of moral rectitude"? Through revelation? This assumption would lead, as it did, into the movement of theological utilitarianism, and ultimately to the positions of Tucker and Paley.[6] Again, however, Locke would not approve. He was convinced that the Gospel was a true code of morality, but he was equally convinced that the discovery of this code did not require a revelation. How then could the true code be found? At this point, Locke's argument petered out inconclusively, and the field remained wide open for the reconstruction of a philosophy of morals. The net result of Locke's speculation, thus, is not a new philosophy of morals but a thorough devastation on which nobody could build anything. The assertion that the position of a moralist is influenced by Locke can be received, therefore, only with caution.[7]

5. Ibid., bk. 2, ch. 28, sec. 8.
6. Abraham Tucker (1705–74), *Light of Nature pursued by Edw. Search* (1768–78); William Paley (1743–1805), *Principles of Moral and Political Philosophy* (1785).
7. The interpretation of Locke in this paragraph follows closely Leslie Stephen, *History of English Thought in the Eighteenth Century* (London, 1876), 2, ch. 9, "The Utilitarians." There is one point, however, that is somewhat obscured by the genteel, Victorian smoothness of Stephen. I hope to have brought it out more clearly: the destructiveness of Locke's habits of philosophizing. The point deserves more attention than it has received, just as Voltaire's irresponsibilities and irreverences, because these habits set a style for the treatment of intellectual problems. Locke's demolition of the assumption of innate ideas may be quite meritorious in itself, but it becomes a somewhat dubious achievement if we consider that he has nothing to offer in its place. The pleasant game of demolishing an opponent is relatively, but only relatively, innocuous as long as the fundamental creed which has found an untenable expression is itself beyond doubt. The purpose of criticism is, of course, not to prove a proposition wrong and to let it go at that, but to clarify, by means of criticism, the insight into the problem that has found an unsatisfactory formulation. If no better insight into the problem is offered, and Locke does not offer it, the result of criticism is the "Waste Land" of enlightenment. Moreover, one should observe the method used by Locke in his attack because it has grown into a pattern for the next century and a half. Throughout his critical analysis of innate ideas, Locke does not give a single concrete reference to a philosopher who has maintained any of the propositions which he criticizes. In the absence of such references it has to remain at least doubtful whether any philosopher was ever asinine enough to maintain, without appropriate qualifications, the propositions criticised by Locke. This technique of pressing a theory into absurd consequences which were not intended by the author, while ignoring the very serious problems which induced the formulation of the theory, becomes one of the fundamental devices of enlightened philosophizing. It accounts for a good deal of the exasperating tone of intellectual superiority which distinguishes so many enlightened persons. When these devices and mannerisms pass on to the lesser lights, and when with a grave face intellectual victories are gained over some nonsense which nobody has ever maintained or ever will maintain, the procedure, as sometimes in the case of James Mill, acquires a touch of the burlesque. These devices and manners become even more destructive in the course of the nineteenth and twentieth centuries, when they are transferred from the criticism of anonymous ideas to the criticism of

What Helvétius owes to Locke can best be gathered from his formulation of what he considered Locke's theory: "Our ideas," says Locke, "come to us from the senses; and from this principle, as from mine, one may conclude that the *esprit* in us is nothing but an acquisition."[8] The *esprit* is an assemblage of ideas, directly or indirectly derived from sense impressions. The nature of man is basically a physical sensibility (*sensibilité physique*). "The physical sensibility is man himself, and the principle of all that he is."[9] All differences between men are due to the differences of the educational process to which the *sensibilité physique* (which is neutrally receptive at birth) is submitted in the course of life. This radical formulation of Helvétius's position, however, is rather to be found in the later *De l'Homme* (published posthumously in 1772) than in the earlier *De l'Esprit*. The principle seems to have crystallized more clearly with the years and Helvétius admits: "In man all is physical sensation. Perhaps I have not developed this truth sufficiently in my book *De l'Esprit*."[10] We see emerging an image of man of impressive simplicity. The content of the mind is a transformation of sense impressions and a complicated structure is conceived as reducible to one explanatory principle, to physical sensibility. And this sensibility is not a faculty of man, but is man himself. Obviously, this is not Locke's conception of the mind, for Locke recognizes two sources of experience—sensation and reflection. The sentence: "*Nil est in intellectu, quod non fuerit in sensu,*" is not applicable to his conception unless at least we qualify the word *sensu* by the adjectives *interno et externo*. The experiences given to the internal sense of reflection—such as perceiving, thinking, doubting, believing, knowing, willing—constitute for Locke a class of experiences independent of sense impressions. The elimination of reflection and the systematic reduction of the internal experiences to sense impressions which we find in Helvétius is rather the conception of the mind that was developed by Condillac in his *Traité des Sensations* (1754). To Condillac rather than to Locke is due the attempt to interpret the structure of the mind genetically and to explain the internal experiences as *sensations transformées*.

About the motives of this radical genetic conception there is no doubt: a science of morals should be constructed "like experimental

---

concrete political ideas of concrete persons. The atrocious polemical manners which characterize the Communist and National Socialist literature are the last—let us hope it is the last—transformation of the polemical manners created by Locke and Voltaire.

8. *De l'Homme*, "Conclusion Générale," *Oeuvres* (1795), 4, p. 413.
9. Ibid., p. 417.
10. Ibid., sec. 2, ch. 1, *Oeuvres* (1795), 3, p. 110.

physics."[11] Into the moral universe, as into the physical, God has injected no more than one principle. Everything else is "necessary development." The principle of matter is force and submission to the laws of motion; out of initial chaos, after many miscarriages, the elements arrange themselves in the balanced, ordered universe that we see today. The principle of man is his physical sensibility, submissive to the laws of pleasure and pain; after initial confusion and many errors, the thoughts and actions of man will achieve the order and balance of happiness in the moral world.[12] The analogy of physics dominates the construction. This desire for fashionable construction is stronger than all critical thought. The reader may have wondered by what miracle we have achieved the transition from a sensualist theory of knowledge to a theory of morals. It was achieved quite simply, through the formula that man is under the direction of pleasure and pain: "the one and the other guard and direct his thoughts, his actions."[13] The "thoughts" (*pensées*) generously include cognitive functions as well as value judgments and emotions. Or, in another formulation: "Man is animated by a principle of life. This principle is his physical sensibility. What does this sensibility produce in him? a sentiment of love for pleasure, and of hatred for pain."[14] It seems almost unbelievable that such cavalier pieces of verbiage should be the foundation of a system of morals in emulation of physics. But, as a matter of fact, that is all there is.

This uncritical construction, again, is not Lockean. It is an ingredient that has entered the style of speculation in the course of the two generations after the publication of the *Essay*. Locke was quite explicit on the point that we have no experience of a causal connection between sense impressions and the feelings of pleasure and pain. "What certainty of knowledge can anyone have, that some perceptions, such as, *v. g.* pleasure and pain, should not be in some bodies themselves, after a certain manner modified and moved, as well as that they should be in an immaterial substance, upon the motions of the parts of body? Body, as far as we can conceive, being able only to strike and affect body; and motion, according to the utmost reach of our Ideas, being able to produce nothing but motion; so that when we allow it to produce pleasure or pain, or the *Idea* of a colour, or sound, we are fain to quit our reason, go beyond our *Ideas*, and attribute it wholly to the good pleasure of our Maker."[15] The ontic realms of mind and matter

11. *De l'Esprit*, "Préface."
12. *De l'Esprit*, *Oeuvres* (1776), 1, pp. 422ff.
13. Ibid., p. 423.
14. *De l'Homme*, sec. 4, ch. 22, *Oeuvres* (1795), 3, p. 384.
15. *Essay*, bk. 4, ch. 3, "Of the Extent of Human Knowledge," sec. 6.

are carefully kept apart and any attempt to reduce the phenomena of the one to phenomena of the other is rejected. And the same holds true when Locke introduces the ideas of pleasure and pain. They are classified as "simple" ideas, irreducible to others, and they may arise either from sensation or reflection. Pleasure and pain can, but need not be, the accompaniment of "bare" sensations or reflections. They can neither be described nor defined, but are accessible to knowledge only through immediate experience.[16] Pleasure, pain and the passions are for Locke an irreducible complex of ideas. In the face of such discrepancies between the actual theories of Locke and the theories of Helvétius which claim Lockean ancestry we have to say that, by the time of the *Esprit*, Locke had become a venerable symbol, lending a certain authority to any attempt at founding a philosophy of morals on the operations of pleasure, pain and passions.

In Helvétius this relationship with Locke is already strongly overlaid by physicism. Its meaning can be seen perhaps more clearly in the earlier reference of Vauvenargues (1715–47) to Locke. In his *Introduction à la connaissance de l'esprit humain* (1746), Vauvenargues quotes Locke almost verbatim to the effect that all our passions turn on pleasure and pain.[17] Moreover, he still preserves the Lockean distinction between sensation and reflection. Pleasure and pain as induced by sensation are immediate and undefinable; the passions, which originate in reflection, are explicable because they are rooted in the experiences of perfection and imperfection of existence.[18] The shift away from Locke is much slighter than in Helvétius, and the motive of the shift is revealed more clearly. Locke's undefinable pleasures and pains do not originate as sense impressions only. "By pleasure and pain, I must be understood to mean of body or mind as they are commonly distinguished; though in truth they be only different constitutions of the mind, sometimes occasioned by disorder in the body, sometimes by thoughts of the mind."[19] The simple, undefinable pleasures and pains, thus, may arise originally from operations of the mind, such as "of rational conversation with a friend, or of well directed study in the search and discovery of truth."[20] And even those which are "occasioned" by sensation belong to the "constitution of the mind." And because they belong to the "constitution of the mind" and not of the body they can

16. Ibid., bk. 2, ch. 20, "Of Modes of Pleasure and Pain," sec. 1.
17. Vauvenargues, *De l'Esprit Humain*, 2, p. 22. Compare Locke, *Essay*, bk. 2, ch. 20, sec. 3: "Pleasure and pain, and that which causes them, good and evil, are the hinges on which our passions turn."
18. Vauvenargues, loc. cit.
19. Locke, *Essay*, bk. 2, ch. 20, sec. 2.
20. Ibid., sec. 18.

produce further experiences of the mind, which Locke calls "internal sensations."[21] These "internal sensations" are the passions; they result when simple pleasures and pains are submitted to consideration by reflection. Here we can lay a finger on the point where Locke himself ceases to be a sensualist and treats the "constitution of the mind" as an autonomous unit, independent of the cognitive functions of the sensations. The sensualist epistemology has no bearing on the internal dimensions of human existence in which are placed the dynamic relations between pleasures, pains, passions, good and evil. In spite of the terminology of sensations which seems to anchor the world of morals firmly in experiences of the external world, the actual analysis throws us back into an atmosphere of internal balances and tensions. We do not know of any good and evil in itself, but only call good and evil that which we associate with pleasures and pains. But there is somehow an objective good and evil which has the peculiar character of causing in us pleasure and pain. Is there, after all, a prestabilized harmony between objective good and evil and subjective pleasure and pain? Locke's *Essay*, as we have seen, does not offer an answer to the question; Locke never elaborated a philosophy of human existence, although he came near the problem through his concept of the "constitution of the mind." This question, left open by Locke, is the question which occupies the French *moralistes* of the eighteenth century. When Vauvenargues takes up the Lockean categories of sensation and reflection, he narrows the meaning of sensation to the meaning of an impression that comes through the senses—and then discards it as uninteresting; and he makes reflection the organ by which we penetrate the structure of human existence. From "the experience of our being" we derive the ideas of "grandeur, pleasure, power"; from the experience of "the imperfection of our being" we derive the ideas of "smallness, subjection, misery"—"*voilà toutes nos passions.*"[22] Pleasure and pain are no longer irreducible, simple ideas; they refer to something more fundamental in the constitution of the mind: beyond pleasure and pain (and, incidentally, beyond good and evil) lies the experience of being, with its precarious balance of power and subjection, of perfection and imperfection, of existence under the threat of annihilation. The shift away from Locke reveals its meaning as the attempt to penetrate beyond pleasure and pain to the foundations of being and to rebuild a philosophy of morals within the framework of a philosophy of existence. The preoccupation with a genetic construction of the moral universe reveals its meaning as the attempt to find the existential foundation of

21. Ibid., sec. 3.
22. Vauvenargues, loc. cit.

morals at a time when the traditional Christian and humanistic foundations had broken down.

The new philosophy of existence

The Lockeanism of Helvétius, thus, is a somewhat confused pattern
of symbols with convergent meanings. From Locke directly stems the
aversion against innate moral ideas, and consequently the necessity to
search for a new basis of morals. When the immediate spiritual experiences have dried up, and when the tradition of faith and morals has
lost its hold, the refoundation of morals is dominated by the symbol
of an inversion of direction. The orientation toward a transcendental
reality is inverted and a new foundation is sought in the direction of
the somatic basis of existence. What specific symbols are used for this
purpose is not so very important; it is anybody's choice whether he
wishes to interpret Helvétius as a materialist because of his insistence
on the *sensibilité physique* as the essence of man, or as a sensualist
because the subjective sense impressions are declared to be the basis
on which the structure of the mind is erected, or perhaps as a hedonist
because the pleasures of the senses play an important directive role in
developing standards of conduct. All these symbols are present in the
work of Helvétius but none of them is decisive for the concrete analysis
of passions. They have an influence on the ideas of Helvétius only as
disturbing factors inasmuch as the concessions to these symbols frequently deflect the main line of the argument. The concessions to the
symbol of happiness as a good in itself vitiate the otherwise quite
admirable analysis of the operations of passions.[23] Setting aside the
disturbing and deflecting effects, the various symbols have the common purpose of directing the analysis toward the fundamental experiences of existence and of developing the phenomena of the moral world
as transformations of elemental forces. To this isolation of the fundamental forces and the analysis of passions we shall now turn.

23. The hedonistic disturbance in Helvétius has been criticised by Nietzsche,
Der Wille zur Macht, no. 751, *Werke*, 16, p. 194. The hedonistic aspect of
Helvétius's ideas, important as it is, has been overemphasized because it was the
aspect that fascinated Bentham. See for instance the presentation of Helvétius in
Henry Sidgwick's *Outlines of the History of Ethics* (1886), enlarged ed. by
Alban G. Widgery (London, 1931), pp. 267ff. On the untenability of this
hedonistic injection into the analysis of moral phenomena the literature is
enormous. See for instance Henry Sidgwick, *The Methods of Ethics*, 5th ed.
(London, 1893), bk. 1, ch. 4, "Pleasure and Desire" and the whole of bk. 2,
"Egoism"; Georg Simmel, *Einleitung in die Moralwissenschaft* (Berlin, 1892),
1, ch. 4 "Die Glückseligkeit"; Nicolai Hartmann, *Ethik* (Berlin, Leipzig, 1926),
pt. 1, sec. 3.

Inertia and ennui

The constituent forces of existence, as they are given to our experience, are on the one hand the forces which make for inertness, on the other hand the forces which counteract inertness and drive man into action. The force which makes for passivity or inertness Helvétius calls *paresse;* we shall use for it the English term *inertia.* Inertness or passivity is natural to man; attention fatigues and man gravitates toward a state of inertness like a body toward its center. And man would remain in this state of inertia unless he were pushed out of it by the counteraction of other forces, forces which Helvétius calls ennui and passion.[24] Ennui is defined as the uneasiness (*inquiétude*) which befalls us when we do not have an active awareness of our existence through pleasure.[25] The ennui is a minor but constant pain (*douleur*). The stronger pleasures of life are necessarily separated by intervals, and we experience the desire to fill these intervals by minor sensations. By a constant stream of new impressions we wish "to be made aware of every moment of our existence."[26] This desire to be agitated, and the uneasiness produced by the absence of impressions, contain, in part, "the principle of the inconstancy and perfectibility of the human mind." This principle compels the mind to agitate itself in all directions and it is the source of the gradual perfection of the arts and sciences and ultimately of the "*décadence du gout.*"[27] The uneasiness of the ennui, however, is normally no more than the continuous undertone of existence. It will drive a man into activities that will procure minor pleasures, but it is not the strong passion which produces a Lycurgus, a Homer or Milton, a Caesar or Cromwell. At best it may produce a military figure like Charles XII. Nevertheless, its importance should not be underrated. Whether the ennui is the driving force of action is determined in the concrete situation to a considerable extent by the general state of society and the form of government. In times when the great passions are chained by custom or a form of government that is unfavorable to their display, as for instance despotism, the ennui has the field for itself alone and under certain social conditions it may become the "*mobile universel.*" The atmosphere of the French court

24. *De l'Esprit*, sec. 3, ch. 5, *Oeuvres* (1776), 1, pp. 380f.
25. *Examen des critiques du livres intitulé De l'Esprit*, *Oeuvres* (1795), 5, pp. 245ff.: "Nous éprouvons continuellement le besoin d'appercevoir notre existence par le plaisir."
26. *De l'Esprit*, sec. 3, ch. 5, p. 381.
27. Ibid., pp. 381f.

of the eighteenth century is for Helvétius the great example of the situation in which ennui combined with feeble ambition are sufficient to explain the conduct of most men. Outside such special situations, the combined operation of ennui and inertia is responsible for a wide-spread state of mind with vast social consequences. For in submission to these two forces, man wants to be agitated to escape the ennui, but not too much so as not to be fatigued: "for that reason we want to know everything without the pains of penetrating it." Men are inclined to accept as true a traditional body of belief because an independent examination would be too much trouble; hence arguments which might disturb the belief are readily rejected as insufficient. Helvétius, when speaking of accepted belief, has his eye specifically on Christianity.[28] But his remarks on the subject are of general importance as an approach to a class of much neglected phenomena which constitute the ground-texture of all social life: the phenomena of conservative belief, credulity, semi-education, enlightened stupidity, resistance to knowledge, cleverly preserved ignorance, for which our awareness has been sharpened by contemporary events.

The role of the passions

From inertia and ennui alone, however, there would never arise the moral universe as embodied in history and society. A stronger force is needed to drive man into the more fatiguing actions and this force is supplied by the passions. The passions are to the moral world what movement is to the physical; they create and annihilate, conserve and animate and without them, there would be general death. Not all types of passion will supply such moving force equally; for the great effects there are needed the passions which Helvétius calls the *passions fortes*. A *passion forte* "is a passion of which the object is so necessary to our happiness that life becomes unbearable without its possession." Only passions of this strength can produce the great actions and induce men to brave danger, pain and even death, and to defy heaven. The great passions are *"le germe productif de l'esprit"*; they entertain the perpetual fermentation of ideas and carry man through the hardships of physical and intellectual adventure.[29] Great passion makes the great man. Great passion is the source of that active intelligence which enables a man

28. A footnote in ibid., pp. 385–388, brings, under the disguise of a Tonkinese myth, a ferocious attack on Christianity as a clerical imposture. Notes of this kind, whose disguise could easily be penetrated, were probably the cause of the storm aroused by the treatise.
29. Ibid., ch. 6.

to distinguish between the extraordinary and the impossible. The absence of great passion, on the other hand, characterizes the sensible man (*l'homme sensible*), that is the mediocrity. On the man of passion depends the advancement of the human mind.[30] The sensible man follows the beaten path, and he will do good not to leave it because he would get lost. He is the man in whom inertia dominates; he does not possess the activeness of soul which opens new perspectives and sows in the present the seeds of the future. Only the man of passion is capable of bearing the fatigue of continued meditation which enables him to see the concatenation of causes and effects stretching into the future. "It is the eagle-eye of passion which penetrates the dark abyss of the future: indifference is born blind and stupid." In social practice this differentiation of human types has the consequence that the "*génie élevé*," which discovers in the little good of the present the greater evil of the future, is treated as a public enemy. In this treatment of the genius virtue seems to punish vice while mediocrity sneers at the spirit.[31]

The genealogy of passions

Not all the passions are of the same type and between the several types there exists a genetical order; one passion is directly rooted in the structure of existence, all others are transformations of this fundamental passion. This relation between the several passions permits Helvétius to develop the idea of a *Généalogie des Passions*.[32] We are already acquainted with the lowermost ranks of this genealogy of passions. They are the principle of physical sensibility and the sentiments of love of pleasure and hatred of pain engendered by this principle. We have now to follow the genealogy beyond these first two ranks. From the operation of the love of pleasure and the hatred of pain arises the *amour de soi*. The *amour de soi* engenders the desire for happiness, the desire for happiness the desire for power, and the desire for power gives rise to the "factitious" passions of envy, avarice and ambition, "which all are, under different names, the love of power in disguise and applied to diverse means of obtaining it."[33]

The genealogy of passions is Helvétius's most fruitful systematic idea and, at the same time, his most disappointing in execution. We

---

30. Ibid., ch. 7, p. 405.
31. Ibid., ch. 7.
32. See the chapter bearing this title in *De l'Homme*, sec. 4, ch. 22. Nietzsche's title *Genealogie der Moral* is perhaps more than a coincidence.
33. *De l'Homme*, sec. 4, ch. 22, "Généalogie des Passions," pp. 384f.

already had occasion to reflect on the flimsiness of the idea of physical sensibility as the essence of man; almost no elaboration is to be found in the work of Helvétius beyond the bare statement of the proposition. We now have to say the same with regard to the further ranks of the genealogy. The cause of this unsatisfactory thinness of the construction is clear: Helvétius tried to combine a genetic construction which we may call materialistic or sensualistic with a genetic construction that relies on the existential experiences of inertia, ennui and passion, and the rungs of the two ladders simply do not coincide. The "genealogy" which we have just presented reveals the dilemma. Helvétius wants to interpret the gamut of passions as a series of variations of one fundamental passion, that is of the passion which he calls the *desir du pouvoir*. Assuming that the idea could be carried out successfully in the concrete analysis, this attempt would fit into the set of his primary assumptions concerning inertia, ennui and passion. The *desir du pouvoir* would be in this triad of concepts the basic passion which unfolds, in certain social situations and under the pressure of biographical circumstances, into the several "factitious" passions. It would be the elemental force which overcomes inertia and assuages the uneasiness of ennui by creating through action an acute awareness of existence. This course, of interpreting the will to power as the elemental force of existence in expansive action, was later taken by Nietzsche. With Helvétius this interpretation is thwarted by the attempt to fit the sense impressions and the pleasure-pain mechanism into the analysis of passion. Hence we find in the *généalogie* the desire of happiness engendering the *desir du pouvoir*. The passion for power loses thereby its function as the elemental force and becomes an instrument for procuring happiness. This perversion of the fleeting accompaniment of action into its purpose would bring Helvétius face to face with the necessity of explaining what kind of pleasure is procured by incurring death—for we remember his definition of the *passion forte* as the passion which braves danger and makes man risk his life. Passion in existence is not a matter of life only, it is a matter of life and death. An exploration of this problem would have compelled Helvétius to revise his genealogy of passions. He escapes this necessity simply by not exploring it.

The amour de soi

The strangest item in the *généalogie*, however, is the rank of the *amour de soi*. Again the *amour de soi* is placed in an instrumental position with regard to pleasure and pain. The *amour de soi* as a permanent sentiment is the guarantee that pleasures are procured and pains are avoided; we may say that the ego is integrated when the *amour de soi* is developed as the permanent control which steers the ego in the direction of pleasure and thereby keeps it in existence. This *amour de soi* is the Augustinian *amor sui*. In Christian psychology the *amor sui* is the passion of existence which prevents man from realizing his creaturely finiteness. The *amor sui* has to be broken by the *amor Dei* which directs man towards his divine origin and fulfillment, but this breaking of the *amor sui* is not entirely within the power of man; it requires assistance by the grace of God, and whether it really is broken is the mystery of Christian existence inaccessible to empirical diagnosis. Helvétius has the concept of the *amor sui* but not of the *amor Dei*, and this isolation of the *amor sui* profoundly changes its meaning as well as its systematic function. When the *amor sui* is used as a category of immanent existence, without regard to its Christian implications, it is difficult to see how it can be distinguished from the *desir du pouvoir* as the fundamental passion of existence. At best the term would emphasize the fact that human existence has as one of its important forming elements the ego, and that the *desir du pouvoir* operates in the form of actions of the ego. In the *généalogie*, however, Helvétius separates the *amour de soi* completely from the passions. Why this strange construction? By its very strangeness the construction gives us at last the key to the understanding of a group of concepts which otherwise might appear as an undigested agglomeration of traditional elements. The *amor sui* is not set by Helvétius into opposition to the *amor Dei*, but it retains from the Christian context a sector of its meaning, that is: its negative value accent. The *amour de soi* which steers man toward his personal happiness is not of itself conducive to virtue; the moral good can be realized only by actions which go beyond the procurement of personal pleasure and have for their aim, incidental to personal pleasure, the achievement of a general interest. This moral qualification of the *amour de soi* introduces a new dimension into the construction, beyond the pleasure-pain psychology and beyond the analysis of existential experiences. In a strict analysis of existence, beyond good and evil, neither the *amour de soi* nor the *desir du pouvoir* should have moral accents; in a strict psychology of the pleasure-pain mechanism, the love of pleasure and the hatred of pain should substitute for all moral considerations. Now we are faced by standards of good and evil, and the whole *généalogie des passions* is moved thereby into the function of an instrument which can be used for the achievement of good or of evil, which may be put to the service of virtue or vice. The curious interlocking of concepts which alternately belong to the pleasure-pain-happiness group or the inertia-ennui-passion group makes sense if it is under-

stood as a manageable means-end concatenation which can be bent to
ulterior purposes by a legislator or educator who is in possession of
the absolute standards of value. We are not surprised, therefore, to
find that Helvétius considers the structure of existence as an acquired
structure, with the exception of the *sensibilité physique* and the
pleasure-pain mechanism. Even the *amour de soi* is an "acquisition."
"One learns to love oneself; to be human or inhuman, virtuous or
vicious. Moral man is altogether education and imitation."[34]

The peculiarities of Helvétius's *généalogie* thus find their explanation
in the instrumentalization of existence. The *amour de soi* can be developed, tempered or deflected through the conditioning of attitudes
by educational rewards of pleasure and punishments of pain. The
desire for happiness can be influenced with regard to the morality of
its content by the previous formation of the ego. The *desir du pouvoir*
will be determined in its direction by the type of happiness which it
has to serve, and the factitious passions can be developed in the direction of antisocial vices, or of virtues serving the general interest, in
accordance with the rewards or punishments held out by the structure
of society in which they operate. The most significant detail in this
process of instrumentalization is the transformation of the *amor sui*
from a fundamental passion of existence into an acquired character.
If we remember the Augustinian origin of the concept, we might say
that in the Christian context the breaking of the *amor sui* is the combined work of human effort and the grace of God, while in the context
of Helvétius the educator takes the place of God: where the grace of
God has failed, the educator may achieve results by a judicious application of the psychology of conditioned reflexes. With the implications
of this divinization of the educational process we shall have to deal
later on in more detail.

For the present, let us consider briefly the influence which the
instrumentalization of the structure of existence has on the analysis of
power. The fundamental passion, from which all other passions derive,
is the desire for power. In the concrete analysis the desire for power is
represented by the desire to find oneself in a position of command, if
possible in the role of a despot. The desire to be a despot is rooted in
the love of pleasure and consequently in the nature of man. Everybody
wants to be happy, and hence everybody wants to have the power to
command other people to contribute to his happiness. The rule over
people can either be a rule according to law or a rule by arbitrary
will. In the first case, the power to command is limited and in order

34. Ibid., sec. 4, ch. 22, p. 384.

to exploit the position of command most effectively for the production of happiness, the ruler will have to study the laws and find the legal means for achieving his purposes. Such study is fatiguing and inertia makes itself felt as the counterforce to action. In order to satisfy his inertia, everyone will strive, if possible, for absolute power, which will avoid the fatigue of studying the law and put men slavishly at his will. *"Voilà par quel motif chacun veut être despote."*[35] Since everybody is a despot by desire, if not in fact, social power is held in high esteem. "One hates the powerful, one does not despise him. . . . Whatever we may say: one does not really despise what one does not dare to despise face to face. . . . The respect paid to virtue is transitory, the respect paid to force is eternal."[36] This state of things is most propitious from the point of view of the educator and legislator. If virtue were a part of the organization of the individual, or a consequence of divine grace, there would be no honest men except those who are organized honestly by nature, or predestined to be virtuous by heaven. Good or bad laws in this case, or forms of government, would not influence anybody. If, however, virtue can be made the effect of the desire for power, the legislator can confer the prizes of esteem, wealth and power on virtuous conduct. Thus "under a good legislation only the fools would be vicious."[37] That all men are inspired by the love of power is the most precious gift of heaven. What does it matter whether men are born virtuous, if only they are born with a passion which makes them virtuous if skilfully managed?[38]

The flaw in this analysis of power as the fundamental passion is obvious: the desire for power, as presented by Helvétius, is not fundamental at all, nor is it much of a passion; it is no more than the attempt to procure happiness, understood in a hedonistic sense, through command over services and commodities. This was the flaw in Helvétius's psychology of passions against which Nietzsche directed his criticism: the idea of an Alexander or Caesar striving for power in order to be happy is preposterous beyond discussion. Helvétius, however, was no fool, and the flaw in his analysis requires explanation. That Helvétius had a keen understanding of the psychology of passions is beyond doubt to the reader of the extended, brilliant discussions of various passions in the *Esprit*. Behind this flaw in the analysis there is a definite will to see the phenomenon of power in a certain light; we have indicated this problem when we introduced the concept of instrumentalization

35. *De l'Esprit*, sec. 3, ch. 17, pp. 497ff.
36. *De l'Homme*, sec. 4, ch. 12, p. 343.
37. *De l'Esprit*, sec. 3, ch. 17.
38. *De l'Homme*, sec. 4, ch. 12, p. 349.

into our interpretation. Now we have to explore a bit farther the motives as they become apparent from Helvétius's analysis.

There is one element in the motivation of Helvétius which is typical for the period of Enlightenment, as well as for theorists of the nineteenth century who were inspired by the pattern of enlightened theory: it is the substitution of a correct empirical observation for the *natura rerum*. Empirically we find, indeed, hedonists who strive for a position of power in order to enjoy the concomitant material benefits, and we also find among those who hold a position of power by circumstance, without striving for it, men whose relation to their position is purely hedonistic. The French court of the eighteenth century could supply Helvétius with ample material in support of his analysis. The elevation of the empirically correct observation into a general theory of power, however, belongs to the same class of phenomena as the Voltairian identification of ecclesiastical abuses of the time with the essence of the Church, or the Marxian identification of the misuse of religion as an opium for the people with the essence of religion. In an earlier chapter we discussed this problem under the aspect of Voltaire's spiritual obscurantism. Now, in Helvétius, another aspect of the problem becomes visible: the willingness to mistake the abuse for the essence in order to continue the abuse, with the best of surface intentions, for a different purpose.

The great temptation in recognizing the abusive instrumentalization of passion as the meaning of passion lies in the possibility for the analyst who makes the mistake to misuse the instrument for his own purposes. In Helvétius's analysis of power we can discern the origin of phenomena which pervade modern politics and are still increasing in importance, the origin of the artificiality of modern politics as engendered through propaganda, education, reeducation, and enforced political myth, as well as through the general treatment of human beings as functional units in private enterprise and public planning. The actual decadence of Western society which occupied the thinkers of the eighteenth century has become the model of social and political practice. The disorder which expresses itself empirically in spiritual obscurantism and the instrumentalization of the life of passion is accepted as the nature of man by the analyst—for others. In Helvétius's analysis we meet a classical instance of the destruction of the integral human person by positing as normal the disorder of the person while denying to man the remedial powers which might restore the order. The possibility of spiritual regeneration of the person, the existence of man in communion with God, the possibility of the *renovatio evangelica* in the Christian sense, are denied. The function of regeneration is transferred to the analyst in the role of the organizing legislator who will create externally the social situation which in its turn will induce the external conformance of conduct to moral standards by a play on the psychological mechanism of disordered man. It is the dream of escape from the mystery of iniquity that has been expressed by T. S. Eliot in the verses:

> They constantly try to escape
> From the darkness outside and within
> By dreaming of systems so perfect that no one
>   will need to be good.

Helvétius has dreamt the dream with radical perfection: in most instances the thinker of this type is satisfied with a Pelagian assumption about the goodness of man, but Helvétius conceives man as a morally neutral force, neither good nor bad. Man is emptied of moral substance, and the forces of good and evil are transferred in their entirety to the analyst-legislator.[39]

Salvation as a social process

The attitude of Helvétius is an early instance of political attitudes which unfold more completely in the nineteenth and twentieth centuries. As always in the early cases, the spiritual processes which lead to the new attitude are more clearly visible than in the later period when the structure of sentiments has settled into conventional patterns. Today we take it more or less for granted that our society is swarming with leaders, left and right, who supply substance to the human automaton. The enormity of the attitude can no longer be sensed so sharply as in the case of Helvétius where it appeared in direct conflict with a living tradition. What happens is, in brief, that the analyst-legislator arrogates to himself the possession of the substance of good in society while denying it to the rest of mankind. Mankind is split into the mass of pleasure-pain mechanisms and the One who will manipulate the mechanisms for the good of society. The nature of man, by a kind of division of labor, is distributed among masses and leaders so that only society as a whole is integral man. Moreover the operations of the legislator on the members of society substitute, as we have seen, for grace and predestination. Society has become a totally closed universe with an immanent process of salvation.

The insight into the spiritual process that occurs in Helvétius will shed some light on the significance of genetic, sensualist psychology, as

---

39. If we translate the construction into Platonic terms, we would have to say that Helvétius dreams of a Politeia without Eros.

well as on the complex of philosophical assumptions attached to it, for the political evolution of Western society. The tenacity of faith in this complex of ideas is certainly not caused by its merits as an adequate interpretation of man and society. The inadequacy of a pleasure-pain psychology, the poverty of utilitarian ethics, the impossibility of explaining moral phenomena by the pursuit of happiness, the uselessness of the greatest happiness of the greatest number as a principle of social ethics—all these have been demonstrated over and over again in a voluminous literature. Nevertheless, even today this complex of ideas holds a fascination for a not inconsiderable number of persons. This fascination will be more intelligible if we see the complex of sensualism and utilitarianism not as number of verifiable propositions but as the dogma of a religion of socially immanent salvation. Enlightened utilitarianism is but the first in a series of totalitarian, sectarian movements to be followed later by Positivism, Communism and National Socialism.

III. HELVÉTIUS AND THE HERITAGE OF PASCAL

As far as the intellectual ancestry of Helvétius is concerned, we have dealt so far only with Locke and with the transformation which the ideas of the *Essay concerning Human Understanding* underwent in the following two generations. In Helvétius's analysis of existence, however, we encountered a group of concepts which does not stem from the English tradition, forces which make for passivity or ennui which Helvétius calls *paresse*. In his analysis of existence in these terms Helvétius moves in the tradition of the French *moralistes* and particularly of Pascal. A comparison with the ideas of Pascal will bring into view further aspects of the new theory of power. This comparison, however, will be confined strictly to the few concepts of Pascal which have a direct bearing upon the analysis of Helvétius.

For Helvétius the forces of existence which overcome the tendency toward inertness are ennui and passion. This initial situation for an analysis of existence is taken from Pascal. The dynamic of existence is determined, for Pascal, by the impossibility of a state of complete quiet or rest (*repos*). "Nothing is as unbearable for man as to be completely at rest, without passion, without business, without distraction, without application to something." In such a state of rest man becomes aware of "his nothingness, his forsakenness, his insufficiency, his dependence, his impotence, his emptiness." Incontinently there springs from the depth of his soul "the ennui, the blackness, the *tristesse*, the chagrin, the spite, the despair."[1] What Pascal tries to describe by this array of terms denoting the facets of a fundamental mood is what is called in modern philosophy of existence since Kierkegaard the "anxiety of existence." The intoxication of activity beclouds the reality of human existence. When passion subsides, the experience of a fundamental emptiness and metaphysical forlornness emerges unobscured, the anxiety of existence springs up crying to be assuaged, and the ordinary method of assuaging anxiety is diversion by new activity. Pascal suggests that "we never are in search of things, but always in search of the search,"[2] because back of all specific miseries of human life lies the fundamental misery of our "weak and mortal state." This state is so miserable "that nothing can comfort us if we think of it closely."

1. Pascal, *Pensées*, ed. Brunschvicg (Paris, 1904), no. 131.
2. Ibid., no. 135.

This anxiety of existence has no specific cause. If man felt safe in every respect, still the ennui would rise on its own account from the depth of the heart since the free-rising, causeless ennui is due to the constitution of man's existence (*par l'état propre de sa complexion*).[3]

The *ressentiment* against this continual misery drives man away from himself into external occupations, into the *divertissements*. The assuaging effect, however, can never be more than temporary. There is no such thing as a happiness in which man can rest because the occupation itself diverts, not its achievement. Nevertheless, the futility of the effort does not deter men from its renewal. "All men, without exception, strive for happiness; whatever means they employ, this is always the aim. . . . This is the motive of all actions of all men, even of those who go and hang themselves." They pursue happiness in spite of the fact that nobody has ever reached it. "What do this avidity and this impotence betray if not that formerly man knew a true happiness of which he has today nothing but the marks and empty traces?" The desire for a happiness which never can be satisfied by finite aims points toward the infinite good which alone can give true satisfaction, toward God.[4] The pursuit of intramundane happiness is the "disease of pride" which detracts man from God, a disease which can be cured only by the Grace uniting man with God—ultimately in death.[5] The happiness in finite action is the shadow of the infinite felicity in the Grace of God, and the memory of "the grandeur of our first nature" transforms the finite aim of such action into the mirage of an infinite aim which, if achieved, would give eternal rest.

Though the pursuit of happiness is futile, it is part of human existence. Pascal does not roundly condemn the *divertissements* of the life of passion. It would be unjust to blame men: "Their fault is not that they seek the turmoil, if only they would seek it as a diversion; the evil is that they seek it as if the possession of the things which they seek would make them truly happy." But men do not admit the escapist character of their *divertissements* and thereby they demonstrate that they do not know themselves.[6] The fleeting consolation that is furnished by the *divertissements* thus becomes the greatest of our miseries, for it is precisely this consolation which hinders us from thinking about ourselves and hence advances us on the road to perdition. "Without it we would be in the ennui, and the ennui would drive us to seek a more solid means to emerge from it. But the diversions amuse us, and

3. Ibid., no. 139.
4. Ibid., no. 425.
5. Ibid., no. 430.
6. Ibid., no. 139.

carry us on insensibly to death."[7] In the worldly dynamic of sentiment, man is thus caught between despair when he visualizes his corruption and weakness, and pride of achievement when he visualizes his possibilities and considers his nature uncorrupt.[8] The way out of this dilemma is pointed by the realization of the supernatural status of the soul in its relation to God. Sentiments of this class, however, cannot be treated in a psychology of passions. The dynamic of these sentiments is transcendental. "The first thing which God inspires in the soul which He chooses to touch truly, is a quite extraordinary knowledge and view by virtue of which the soul considers the things and itself in an entirely new manner."[9] This "new light" changes the appearance of the *divertissements*, the perishable aims appear as perishable, even as perished, and in this light the world of passion is annihilated as a realm of true happiness. The anxiety at the core of existence (*la crainte*) also takes on a new dimension. The soul experiences its own ultimate nothingness and in penetrating to the abyss of this nothingness it finds itself in its creatureliness in relation to the infinity of God, the Creator.[10] As a result of this realization the soul will be possessed of a sacred humility which God lets outgrow the pride and it will embark on the search of the true supreme good, which is God.[11]

In the perspective of the existence that has been touched by God, the natural ego with its passions will appear as hateful. "*Le moi est haissable*" is Pascal's doctrine with regard to the worldly ego.[12] The ego is hateful because it is unjust, and it is unjust to the structure of existence because, under the pressure of the experience of death, it erects itself into a "world-all," a total of meaning which blots out the meaning of everything else in the world. "Everybody is an all to himself, for when he is dead, all is dead to him. And hence it comes that everybody considers himself all to all."[13] This fundamental injustice can be tempered superficially through a diversion of passion into public service. But the system of ethics and the moral conduct resulting from such diversion is "a false image of true charity." Pride has assumed in virtuous social conduct a new form; it is not extirpated. At bottom, there is still the hatred with which man hates the other

7. Ibid., no. 181.
8. Ibid., no. 435.
9. Pascal, *Sur la conversion du pécheur, Oeuvres Complètes* (Paris, 1904–14), 2, p. 37.
10. Ibid., p. 39.
11. Ibid., p. 38.
12. Pascal, *Pensées*, no. 455.
13. Ibid., no. 457.

man's ego as the rival to his own world-filling ego.[14] One does not hate
in the ego only its potential dangerousness, but the fundamental injustice which is only covered by just conduct. "Every ego remains the
enemy and would like to be the tyrant of all others."[15]

The ideas of Pascal are of relevance in the present context because
they show the origin of the concepts of Helvétius and because, at the
same time, they contain the critique of the use which Helvétius made
of them. Pascal's analysis is deeply embedded in the Christian tradition, but it also contains a decisive step beyond the Christian tradition
insofar as it recognizes, as a new phenomenon of mass relevance, the
man who is obsessed by the pursuit of happiness to the point of being
blind to his creaturely finiteness. The extended analysis of passion appears in Pascal for the same reason for which it appeared in the contemporary work of Hobbes: in France as in England, the mass appearance of men who are passionately engaged in intramundane action
and have lost the sense of their creaturely existence engages the attention of thinkers. The Christian *contemptus mundi* is on the point
of being forgotten and action in the world becomes the absorbing passion of man. In Pascal, even more than in Hobbes, the analysis of
passion implies the condemnation of the new type; but the analysis is
made nevertheless, and later thinkers who do not condemn may use
the analysis in a positive way for their own purposes. This peculiar
critical position of Pascal anticipates the later analysis of passion and
reveals its faultiness. Pascal recognizes, as Helvétius did later, the
uneasiness of existence, the ennui, as the mood which drives man into
diverting action. But, unlike Helvétius, he recognizes the diverting
character of action and he knows that the ennui may be overcome by
searching in another direction than that of the release of passion. The
return into the creatureliness of existence in order to meet the Grace of
God is the Christian answer to the anxiety of existence; the life of
passion which blots out this possibility becomes the source of misery
and is hateful. From the Christian position of Pascal, the analysis of
passion and of the pleasure-pain mechanism in the tradition of Locke
and Condillac touches only one half of the problem of existence, and
it touches precisely the half which is destructive of the true self if it
is taken for the whole.

The two selves

Helvétius was well acquainted with the work of Pascal and especially
with this problem. His method of coping with it will let us gain perhaps

14. Ibid., nos. 451, 453.
15. Ibid., no. 455.

the profoundest insight into the new type of anti-Christian religiousness which inspires a new approach to politics. The problem becomes topical in the *Esprit* when Helvétius suddenly experiences the necessity of penetrating "*Jusques dans l'abyme du coeur humain.*"[16] After having explained that passions are morally indifferent and that it depends on the form of government whether they serve virtue or vice, he finds that there is a residual phenomenon requiring explanation: the phenomenon that even under the best form of government men of most reliable virtue show flaws of conduct. Brutus and Cato are for Helvétius models of virtue, but even Brutus once used his political influence to gain a favor for a member of his family, and even Cato, on one occasion, seems to have used government funds for pocket money. Even if most properly directed toward virtuous action, the heart of man seems to remain a battlefield for virtue and vice. In order to solve this moral problem "we have to search the cause of the alternate states of unrest and quiet of conscience, of these confused and variegated movements of the soul, of these internal struggles which the tragic poet presents with so much success on the stage because the spectators have experienced similar ones themselves"; in brief: "we have to ask what are these two selves which Pascal and some Hindu philosophers have recognized in man."[17]

At first sight, the reader might suspect some grotesque misunderstanding. What have the *deux moi* of Pascal to do with the civic honesty of the two Roman models of virtue? And we have to ask this question particularly because under the title of "the other self" Pascal has dealt with the problem raised by Helvétius. We are not satisfied, says Pascal, with "the life that we have in us and in our true being: we want to live an imaginary life in the minds of others, and for that reason we force ourselves into appearance. We work incessantly to embellish and conserve our imaginary being and we neglect the real one. If we are possessed of tranquillity, or generosity, or loyalty, we endeavor to make it known in order to attach these virtues to our other self, and we remove them even from our true self in order to join them to our other self: we would readily commit an act of cowardice in order to acquire the reputation of being courageous. This characterizes the nothingness of the true self that we are not satisfied by the one without the other, and that frequently we even exchange the one for the other! For a man who would not die to conserve his honor would be infamous."[18] The problem of virtuous action belongs to the process of building the imaginary, other self. The misdemeanors of Brutus and Cato, which

16. *De l'Esprit*, sec. 3, ch. 16, p. 482.
17. Ibid., p. 486.
18. Pascal, *Pensées*, no. 147.

aroused the misgivings of Helvétius, are a problem insofar as the public image of the self is disturbed. From the perspective of Pascal, the misdemeanors would quite possibly be the only instances in the lives of the two gentlemen when for once they had forgotten their stage-act of Roman virtue, when for once they had been loyal to their true self.

Helvétius, however, has not misunderstood Pascal at all. He continues his remark on the *deux moi* by a reference to the parallel insight in Hindu mysticism, and he explains carefully that he is referring to the two principles of Vedanta philosophy. The positive principle is that of the true self, the negative principle is that of the *maya*, of the veil of appearance. Wisdom consists in deliverance from the *maya* through return into the infinite, divine ground of the true self.[19] He does not misunderstand the meaning but deliberately projects the meaning into the universe of passionate action. Hence the question why even the most virtuous men are not without their flaws has to be answered by exploring the mechanism of passions. If man were possessed by a solitary passion only, such as the *amour de gloire*, his actions could be directed uniformly toward virtuous aims. Since he is possessed, however, by a plurality of passions, a virtuous man has to be defined as a man in whom the passion leading toward virtuous results is predominant while the other passions are comparatively weak in their effects.[20] And this virtuous man is only possible concretely if the *amour de gloire*, the desire for social esteem, can find its satisfaction in actions which serve the public interest. "It is the happy conformance between our personal interest and the public interest, the conformance which ordinarily is produced by the desire for esteem, which produces tender sentiments for other men and experiences their affection as a sufficient reward."[21] If this conformance is not provided for by the social structure, there will be no virtuous men. "The virtuous man is not the man who sacrifices his pleasures, habits and strongest passions to the public interest; he is the man whose strongest passion is in so close conformance with the public interest that practically always he is compelled to be virtuous."[22] And how can this lucky conformance be procured? Again we are referred to the legislator as the savior.

We can now formulate the problem more clearly. Helvétius agrees with Pascal on the general principles of the interpretation of passions. The life of passion builds, for Pascal, the imaginary self for the public eye; it weaves, for Helvétius, the veil of *maya*, using as its forces the

19. *De l'Esprit*, sec. 3, ch. 16, p. 486.
20. Ibid., p. 488.
21. Ibid., p. 489.
22. Ibid., pp. 490f.

amour de soi and the *amour de gloire.* For Pascal this texture of pride can be torn only by a radical change of direction toward creaturely nothingness and the building of the true life, without passion, in openness to the Grace of God. For Helvétius, man cannot change his course, the life of passion is his fate, and all one can do is to provide a social situation in which the results of passionate action are virtuous. The legislator has the function of entangling man in the veil of *maya* in such a manner that the fabric shows a surface iridescence of virtue. Man is left in the life of appearance but, by means which remind us of Hegel's *List der Vernunft,* the appearance is overlaid by a further appearance of virtue. As the spider in the web of appearances sits the managing legislator—the intramundane counterforce to God—guiding the spectacle of the struggle which has so much success with the audience because everybody recognizes in it his own struggle.[23] This truly Satanic vision reveals the extent of the catastrophe of the Western spirit even in the eighteenth century. Helvétius, as we have said, did not misunderstand Pascal, he simply was dead to the possibility of a Christian existence. The problems of Pascal are retained, but the new religiousness of the closed intramundane person determines a new image of man and a new interpretation of the old problems. Helvétius was neither a great thinker, nor a great soul. He could advance his position with comparative unawareness of its implications. The catastrophic end of this new religiousness which severs the relations with the *realissimum* we shall see, a century later, in Nietzsche.

From this excursion into the Satanic depths of happiness and virtue, let us now return to the surface problems of politics whch tempt the children of the world.

Happiness and virtue

A spider is a purposeful little animal: it does not want to weave a net only, it also wants to catch the fly. Catching the fly is the great lust both of the thinker and the man of action who want to create the

23. After I had written this sentence I found that my imagination cannot outrun reality. Bentham, in the *Panopticon,* praises as the great advantage of his plan for the perfect prison "the *apparent omnipresence* of the inspector (if divines will allow me the expression), combined with the extreme facility of his *real presence*" (*Panopticon: or, The Inspection House, Works,* ed. Bowring [Edinburgh, 1843], 4, p. 45). The *Panopticon* is one of the most fascinating documents for the pneumapathology of the eighteenth century. It should be read in comparison with novels of Franz Kafka: the dream-like situations which the poet uses as his instrument for expressing the anxiety of existence have become reality in the life and work of Bentham. The reader of the *Panopticon* is haunted by the suspicion that Bentham is a figure that has escaped from a novel of Kafka.

happiness of man in society. We remember Pascal's remarks on the false image of true charity, and on the ego that would like to be the tyrant of all others. Let us first get our bearings on this subject matter through a famous passage of Bentham's, reflecting the influence of Helvétius: "If one could find a method of becoming master of everything which might happen to a certain number of men, to arrange everything around them so as to produce on them the impression that one wishes to produce, to make sure of their actions, of their connections, and of all the circumstances of their lives, so that nothing could escape, nor could oppose the desired effect, it cannot be doubted that a method of this kind would be a very powerful and a very useful instrument which governments might apply to various objects of the utmost importance."[24] The passage is so rich that it could serve as the text for a sermon of book length. We shall only note the Gestapo dream of complete physical and mental control over a group of human beings, the suggestive association of powerful and useful, and the suppressed desire to lay one's hands on a government in order to apply the instrument "to various objects of the utmost importance." Bentham was born a hundred years too early—a century later, circumstances would prove more favorable for the realization of his dream. On the eve of the Russian Revolution, Lenin evoked the vision of the happy state when the majority of the people will rule the exploiters and operate the government as a vast institution of accounting and control: "When the *majority* of the people begin everywhere to keep such accounts and maintain such control over the capitalists (now converted into employees) and over the intellectual gentry, who still retain capitalist habits, this control will really become universal, general, national; and there will be no way of getting away from it, there will be 'nowhere to go.'— The whole of society will have become one office and one factory, with equal work and equal pay."[25] In Lenin, as in Bentham, we see at work the sadistic imagination devising circumstances that will leave to the victim only the choice between submission and suicide. The legislator expects the victims to get "accustomed" to the conditions and ultimately to feel free in their network; at the latest, the next generation, "reared

24. Jérémie Bentham, *Traités de Législation Civile et Pénale*, ed. Dumont (Paris, An X [1802]), 3, p. 209. The passage quoted is the opening paragraph of the *Mémoire* on the *Panoptique*, of 1791. The formulation is Dumont's, but it was approved by Bentham. The passage continues: "L'éducation, par exemple, n'est que le résultat de toutes les circonstances auxquelles un enfant est exposé. Veiller à l'éducation d'un homme, c'est veiller à toutes ses actions: c'est le placer dans une position où on puisse influer sur lui comme on le veut, par le choix des objets dont on l'entoure et des idées qu'on lui fait naître."

25. Lenin, *State and Revolution* (*Collected Works*, 21, p. 230; *Sochineniya*, 21, p. 440).

under new and free social conditions" (Engels) will acquire the habit of feeling unoppressed and happy in the new world.[26]

The greatest happiness principle

We have marked out the general path of happiness and virtue at the beginning of which we find the ideas of Helvétius. His fundamental thesis for practical politics is the moral neutrality of man; men are neither good nor bad, they follow their interest. "The cries of the moralists will not change this motive force (*ressort*) of the moral universe. One should not complain of the badness of man but of the ignorance of legislators who have always put private interest into opposition to the general interest."[27] The excellence of laws is the condition of virtuous conduct. And when are the laws good? When they are consistent among themselves, and they are consistent only when they are animated by a single, simple principle, as for instance by the principle of public usefulness (*utilité public*), that is of usefulness "to the greatest number of men under one governmental organization." This principle contains in nucleus "all morals and legislation."[28] These propositions have their practical importance because man by nature is made to be virtuous. This virtuousness "by nature" is not a contradiction to the earlier assumption of moral neutrality since "by nature" means that massive force is on the side of justice. The principle of the greatest number is not to be understood as a mathematics of happiness in the sense that the majority should be happy rather than the minority. Rather, it involves the recognition that "the greatest number" is a political force. "If we consider that the power essentially resides in the greatest number, and that justice consists in the practice of actions useful to the greatest number, then it is evident that justice, by nature, is always equipped with the necessary power to suppress vice and to compel men to be virtuous."[29] If justice is in harmony with power, why then is justice not realized in the concrete society of the day? Because the mass of the people is held in ignorance with regard to this truth by the ruling minority, that is by Church and Court. The critique of contemporary society given by Helvétius is extensive but cautious in the decisive formulations. He takes pains to avoid a direct attack on King and Church, and rather concentrates on the obviously abusive

26. Ibid. (*Collected Works*, 21, p. 214; *Sochineniya*, 21, p. 426).
27. *De l'Esprit*, sec. 2, ch. 5, pp. 96ff.
28. Ibid., sec. 2, ch. 17, p. 228. Another formulation is to be found in sec. 2, ch. 23, pp. 291f.: "the public interest, that is the interest of the greatest number, on which always ought to be based the principles of good morals."
29. Ibid., sec. 2, ch. 24, pp. 300f.

part of the minority whom he calls the *"fanatiques"* and the *"demi-politiques,"* the religious fanatics who indulge in persecutions and the parasitical hangers-on who prevent the enlightenment of the people.[30] The next question would have to be: how did the minority which opposes the interest of the people ever gain its ascendancy? The answer to this question can only be furnished by a theory of the historical evolution of society.

The historical evolution of society

Helvétius's theory of social evolution is of considerable importance in the history of political ideas as well as for the understanding of certain systematic issues in later theories of politics. As far as the history of ideas is concerned, Helvétius has seen clearly for the first time that a philosophy of social justice has to rely on the historical evolution of economic institutions as its basis, if and when the insight into spiritual values is lost. As far as the systematic issue is concerned, we find in Helvétius the problem of the happiness of the greatest number still connected with the concrete issues of social revolution. In the later development of systematic ethics the greatest-happiness principle lost this connection with the concrete issue that had given it meaning and it was advanced and criticized as an abstract principle of morality. With Helvétius, the greatest number whose happiness is supposed to be the standard of social justice is not a mathematical maximum but quite concretely the "people," that is the middle class, the peasants and the workers. And the smaller number whose happiness may be neglected is not a group of idiosyncratic individuals on the fringe of mass normality, but quite concretely the ruling class of France. In its origins, with Helvétius, the greatest-happiness principle is clearly related to the differentiation of economic classes and to the problem of class struggle. English utilitarianism and Marxism are both off-shoots from the original position of Helvétius, the one stressing the middle class as the greatest number whose happiness has to be secured, the other the proletariat.

In *De l'Esprit* and *De l'Homme*, Helvétius has formulated his theory of social evolution more than once. We have to distinguish two main variants of the theory. In one of the accounts, the emphasis lies on the issue of nationalism or internationalism: should the greatest number be the majority within a nation or the majority of mankind? In a second account, the emphasis lies on the issue of the class struggle: who specifically are the greatest number and wherein does their happiness

---

30. Ibid., ch. 23. The later *De l'Homme* is more outspoken in the critique.

consist? We shall deal first with the account that emphasizes the issue of nationalism or internationalism.

The question of social evolution arises with the problem why justice should be defined in terms of the general interest. The physical sensibility and the pleasure-pain mechanism are the only principles admissible in the interpretation of man; we have to ask, therefore, how the general interest can be explained as a transformation of individual interest. As long as this question is not answered, the demand addressed to the legislator that he should, by his laws, produce conformance between private and public interest, hangs in the air, and we may ask legitimately why there should be a conformance of this kind. The theory of social evolution has the purpose of showing that genetically the general interest is an outgrowth of private interest; the state of predominant private interest is a primitive social state and evolution toward the general interest marks the advancement of the social state. The phases of this evolution are the following: (1) we have to assume an initial stage of isolated families who provide for their necessities of life; (2) population increase produces neighborhood relations in which rivalries for food and women will result in quarrels and combat; (3) life in perpetual fear will induce agreements and the creation of magistrates for their enforcement; (4) up to this point the development has taken place under the economic conditions of forest life, and of a hunting and fishing civilization; further increase of population and scarcity of food supplies will compel the transition to cattle-raising and nomadism; (5) the same factors will produce in due course agriculture and the development of landed property; (6) the necessities of a barter economy will result in the creation of money, and with this invention the primary equality is broken; society is on its path toward stratification into the rich and the poor; (7) since wealth procures pleasure, the desire to belong to the economic upper class produces the factitious passions and, generally, the texture of sentiment which characterizes civilized society. Society has become a body of men who are bound together by their economic interdependence; the destruction of this body would result in misery for all, hence its preservation is everybody's private interest. Under these circumstances, a differentiation of interests that would result in cleavages in the social body along class lines has to be avoided; the pursuit of the "general interest" means therefore the creation of social attitudes, in the concrete society of the eighteenth century, that will forestall a revolutionary disintegration of the nation, with the inevitably ensuing misery for all.[31]

The "general interest" thus is the stable balance of the private in-

31. Ibid., sec. 3, ch. 9, pp. 423ff.

terests of the members of a society.[32] This stable balance can be created only by law and its effective enforcement. If the magistrates are not equipped with the necessary powers of enforcement, the greatest number of men will violate the law, and in this case it would be violated justly by the single individual in pursuit of his private interest. A law that is not enforced is useless, and with its uselessness it loses its validity.[33] The questions of the greatest number and the general interest are closely bound up with the existence of an organized body politic and the economic interdependence of its members. The insight into this connection determines Helvétius's analysis of the question whether the principle of the greatest number and their general interest can be extended beyond the national state into international relations. This question cannot be answered by a simple yes or no. The international community is no more a fit object for wishful thinking than is the national community; both are stages in the scale of evolution. The principle of the general interest is applicable to the national state because the national state exists historically. Whether it is applicable to the international community of mankind depends on whether this community exists. As a matter of fact, it exists only in a very rudimentary form, as evidenced by the fact that acts of violence in international relations are not considered dishonorable in the same degree as violent acts within the national body politic. The nations have hardly reached in their relations the stage of conventions; they have not even guaranteed each other their possessions as have the individuals within the state. And they have not done it because, hitherto, they had no pressing interest to do it; they are able to coexist without a legal order and a machinery of enforcement. The Church and the kings permit slave trade and the same Christian who condemns a disturbance of family life at home gives his blessings to the merchant who breaks up native families and purchases their members in exchange for Western products. These facts indicate that in public opinion the relations between peoples are still governed by nothing but force and cunning. Even when, in single instances, the stage of conventions is reached, the treaties have the character of a truce for they are always concluded with the tacit understanding of the *clausula rebus sic stantibus*. The actual state of brigandage among nations will not cease until the majority of them will have entered into general conventions and until a federal league is concluded between them, with powers of enforcement, following such plans as those of Henri IV and the Abbé de Saint-Pierre. Only

32. Ibid., ch. 4, p. 364: "l'intérêt commun, c'est-à-dire, l'assemblage de tous les intérêts particuliers."
33. Ibid., p. 363.

when the international community exists in fact, and that means as an organized body with enforcement of its order, can speculation concerning the greatest number and their interest be extended beyond the national scene.[34]

The class struggle

In his late work, *De l'Homme*, Helvétius has given the second account of evolution, which emphasizes the problems of class struggle. The outline of phases, on the whole, is the same as in the *Esprit*. The new elements are introduced into the analysis at the stage where society has increased to the size of a nation on a considerable territory, when economic interdependence is highly developed through division of labor, and when the differentiation of social strata is expressing itself in the growth of towns and particularly of a capital city which overshadows the rest of the country by its splendor; in brief: the situation in France. At this stage, the single member of the community has ceased to be an active citizen, and he can participate in politics only through "representatives"; the economic man separates from the political man; politics becomes a differentiated social function and with it enters the possibility of abuse. For the people are now divided into economic classes and it is not possible that the interests of the various classes should always be in harmony. Nothing, for instance, is more contrary to the national interest than a great number of men without property. They are so many secret enemies whom a despot might arm at his discretion against the property owners. The business community, on the other hand, has an interest in great numbers of poor people; the needier they are, the less a businessman will have to pay in wages. The interest of the business community thus is opposed to the public interest, and a business community (*un corps de négocians*) is frequently a power in trading nations because it is the great employer. When a people thus is composed of a plurality of peoples with conflicting interests, there will be no uniform national interest on which all are ready to agree. The ruling "representatives" can play off the various groups against each other, and in the general confusion they will increase their power and wealth until it equals the power and wealth of the nation. The country is split into the rulers and the ruled; the people have lost their power over the "representatives" and can hardly hold their own against them. For wealth has a tendency to accumulate in an ever smaller number of hands of the ruling class,

34. Ibid., ch. 4, pp. 365–368.

and the number of independent proprietors, the mainstay of liberty, will decrease. The end is an economic despotism of a small minority which rules the people for its private interest. This evolution has been the cause of the fall of many empires in history.

What can the legislator do to prevent a similar misfortune in the concrete case under discussion? Helvétius suggests a number of measures for a solution of the problem, such as abolition of inheritance for great fortunes and redistribution of accumulated wealth on the death of the owner, or a progressive land-tax which for land holdings over a certain acreage will be higher than the profit. These measures, however, do not have the purpose of equalizing wealth—economic inequality cannot and should not be abolished, only excess accumulation should be prevented in order to preserve the political stability of the nation.[35]

The Jesuit Order

Our survey of the politics of Helvétius is drawing to its close. At the end, let us return to the beginning, to the legislator who bends men and their passions toward the general interest. In his capacity as the presumptive legislator, Helvétius is strongly disturbed by the existence of a group of men who have organized themselves effectively for the operations of bending men to their will. The previously described differentiation of society into economic classes with conflicting interests is a grave danger to the general interest. This danger, however, pales before the danger presented by a particular interest group which has organized itself as what we would call today "a state within the state," and which uses its efficient organization for the purpose of establishing itself as a ruling class against the general interest. This efficient organization is the Jesuit Order. Helvétius is deeply interested in the means by which the Jesuit Order achieves its success. This "masterpiece of politics" combines the advantages of monarchical and republican government. It depends equally on secrecy and promptitude of execution, and on an ardent love for the grandeur of the Order. At the head of the organization is an enlightened despot, who at the same time is an elective officer. This chief is carefully chosen from a number of prospective, well-trained candidates. He is under the same rules as the rank and file, has made the same vows, has renounced, like his brethren, all dignities and all bonds of love and friendship. He has no other interest than the grandeur and power of the Order and in his subjects he has the perfect instrument of execution. His independ-

35. *De l'Homme*, sec. 6.

ence from temporal powers is secured through his residence at Rome. From his cell, "like the spider from the center of its web," he instructs his sons in all Europe, and there he receives from them the intelligence of what is going on in the capitals of the world. His peculiar power and the terror which he inspires is not due to his principles (which are, on the whole, not different from those of the Church), but to the perfection of his governmental organization.[36] The members of the Order are chosen with equal care among fanatics. In the monastic environment, surrounded by other fanatics, the sentiments of the recruits are formed in the proper direction. Enthusiasm, as Shaftesbury said, is a communicable disease. Among all religious Orders that of the Jesuits is "at the same time the most powerful, the most enlightened and the most enthusiastic." No other Order could exert a similar fascination over the imagination of a fanatic. The *esprit de corps* gives each member a feeling of security and, consequently, full freedom of the mind to concentrate on the task at hand.[37]

Helvétius hates the Jesuit Order. He analyzes its organization because it is the most dangerous enemy to the general interest and he rejoices in its fall. Nevertheless, throughout these chapters on the Jesuits there is an undertone of admiration and envy. "The true crime of the Jesuits was the excellence of their government. Its excellence was altogether destructive to public happiness." Still: excellence was the crime. And could such excellence not be used some day for virtuous purposes? "We must admit that the Jesuits have been the most cruel scourge of the nations; but without them we would never have gained a full insight into the power which a body of laws inspired by one purpose can have over men." "No legislation has ever realized with so little means so perfectly the great object of power and wealth." Regrettably, no people has a legislation of comparable excellence; and in order to create it "one would have to found a new empire like Romulus." Unfortunately, the legislator is rarely in this situation; "and in any other situation it is perhaps impossible to give an excellent legislation."[38] Helvétius ends on a melancholy note. His dream of excellence could not be dreamed into history in the eighteenth century. Still, he had the right instinct: the political cadre has become the great instrument for making the greatest number as happy as only the leaders of such cadres can make them.[39]

36. Ibid., sec. 7, ch. 5.
37. Ibid., ch. 10.
38. Ibid., ch. 11.
39. Compare the parallel attitude in Bentham. In the *Panopticon*, in the chapter on "Schools," Bentham discusses the arguments against the merits of an

Conclusion

The historian of ideas has to do more than to report the doctrines advanced by a thinker or to give an account of a few great systems. He has to explore the growth of sentiments which crystallize into ideas, and he has to show the connection between ideas and the matrix of sentiments in which they are rooted. The idea has to be studied, not as a concept, but as a symbol which draws its life from sentiments; the idea grows and dies with the sentiments which engender its formulation and, with the great thinkers, its integration into a system of thought approximating the asymptote of rationality. Only insofar as the idea is understood as the approximately rational expression of the life of sentiments can we understand it as a historical entity. For the interpretation of ideas in this process of historical growth, the minor thinkers sometimes may be more important than the great ones in whose systems the motivation of ideas through sentiment is covered by the exigencies of immanent logical consistency. Helvétius was a thinker whose awareness of systematic exigencies was strong enough to make him face the major problems raised by his approach to politics, but his desire to elaborate a system of politics was not so strong that it abolished the essentially aphoristic style of his work. Aphoristic style means, as was later clarified by Nietzsche who used it deliberately, that the author preserves in the presentation of his ideas the connection with the experiences and sentiments which produce the ideas. This aphoristic character of the work of Helvétius makes it unusually valuable for the historian of ideas because here he will find ideas, which in themselves are elaborated more clearly and consistently in later systems, at the point where they begin to separate as symbols from the matrix of sentiments and where the motives which animate their creation are still visible. We now have to summarize briefly the rich aggregate of sentiments and motivations which determines a considerable sector of political thought in the period of Enlightenment and the subsequent crisis of the nineteenth and twentieth centuries.

"inspection-school." The opponent might raise such questions as: "whether the liberal spirit and energy of a free citizen would not be exchanged for the mechanical discipline of a soldier, or the austerity of a monk?—and whether the result of this high-wrought contrivance might not be constructing a set of *machines* under the similitude of *men?*" Bentham's answer to such questions would have to recur to the end of education: "Would *happiness* be most likely to be increased or diminished by this discipline?—Call them soldiers, call them monks, call them machines: so they were but happy ones, I should not care" (*Panopticon, Works,* ed. Bowring [Edinburgh, 1843], 4, p. 64).

The structure of sentiments which appears in Helvétius can be characterized generally by the term of intramundane religiousness. In the conflict with the Christian tradition the new religiousness expresses itself through the inversion of the direction in which the *realissimum* of existence is to be sought. The new attitude had become visible by the time of Hobbes when the orientation toward a *summum bonum* was replaced by the flight from the *summum malum* of death in civil war. The inversion of direction becomes now established, under the title of genealogy, as the principal instrument for interpreting the internal order of human nature. Whether it be the materialistic, the sensualistic, or the hedonistic variants—the strata of human nature are interpreted genetically as derivatives of a physical or biological substance at the bottom of existence. The internal structure of man is no longer ordered toward a transcendental aim but is to be explained by the operations of physical sensibility or of a pleasure-pain mechanism. This inversion of direction becomes from now on the symbol of the anti-Christian anthropology in politics—whether it assumes the form of economic materialism, or of biologism, or of psychologism. With the most important inversion, the inversion of Hegel's idealism by Marx, we shall have to deal in some detail in a later context.

The inversion of direction is accompanied by the perversion of the idea of order: the disorder of passions is accepted as the normal order of the human soul. The problem of perversion as such is of long standing. As far back as in the *Policraticus* of John of Salisbury, one can observe an incipient psychology of the *homo politicus*, the man of secular passion, as the normal type of man. The problem is realized in its full importance in the seventeenth century by Hobbes and Pascal. To the madness of the inflated ego Hobbes finds the practical answer of crushing the proud by the Leviathan; Pascal tries to awaken the insight into the life of passion as *divertissement* and counsels the return to a life in communion with God. Both analysts of the disorder of passion still recognize the disorder as such—though in Hobbes we already see the dangerous attempt to replace the spiritual process of contrition by the external process of submission to governmental power. Helvétius resumes the analysis of passion but in his treatment the passions have lost their character as a source of disorder in the soul and have become the fundamental force on which all order in the conduct of man has to rely. The return to the ground of existence and to the experience of creaturely nothingness have lost their function in the order of the soul.

The perversion of the idea of order is intimately connected with the problem that we designated as the instrumentalization of man. Man is no longer an entity that has its existential center within itself; he has become a mechanism of pleasure, pain and passions which can be harnessed by another man, the "legislator," for purposes of his own. Instrumentalization proved to be a peculiarly rich complex of sentiments and ideas. First of all, the ground of existence in the Pascalian sense is denied to man. Here we are at the key point of the anti-Christian attack on the existence of man. Only when the spiritual center of man, through which man is open to the transcendental *realissimum*, is destroyed can the disorderly aggregate of passions be used as an instrument by the legislator. The Kantian, rational-Christian, ethical rule, that every man must be considered an end in himself and not an instrument for ulterior purposes, is perverted into its opposite through the thesis: man is no end in himself but merely an instrument to be used by the legislator. This is the new basic thesis for collectivism in all its variants, down to the contemporary forms of totalitarianism.

Once the disorder of the soul is established as the nature of man, and order can be instilled into this blind field of psychic forces only from an acting center outside of man, that aspect of instrumentalization comes to the fore which we designated by the term of artificiality in politics. The growth of the soul through an internal process which is nourished through communication with transcendental reality is replaced by the formation of conduct through external management. Here is the origin of the managing and organizing interference with the soul of man which, from the position of a spiritual morality, is equally reprehensible in all its variants: whether it is the propagandizing formation of conduct and opinion through such political movements as the Communist or National Socialist or an educational process which relies on the psychology of conditioned reflexes and forms patterns of social conformance without raising the question of the morality of the pattern or of the morality of conformance. This process of general education for the purpose of forming the useful member of society, while neglecting or even deliberately destroying the life of the soul, is accepted as an institution of our modern society so fully that the awareness of the demonism of such interference with the life of the soul on a social mass scale, and of the inevitably following destruction of the spiritual substance of society, is practically dead. Only when the instrument is used for the inculcation of patterns which differ widely from the survivals of Christian tradition, and when the success of such use has demonstrated the previous destruction of the soul without which such success would be impossible, a sudden wave of alarm and indignation springs up. But even then (we are speaking of the contemporary situation) the indignation is not directed against the methods which destroy the life of the soul but against the new patterns of conduct inculcated by political movements. The remedy against the pattern of which we disapprove is the use of the same destructive method for a different purpose, under the ominous symbol of "re-education."

Artificiality in politics means that the leadership of Western political units has to rely increasingly on the mechanism of passions and interests of the social group as the source of power and policy; it can no longer rely with assurance on engaging as a source of power a spiritual substance that would be living in a socially relevant stratum of the body politic. An aggregate of passions and interests, however, is an ephemeral force; it needs constant watching and the leaders of the moment have to beware that a skillful reshuffler of passions and interests will not, in a surprisingly short time, create a differently shaped aggregate for his own purposes. Once the spiritual destruction has achieved a certain degree of success, the structure of political sentiments in a society is in a precarious balance that can be destroyed by any untoward event, as for instance an economic crisis. The struggle between political leaders for the shaping and for the control of the labile aggregate of passions and interests will become the content of politics. This aspect of the problem of leadership appears in Helvétius under the title of the "legislator." The legislator, as we have seen, provides in his person the directive center of which the soul of the man of passion and interest has been deprived. The leader becomes the new center of human life when God has been abolished. The spiritual drama of salvation which takes place in the Christian soul has become externalized in the drama of a society under the leadership of a "legislator." At this point we should note a certain difficulty of terminology. The new attitude which appears in Helvétius is usually termed social immanentism. There are reasons to use the term but we must be aware that what actually takes place is the externalization of processes of the soul and their enactment on the stage of society. The religious life of man is not abolished (as is so fondly believed by even such a notable figure as the author of *The Future of an Illusion*); rather, the life of the soul has become perverted and the religious symbols which express the perversion dominate the scene.

The religion of social Satanism expresses itself in certain symbols. Some of these symbols were developed by Helvétius at least in their outline. Let us mention first the new aspect of the idea of equality. The idea of equality as such has absorbed more than one component of sentiment. In earlier contexts we have seen the roots of equality in the matriarchal idea of the sons who are all born equally from the same mother, as well as in the patriarchal idea of the spiritual sons of the same father; and we have seen further components of Western equality which stem from the aristocratic spiritualism of the high Middle Ages with its generous extension of the idea of the spiritually mature person to all men. We now have to observe a further component which becomes of increasing political importance in the nineteenth and twentieth centuries: the idea of the equal pleasure-pain mechanisms who all are engaged equally in the pursuit of happiness. This new component of equality is intimately connected with a second symbol, the symbol of the elite who set the standard of the happiness that is to be pursued by the mass of the equal automata. The egalitarian and elitarian ideas of political order can be conceived as mutually exclusive if we concentrate our attention on those components of the idea of equality which stem from the Christian and medieval aristocratic tradition. They do not at all exclude but, on the contrary, require each other if and when the equality of passions, interest and happiness in the sense of Helvétius comes to be the component which is experienced as the decisive one in a socially relevant degree. Helvétius understood this connection very clearly when he warned of the dangers of accumulation of wealth and of the corresponding impoverishment of the people; for in this situation the happiness of the greatest number who are all equal in their lack of property could be satisfied by a despot who abolishes the Western structure of society. The social mechanism by which Napoleon III rose to power gave Europe the first object lesson in the possibilities of plebiscitarian dictatorship which Helvétius had seen on the social horizon. This rise of Napoleon III released the great critique of parliamentary democracy and of universal suffrage in the second half of the nineteenth century and the predictions concerning the end of liberalism and the emergence of the age of the masses.

And, finally, we have to recall the symbol of social evolution. Systematically the idea of social evolution had to supply for Helvétius the standard of the happiness of the greatest number. The dangers to the stability of French political society which arose from the differentiation of class interests were to be averted by the standard of a heroic middle-class republic. This idea was revolutionary insofar as it implied the abolition of the aristocratic and financial ruling class; it was conservative insofar as it wanted to stabilize the revolution on the level of the middle-class republic and to prevent its progress toward a plebiscitarian dictatorship. This is the conservative French republican idea which was broken by the successive waves of Napoleonism, by the emotional leadership in the first decades of the Third Republic, and by the Dreyfus affair. The structure of sentiments which animate the idea, however, has an importance far beyond the immediate French problems. The symbol of evolution creates a new ontology as the basis for the meaning of human existence in society. The Christian order of the soul as the standard of meaning is abolished but it is replaced by an external order of objective evolution of civilization through population pressure and scarcity of goods. Human existence under the new dispensation finds its meaning through the conformance of private interest to the general interest that has evolved objectively at the time. The meaning of life has been transformed from the internal growth of the soul in orientation toward the transcendental *realissimum*, into the external harmony of the private interest with the historically objective fact of the general interest. Obviously this construction raises serious questions: what will happen if evolution goes on? if a new situation of fact arises? if the greatest number develops interests far different from the standard envisaged by Helvétius? In this case do we have to revise our ideas of what constitutes the happiness obligatory for everybody? At this point Helvétius, like every radical social Satanist after him, has to take his leap into eschatology. One answer to these questions would be the relativistic drifting with evolution that has become an important characteristic of the movement of historicism: any situation of fact is as acceptable as the previous one because the standards of value and meaning are surrendered. A personality of the strength of Helvétius's cannot be satisfied with this escape. We have seen his awareness of the dangers of plebiscitarian despotism and his will to stabilize evolution at an earlier point. This idea of stabilizing evolution at a given point will inevitably occur to a man who takes seriously his function as the social savior of his benighted fellowmen. Evolution has reached a certain point, but now society must cease to evolve. The present situation of fact has arisen objectively through evolution and draws its authority from this objectivity, but no future different situation must arise; history has to stop. The eschatology of stopping history, of a last historical phase that will not be superseded by an entirely different one, has become one of the great symbols of politics after Helvétius. In our time this Satanic mirage has become one of the great paralyzing forces in Western politics in the form of the idea that democracy, at the phase which it has reached historically, can be stabilized and perpetuated by "stopping" this or that—for instance, a Hitler or a Stalin. The symbol has found its classical formulation in the Marxist idea that social evolution up to the present is "prehistory," and that after the revolutionary stabilization of a situation of fact "real history," without further profound changes, will begin.

IV. POSITIVISM AND ITS ANTECEDENTS

What is sometimes referred to as the crisis of Western civilization is not an event that occurs at a definite point in time. It is a process which extends by now over more than a century and a half and which, for all we know, may be protracted for another century. The crisis does not belong to the past, it is a living present. Every day adds to our experience of its extent and profoundness, and in the light of these experiences we are compelled, if we want to understand it, to revaluate the past phases of the crisis. Events which seemed to be irrelevant accidents or momentary outbursts in their time appear, in the light of contemporary experiences, as prefigurations of later horrors. Ideas which seemed to be side issues, exaggerations, idiosyncrasies or absurdities, now reveal their full meaning when they become concretized in political actions and institutions. Men who seemed to have a somewhat limited importance grow into sinister giants who cast their shadow over the present and into the future. This revaluation proceeds, and will continue to proceed, with our expanding experience of the crisis itself.

Auguste Comte (1798–1857) is the first great figure of the Western crisis. Comte belongs to our historical present in the same sense in which Marx, Lenin and Hitler belong to it. While we cannot know the ultimate form which the course of the crisis will assume, we know much more about it than Comte and his contemporaries and we know a good deal more than even the generation which preceded us. We know above all that the Western crisis is not a brief episode that will reach its end within a few decades. This belief, in which Comte indulged in the 1840's, will hardly be entertained by anybody today. Moreover, we know today that the crisis is not a political disturbance, in the restricted sense of power politics, which can be settled by wars and subsequent peace treaties. We know that it is essentially a crisis of the spirit and we are acquainted today with some of the attempts at a solution of this problem through political religions such as National Socialism and Marxism.

Although Comte misjudged the duration of the crisis, he neither misjudged its scale nor its nature. While his attempt at a solution was as abortive as the contemporary ones, at least one important cause of the failure was the close relationship between Comte's ideas and the totalitarian practice of our times. After a century of misunderstanding we are approaching today, on the basis of more recent experiences, a more adequate view of Comte in his quality as an astute and perspicacious philosopher of history as well as in his more sinister quality as a spiritual dictator of mankind. The history of the misunderstanding of Comte and of the gradual dissolution of these misunderstandings is, at the same time, the history of our growing insight into the meaning of the Western crisis.

Positivism, as it was formed through the person and work of Auguste Comte, has its effectiveness as a European movement because it had absorbed a rich tradition of sentiments and ideas. The pseudo-prophetic personality of Comte was necessary to achieve the fusion and to penetrate it with religious enthusiasm, but the elements which entered into the composition of the system had accumulated in the course of a process which had started more than a century before Comte shaped the *Politique Positive* as the keystone of his thought. Hence the nature of Positivism and its broad appeal cannot be properly understood without a survey of its prehistory. Without this prehistory the momentum would be inexplicable. Such a survey, however, has its difficulties because of the volume of tradition that crystallized in the system of Comte and it would have to encompass an appreciable sector of the intellectual history of a century. In order to reduce the problem to manageable proportions we shall endeavor to assemble some of the more important elements which have entered the Comtean edifice of ideas. Among these elements was the idea of the eighteenth-century French *Encyclopédie* as developed by d'Alembert in his *Discours Préliminaire*.[1]

D'Alembert's Discours Préliminaire

The *Discours* was originally published as the editors' preface to the first volume of the *Encyclopédie* in 1751. It soon gained prominence, independent of this function, as the classic expression of the encyclopaedist spirit as well as of the idea of the *Encyclopédie*. It was made required reading in the educational institutions of France and influenced several generations of young Frenchmen, among them Auguste Comte.[2] The purpose of the *Discours* was to inform the readers of the *Encyclopédie* about the principles underlying the great work. It was supposed to be a systematic collection of human knowledge (*connaissances humaines*) in the sciences, the liberal arts and technology. The collection was not to be indiscriminate but would embody only relevant and valid knowledge. The execution of this program required criteria of relevance and completeness and the *Discours* endeavored to furnish

---

1. D'Alembert, *Discours Préliminaire de l'Encyclopédie*, ed. F. Picavet (Paris, 1894).

2. See on this point Picavet's "Introduction," ibid., p. xlvii.

the criteria. This attempt at a theoretical clarification of the issues involved gave the *Discours* its importance beyond that of a preface.

It was, as a matter of fact, the revolutionary manifesto of a new attitude towards man and society. It was inspired by the pathos of the scientist, and more specifically, of the mathematical scientist, who tries to orient man in society and the universe by means of the methods which have shown their value in the mathematical and physical sciences. This pathos expressed the momentum which science had gained in the century of Descartes and Pascal, of Huyghens and Newton, of Boyle and Locke, of Leibniz and of d'Alembert himself. In the consciousness of this revolutionary expansion of the horizon of knowledge, the enterprise could be conceived as surveying systematically the present state of knowledge, using as ordinates of relevance and completeness the methods of science which were considered valid at the moment. In this perspective, the *Encyclopédie* is the modern counterpart of the medieval *Summa*. The *Summa* of the type that was fixed by St. Thomas embraced systematically what appeared as relevant knowledge within the categories of the Christian view of man in the universe; the *Encyclopédie*, at least in the original conception of d'Alembert and Diderot, attempted the equivalent organization of relevant knowledge within the categories of the new anthropology that had become fixed by the middle of the eighteenth century. Within the narrower perspective of French intellectual history, we may say that the *Discours* of d'Alembert is the sequel to the Cartesian *Discours de la méthode*. The principles developed by Descartes have unfolded in the advancement of science, and the *Discours* of d'Alembert amplifies these principles by applying them encyclopedically to the whole body of human knowledge.

The principles of the Encyclopédie

The principles used by d'Alembert for securing relevance and completeness are, on the whole, an elaboration of Helvétius's ideas of the genealogy of passions and of social evolution; they reappear in d'Alembert as the genealogy of knowledge and the history of the progress of the human mind. The genealogy of knowledge is constructed, in substance, in the same manner as the genealogy of Helvétius. The direct experiences of human existence and of the external world are the foundation; all other knowledge is interpreted as the product of reflection on their basis. The construction in the form of the genealogy is supposed to furnish the reliably complete register of the *connaissances*, from the immediate experiences to the reflective derivatives. For the purposes of the *Encyclopédie*, the resulting table of *connaissances* is rearranged, according to subject matters, as an *arbre généalogique* or *encyclopédique*. The titles in the alphabetic order of the *Encyclopédie* are referred to the *arbre généalogique* so that the reader of the respective article is clear about the position of the subject matter in the system of science. The history of the progress of the human mind, in its turn, has the same function as Helvétius's theory of social evolution. The history of intellectual progress carries with it the authority of its facticity. That a certain stage is reached at present *de facto* endows this stage with an authority by which it is superior to previous phases in the intellectual history of mankind. When the idea of a creative, transcendental reality pales, the idea of the authoritative present takes its place. These two ideas, the genealogy and the history, determine the organization of the *Discours* in its two parts. And, by anticipation, we may say that these two cornerstones of the Positivistic edifice will reappear in the system of Comte as his two great conceptions of the hierarchy of the sciences and of the law of the three stages in the progress of the mind.

Let us now examine the two ideas in order, first the idea of genealogy. The actual genealogy and the resulting *arbre encyclopédique* are of no interest to us. In the course of their development, however, there appear certain problems which are symptomatic of the complex of Positivism and are relevant for the understanding of the later history of political ideas.

The first of these points concerns the derivation of the ideas of justice and of moral good and evil. For d'Alembert the idea of justice is provoked through a situation of oppression. His assumption seems to be that the equal somatic constitution of men induces the idea of equality of men as a "reasonable" idea and that the violation of a "reasonable" state of equality through the stronger arouses resentment and resistance. "From there stems the notion of the unjust, and consequently of moral good and evil, of which so many philosophers have searched the principle, and which the cry of nature, echoing in every man, makes understood by all people, even the most savage."[3] D'Alembert makes the attempt to derive the idea of good and evil from the fundamental experience of revolt against oppression and rejects a religious or metaphysical foundation of morals. The value of this derivation for a theory of morals is not very great. But we find in it the expression of a sentiment that has appeared earlier in French history of political ideas, in La Boetie's *Servitude Volontaire*, a sentiment that gains considerable popular acceptance in the later history of Anarchism and Syndicalism:

3. Ibid., p. 20.

namely, the sentiment of revolt in the sense of an immediate, violent reaction against a social state that is experienced as oppressive. We have seen that d'Alembert has no direct access to the idea of justice; the primary experience is that of oppression. The idea of an unjust state of things precedes that of a just one. The sentiment of revolt overshadows the idea of order much more strongly than in Voltaire, whose indignation at injustice was oriented towards a clear code of secular, utilitarian morality. At the same time, the derivation is a consistent attempt to gain an idea of justice within a philosophy of existence which relies for its construction on the symbol of the genealogy. D'Alembert certainly faces the problem of ethics more seriously than did Locke with his inconclusive drifting in the surviving tradition of Christianity, or Helvétius with his transfer of the moral substance of man to the legislator. This seriousness of the attempt holds its appeal for later thinkers who on the one hand adopt an anthropology based on the symbol of genealogy but who, on the other hand, are neither willing to accept a traditional morality without foundation, nor without qualms to subscribe to an idea of collectivist salvation which denies the moral substance of man. This sentiment of revolt has found its radical expression in Bakunin. For Bakunin the experience of revolt is an irreducible factor in human existence, independent of the somatic basis which provides the dynamic of revolution. This instance is of particular interest because Bakunin favors, side by side with the idea of revolt, the incompatible idea of collective salvation through a revolutionary leader. Here we find fully developed in the same person both of the principal solutions which can be given to the problem of ethics within the framework of the Positivistic creed.

The disappearance of the bios theoretikos

A second point that invites attention is d'Alembert's derivation of that type of knowledge which is not of a strictly utilitarian nature. He differentiates between knowledge which serves the satisfaction of human needs, and knowledge which, at least at the time of its discovery, has no practicality. The acquisition of useful knowledge is considered quite intelligible, but why should men devote their energies to the acquisition of useless knowledge? The answer is to be found in a general disquietude, expressing itself in curiosity, which casts around for escape from a not quite satisfactory situation. The satisfaction of curiosity is in itself a pleasure and to this pleasure we owe the discovery of useless knowledge. Since sometimes useless knowledge later turns out to be useful, we continue to satisfy our curiosity through systematic scientific research in the hope that ultimately it may serve a useful purpose.[4] Again, the derivation itself is of little value for a theory of knowledge. But in the frankness of its statement, it reveals more clearly than the later conventionalized expressions of the same idea the sentiments which underlie the Positivist creed. D'Alembert, apparently, has never experienced either the desire for, or the obligation to pursue, that life of contemplation which Aristotle describes as the *bios theoretikos*. He ignores the fact, or does not know, that the life of man does not exhaust its meaning on the level of utilitarian desires and needs, and that the life of contemplation, resulting in the understanding of man himself and of his place in the universe, is a fundamental spiritual obligation quite independent of its contribution to "useful" activities.

Insofar as the origin and the obligation of the *bios theoretikos*, and with it the meaning of humanistic civilization, are unintelligible from the pragmatic perspective of utilitarian values, we find in the attitude of d'Alembert an indication of the profound antihumanism underlying the Enlightenment and the Positivist creed. This important component of Positivism is frequently underrated or overlooked entirely, perhaps because the attempts to stabilize the remnants of tradition at the level of disintegration which they had reached at the moment disguised the radical incompatibility of the new attitude with the values of classical and Christian civilization. As a result, the deceptive picture of a progressive civilization arose in which the advancement of science seemed to compensate amply for the atrophy of other civilizational values. When the breaking point in this process of undermining the central values of civilization has been reached, as it has in our age, the impression is widespread that entirely new ideas are in revolt against the traditions of progressive Western civilization, but in fact the wrecking operations of the present only consummate a work of destruction that has been going on for the last four centuries. It is a serious misunderstanding of historical forces to believe that a handful of men can destroy a civilization before it has committed suicide, to use the phrase of Toynbee.

Towards a new pouvoir spirituel

D'Alembert's attitude towards Christianity and religious cults is the third point which needs our attention. Since the experience of the *bios theoretikos* is missing in d'Alembert, it is not surprising that with

4. Ibid., pp. 23f,

regard to religious experiences he shares the spiritual obscurantism of Voltaire. D'Alembert accepts, like Voltaire, certain "*notions purement intellectuelles*," such as vice and virtue, the necessity of laws, the spirituality of the soul, the existence of God, and the obligations of a cult. For the rest, he refers the reader to revealed religion which instructs man concerning subject matters of which he has no natural knowledge. This instruction, however, does not amount to much; it is confined to "a few truths of faith," and "a small number of practical precepts." A spiritual penetration of the problems of faith d'Alembert has never attempted.[5]

This somewhat vague attitude of 1751 crystallized, in d'Alembert's later years, into more precise ideas. In a letter to Frederic II (November 30, 1770), d'Alembert wrote that Christianity was originally a pure deism, and Jesus "a sort of philosopher." Jesus hated persecution and priests, he taught goodwill and justice, and reduced the law to the love of fellowman and the adoration of God. This simple religion was changed by St. Paul, the Fathers and the Councils. "One would do a great service to mankind if one could make men forget the dogmas; if one would simply preach them a God Who rewards and punishes and Who frowns on superstition, Who detests intolerance and expects no other cult of man than mutual love and support."[6] The King was not quite convinced by d'Alembert's idea since he thought that the people would want something more than a merely reasonable religion. D'Alembert answered (letter of February 1st, 1771) that he would ask the King, if the Treaty of Westphalia permitted a fourth religion in the Empire, to erect "a very plain temple" in Berlin or Potsdam "where God would be honored in a manner worthy of Him, where nothing would be preached but humanity and justice." If the masses would not flock to this temple in a few years, only then would he admit that the King was right.[7]

These passages from the letters indicate certain trends in Positivism which later unfold prodigiously. In itself the deistic creed of d'Alembert is rather conventional for its time. More unusual is the idea that deism is not a rational progressive transformation of Christianity, but that it represents a return to original Christianity before its corruption by St. Paul, the Fathers and the Councils. This conception implies that deism is a "reform" of Christianity, more radical than the Protestant because it goes back to the origins even before St. Paul. Nevertheless, this "reform" does not imply a *renovatio evangelica*. It does not have its source

5. Ibid., pp. 21f., 35. Cf. n. 25, 26 by Picavet.
6. Picavet, "Introduction," ibid., p. xv.
7. Ibid.

in a mystical experience and it implies no more than a rationalist purification of Christian symbols, including the divinity of Christ, so that in the end Jesus appears as a "sort of philosopher" who counsels mutual love and support without any intelligible authority or foundation for such counsels. We can observe here in formation the highly important merger of spiritual obscurantism with the apprehension that a religious substitute for Christianity might be necessary, and that the substitute would even have to include a cult. In the suggestion to Frederick II to build a temple in Berlin or Potsdam for the purposes of a worthy cult to the rationally purified God, we see prefigured the cults of the Revolution, and in particular Robespierre's cult of the *Être Suprême;* and foreshadowed in the farther distance are Saint-Simon's *Nouveau Christianisme* and Comte's cult of the *Grand-Être*. Side by side with the pathos of positive scientism, the idea that the new Positivist civilization needs a *pouvoir spirituel* that will take the place of the medieval-Christian is beginning to take shape. With Comte the idea of the new *pouvoir spirituel* becomes the center of the Positivist creed, and ever since Comte it has remained the key problem of the new political movements until the *pouvoir spirituel* is joined with the temporal power of the state in the foundations of Lenin and Hitler.

The fourth and last point on which we have to touch is d'Alembert's attitude towards the problem of a moral code. We have seen that his source for the idea of justice, or rather injustice, was the experience of revolt; and we remarked that with d'Alembert this experience is not balanced, as with Voltaire, by a positive code of morals. Moreover, we have seen that an ethics of the Aristotelian type (with a scale of values oriented toward the *bios theoretikos*), or a spiritual morality of the Christian type (determined by the experience of the common ground in a transcendental reality), are beyond his reach. On the other hand, d'Alembert took very seriously the problem that faced him: of finding sources for a moral code other than the theoretical or spiritual sources. His hope to reach this aim was supported by a revealing misunderstanding of the foundations of Greek and Roman ethics, a misunderstanding that has continued on a socially relevant scale to this day. The idea of an autonomous ethics, without religious or metaphysical foundation, strikes d'Alembert as a possibility because in his opinion such a code of ethics was realized once among the "pagans."[8] Rules of ethics existed before Christianity, and since religion is for him synonymous with Christianity, the Greeks had an ethics without religious foundation. Explicitly or through tradition, this misunderstanding has

8. Picavet, "Introduction," ibid., p. xxx.

survived, and we can recognize the effectiveness of this identification of Christianity with religion even today in the widespread resistance to admit the character of modern political movements as new collective religions, as well as in the difficulty of explaining to the layman that radical atheism may be anti-Christian, but that it is not an antireligious attitude, that, on the contrary, it expresses another type of religiousness. Inspired by this misunderstanding, d'Alembert was greatly interested in developing an autonomous code of ethics.

The idea of a *catéchisme de morale* occupied him even in his later years, but he never wrote one and for excellent reasons. These reasons he discussed in his correspondence with Frederic II. In a letter to the King on January 21, 1770, he wrote that the source of morals and happiness was the harmony between enlightened self-interest and the fulfillment of duties. D'Alembert is plagued by a question he finds difficult to answer, namely: "There are those who have nothing, who give everything to society and to whom society refuses everything, who hardly can feed a numerous family by their work and perhaps not feed it at all. Can these people have another rule of conduct than the law? and how could one persuade them that it is their true interest to be virtuous, if, without fear of punishment, they could not be virtuous?" "If I had found a satisfactory solution to this question, I would have written my catechism of morals long ago." In subsequent letters, of March and April of the same year, d'Alembert elaborates his point. The fear of the law and the hope for charity may restrain the indigent. But what happens when there is no hope and when the indigent sees a possibility to take part secretly of the abundance of a rich man for his own subsistence? "I ask you: what should he do in this case? Can he, or even should he, let himself and his family die from starvation?" "In the case of absolute necessity, theft is permitted, and even an act of justice." It is not wise to put such a doctrine into a catechism of morals because greed or *paresse* might misuse it. "That is the reason why it is impossible to make a catechism of morals that would be equally valid for all members of society." The root of the evil is that "the distribution of wealth is monstrously unequal, that it is atrocious as well as absurd to see some people gorging themselves in abundance and others lacking the necessities of life."[9]

There is only a step from d'Alembert's "theft is an act of justice" to Proudhon's "property is theft." We can now understand more clearly the meaning of the "oppression" against which d'Alembert experiences revolt. In part it is religious intolerance and persecution, as with

9. Ibid.

Voltaire, but more decisively it is the oppression which stems from an excessive inequality of wealth. The principle of utilitarian ethics, in order to be applicable concretely, requires a certain degree of economic homogeneity in a society. Even if the indigent should be a minority so that, indeed, the greatest number would be happy, the presence of the indigent minority would mean that the code of utilitarian morals is not equally applicable to all members of society. The distance from Helvétius is not very great, but we should note the difference of accents. For Helvétius, the minority which aroused misgivings was still the ruling class of France; once the iniquity of the minority would be abolished, the happiness of the greatest number would be secured in the form of a middle-class republic of small property owners. For d'Alembert, the accent has shifted to the indigent whose lot would not be changed, on principle, by the abolition of the ruling minority and the establishment of a middle-class republic. The component of utilitarianism becomes more clearly discernible which leads to the demands for a redistribution of wealth and ultimately to the idea of a socialist, planned society in order to make society a homogeneous field for the application of one principle of ethics for everybody. This component becomes dominant during the Revolution in Babeuf; we see it continued strongly in Saint-Simon and Comte and ultimately victorious in Proudhon and the Anarchist and Syndicalist sequels.

The idea of progress and the "authoritative present"

The second principal doctrine of d'Alembert concerns the progress of the human mind. We have indicated earlier why this doctrine forms an indispensable part of the Positivist creed. When the intellectual and spiritual sources of order in human and social life dry up, there is not much left as a source of order except the historically factual situation.

When, however, a situation of fact is to be used as a source of order, the situation has to be surrounded by a body of doctrine which endowes it with a specific legitimacy. Hence, one of the typically recurrent ideas in this contingency is the assumption that the situation of the moment, or a situation which is envisaged as immediately impending, is superior in value to any prior historical situation of fact. The idea of progress through several phases of history, supported by an array of materials which show the increase in value through the successive phases, furnished the basis for this first necessary assumption. The idea of progress, however, creates legitimacy for the present only insofar as it evokes its superiority over the past. Hence, typically in the doctrine, a second idea recurs which is destined to protect the present against invalidation by the future. With Helvétius, this desire for protection against the future took the form of "the leap into eschatology": the present is considered the last phase of human history; no situation of the future ought to differ in substance from the situation envisaged as the desirable present. This element of "stopping" or "freezing" history into a perpetual present is usually overlooked in the analysis of the idea of progress because it is in overt contradiction with the idea of progress itself. This contradiction, however, that a situation cannot be static and progressive at the same time, lies only on the surface. The idea of progress is, indeed, the idea of a static situation insofar as it envisages the future as "an addition to," or "an elaboration of" the present. The idea that possibly the values of modern Western civilization might be superseded in due course by a civilization with a value structure as different from the present Western as is the Hellenic from the Chinese, does not enter these speculations on progress. Insofar as the future can bring nothing but a perfection of the values embodied in present civilization, and as the open future of man in history is transformed into a present aim projected into the future, the idea of progress is static. From this static element in the idea of progress stems the reactionary, paralyzed attitude of progressives in the face of new developments (not envisaged in a project which, in substance, is rooted in the eighteenth century) as well as the wrathful impotence of the progressive intellectual to answer with a positive, ordering will the disintegration of Western civilization. Thus the historical situation of fact, in order to become a source of order, has to be safeguarded against the future as well as against the past. The idea of progress fulfills both these functions. The peculiar character of the situation which is created by these doctrinal means we shall designate by the term "authoritative present." Through this analysis and through the introduction of this term we have gained a position from which we can see the problem of progress in its correct perspective: the idea of progress in general does not imply a scientific proposition which can be submitted to verification; it is an element in a doctrinal complex which purports to evoke the idea of an authoritative present. This idea, in turn, is needed for the adequate expression of intramundane religiousness in politics. A merely empirical present is a brute fact without superior authority in comparison with any past or future present. When the critical standards of civilizational values which stem from the *bios theoretikos* and the life of the spirit are abandoned, when the empirical process itself has to furnish the standards, then a special doctrine is needed to bestow grace on the present and to heighten an otherwise irrelevant situation of fact into a standard by which the past and the future can be measured. This act of grace, bestowed by the intellectual leaders of Enlightenment on themselves and on their age, is the source of the genuine revolutionary pathos that animates the idea of progress, as well as of its plight when the by no means negligible values of utilitarian scientism have run their course. This end seems to have come in our time, when the "revolutions" are becoming "reactions" and spiritual regeneration is the burning problem of the age.

Security against the past

Into this outline of the theoretical problem we now have to fill the materials which d'Alembert uses for the construction of his doctrine. The progress of the mind (*les progrès de l'ésprit*) begins with the Renaissance.[10] It has moved through three distinct phases. The first phase was the new erudition of the humanists, the second phase was the revival of the arts and the third was the advancement of philosophy. The sequence is determined by historical necessity. When man emerged from the "centuries of ignorance," when he was jolted out of "barbarism" by the fall of Constantinople and the penetration of Eastern knowledge into the West, he found himself in a state of infancy. Languages and facts had to be regained and ideas had to be accumulated, while the systematic organization of knowledge lagged behind. This period of predominant erudition, without the balance of theory, employed chiefly the faculty of memory. Next, imagination was aroused through the aesthetic appeal of ancient literature and art, with the consequent Western revival of art. And only in the end could reason embark on the labor of organizing systematically the newly gained knowledge. This systematic organization of knowledge d'Alembert calls philosophy, including under the term the sciences. Philosophy, in its beginning, was severely hampered by the survival of prejudices. "Scholastic philosophy, which exhausted the sham science (*science prétendue*) of the centuries of ignorance, still hampered the progress of true

10. Ibid., p. 76. The reason for starting the history of progress at this particular point is given briefly by the phrase: *"Pour ne point monter trop haut."* The reader should note this phrase because it is characteristic of the style of enlightened theorizing. Unfortunately we do not yet possess a monograph on the typical phrases of progressive intellectuals by which they dispose of those millennia of history which do not fit into the construction of their doctrine. With d'Alembert, a phrase of this kind can still be considered to be used in objective good faith; he could sincerely believe that he need not bother about some 1500 years of Christian history and several centuries of Hellenism. Similar phrases, when they are used in our time, have the less laudable function of covering an inexcusable illiteracy on the part of their authors.

philosophy in this first century of light."[11] In reflecting on the motives of prejudiced resistance d'Alembert achieved one of the finest, involuntary revelations of the progressive mind, by projecting it into the past, when he wrote: "Many people who are born and confirmed in error by education believe themselves most sincerely on the path of truth because there never has occurred to them the slightest doubt on this point."[12] The resistance, however, has been broken and with Bacon begins the advancement of philosophy in the sciences.

Security against the future

The present, thus, is secured against the past. The "very imperfect philosophy" of the ancients has become obsolete, the "centuries of ignorance" can be passed over in silence, the revival of the *esprit* is culminating, today, in the systematic organization of knowledge. But how can this present be secured against the future? The basic sentiment which inspires this second part of doctrinal construction is expressed in the passage quoted above: there is no doubt that we are on the path of truth. We are not in the future to which this path will lead, but we are right on the path and we definitely know its direction. In this spirit the idea of the *Encyclopédie* is conceived and its function understood. The realm of the sciences and arts is rich in discoveries but the reports on them are sometimes unreliable. The *Encyclopédie* has to inform the reader reliably of the true discoveries and to warn him of the errors; it has to fix a starting point in order "to facilitate the search for what remains to be found."[13] The present state of knowledge has to be ascertained in order to gain a clear view of the means for its perfection. When the *Encyclopédie* shall have attained this aim "then the *bons esprits* will no longer occupy themselves with searching what one knew before them."[14] This sentence is the classic formulation of the progressive dream: the state of human knowledge will be incorporated in a textbook of gigantic proportions and nobody will have to read anything that was published prior to the encyclopaedic textbook. All we have to do in the future is to make new editions which incorporate the "contributions" which have accumulated since the last one. Mankind will have behind it the *Encyclopédie* and ahead of it the path determined by it. This determination, furthermore, is austere. To a critic of the *Encyclopédie* d'Alembert answered with a defiant justification of his

11. Ibid., p. 88.
12. Ibid.
13. Ibid., p. 139.
14. Ibid., p. 140.

principles of the one and only truth. If people are astonished, he wrote, to find articles on philosophers but none on Church Fathers, the answer is that philosophers are creators of opinions while the Fathers, who only preserved a tradition, had nothing to teach mankind. If nothing is to be found on the saints, on the genealogy of princes, or on the conquerors who have devastated the earth, the *Encyclopédie* compensates by the space which it gives to the genealogy of science and to the immortal geniuses who have enlightened mankind. "The *Encyclopédie* owes everything to talent, nothing to titles; it is the history of the mind, not of the vanity of man."[15] This highly elastic categorization of *esprit* and *vanité* makes it possible to project the future as a directed development of the present. If anything should actually interfere with this future course, it would not belong to the progress of the *esprit* but would have to be classified as a disturbance by vanity, or a relapse into barbarism. A passage from Diderot will be the best summary for this part of the doctrine: we are, says Diderot, the spectators and historians of the progress of the sciences and arts; we transmit them to posterity. May posterity, in opening our Dictionary, say that this was the state of science and art in our time. May it add its own discoveries to those which we have registered so that the history of the human mind and of its productions may go on and on to the most remote ages. May the *Encyclopédie* become the sanctuary where the knowledge of man is sheltered against time and revolutions. What could flatter us more than to have laid the foundation for this development?[16]

The role of technology

One detail of the doctrine has to be enlarged upon because it has become a rather persistent part of the later Positivist creed: that is the overemphasis on technology. This accentuation has to follow inevitably when the *bios theoretikos* as a standard is abandoned. In this case, the criteria of value have to be found on the utilitarian level. And there can be no doubt that technical inventions are more useful to mankind than the expressions of the contemplative intellect. D'Alembert attacks forcefully the overrating of theoretical science and of scientists. Whatever superiority the liberal arts may have over the mechanical by virtue of the labors of the intellect and of the difficulties to excel in them, is amply compensated by the superior utility of the latter.[17] The discovery of the

15. Picavet, "Introduction," ibid., p. xlv.
16. From the *Prospectus* of the *Encyclopédie*, written by Diderot and incorporated by d'Alembert into the *Discours Préliminaire*, ibid., p. 143.
17. Ibid., p. 53.

compass is not less profitable to mankind than the explanation of the magnetic phenomenon would be to physics.[18] The underrating of the mechanical arts has brought neglect even to the inventors. "The names of these benefactors of mankind are almost all unknown while the history of its destroyers, that is of the conquerors, is known by everybody."[19] Why should the inventors of the mechanism of a watch be held in less esteem than the thinkers who have perfected algebra?[20] Diderot is even more aggressive when he writes that the superiority which we accord to the liberal arts is a prejudice which tends to fill the cities with proud talkers and useless contemplators and the countryside with ignorant, lazy and haughty petty-tyrants.[21] We need not linger on a melody which rings in our ears every day. The breakdown of Hellenic anthropology is as complete as that of the Christian.

The historism of Turgot

The movement of Positivism has absorbed a highly diversified aggregate of sentiments and ideas. The scientistic radicalism of d'Alembert is no more than one strain in the texture of the whole. A second strain, of equal importance, is to be found in the historism of Turgot. The principal sources for Turgot's ideas are the two *Discourses* which he delivered at the opening and closing sessions of the Sorbonne in 1750, when he was 23 years of age. To these have to be added his fragments of the *Discourses on Universal History* of the same period; and, perhaps the richest in ideas, the project of a *Political Geography*. The theory of knowledge which Turgot implied in these works he set forth in a formal manner in the article *Existence* in the *Encyclopédie.*[22]

Let us begin with that idea of Turgot's which has become the centerpiece of Comte's philosophy of history under the title of the law of the three stages. Turgot was concerned about the different rate of progress

18. Ibid., p. 54.
19. Ibid., p. 54.
20. Ibid., p. 55.
21. The passage from Diderot quoted by Picavet in n. 40, ibid., p. 214.
22. *Discours sur les avantages que l'établissement du christianisme a procurés au genre humain* (July 3, 1750); *Discours sur les progrès successifs de l'esprit humain* (December 11, 1750); the fragments of the project on Universal History consist of (1) *Idée de l'Introduction,* (2) *Plan du premier discours, sur la formation du gouvernement et le mélange des nations,* (3) *Plan du second discours, dont l'objet sera les progrès de l'esprit humain,* and various minor fragments; the fragments on political geography consist of (1) *Idées générales* and (2) *Esquisse d'un plan de géographie politique.* All of these pieces, as well as the reprint of *Existence,* are to be found in *Oeuvres de Turgot,* ed. Daire and Dussard, vol. 2 (Paris, 1844).

in the various sciences, particularly of mathematics and physics. The development of mathematics begins earlier and its advancement is more rapid than that of physics. What is the cause of this difference? In search of an explanation Turgot goes back to Locke's theory of knowledge, in the radicalized, monistic form which it had assumed in France. All knowledge starts with sensation; all ideas are derived reflectively from sensation. Mathematics and physics have different rates of progress because in mathematics, reason has to operate with ideas only, while in physics the symbols of science refer to events in the external world. In physics we search for the causes of events which impress themselves on our senses. We try to ascend from effects to causes, from the senses to bodies, from the present to the past, from visible to invisible bodies, from the world to the Divinity.[23] In this search we do not combine and compare ideas as in mathematics, we try to ascertain the structure of corporeal existence. Errors are inevitable and corrections are slow. Among the various sources of error, one is of specific relevance because it determines a style of hypothesis which stands at the beginning of our interpretation of the external world, and can only slowly be overcome in the history of science; that is the penchant for analogical thinking. In searching for the causes of effects, the first hypothesis which offers itself is the assumption of intelligent, invisible beings, similar to ourselves, who cause the events which impress us. Everything that happens and that cannot be attributed to a human agency must be due to a god who is conceived analogically to man. For this first phase of interpretation Turgot himself has not coined a term; it has been termed successively the fetishistic, or animistic phase of thinking but closest to Turgot's meaning would be the term anthropomorphic. The second phase of interpretation is characterized by a critical, philosophical attitude. The anthropomorphic interpretation of natural forces is abandoned in favor of "abstract expressions," such as essences or faculties, "expressions which explain nothing and about which one speculated as if they were beings, new divinities substituted for the old ones." Only in a last phase were the mechanical interactions of bodies properly observed and interpreted in such a manner that they could be expressed in mathematical terms and verified by experience.[24]

Turgot and Comte

This sequence of phases is in substance the sequence which appears in the system of Comte as the progress of the human intellect from its

23. *Histoire Universelle, Oeuvres de Turgot,* 2, p. 649.
24. Ibid., p. 656.

theological, through its metaphysical, to its positive phase. The fact in itself is well known, but not until quite recently have historians begun to draw the inevitable consequences for the interpretation of the Positivist movement. In the older interpretation, the great achievements of Comte were considered to be his ideas of the hierarchy of sciences and of the law of the three stages. By now we have seen that these principal doctrines go back to d'Alembert and Turgot; Comte may be accorded the merit of having elaborated them, but certainly the ideas themselves were not created by him. They are fully developed and fixed by the middle of the eighteenth century. A firm insistence on this point is necessary in order to bring into focus the real significance of Comte in the history of the Western crisis. This significance does not consist in the reiteration and elaboration of the ideas of d'Alembert and Turgot but in his creativeness as a religious personality. Comte would be a rather insignificant figure in the history of political ideas if he were not the *Fondateur de la religion universelle* and the first high priest of the new religion. Pseudo-prophetic charisma is the strength of Comte, and while his church was not much of a success, his religious enthusiasm was strong enough to endow a body of ideas, although of dubious scientific value, with the glow of a revelation on whose acceptance depends the salvation of mankind. Comte has not added much as a thinker to the complex of Positivist ideas; he has added to them in his capacity as a religious founder by shifting them to the level of a dogmatic religion.

The law of the three stages was transposed by Comte from the context of a primarily scientific study as we find it in the *Discourses* of Turgot, to the context of a new Koran—for, indeed, that is the character of the main work of Comte, just as it was the character of the *Institutes* of Calvin. Through this transposition much of the original flavor of Turgot's idea was lost, and the original meaning is of considerably greater interest for the further history of political science than the religious-dogmatic meaning of Comte. The misplacement of emphasis on the content of Comte's law of the three stages, instead of on its dogmatic character, not only has distorted the picture of Comte, it also has obscured the original problem of a philosophy of history that was raised by Turgot. A complete exposition of Turgot's ideas concerning a philosophy of history cannot be given here, but we shall indicate at least the principal problems.

Definition of progress

First of all, the sequence developed by Turgot is not a general law of history but definitely a series of phases through which our interpretation of the external world passes. The question whether there are three or more phases is quite irrelevant; the crucial point is that the mathematized science of the external world disengages itself historically from a context of anthropomorphical symbols which in themselves may be at various stages of rationalization. The critical purification of science from anthropomorphisms is the problem. Turgot designates this process of purification as progress. This designation is valuable in various respects: (1) it attributes to the term progress a clear meaning, (2) it fixes the empirical core of the idea of progress and (3) by this fixation it enables us to distinguish the political, evocative meanings of progress from this by no means unimportant but politically not very exciting core. In particular, the clearness of Turgot gives us a precise criterion for the political misuse of the idea. This misuse can assume two main forms: (1) when the idea of purification from anthropomorphisms is transferred indiscriminately as a criterion of value from the realm of mathematical physics to other spheres of intellectual and spiritual expression, and (2) when the evolution of mathematical physics, however valuable and progressive in itself, is uncritically used as the criterion of the value or progress of a civilization.

The political, evocative amplification of the idea is not absent from the work of Turgot, but the amplification of the sequence is carefully distinguished from its basic meaning. The distinction must be a grave problem for a conscientious thinker because, taken in itself, the emergence of mathematized science has no connection with the problem of meaning in history. What are the considerations which would induce a thinker to make this specific process a symbol for historical meaning? The title of the fragments: *Discours sur l'Histoire Universelle*, contains the key to Turgot's considerations, for the title resumes consciously the problem of Bossuet's *Discours*. Turgot grapples with the problem of meaning in history after the Christian meaning is lost. In this respect he is the rival of Voltaire, though he far surpasses Voltaire in his penetrating, theoretical analysis of the problem. He knows that encyclopaedic completeness is no substitute for the universality of the Christian drama of fall and redemption and the profoundness of his historical knowledge does not permit him to relegate the whole history of mankind into some prehistoric abyss and to let meaning begin with the Renaissance. The thinker who tries to find meaning in human history from an intramundane position must, in the first place, establish that there is such a thing as mankind at all, that the succession of human generations in time has a discernible structure which possibly could lend itself to a construction of meaning. Turgot thinks that he can see such a structure by which the succession of men in time is integrated into a whole that can be called mankind. In nonhuman nature he finds the cycles of growth and decay as the fundamental structure. The successive generations of vegetables and animals reproduce the same state over and over again and there is no structure overlapping the single generations. In the succession of human generations we do not see repetition but infinite variety by virtue of the operations of reason, the passions and freedom. This infinite variety, furthermore, is not a discontinuous variety but is held together in time by the chain of cause and effect which links every present generation to all past ones. And, finally, the chain is not a simple continuum, for the intellectual and spiritual life of previous generations is preserved through language and script in the life of the later generations. A *"trésor commun"* accumulates that is transmitted from one generation to the next and passed on, with new increments, as a heritage which grows from century to century. The unity of mankind, thus, is constituted through three principles: (1) the historic individuality of every man, the substance out of which the whole can be built; (2) continuity through the chain of cause and effect linking the generations and (3) accumulation of substance through the collective memory in language and script.[25]

The masse totale *as the Carrier of Meaning*

The continuously accumulating substance is mankind itself and this mankind is conceived as a carrier of meaning. But does this process of accumulation have a meaning as a whole? The meaning of the whole, however, is inaccessible to the intraworldly thinker because he is living in the finite present and the whole, extending into an infinite future, is unknown to him. The meaning of the whole is an unsolvable problem from the intraworldly perspective. Hence Turgot can do no more than search for finite lines of meaning which may have become visible in the known history of the arts and sciences, of morals and politics. Such lines of meaning can be found in great numbers—lines of growth, of decay and of recuperation. But are there any lines which run through the whole body of known history up to the present? Are there lines of growth, not of decay? Turgot thinks that he can discern such lines and he names them as the softening of the mores, the enlightenment of the mind, and the intensified commerce between formerly isolated nations to the point of global intercourse.[26] These lines do not run an even course through history. They suffer frequent interruptions and not all men participate equally in this meaningful increase of human substance.

25. *Second Discours en Sorbonne, Oeuvres de Turgot*, 2, pp. 597ff.
26. Ibid., p. 598.

But in spite of all retardations of the process, in spite of interruptions, and in spite of the distribution of the process over a multitude of civilizations and nations who do not all move at the same speed, while some do not move at all—in spite of all this "*la masse totale*" of mankind marches towards an ever increasing perfection.[27]

The considerations of Turgot offer the rare opportunity to watch a progressive philosophy of history *in statu nascendi*. We are not faced yet by a final dogma, as in Comte, and we can trace the motives and the means of construction. The decisive instruments in the construction are the lines of meaning which run through the whole process of known history and the idea of the *masse totale*. The process of history in its full broadness has no meaning, not even a finite one; that much Turgot admits. The lacunae in time through the interruptions in positive growth of substance, and the restriction of the growth to a tiny trickle of men as its bearers while the vast majority participate in progress only at a respectful distance, reduce the field of actual progress to a comparatively small area in the total flux of human history. One has to look very hard indeed in order to find in this rather turgid flux "*le fil des progrès*" at all. And if we have found such a "thread," of which the critical purification of physics is an instance, what have we gained? Of what concern can it be to a man, who lives and dies in his finite present, whether mankind has progressed in the past or will progress in the future, if he himself leads a miserable life in an unenlightened, isolated community where the mores are restrictive? Turgot's answer is the *masse totale*. The triumphant brutality of the answer is unsurpassable. History has no meaning for man. What does it matter? It has meaning for the *masse totale*.

The loss of the Christian meaning of history

This answer is heavily fraught with implications. Let us first see what has happened to the problem of meaning in history. In the Christian philosophy of history, as it was still represented by Bossuet, the problem of meaning is solved by means of the dichotomy between sacred and profane history. Profane history has no autonomous meaning and the problem of meaning is concentrated in sacred history. Sacred history has meaning insofar as it is a spiritual drama, beginning with the creation of man and ending with the second coming of Christ. The drama is known from the first to the last act and for this reason it is a true line of universal meaning. The drama of salvation has a meaning

27. Ibid.

of human relevance because involved in it is the spiritual destiny of
every single human being. Precisely because it has this bearing on every
single human destiny, because it is not the drama of a *masse totale*, we
see certain thorny questions of doctrine arise in the history of Christianity, such as: what happens to men who lived before Christ, what
happens to those who lived after Christ but have never heard of him,
what happens to those who have heard of him but resist the Evangel,
what happens to those who are called but not elected? The sacred line of
meaning which runs through history is inseparable from the meaning
which it has for the individual person. Without meaning for man,
understood as the concrete person, there is no meaning in history.
Turgot transposes the Christian dichotomy of sacred and profane history
into the context of intramundane thought through his dichotomy of the
"thread of progress" and the vast ballast of historical ups and downs
which have no meaning in themselves. However, he cannot extract
from the "sacred" thread of progress a meaning for the spiritual destiny
of the concrete person. At this point, therefore, the evocative amplifica-
tions have to be introduced. Since the finite lines of meaning, which can
be found in the civilizational process, can have no meaning for man as
a spiritual person, man and his concrete problems have to be brushed
aside. Since concrete man cannot be the subject for whom history has a
meaning, the subject has to be changed—man is replaced by the *masse
totale*. The *masse totale*, however, has no concrete existence, nor is the
masse given to human experience. It is the evocation of a carrier of
meaning, of a new divinity, into which a man who has lost his openness towards transcendental Being has projected his desire for salvation.
The *masse totale* is not a reality in the experiential sense, rather it is the
tentative evocation of a new worldly divinity. In Comte we shall see
the new god finally enthroned as the *Grand-Être*, together with a clergy
and a rite.

The loss of the Christian idea of man

Let us now consider what happened to man through the creation of
the *masse totale*. The reader will have noticed that in the preceding
paragraph we did not speak simply of man, but several times used the
term "concrete man." The necessity for such usage, in order to make
clear the intended sense of the word "man," illustrates best the
terminological difficulties which have been created through the Positivist dogmatism and its uncritical acceptance. It ought to be a matter-
of-course that the term "man," when used in a philosophical or political
discourse, should denote the "concrete man," that is the concrete human

person in the fullness of his dimensions, including the intellectual and spiritual. Unfortunately, this is no longer a matter-of-course. The thinkers of the eighteenth century have mutilated the idea of man beyond recognition. In the case of d'Alembert, for instance, we have seen that man was deprived of his *bios theoretikos* and reduced in essence to the utilitarian level of a *homo faber*. In Voltaire we have seen the fierce attack on the life of the spirit and its elimination from the "true" idea of man. Diderot has spoken of the "useless contemplator." Bentham has excluded from his political speculation the "ascetic" type as a repulsive abnormality which ought to be neglected by the philosopher. Turgot, in his capacity as Prior of the Sorbonne, delivered a discourse on the ominous subject of the "profits" which mankind has derived from the establishment of Christianity, and the editor candidly notes that the *Discours* originally contained an opening paragraph in which the author disagreed with those who believe that Christianity is "useful" only for the other life.[28] This reduction of man and his life to the level of utilitarian existence is the symptom of the critical breakdown of Western civilization through the atrophy of the intellectual and spiritual substance of man. In the progressive, Positivist movement since the middle of the eighteenth century, as well as with the followers of the movement, the term man no longer designates the mature man of the humanist and Christian tradition, but only the crippled, utilitarian fragment.

The loss of the Christian idea of mankind

A crippled man, however, does not cease to be a man. Spiritual obscurantists, or antihumanistic utilitarians, are not animals; they continue to function as humans. Still, they can no longer solve human problems rationally, or on the basis of the spiritual experiences the possession of which characterizes mature man. Hence there appear the curious transpositions of the problems of mature Western civilization to the new level of utilitarian immaturity. There arises the necessity of substituting for transcendental reality an intraworldly evocation which is supposed to fulfill the functions of transcendental reality for the immature type of man. As a consequence, not only the idea of man but also the idea of mankind has changed its meaning. The Christian idea of mankind is the idea of a community whose substance consists of the Spirit in which the members participate; the *homonoia* of the members, their likemindedness through the Spirit that has become flesh in all and

28. Ibid., p. 586.

each of them, welds them into a universal community of mankind. This bond of the spirit is timeless. The Spirit is not more present today than it was yesterday and it will not be more present tomorrow than it is today. Only because the Spirit is transcendentally out of time can it be universally present in time, living in each man equally, irrespective of the age or place in which the man lives. Only because the source of the community is out of time is mankind a universal community within historical time. Turgot's evocation of the *masse totale* transposes the Christian idea of mankind into the utilitarian key. Man is no longer a spiritual center but a mere link in the chain of generations. The spirit which welds the plurality of men into the unity of mankind is no longer a transcendental reality to be experienced by every individual soul but has become a thread of meaning to be touched at one point by a man if he is fortunate but beyond the reach of the vast majority of mankind. And the eternal presence of the Spirit to every soul that willingly opens itself is transposed into a precarious, fleeting meaning which can be ascertained only with some difficulty by scholars who know a good deal about the problems of mathematized science. At first sight, this whole transposition looks so much like an infantile insult to the dignity of man that the mass appeal, which the idea undoubtedly has to this day, is hardly intelligible.

The appeal to utilitarian immaturity

Let us consider therefore, finally, the conditions under which this idea of man can appeal to men. Obviously it can have no appeal to a mature humanist and Christian, and whenever Positivist ideas spread in a socially menacing form, the clash with the traditions of Western high-civilization is inevitable. With equal obviousness the mass appeal exists. In quest of its conditions we have only to summarize various remarks which we had to make incidental to the previous analysis. The idea of being in substance a member of a *masse totale* can only appeal to a man who has not much substance of his own. His personality must be sufficiently underdeveloped, that is to say it must be deficient in spiritual organization and balance to such a degree, that the anxiety of existence cannot be controlled and absorbed by the normal processes of the mature, meditative life. As a consequence he will be plagued by insecurities, frustrations, fears, aggressiveness, paranoic obsessions and uncontrollable hatreds. The great escape for the man who cannot extricate himself from this state through the personal solution has always been, and will always be, to submerge himself in a collective personality which he either will find ready at hand in his environment, or which he can evoke for the occasion. Tribalism is the answer to immaturity because it permits man to remain immature with the sanction of his group.

A man who is not much of a person can still be quite a useful individual. Hence a tribe of immature utilitarians can be a highly efficient and very powerful community and at the same time a very dangerous one if its insecurities, its provincialism, its xenophobia and paranoia turn, for one reason or another, aggressively towards others. The tribes which emerge in the crisis of a civilization can display a considerable political effectiveness while they last. Immaturity is no argument against political power. The political effectiveness and survival value of a tribalist movement not only add to its appeal but make it possible as a form of political existence, of appreciable duration, for the masses of men who, in increasing numbers, are set free for reorganization in new political forms in an age where the institutions of a high civilization begin to break down, as they did in the eighteenth century. The conditions for a successful tribalist evocation are present: there is given the type of man which exists at all times in large numbers; there is given the situation of a civilizational breakdown in which masses of this type are ready to respond to a new appeal (the internal proletariat, to use Toynbee's term); and, finally, there is given an idea which has the twin merit (1) of being close enough to the tradition (because it is a transposition of traditional ideas) to deceive the not so discerning, and (2) of supplying a collective personality to those who want to paddle through life with that minimum of effort that goes by the respectable name of usefulness.

The tribalism of mankind

We have surveyed the general conditions which make a tribalist idea attractive to the members of a community and which offer a certain guarantee of durable political existence. We have not yet, however, exhausted the particular charms of a tribalism of mankind. Tribalism as such exhales a bad odor in a civilization which is still permeated by traditions of Christian universalism. The various tribalist movements which have sprung up in the period of the crisis have run into conflicts with Western tradition. But not all of them have developed conflicts of the same severity. The differences in the violence of tension are caused by the different contents of the tribal evocations in the several totalitarian movements. A combination of nationalism with racialism, of the type in which the National Socialist movement indulged, is apt to arouse considerable tensions, as it actually did, because the vast majority of mankind cannot acquire membership in the *masse totale*. The universalist aspiration, combined with the restrictive content of the idea, must result in the extinction of the evocation when the tribe that was constituted by the idea meets defeat in an armed clash. The Communist tribal evocation is in a much more favorable position. The tribe also is restricted in principle, but it is restricted to "toilers." And toilers exist in great number in every society on earth. Moreover, nontoilers can be converted into toilers by the simple device of taking away their possessions. The universal aspirations of the Communist idea can be implemented "in the flesh" through changes in the economic structure of society and through the application of the great clyster which purges the *masse totale* of unassimilable elements by their liquidation. The end of Western civilization through diarrhoea is so much wider in its appeal than the end through gas-chambers and incinerators because the number of those who are made happy by the process can be envisaged at some date to be coextensive with the number of those who survive. The progressive, Positivist evocation, finally, is obviously in the most favorable position because it can use the symbol "man" for the designation of membership in the *masse totale*. The difficulty of distinguishing between tribalism and universalism, which is serious even in the case of the Communist idea, is practically unsurmountable for a progressive intellectual (who himself belongs to the *masse*) when the tribe is co-extensive with mankind at any given point of time.

The appeal of the *masse* for the common man, in the progressive version of Turgot, lies in the possibility of obtaining the benefits of mankind without incurring its obligations. All he has to do is to make himself useful to the extent of earning a living; for the rest, he can feel himself on top of the historical world by identifying himself with the progress of the *masse*. This is the appeal for the ordinary member of the movement. For the leaders, the idea holds the added appeal which we studied in detail in the chapter on Helvétius. The thinkers who evoke the idea, and the group of men who represent progress actively, are the measure of meaning in history. The *masse totale* is in progress as a whole because select individuals and groups are actively in progress. If intramundane mankind as a whole is the new *realissimum*, its standard-bearers are the god-men. The *masse totale* holds great temptation for the active elements since they can place themselves at a comfortable rank in the hierarchy. Turgot does not go to the extreme of Comte, that is of making himself the Messiah and the Pope rolled into one; nevertheless, the clerical pride cannot be overlooked. The mass of mankind certainly does not progress at an even speed. Some groups are leading, some are lagging behind, still others are in the most primitive stages of barbarism. "The present state of the universe contains at the same time on earth all the shades of barbarism and civilization; at one glance we can see all the monuments and traces of all the steps of the human mind, at one glance the picture of all the grades through which it has passed, at one glance the history of all the ages."[29] By no means do Turgot and the French nation hold the most insignificant place in the simultaneous picture of the chronological stages. As a matter of fact, they are the authoritative present and consequently the summit of the hierarchy. Bacon and Galilei, Kepler and Descartes, Newton and Leibniz receive their due as the bearers of the torch, but the climax is France. The second *Discours en Sorbonne* closes with the apotheosis of the King and the praise: "Thy happy people has become the center of civilization (*politesse*)."[30] The idea of the *masse totale* blends with nationalism. What might be the innocuous pastime of an exultant intellectual becomes a political force because it gains, on the international scene, the momentum of a powerful state if it can capture the nation to the degree that the national mass identifies itself with the leadership of mankind. In its outline we see the idea of mankind dominated by a chosen people which embodies the progressive essence of humanity. In historical actuality that would mean a totalitarian organization of mankind in which the dominating power would beat down in the name of mankind and freedom everybody who does not conform to its standards.

Profane history versus sacred history

There is evil in Turgot as in every totalitarian but in him it is not yet more than a spark. Turgot was much too deeply imbued with the spirit of Bossuet to fall naively into the radicalism of a new salvation. The "thread of progress," that is the new sacred history, is certainly his dominating idea, and the *masse totale* is his obsession.[31] However, this aspect of Turgot's historicism is balanced by a wideness of the historical horizon, as well as by a surprising penetration of historical forms, which is peculiarly his own. A good deal of this historical openness has become the precious heritage of Comte but most of it was lost to the later development of progressivism, and it was not only lost to progressivism. We must say quite generally that, setting aside such

29. Ibid., p. 599.
30. Ibid., p. 611.
31. Besides the passage on the *masse totale* quoted before, the reader should also compare the passage on the same subject, as well as its context, in the *Discours sur l'histoire universelle*, op. cit., p. 633, in order to appreciate that the idea is the backbone of Turgot's philosophy of history.

landmarks as Hegel, Burckhardt, Spengler and Toynbee, there is not much in the average occupation with problems of politics and history that can equal in breadth of conception or flair for problems the work of Turgot. This richness of Turgot's historical perspective is due to the momentum, not yet exhausted, of Bossuet's treatment of profane history.

We have hitherto neglected the profane section of the Christian philosophy of history. We have dealt only with the particular line of meaning which assumed for Turgot the function of sacred history, and we have not yet dealt with the problem that such a finite line of meaning could be found at all and that its discovery did not create a sensation. It did not create a sensation because the traditional profane history abounded in finite lines of meaning. The problem for Turgot was not to discover such a line for the first time; rather, his problem was to discover a line that would cut across the plurality of lines already known in such a manner that history could be interpreted as a meaningful whole from its beginnings to the present. We have insisted repeatedly that the meaning of history as a whole is inaccessible from the intramundane position but from this inaccessibility it does not follow that history does not have a finite structure of meaning, that is, that it does not have a recognizable meaningful articulation into the finite histories of civilizations and peoples. This finite meaning, since it is not a universal meaning, cannot touch the whole of human existence, but it touches very strongly the finite existence in community, as well as the civilizational values of which the community is the carrier. The understanding of this finite meaning, the insight into the order which prevails in it (if such an order should be discoverable empirically), is a human concern because it enables man to orient himself in his own historical situation and by virtue of this positive orientation to gain also the proper distance to the realm of civilizational values, that is: the Christian *contemptus mundi*.

The structure of history, however, can become a human concern in this sense only if it is understood as the structure of profane history, as a realm of finite meaning. As soon as any part of the profane structure is hypostatized into a process of universal meaning, the finite structure is falsified and orientation becomes impossible. This consequence of an intramundane construction of sacred history is rarely appreciated in its full importance. Once a strand of history is isolated and endowed with a sacred meaning, the tendency is irresistible to neglect all other structural elements of history as irrelevant. The "sacred history" becomes a restrictive principle of selection for historical materials. Within the Positivist movement we have to observe, therefore, a characteristic swelling and sinking of historical understanding. With Turgot, at the beginning of the movement, the view of history is still surprisingly full and well balanced, on the whole. The "thread of progress" is singled out from a historical manifold which for its greater part is not progressive at all. With Comte the construction has already become rigid—the wealth of materials is still considerable but the materials fit with a suspicious willingness into the sweeping course of progress. With the later Positivists the construction degenerates into a progressivism so thoroughly selective that selection becomes indistinguishable from ignorance. A movement which originates as a reinterpretation of history ends in the dogmatic destruction of history. Moreover, the tendency towards the destruction of contemplative history is not confined to the Positivist movement. In the course of the nineteenth century it prevails generally where ever history is written with a view to legitimate an authoritative present. The Whiggist misconstruction of English constitutional history is a match for the nationalist misconstructions of German history. The nonsense written about the medieval emperors who betrayed the German national interest through their hankering after Rome is the counterpart to the nonsense written about the Magna Carta. And the nationalist and progressive misconstructions are even surpassed by the nightmare of Marxist and National Socialist historical writing. Towards the end of the nineteenth century, this writing of selective history with a view to support a contemporary political interest was even theorized through a logic of historiography chiefly through the efforts of German methodologists. In this movement, the writing of history was considered to be a selection of materials in orientation towards a "value" (*Wertauswahl*) and correspondingly it was considered to be the function of the historian to impose meaning on history (*Sinngebung*). The immanent logic of this attitude could hardly lead to any other conclusion than the postulate that history has to be rewritten in every generation to suit the new political developments.

The resulting anarchy of liberal and racist, of progressive and Marxist history, and, in addition, of as many nationalist histories as there were nations, spelled the end of history as a science. Or, rather, it would have spelled the end unless remedial forces had been at work which tended towards a restoration of contemplative history. The awareness of this problem had never died completely. Ranke held fast to the principle that all periods of history are equal in their immediacy to God, and Burckhardt knew that all civilization is not worth the death of a single human being. In the twentieth century the restorative tendencies became strongly visible, particularly through their first great summary in Toynbee's *Study of History*. Nevertheless, there is not yet much cause to rejoice. The restorative movement is a comparatively think trickle of little effectiveness. In areas in which an intramundane political religion has become institutionalized as the state church, as for instance in the Soviet Union, history as a contemplative science cannot live in the person of even a single individual because the body-killing governmental terror would be immediately used against it. In a society like the American the chances of development are slim in the face of the soul-killing social pressure of the progressive creed, and whether the remnants of the European national societies can resist the advancing civilizational destruction is a question which only the future can answer. Still, the restorative movement exists for the time being and the problem of a science of profane history has been reopened. As a consequence of this curious course of historical science, we have returned today to approximately the point where Turgot began to depart from the classical treatment of profane history. To be sure, our knowledge of historical facts has increased greatly in the two centuries which have passed, but the categories of interpretation have not changed decisively. A few reflections on Turgot's principles of historiography have, therefore, the double function (1) of showing the state of the problem at the time when profane history begins to separate from its traditional, Christian context, and (2) of showing in what respects the problem has changed in the present.

Turgot's categories of history

Let us survey first the basic stock of categories employed by Turgot in the classification of historico-political phenomena. This stock of categories is drawn from a number of sources which are still clearly distinguishable in the analyses. The principal ones are: (1) the Christian tradition, (2) the Graeco-Roman tradition, (3) the events of the migration period, (4) some knowledge of the origin of government through the conquest of sedentary tribes by nomadic tribes, (5) speculation about the stagnation of Far Eastern civilizations, (6) the complex of problems which arises through the assumption of a "thread of progress." A few examples will illustrate these sources.

From the tradition of Augustine-Orosius stems the general view of the ups and downs in history, that is of the rise and fall of empire, of the succession of laws and forms of government and of the retardations and accelerations of the arts and sciences.[32] The *metathesis*, the transfer of empire from one people to the next, in such a manner that the great

32. *Second Discours en Sorbonne*, op. cit., p. 598.

periods of history are characterized by the succession of imperial peoples, is the first category determining the structure of history. In his use of the *metathesis* Turgot emphasizes the cultural domination which accompanies political domination more strongly than does the tradition, but his use of the category does not go, on the whole, beyond the practice that had been established by Machiavelli's idea of a wandering of the *virtù* from one leading nation to another. It is the pattern of history which we still find in Hegel. In one decisive point, however, Turgot's use of the *metathesis* differs from that of Orosius or Hegel: for him the rise and fall of empire is not the exhaustive structural principle of profane history. History is not organized as a strict sequence of no more than four empires like the Orosian, nor as a strict sequence of "worlds" like the Hegelian. The category of empire is no longer the focus as it was under the impression of the world-filling importance of the Roman Empire, and the category of the civilization (Chinese, Hellenic, Roman, Western) which determines the Hegelian speculation is not yet developed. The rise and fall of the political units is an open movement with an average of progress running through the ups and downs. Moreover, other structural features overlap with the structure of dominating peoples.

One of these overlapping features is the rhythm of political form within any of the nations which in succession may characterize one of the great historical epochs. This category of the internal rhythm stems from the Graeco-Roman tradition, though it is possible that the history of the Italian city-states has had some influence on its formation. The problem of internal rhythm is formulated on one occasion in such a manner that obviously the history of the Hellenic polis from the primordial kingship to Alexander, or of Rome from the first kings to the principate, is the model. On this occasion Turgot speaks of "the flux and reflux of power" from the prince to the multitude and back from the multitude to the prince, with the result of a more stable situation because in the course of flux and reflux the smaller political units are replaced by an empire which enforces peace within its borders.[33] On another occasion Turgot analyses the internal rhythm specifically for the case of the city-state. The sequence of governmental forms begins with kingship. This form is unstable because abuse of power in the small confines of a town will be easily detected and resented and, in due course, will engender a revolution. The resulting aristocratic republic again will be unstable and tend towards democracy because the tyranny of a republican oligarchy is even more unbearable than

33. Ibid., p. 599.

that of a king, and it is more unbearable because the abuse of power through a group will always assume the disguise of virtue and thus add insult to injury.[34] The explanation of causes differs from the Platonic discussion of the same typical sequence but the sequence itself, from kingship to democracy, and to a final despotic monarchy, is substantially the same.

The combination of the *metathesis* with the internal rhythm alone would result in a picture of the structure of history both richer in content and empirically more adequate than the later progressivist constructions, for this combination permits the assumption of a thread of progress running through the sequence of the larger historical units (empires or civilizations), while it does not neglect the rhythms of growth and decay within the units. Turgot's combination makes a theory of progress compatible with a theory of civilizational cycles. A civilization may decay, and still mankind may advance. Turgot, at least, would not run into the emotional impasse of contemporary intellectuals who howl with anxiety that civilization is at stake when our particular Western civilization will have reached the end of its course. But he adds further factors to the combination which build the periods of decay into a theory of historical dynamics. We have seen that the flux and reflux of power from the prince to the multitude and back to the prince does not produce a neutral sequence of governmental forms, but that in the course of the process the smaller units are absorbed into a larger imperial unit which enforces peace. The process is a rather bloody one, but from the struggle of the smaller units emerges the peaceful order of the larger unit—a progress for Turgot, though it would not be considered one, for instance, by Burckhardt. The violent upheaval (*les bouleversements*) becomes in Turgot's speculation the vehicle of progress. No advance is possible without decadence and destruction. The forests of America are the model of the historical process: trees grow and fall in the virgin forest and their decay fertilizes the soil for new growth. In the same manner, on the surface of the earth, governments succeed each other and empires rise on the ruins of empires. Only through bloody revolution has despotism learned to moderate and liberty to regulate itself. "And thus, by alternatives of agitation and calm, of good and evil, the *masse totale* of mankind is marching steadily towards perfection."[35] Here again the *masse totale* makes its ominous appearance—as if it were a satisfaction to the victims of an upheaval (for instance to those who were cremated in Auschwitz) to be the

34. *Discours sur l'histoire universelle*, ibid., p. 635.
35. Ibid., p. 633.

fertilizer for the progress of mankind. But the progressivist is happy because "no upheaval has ever occurred which has not produced some advantage." Nevertheless, we must stress the importance of the "upheaval" as an empirical category for the interpretation of political history. While the upheaval does not result in progress, it certainly results in the destruction of old political forms and the growth of new ones. And the dynamics of disintegration and growth are a problem in contemplative history quite independent of the question of whether a line of meaning runs through the succession of political forms.

With regard to this problem, Turgot has laid foundations which can be improved upon in detail but hardly in the essentials. Under the title of *mélange des nations* he has classified the processes in which existing communities break up and new ones are formed. The classic instance of such formation is the growth of the Western nations from the *mélange* of the original settlers and the Germanic conquerors. Both elements of the symbiosis lose their former identity and a new political entity, the nation, emerges from the mixture. These processes are noticed and remembered only when they occur on the level of civilized groups with written records. The principle, though, has to be applied generally to the dynamics of communal growth. Hence Turgot extrapolates the process from the migration case into more primitive social relations and develops the theory that differences of economy are the first incentive towards the *mélange*. Nomadic and agricultural tribes are differentiated by their ability to move: sedentary populations are by nature not conquerors; nomadic tribes are ready to move, and compelled to move if pasture is exhausted, and are inclined to descend on agricultural communities for plunder. Hence the permanent tensions between these two types in which the nomads have the role of aggressors and conquerors. The agricultural economy, on the other hand, creates more wealth and gives rise to towns with their technological and commercial civilization, so that the war potential of agricultural communities is comparatively high if they are pressed on the path of defense and defensive expansion. From the clashes result conquests with subsequent symbiosis of the warring elements, amalgamation of larger populations on larger territories, diffusion of culture and the incorporation of slaves and lower-class populations.[36] In brief: Turgot outlines a complex of problems which later was elaborated in Gobineau's theory of Western civilization as the symbiosis of sedentary with conquering populations, in Franz Oppenheimer's theory of the origin of the state through conquest and, more recently, in Toynbee's compre-

36. Ibid., pp. 631f.

hensive analysis of "upheaval" through the internal and external proletariat.

The enlargement of the historical horizon beyond the Mediterranean
area to the Far East has introduced into the speculation on progress a
problem for which Turgot does not find a quite satisfactory solution.
Still, he recognized it and did not evade it. Even under the assumption
of the *masse totale* as the subject of progress, the overall picture is
somewhat marred by the fact that the great Asiatic civilizations, in
particular the Chinese, do not seem to participate in what we fondly
consider our progress. The Asiatic "stagnation," which is the form of
existence for a vast part of mankind, does not fit easily into a picture
of progressing mankind and at least requires some explanation. Turgot
suggests that in China, India and Egypt the earliness of civilizational
achievement is the very cause of stagnation. The respect which the
nascent philosophies commanded tended to perpetuate the first opinions. "Pride is nourished by ignorance; the less one knows, the less one
doubts; the less one has discovered, the less one sees what remains to
be discovered." As a further retarding factor he considers the governmental regulation of studies, particularly in China, and the integration
of an early, comparatively high state of science, into the political institutions—which inevitably makes for mediocrity. We may agree with
Turgot's excellent common sense suggestions and still not be quite
satisfied with the explanation. Nevertheless we have to acknowledge
Turgot's merit in having tackled a problem which even today we have
not penetrated sufficiently. This is not the occasion to offer our own
solution; may we only suggest that the first step towards a solution of
the very real problem of differences in civilizational structure between
East and West lies in the recognition that the "stagnation" of the East
is quite as unfounded an idea as the "progress" of the West. If we drop
the category of Western "progress," the category of Eastern "stagnation" will disappear automatically.

Systematically of the greatest interest are, finally, those categories
of Turgot which support the assumption of progress itself. That progress seems to be possible only in the *masse totale* but not uniformly
throughout mankind is, after all, disquieting. Could this inequality of
progress perhaps be caused by inequalities between the various communities or between single individuals? Turgot rejects inequality between communities or races, but admits inequalities between individuals. The *esprit humain* is uniformly endowed with the possibilities
of progress throughout mankind, but nature has given an abundance
of talent to some which it has refused to others. Circumstances develop talents or leave them in obscurity and from the infinite variety

of circumstances derive the differences of progress in the several societies. This principle implies that primitive conditions put approximately the same type of obstacles in the way of everybody. "A state of barbarism equalizes all men."[37] Only when the first steps of progress in the face of the general obstacles have been taken and when the changes wrought in the environment by these first steps have created circumstances more favorable to the unfolding of talents can differences of progress appear as the result of a more accelerated or more retarded accumulation of such steps.

Again we have to praise Turgot's rare honesty in facing a problem and his skill in offering a methodologically clean solution. Inequality at some point has to be assumed in order to explain the panorama of civilizational inequality which lies before our eyes. Since a clear relation between natural factors and civilizational differences cannot be found, the source of inequality must lie in man himself even if we reduce this inequality to small initial differences between men and explain major civilizational differences as the result of retarded or accelerated accumulation. We are driven back to inequalities between men—a formidable problem metaphysically as well as empirically. "Genius is distributed among mankind approximately like gold in a mine. The more mineral you take out, the more metal you have gained. The more men you take, the more great men you will take."[38] What then makes the great man? First, natural differences may be a factor in human quality: a lucky arrangement of the cells in the brain, strength or delicacy of the senses or of memory, or differences of blood pressure. Beyond these natural factors, which are too rough-hewn to be used in explanation of the nuances of human differences, lie the strength and character of the soul. And the souls "have a real inequality the causes of which will always be unknown to us, and can never be the object of our reasoning."[39]

This is the finest early exposition of the problem of human inequality in civilizational action. If we make the implications explicit, we would have to render them in the following manner: (1) human civilization is not uniform throughout mankind but shows empirically various degrees of differentiation in the several communities, (2) the natural environment is a factor in the differentiation but the factor does not suffice to explain exhaustively the actual differences, (3) the explanation through inequalities between human groups is inadmissible because the human groups are not constants—*mélange* is the principle

37. *Second Discours en Sorbonne*, op. cit., p. 599.
38. *Discours sur l'histoire universelle*, op. cit., p. 645.
39. Ibid.

of historical dynamics, (4) the source of the differences must lie ultimately in inequalities between single human individuals, (5) this
source must not be sought in a radical inequality between men which
would touch the equality of spiritual substance in the Christian sense,
(6) it may be found in part in physiological inequalities—a slightly
higher reaction speed, as we would say today, may affect the course of
a human life and be the cause of differences between mediocrity and
brilliance, (7) all this still leaves an irreducible residuum which
Turgot characterizes as "talents" or "strength and character" of the
soul. The recognition of this last factor, however insufficiently described, is the methodological masterpiece. It does not abolish the
spiritual equality of men but it recognizes as an irreducible factor the
stratum in the nature of man which is characterized by such functions
as imagination, sensitiveness for minute differences of value, loyalty to
work, intellectual energy, ability to concentrate and to give form to an
idea, the ability to have "good ideas" and to grasp them when they
come. In the possession of this stratum, of course, all men are equal,
but it is a stratum which has a considerable amplitude of degrees and
in this amplitude is room for such differences as dullness and brilliance,
mediocrity and greatness.

Turgot's dilemma

In recognizing this irreducible stratum as the source of civilizational
differentiation, Turgot has gone almost to the limit of invalidating his
metaphysics of progress in history. The assumption of superior talents
which at all times are distributed among mankind in approximately the
same proportions and which, therefore, constitute the perpetual ferment
of progress excludes from progress man himself. However much civilization progresses, man does not progress. The social environment may
change in such a manner that it favors the unfolding and effectiveness
of talents, but the talents do not change. "If Racine had been born
among the Hurons in Canada, or in the Europe of the eleventh century,
he would never have unfolded his genius."[40] But, though he could unfold it in the seventeenth century, his peculiar gifts at the later point
did not differ from those which he would have had at the earlier point.
The nature of man remains constant, including its amplitude of higher
and lower endowment. Thus the locus of progress is the objective structure of civilization with its works of art and science, its technology, its
mores, its organizational knowledge in economics and politics. The

40. Ibid., p. 646.

problem of man is the same, whether he is placed in the civilization of an African native tribe or in that of a modern Western nation. A higher degree of differentiation in the objective structure does not mean that the men who are born into it have a superior ability for grappling with its problems. On the contrary, the differentiation may become so complicated that the "talents" in the society are no longer sufficient to penetrate it and to develop it further. A crisis of this kind is apt to issue in a social upheaval in the course of which the great "simplifiers" (to use Burckhardt's term) destroy the complicated civilizational structure and make room for a fresh and simpler start. The possibility that the complications of the civilizational structure might outrun the human ability to deal with it does not seem to have occurred to Turgot although in the eighteenth century it was a concern of such thinkers as Rousseau and Ferguson.

V. THE CONFLICT BETWEEN PROGRESS AND POLITICAL EXISTENCE AFTER TURGOT

Turgot presses his analysis far enough to make it clear that the central problem of history and politics is always man in society. On the other hand, he makes the objective content of civilization the center of his philosophy of history. Both problems must concern the theorist of politics but Turgot did not achieve their integration into a system. The emphasis on civilizational content to the neglect of the existence of man in society is characteristic of progressivism in all its variants. The emphasis on political existence to the neglect of civilizational content has become characteristic of various countermovements to progressivism.

Let us restate the problem. The "thread of progress" is concerned with the meaningful differentiation of a civilizational content, especially with the rationalization of our view of the external world. Assuming the description of the thread to be empirically correct, nothing would follow from the existence of the thread for the healthy state of a concrete society at any period of history. A highly developed system of mathematical physics means nothing to people who do not understand it and for societies who can master it and translate it into technology it may become a factor contributing to social disintegration. The problems of a concrete political society can be strongly affected by the "thread of progress," favorably as well as unfavorably, but their course has, nevertheless, a high degree of autonomy. In the more extreme variants of progressivism (which command mass appeal in our time) this autonomy of the course of a political society is so strongly neglected that the historical process assumes the character of an automation which can be depended upon to deliver ever further installments of progress. When the concrete societies follow their own course and disturb the dream of automatic progress, the reaction is indignant surprise, expressed, for instance, in the formula: it is outrageous that such things should happen in the twentieth century—for the twentieth century is, of course, better than the nineteenth as the nineteenth is better than the eighteenth. Back of this attitude lies the identification of the "thread of progress" with the state of the concrete society. That this identification is inadmissible did not remain hidden from the more discerning thinkers, not even from the progressivists. Saint-Simon and Comte understood well that the progress of science and industry is no substitute for the order of society. To prevent the disintegration of Western society, a danger which was felt to be imminent, it would be necessary to devise new institutions with an authority equivalent to the authority of the decaying institutions. This was the purpose they wanted to serve with their idea of a new *pouvoir spirituel*. The internal coherence of society through leadership and hierarchy thus became the absorbing problem even within the Positivist movement itself. Later political events increased the awareness of the problem, and after 1848 we have to observe an intensive occupation with the questions of political existence, resulting in such expositions as Mosca's and Pareto's theory of the ruling class and of the circulation of elites, and, in our time, in Toynbee's broad survey of the functions of a "creative minority" in the course of a civilization.

The analyses of Mosca, Pareto and Toynbee are the principal instances of a theoretical penetration of the problem that was neglected by Turgot. At the same time, however, the question received increasing attention on the part of political activists who sensed the decay both of the old institutions and of the minorities supporting them, and experienced the call to supply a new elite, and therewith a new coherence, to society. Helvétius had cast envious looks on the Jesuit Order as the model of a new elite. Saint-Simon and Comte attempted to create a new hierarchy and after 1815 this creation of new elites becomes a permanent occupation among political intellectuals. There is a continuum of elitarian formations running from the political clubs of the eighteenth century, through the clubs of the French Revolution, the conspiratorial organizations of Italy, the progressivist, nationalist, and internationalist groupings of the nineteenth century, to the twentieth-century organizations of elites in the Communist, Fascist and National Socialist movements. In appraising the meaning of this continuum, however, we have to beware of the temptation to project into the beginnings the meaning which ultimately emerged and to avoid labeling these formations indiscriminately as Fascist. In spite of the close relations between certain ideas of Blanqui and Rousseau, or of Mussolini and Mazzini, or of Hitler and Fichte, or of Lenin and the French philosophers of Enlightenment, it will be advisable to use a neutral term for designating this phenomenon and as such a neutral term we shall use "the short-circuit evocation of elites." By this term we mean to say that the persons engaged in the evocation of elites are agreed in the insight that the traditional "creative minorities" (Toynbee) can no longer cope adequately with the complications of an industrialized Western society, that they have become (to use Toynbee's term again) "dominant" minorities devoid of competence and authority, that the Western societies depend for their continued existence and internal cohesion on the formation of new creative minorities and that, moreover, in their judgment concerning the traditional social structure of

Western society and its survival value, the political activists are all pessimists. By characterizing the attempts at creating new elites through the adjective "short-circuit," we mean to say that, on the basis of an analysis which in itself is fundamentally correct, the political activists rush into the formation of elites with a blissful ignorance concerning the difficulties of the enterprise. This ignorance, of course, has degrees. Bakunin, for instance, was acutely aware that the formation of a new elite without a profound spiritual renovation was senseless. Marx, at least in his younger years, knew quite well that a change of economic order without a change of heart was no remedy for the evils of the capitalist system, and even Lenin was aware of this point, though he assumed naively that one could start on a communist order of society organizationally and that the spiritual reform would take care of itself in the course of time. Nevertheless, the political activists, on the whole, did not sense clearly that a renovation of society through a new elite would have to rest on deeper foundations than any of them were able to lay. The readiness to embark on the task of forming a new elite, without properly gauging its magnitude, is what we designate by the "short-circuit" character of the attempts.

Emphasis on political existence

The cross pattern of civilizational progress and of the autonomous course of political society in history, of theoretical penetration of the problem and of political action for its practical solution, has resulted in a curious interlocking of ideas. Today unfortunately this relationship is rather obscured by interpretations in partisan terminology. Let us try to clarify the main outlines of these relations.

Turgot's analysis has led to the point where the conflict between an emphasis on progress and the autonomous problems of political existence became clearly visible. One course to be taken in this situation would have been to drop the emphasis on progress and to cope with the problem of political existence. This was the course taken by the contemplative critics of Western civilization who discerned the disintegration of society behind the facade of progress. The short-circuit evocations by political activists, on the other hand, are characterized by the attempt to solve the problem of political existence and at the same time not to surrender the amenities of progress. It is still too little realized that the great elitarian movements of Communism, Fascism and National Socialism have a factor in common which, moreover, they share with the variants of progressivism: that is their adoration of science, of the industrial system and of the values of technology. However widely they may differ with regard to the solutions which they offer for the problem of political existence, they all agree that the industrial system has to be developed to the limits of its potentialities as the basis of the welfare of the people. This is the factor through which the modern political mass movements are the heirs of the progressivism and positivism of Saint-Simon and Comte.

In other respects, however, there persists a hysterical enmity between the various activist movements. The optimism of the progressivist creed is in conflict with the civilizational pessimism which lies at the basis of the elitarian movements. From this conflict stems the hatred of progressivists, not only against the elitarian activists, but against the thinkers who inquire into the problems of political existence. Every political scientist or historian who recognizes that there exist such problems as the cohesion of society through a ruling class or creative minority, or who considers the question that a society may be in full decline in spite of the advancement of science, or who indulges in the supreme insolence of recognizing that Communist Russia owes its coherence to an elitarian ruling class just as much as did National Socialist Germany, becomes the target of calumniations as "Fascist"— whether he be Pareto, or Mosca, or Nietzsche, or Spengler.[1] In such judgments we reach the point where selectiveness in historical interpretation shades off into plain ignorance: when progressivists fly into indignation at the mere mention of the name of Spengler. They simply do not know that Spengler has not discovered the decline of the West, but that the topic has been under continuous discussion for the last two centuries. On the other hand, we have to observe the political activists who claim eagerly that their courses of action are justified by the critics of Western civilization. When the critics are still alive, such claims may lead to tensions and disappointments for the activists, such as the National Socialists experienced with Stefan George, Ernst Juenger and Oswald Spengler. When they are dead, the game is easier: Renan could not defend himself against the title of *prefascista* bestowed on him by Mussolini, and Nietzsche is defenseless against National Socialists in search of ancestry.

Emphasis on progress

In the face of Turgot's dilemma, one course that was open, as we said, was to drop the emphasis on progress and to concentrate the inquiry on the problems of political existence. There is, however, another course open: to take Turgot's "thread of progress" seriously and to

1. Toynbee had the good luck that his *Study of History* began to appear at a time when National Socialism was well on its way to power. Otherwise he also would have been classified as a "cause of Fascism" like Nietzsche and Spengler.

explore its meaning without hypostatizing it into a total meaning of human history or making it the dogma of a religion of the Comtean type. At first sight this seems to be a quite sober suggestion. The dissolution of the anthropomorphic interpretation of the external world, and the substitution of a rational view, is a historical process which can be observed empirically. It would be a finite line of meaning among others and, divested of the progressive emphasis, reveals itself as a line of meaning of some importance, at least for Western civilization if not for the history of mankind. Unfortunately, a closer inspection does not render such a comparatively innocuous result. Turgot's "thread of progress" is not as simple a sequence of phases as it seems to be in his *Discours* and neither does the sequence of phases in the Comtean version have the simplicity which it seems to have before analysis.

Let us turn to Turgot's text in order to establish precisely the problem involved in the "thread of progress." The first phase of our interpretation of the external world, the anthropomorphic phase, is characterized by Turgot in the following terms: "before one knew the interrelation of physical effects, there was nothing more natural than to suppose that they were produced by intelligent beings, invisible and similar to us." We can omit the second, transitional phase as irrelevant to our problem. In the third phase "the mechanical interactions of bodies were observed" and only then "hypotheses were evolved which could be formulated by mathematicians."[2] Comte's formulation of the law of the three phases is more polished, but does not add anything to the substance of Turgot's idea. Nevertheless, it will be good to have the text before us: "In whatever way we study the general development of the human intellect, whether according to the rational method or empirically, we discover, despite all seeming irregularities, a fundamental Law to which its progress is necessarily and invariably subjected. The content of this Law is that the intellectual system of man, considered in all its aspects, had to assume successively three distinct characters: the theological, the metaphysical and, finally, the positive or scientific (*physique*) character. Thus man began by conceiving phenomena of every kind as due to the direct and continuous influence of supernatural agents; he next regarded them as products of various abstract forces, inherent in the bodies, but distinct and heterogeneous; and, finally, he restricts himself to viewing them as subject to a certain number of invariable natural laws which are nothing but the expression in general terms of relations observed in their development."[3]

2. Turgot, *Discours sur l'histoire universelle, Oeuvres de Turgot*, 2, p. 656.
3. Comte, *Considérations philosophiques sur les sciences et les savants* (November, 1825), reprinted in the appendix of *Système de Politique Positive*, 4th

In spite of slight variants between the texts of Turgot and Comte, there can be no doubt about the intention of the theory. The *esprit humain*, or human intellect, is the subject for which a certain necessary evolution is predicated. The title "progress" given to this evolution implies a positive evaluation but it adds nothing to the content of the law itself, and the human intellect is not defined in any other terms but those of the characteristic phases through which it passes. Hence we must concentrate the analysis on the description of the phases themselves. When, however, we try to trace the identity of the intellectual functions through the three phases, we discover that the functions which are supposed to assume three successive characteristics are not identical in the three phases. Since the functions are not identical, or, since there is no identical subject of which successive characteristics could be asserted, there are no three phases—progressive or otherwise. The evolution described by Turgot and Comte is not an evolution of the human intellect in general at all, but rather the evolution of a very specific problem that is well known to us, that is, the problem of phenomenalism. The transition from the anthropomorphic to the positive phase does not mark a progress in our understanding of the external world; it is the transition from speculation on substance to the science of phenomena. In the anthropomorphic phase the knowledge of phenomena is still embedded in the knowledge of substances; in the positive phase the knowledge of phenomena is differentiated into the critical system of mathematized science. This development in itself certainly is an advance of our knowledge of phenomena, but it is not a progress of the human intellect. On the contrary, insofar as the knowledge of the universe is now restricted to the knowledge of phenomena, the knowledge of substance is lost. As far as the development of the integral functions of the intellect and spirit is concerned, the transition is distinctly a retrogression. This was the problem of Giordano Bruno in his attack on a science of the "accidences of the accidences," it was the issue in the debate between Kepler and Fludd, and in the Kantian distinction between noumena and phenomena; it is the problem to which Schelling gave the solution of the *Potenzenlehre* and the philosophy of the unconscious.

Hence a serious occupation with Turgot's and Comte's idea of progress can lead nowhere but to a dissolution into its component parts. On the one hand, we can isolate the advances of our knowledge of phenomena, and this results in the flourishing discipline of the history

---

ed. (Paris, 1912), 4, p. 137. For an English edition see Comte, *Early Essays on Social Philosophy*, ed. Hutton and Harrison (London, n.d.), p. 218.

of science. On the other hand, we can isolate the speculation on the substance of the universe. This isolation, in the wake of Schelling, results in the philosophy of history. This latter development deserves our attention because it forms an increasingly important strand in the fabric of modern political ideas. In spite of its confusion, the law of the three stages touches upon a very serious problem in the philosophy of history. The construction of Turgot-Comte was defective because in the concept of the third stage the problem of substance was not shown in a further phase of development, but was simply excluded from consideration. If we do not exclude it, but conscientiously continue the line of thought initiated in the description of the first phase, the question will arise: what becomes of the problem of substance once it has passed beyond the stage of anthropomorphic symbolism? We know the answer given by Schelling in his philosophy of the theogonic process and in the new roles assigned to the protodialectic experiences and their dialectical elaboration. But we also know Schelling's ultimate dissatisfaction with a type of philosophical speculation that is a poor substitute for the forceful imagery of mythology, a dissatisfaction that leads him to expound the necessity for a new myth of nature. When it comes to the symbolization of substances, the myth is a more adequate mode of expression than a critical concept which can only clarify our experience but cannot incarnate the substance itself. Through the critical disintegration of the myth, both pagan and Christian, a universe of symbols has been destroyed, the *koine* in which communities of men could express the identity of the ground in themselves with the ground in the universe. The weakening and destruction of the myth is at the same time the weakening and destruction of the sacramental bond between men who hold it in common. The answer to this destruction of the myth, to the dedivinization (*Entgötterung*) of the world, is again twofold, as it was to the problem of political existence—it is either contemplative or activist.

The contemplative response to the disintegration of the myth is contained in Schelling's *Philosophie der Mythologie und der Offenbarung*. The spiritual process in which the symbols of myth and dogma are created is recovered from the unconscious through *anamesis* (recollection), and the symbols actually created in the course of human history are interpreted as meaningful phases of the theogonic process, manifesting itself in history on rising levels of spiritual consciousness. In this contemplative attitude the myth of the past need not be abandoned as the aberration of an undeveloped intellect but can be understood as a necessary step in the expression of spiritual reality. It can be superseded historically but not invalidated in its own place by subsequent fuller and more differentiated symbolic expressions. This was the method already employed in principle by St. Paul when he interpreted the Natural, the Hebrew and the New Laws as successive phases of divine revelation. Schelling draws into the orbit of his interpretation a vast historical material, including the pagan myth, Oriental symbolisms, and the Catholic and Protestant Churches, and the further enlargement of this orbit, particularly through the inclusion of primitive symbolisms and of the Oriental civilizations, is the principal problem for a philosophic history of the spirit after Schelling. Of more recent attempts in this direction I mention only Bergson's *Deux sources de la morale et de la religion*, written strongly under the influence of Schelling. Bergson's treatise has become of special interest because Toynbee, in his *Study of History*, has drawn considerably on Bergson's principles for his own construction of historical evolution.

The activist response, as we have seen, begins in the Positivist movement itself through the religious foundations of Saint-Simon and Comte. The speculation on substance, which was eliminated from the third of the Three Phases, is reintroduced in the integral system of Comte in the form of an evocation of a new *pouvoir spirituel*. The foundation of Comte, as well as the later activist attempts to solve the spiritual problem through the foundation of political religions, are incidental to the previously surveyed attempts at solving the problem of political elites and they share with them their "short-circuit" character. This question of the spiritual "short-circuit" forms part of the general problem of the pneumapathology of the crisis.

In this context we shall touch only on the political tensions which develop between the "short-circuit" political religions and the new philosophy of the spirit in history and politics which is represented by Schelling. The political fronts determined by this issue differ somewhat from the fronts determined by the issue of political existence. Concerning this latter issue, the progressive activist (with the exceptions stated above) will not be inclined to recognize the problem of the creative minority and he will even condemn the mere contemplative occupation with it because of its pessimistic implications. The activist of the Fascist or National Socialist type will be in sympathy with the thinkers who recognize the problem—though the sympathy will not always be reciprocal. Besides the various types of activists will be at odds with each other. Concerning the spiritual issue, the political front follows a much simpler line: the "short-circuit" activists are all agreed on the intramundane character of the new divinities—whether it be the progressives' tribalist idea of mankind, or the nation, or the race, or the proletariat; moreover, they are all agreed that under no circumstance can the "inner return" (in Schelling's sense) to the sources of spirituality be tolerated. As a consequence the spiritualist is faced implacably by the united front of liberal progressives, Fascists, Communists and National Socialists. With regard to their antispiritualism, the great activist movements are again in harmony, in the same manner as they are with regard to their insistence on preserving the amenities of industrialism however widely they may differ in their elitarian solutions.

The Géographie Politique

We have analysed Turgot's categories of profane history as well as the thread of progress which marks the sacred line of meaning, but we have not yet seen how these various conceptual instruments are applied to the concrete historical materials in the building of an integrated view of world history. Such a view Turgot has unfolded in his fragments concerning a *Géographie Politique* rather than in his better known *Discours*. We have indicated previously that these fragments are particularly rich in ideas. For our purpose we have to select only one or two leading ideas which have a direct bearing on the problems of Positivist history and politics.

The title of the fragments, with its amalgamation of geography and politics, indicates the basic idea which Turgot employs in his construction of history. We have touched on this idea before, when we dealt with Turgot's criteria of progress. The line of progress from anthropomorphism to science is only one of the strands in the "thread of progress" running through history, namely the line which Turgot called the enlightenment of the mind. The other two lines were the softening of the mores and the intensified commerce between formerly isolated nations to the point of global intercourse. This problem of global intercourse, drawing all mankind into the actual unit of enlightenment, is now coming to the fore in the construction of a positive philosophy of history. The magnitude of the problem may easily escape the modern reader and that is probably the reason why this part of Turgot's speculation has received scant attention. Today we have become so thoroughly accustomed to such terms as world economy, world government, global politics and global warfare that the awareness of the formidable metaphysical problem involved in this terminology is all but dead. Again the work of Turgot has its extraordinary importance because here we can catch the problem *in statu nascendi*. It is a problem which had to emerge, like the "sacred" line of enlightenment, at the juncture when the Christian philosophy of history was disintegrating and the Christian problems had to be transposed into the secular key. The problem of geography in politics, down to its modern crystallization in geopolitics, can become intelligible only when it is understood as the secular variation on a Christian theme that was transmitted to Turgot by Bossuet. It is the problem of the function which the earth has in the existence of man in society.

In the Christian view of the world, the earth is the symbol of the substance from which we come and to which we return bodily. In birth and death it binds and frees the soul, and the brief interval of earthly life is passed in the mysteriously ordained tension between the two duties of keeping soul and body together physically and of preserving the integrity of the soul against the spiritual temptations of the earth. In the Christian hierarchy of existence, the earth is, furthermore, in its morphological features as well as in the realms of being which it carries, the gift of God to man as the field of his sustenance and of his civilizational achievement. In the eighteenth century, with the atrophy of Christianity and the growth of the intramundane ideas of man and mankind, this problem of the earth does not disappear but assumes a corresponding intramundane form. The substitution of the thread of progress for the drama of salvation is paralleled by the substitution of political geography for the Christian mystery of the physical creation as the scene of the pneumatic drama. The tribe of mankind now has the globe for its habitat, the globe understood as a physical object among others of which we wish to give a description as it would be given "by an observer from the moon with good telescopes"[4]—*rien que la terre.* The intramundane progress of the *masse totale* means the increase of knowledge concerning this habitat and its increased technological exploitation. The abysmal mystery of creation has become the phenomenal mastery of a spherical surface and its resources. The history of mankind would have to proceed, therefore, from "the nations isolated by their ignorance in the middle of other nations," to the contemporary situation of general commerce between all men.[5] The dogma of progress is supplemented by the correlations of ignorance and isolation, of enlightenment and global intercourse.

In spite of the concentrated form of the fragments, there is again clearly discernible Turgot's oscillation between a contemplative history in the tradition of Bossuet's profane history and the intramundane meaning of the whole which corresponds to the Christian sacred history. The oscillation expresses itself through a variety of suggestions for the organization of the subject matter and in some hesitation concerning the course which should be taken ultimately. Well within the range

4. *Géographie Politique,* op. cit., p. 614.
5. Ibid.

of contemplative history is a first series of suggestions concerning the
topics to be included, such as: (1) the morphological features of the
earth in their relation to the distribution of peoples, the geographical
facilities for, and obstacles to, the formation of larger political units;
(2) the natural resources of the various nations and the effect of their
distribution on commercial relations; (3) the facilities of communication (rivers, oceans), their effect on the friendly or hostile relations
between peoples, and on the type of commerce that can be carried on;
(4) geography in its relation to the national character, its genius,
courage and industry. The last point stems from the tradition of the
Ptolemaic theory of climates and from Bodin. Turgot qualifies it cau-
tiously by the suggestion that we separate the "moral causes" from
the physical and inquire whether and how the physical causes have a
part in this question at all.[6]

Climatic conditions, natural resources and means of communication
are factors which have to be taken into account in history and politics
as empirical sciences. Physical factors of this type have their effects on
the technological possibilities, the wealth and the historical course of
political societies, but not much can follow from them for those central
problems of a philosophy of history that are concerned with the human
factor. The difficulties of Turgot begin when he tries to go beyond the
analysis of physical factors and their effects and to construct the
whole of human history as a function of the geographical factors. For
he attempts, indeed, to establish a *géographie politique* as an independent science. This science will consist of two parts: of a theoretical
géographie politique and of a positive or historical *géographie politique*.
The theoretical part is supposed to deal with the relations of the art
of government to physical geography. But a misgiving arises: "Since
the earth is the theatre of all human actions, this part would include
practically the whole art of government; in order not to include it in
this part totally, one would often have to do violence to the systematic
development of ideas." After this admission, Turgot quite rightly asks
himself why a treatise on government should be disguised under the
strange name of political geography. "Would it not be better to present
the part under the name of the whole than the whole under the name
of the part, however important the part may be?" We have to agree
with Turgot: why, indeed, should one resort to this strange device? It
is the same question that we would have to ask with regard to the later
development of geopolitics. But Turgot does not answer his question
explicitly. We can only assume that the subsequent development of the

6. Ibid., pp. 611f.

positive political geography is supposed to explain his insistence on the strange course.[7]

The positive political geography is subdivided into two parts: the present and the past. By the present Turgot means "*l'état actuel du monde politique*," that is, the manifold of national forces under their physical, moral, and political aspects. A national force has to be expressed in terms of population, the wealth of a state, the character of its inhabitants, the ease or difficulty of aggrandizement arising from the nature of the government. In the relations between nations we have to observe the national commerce, the respective pretentions, the true or false national interests, the policies which the nations pursue at the moment and their direction towards further progress or towards decadence.[8] The political unit in the field, thus, is a national force on a given territory and the political problem is the potential of aggrandizement. At this point, Turgot reveals the function of his *géographie politique* as a source of advice to governments concerning the question of aggrandizement. This does not mean, however, that Turgot favored a policy of national aggrandizement. On the contrary, his standard of right policy was the coincidence of territorial expanse with "*un corps de nation*." Acquisition of provinces beyond the national territory he considered "unnatural." His "natural order" is the balance of national powers, and his criticism is directed against the principles of public law which rely on succession treaties for the establishment of order. In clarifying this point, he uses as his conceptual instrument the distinction between state (*état*) and power (*puissance*). Charles V had a power but not a state, and Spain remained a power until Philip V. "The King of Prussia is a power; the King of France has a state." A power becomes a state when it reduces itself to the limits which nature has assigned to it. Political geography has drawn the limits of the state, public law forms the powers; but in the long run political geography is stronger than public law, "because always in the long run nature is stronger than the laws." Political geography, thus, is a normative science which establishes the natural law that the long-range order of Europe is the division into national territorial states of the French type. At least one of the reasons for the overemphasis on the geographical aspects of politics is Turgot's interest in the territorial reorganization of Europe according to the national principle. The political principle determining the "present" *ought* to be the organization of the nation, and the nation covers a delimited area on the surface of the

7. Ibid., p. 613.
8. Ibid.

globe. Principles of politics which disregard the territorial settlement of the nation, that is principles which lead to the formation of a *puissance* without regard to territorial limitations, should be abolished.[9] The standard example for the disregard of the national principle is the attempt of Spain and Austria to maintain the possession of the Low Lands. The political acumen of Turgot shows itself more clearly in the prediction (in 1750) of the inevitability of American independence.[10] And he is acutely aware, as we have seen, of the peculiar Prussian problem as a *puissance* which has not yet become a state—leaving open the question whether the state of the Prussian *puissance* has to be achieved by reduction, like the Spanish, or by further expansion. The political front of Turgot is turned against the past with its distribution of power according to the dynastic principle; his "present" is dominated by the idea of the nation as determining the territorial division. But in principle his argument opens the way for any collectivist idea which may supersede the nation as the unit which occupies a territory.

The absorbing interest in the geography of the "present" induces Turgot's fascinating construction of the "past" as a series of "presents" leading up to the actual present. This construction is perhaps the most convincing document for the devastating consequences of the assumption of an "authoritative present." Turgot is aware, of course, that a geography as the *tableau du présent* is a somewhat ephemeral affair because tomorrow the present is past and the new present would require a new political geography. But he is not to be deterred. "All that is past has been a present; history, which is a recital of the past, should consequently be a sequence of the *tableaux* of world-history at each moment." Human existence in society has two dimensions: space and time. Geography in the present tense is the spatial dimension: historical chronology is the temporal dimension. Geography and chronology place men at their distances in a system of ordinates: "The one expresses the ordinate of space, the other the ordinate of time." Both together determine the "situation." "*Voilà l'histoire universelle.*" "Each moment has its peculiar political geography; and this title is especially appropriate to the description of the actual present in which terminate of necessity the various courses of events."[11] In this conception we see the metaphysics of "current events" fully developed. The historicity of existence is abolished—all events are "current" in space-time, history is a film of such events which are current in their place and the substantially eternal presence before God is replaced by the phenomenally current

9. Ibid., p. 625.
10. *Discours en Sorbonne*, op. cit., p. 602.
11. *Géographie Politique*, op. cit., p. 613.

present before the photographer or "observer." Not even the fine nuance is missing in the formulation of Turgot that the actual present is a little more present than the presents which are already relegated to the limbo of the past.

Religion and political geography

The *Esquisse d'un plan de géographie politique* itself we shall not analyse. We shall extract from it only one idea: that of the impact of religions on the problems of political geography. Religions, in the opinion of Turgot, have not always had a bearing on political geography. In the age of polytheism the gods and their cults were compatible with each other; the gods were different, the religion was the same. There may have been an occasional war for religious reasons, like the sacred wars of the Phoenicians, but such wars were intended to take revenge for a particular injury done to a sacred place. "The peoples fought for their gods like our knights for their ladies." Political problems make themselves felt only with the rise of exclusive religions. If an exclusive religion was confined to one people, like the Hebrew, the political consequences were still not great since they would consist mainly in separation. Only when the object of religions becomes truth, "as in some philosophical sects," and when, in addition, the truth did not remain sectarian but was propagated with the intention to embrace all men and nations, do the political problems begin. To claim possession of truth is "a sort of injury to the rest of mankind" and the attempt at conversion cuts politically across the national organization. Such religions are Christianity and Islam.[12]

The problem presented by the rise of the universal religions is in itself well observed. The consensus of the faithful as a new type of community in politics has become the topic of one of the more convincing chapters in Spengler's *Decline of the West*, under the title of the Magian nations, and the function of the universal church as the "chrysalis" of a new civilization has been clarified by Toynbee. The rise of the universal religions in the epoch between two "generations" (Toynbee) of civilizations is, indeed, one of the great morphological features of world history. Though he recognizes its importance, Turgot regards it with clear disfavor as a disturbance of the clean geographical affairs of history. The religions *should* not exert an influence in political geography because they disturb the territorial political order. If several religions with equal universal claims find adherents in the same nation,

12. Ibid., p. 621.

the stronger will suppress the weaker and wars for the freedom of conscience will result. The persecuted subjects of one prince will form alliances with neighboring princes who are their coreligionists and under such conditions a nation cannot live in peace on its territory. The solution for such evils is unconditional tolerance on the part of the state, including the freedom of worship. "Only then will religions cease to be a factor in political geography; if for no other reason, because a state governed by the principle of tolerance will be wealthier and more populated than any other."[13] The principle of the universal Church must be abandoned, just as the dynastic principle, because it interferes with the existence of the organized nation. What Christianity has given to the world should not be belittled, but the best it has given was "to inspire and propagate natural religion." The characteristics of this essence of true Christianity are "sweetness and charity" which permit the nation to live in peace, without mutual persecutions of its citizens.[14] And what will the nation do when it lives in peace? The future is full of promise. Hitherto we have lived on the globe like savages, exploiting the fertility of the soil. This was possible because there was enough fertile soil for the comparatively small number of men. In the future, however, mankind will increase, and the increased mankind will have to use its ingenuity on lands which have been hitherto uncultivated. There is no reason to despair of this future; the technology of soil improvement and the technical means of artificial water-supply are well developed. Mankind faces a rich and meaningful existence through artificial fertilizers and irrigation projects.[15]

The three strands in the thread of progress, that is (1) the enlightenment of the mind, (2) the intensification of global intercourse, and (3) the softening of the mores, thus, are intertwined in the authoritative knot of the present. In spite of the nearness to Bossuet, in spite of Turgot's conscientiousness, and in spite of the impasses and honest hesitations, the intramundane sentiment predominates and the anti-Christian dogmatism outweighs the contemplative elements. Still, Turgot is so close to the Christian tradition that the lines of derivation through which the Positivist creed is connected with Western high civilization become visible in every detail. The creed is fully developed as an intellectual position but it has not yet acquired the characteristics of a conscious religious movement. Nevertheless, just as d'Alembert's radical progressivism, the variant of Turgot represents a definite phase in Positivism which has its historical importance independent of the

13. Ibid., p. 623.
14. *Lettres sur la tolérance*, op. cit., p. 687.
15. *Géographie Politique*, op. cit., p. 626.

Comtean additions. In Turgot's speculation, the creed of enlightenment, despiritualized morality and technology has entered into the momentous combination with nationalism. The national state of the Western type is supposed to be, and to remain, the vessel of progressive civilization. This particular evocative aggregate of ideas has profoundly influenced the course of Western political history insofar as it has become one of the great obstacles in adjusting political forms to the necessities of an industrialized society. Toynbee has given a thorough analysis of the problem which arises when democracy and industrialism, both of which require larger political units for their functioning, have to function within the unsuitable framework of the European national state. The amalgamation of the Positivist aggregate of ideas with nationalism has an aggravating, parallel effect on the resistence of national political units against their blending into larger communities.

Condorcet and the gospel of progress

When we turn to an analysis of Condorcet's *Esquisse* we are getting deeper and deeper into a class of literature which has little value as contemplative science or spiritual expression, but which nevertheless is of great historical importance because it contains a naive political dogmatism of broad social effectiveness. Turgot's evocation of the *masse totale* in progress does not remain an ephemeral idea: the *masse* gains flesh through the penetration of human minds with ideas propagated by a vast publicist literature. This, of course, does not mean that the *masse* is engaged in anything which remotely resembles a progress. On the contrary, penetration by the idea of progress means the ideological destruction of the intellectual and spiritual personality. The actual evocation of the *masse* creates the social state which we call the crisis of Western civilization. Condorcet's *Esquisse* holds a key position for the understanding of this process because, on the one hand, it presents a new step in the fixation of the dogma for mass consumption, while, on the other hand, it takes the step deliberately, with a clear insight into the atrocities of vulgarization. The *Esquisse* is consciously a work of the progressivist apostolate, a work which tries to create the *masse* by carrying the message into it. It certainly is not the first work with apostolic intentions; a good deal of the political literature of the eighteenth century serves the apostolate of enlightenment. But it holds a place in the Positivist movement which may be compared to that of a gospel of the Johannine type in the Christian evangelical literature. It is an authoritative summary of the creed for the community, a testament in more than one sense, for it was written by Condorcet while he was hiding as a fugitive from justice, as his last service to mankind, in the expectation of the guillotine.[16]

To carry the progressivist idea to the masses is Condorcet's great desire. The gulf has to be bridged between the few who actively carry the progress of mankind and the vast majority who participate in it only slightly. This bridging of the gulf has already begun. In his survey of the progress of mankind, Condorcet pays particular attention to the decisive historical epoch when progress ceases to be the privilege of an active elite and is brought within the reach of the common man. "Hitherto we have shown the progress of philosophy only in the men who have cultivated, deepened and perfected it; now we have to observe the effects on the *opinion générale*." Reason not only has purified our methods of knowledge and guarded us against the errors into which we were led "by respect for authority," it also has destroyed, in the *masse générale* of men, the prejudices which for so long have corrupted the human species. At last the right has been recognized to use one's reason as the sole criterion of truth and no longer to rely on the word of another man. "The abasement of reason before the delirium of a supernatural faith disappeared from society, as it has disappeared from philosophy."[17] The social instrument for bringing about this happy state was a new class of men "who were less interested in the discovery of truth than in its propagation; who pursued the prejudices into the recesses where the clergy, the schools, the governments and the old corporations had amassed and protected them; who set their pride rather in destroying popular errors than in pushing farther back the limits of human knowledge; who developed this indirect manner of serving progress, which was not the least perilous nor the least useful."[18]

With a few masterful strokes Condorcet has sketched the new type of intellectual parasite whose zeal to teach others is stronger than his willingness to submit to intellectual discipline, who thrives on the fallacy that truth is to be found in the solutions of problems rather than in their discovery, who believes that truth can be dispensed as a body of doctrine, who transfers the characteristics of revealed truth to the finite human search for knowledge; who consequently, through vulgarizing problematical knowledge into dogmatic results, can make the innocent

16. Condorcet (1743–94) wrote the *Esquisse* while he was in refuge with Mme. Vernet. The manuscript was completed by October 1793. It was published for the first time An III. For a brief life of Condorcet and the question of MSS and publication see the "Introduction" and "Avertissement" by O. H. Prior in his edition of the *Esquisse* (Paris, 1933).

17. *Esquisse d'un Tableau Historique des Progrès de l'Esprit Humain. Ouvrage posthume de Condorcet* (n.p., 1795), p. 242.

18. Ibid., p. 243.

believe that they enter into the truth if they accept faithfully as dogma a proposition which no conscientious thinker would accept without far-reaching qualifications, who create in their victims the belief that instruction is education, who destroy intellectual honesty through their separation of results from the critical processes which lead up to them, who build up in the masses the unshakable brutality of ignorant conviction and who, for their murderous work of destruction, want to be applauded because it is "not the least perilous, nor the least useful" to society.

The techniques employed by these men are described by Condorcet with the competence of first-hand knowledge. They employ "all the arms which erudition, philosophy, brilliance and literary talent can put at the disposition of reason; they assume all the tones, use all the forms, from pleasantry to the touching, from a vast and scholarly compilation to the novel or pamphlet; they cover truth with a veil in order not to frighten the weak, and to leave the pleasure of surmise; they are skillful in catering to prejudices in order to deal even more effective blows; they neither attack them all at the same time, nor one quite thoroughly; sometimes they give comfort to the enemies of reason by pretending that in religion they do not want more than semi-tolerance, or in politics more than semi-liberty; they are moderate towards despotism when they fight the absurdities of religion, and towards the cult when they rise against tyranny; they attack the two scourges on principle when they seem to castigate only some revolting or ridiculous abuses; and they strike the tree at the roots when they seem to trim only some rank branches."[19] The passage sounds as if it came from an instruction sheet, issued to his staff by a National Socialist Minister for the Enlightenment of the People. We should note the tone of implacable hatred; the radical will to strike at the root of institutions, even when the overt criticism extends only to reformable abuses; the technique of apparent compromise by which the propagandist whittles down resistance step by step until he can deal the final blow; the intentional dishonesty of "veiling," that is of half-truth which may tempt the uncritical mind; the playing of sentiments against each other until the institutions are equally engulfed in a social catastrophe; in brief: the catalogue of techniques, which we all know too well, employed by the political intellectual in undermining the authority of institutions and in transforming bewildered individuals into a disoriented mass.[20]

19. Ibid., pp. 243f.
20. The force of hatred in Condorcet is significantly revealed in a discourse celebrating the destruction of papers relating to the history of noble families of France: "To-day Reason burns the innumerable volumes which attest the vanity

The effective use of these means is conditioned by the invention of printing. This invention marks for Condorcet one of the great epoch-making events in the history of mankind because it has placed in the hands of the intellectual the instrument by which he can approach the individual directly, circumventing the educational institutions which are in the hands of the vested interests. However rigid the control of the schools may be, and however watchful governmental interference with the circulation of subversive literature, governments are ultimately powerless against the dissemination of ideas through books and pamphlets. This observation of Condorcet is correct to the point of triviality. Nevertheless, it should be stressed in the face of the contemporary widespread, erroneous opinion that people get their ideas in schools, that, for instance, political attitudes in pre-Nazi Germany originated in schools and can be eradicated through "reform" of the schools and the revision of school-books. The totalitarians, like Condorcet and his modern successors, have a better insight into the helplessness of schools in combating the influences which press upon the individual from much more powerful sources in the environment.[21] Hence, when totalitarians capture a government, quite consistently they supplement the control of schools by a system of licensing writing for publication and by the physical control of all printing establishments and of the paper supply.

In order to be effective, the techniques must be employed with a purpose; in the network of deceit, veilings, fake compromises there must be a point of integrity. This point is for Condorcet "the independence of reason and the freedom to write"—here lies the fundamental "right and the welfare of mankind." With indefatigable energy the intellectual has to rise "against all crimes of fanaticism and tyranny," and "he will take for his war-cry: *reason, tolerance, humanity.*"[22] Ani-

---

of a caste. Other vestiges remain in public and private libraries. They must be involved in a common destruction" (I owe this quotation to F. A. von Hayek, the "Counter-Revolution of Science," *Economica* [February, May, August, 1941], p. 13). This is not the place to go into details of this kind. But the reader should be aware that this instance of burning documents and books is not the only point of contact between Progressivism and more recent totalitarian movements. A careful monographic study would reveal that there is not much in the techniques of intellectual and moral destruction of human beings, and of mobilizing the dregs of vulgarity and the basest of sentiments, which today we associate with National Socialism and Communism, which does not stem from the arsenal of Progressivism.

21. Op. cit., pp. 180ff. The argument of Condorcet has to be qualified, however, on one point. While the art of printing has greatly increased the leverage of social influence for the intellectual, mass movements could be influenced decisively through literature even in the time of manuscripts.

22. Ibid., p. 245.

mated by "universal philanthropy" the intellectuals spread the knowledge of the natural rights of man, of the freedoms to think and to
write, of commerce and industry, of the welfare of the people, of the
abolition of torture and cruel punishment; they foment the indifference
to religion which at last is placed among the superstitions, the hatred
of tyranny and fanaticism and the contempt of prejudice. Thanks to
the incessant propaganda of the last generations there has been formed
by now a fairly general *opinion publique* in some countries, and this
public opinion has gained sufficient prestige so that even the *masse du
peuple* seems to be ready to let itself be led by it and to obey it.[23] The
passages are a *locus classicus* for the welter of genuine social grievances,
of moral indignation and justified demands for reform, of compassion
for human misery and sincere social idealism, of *ressentiment* and
hatred of the System (Goebbels), of the contradictions of universal
philanthropy and murderous intentions against the enemy, of contempt
of prejudice and fostering of still worse ones, of common sense in
details and obscurantism in fundamentals, of the fanatical attack on
fanaticism, of bigotry in the name of tolerance, of freedom of thought
through suppressing the thought of the enemy, of independence of
reason through hammering the *masse du peuple* into a dazed obedience
to a public opinion which itself is produced by the propaganda barrage
of dubious intellectuals—that is, for the welter from which rises the
sanguinary confusion of Condorcet's time and of our own.

Condorcet was a mathematician and his special interest was the recently developed calculus of probability and its application to social
mass phenomena.[24] The problem of the progressive *masse totale* in
the meaning of Turgot blends for Condorcet with the problem of
society as a mathematical mass with calculable and predictable features. Hence the historical survey of the progress of mankind culminates in the *tableau des espérances* for the progress of future generations which seems assured through the constancy of nature. We have
to understand that nature has created an unbreakable bond between
"the progress of light and that of freedom, virtue and the respect for
the natural rights of man." Once this bond is understood and has become a reality "in the whole class of enlightened men," then progress
is assured through the concerted and well-directed efforts of the friends
of humanity for its perfection and happiness.[25] Progress will no longer
be a line of meaning to be discovered by the historian, it will be a

23. Ibid., pp. 250f.
24. On this point see the works and passages of Condorcet quoted in F. A. von
Hayek's "Counter-Revolution of Science," pp. 12f.
25. Condorcet, *Esquisse*, p. 14.

direction in the process of mankind, intelligently accelerated by the enlightened elite.

In the analysis of d'Alembert's *Discours Préliminaire* we have found the idea of the authoritative present already well developed, securing the model value of the present against the past as well as against the future. The attempt to secure the present against the future did not, however, go beyond the comparatively mild form of organizing the *Encyclopédie* as the monumental source of obligatory knowledge for the future. The attempt certainly shows the characteristics of megalomaniac aggressiveness which is typical for the enlightened intellectual. Nevertheless, all a healthy human being had to do in defense against this attempt at intellectual terrorization was to shrug his shoulders and ignore the *Encyclopédie*. In Condorcet the idea of security against the future has gained a new activist momentum. We see the idea of a directorate of mankind emerging, fixing the standards of the good society and formulating a policy for its accelerated realization.

The basis for such directive action is the predictability of consequences which will result from actions of the directorate. If the existence of man in society contained an element of contingency which would frustrate the policies of long-range management, the idea of direction would break down. Condorcet's argument for predictability has become the staple of the progressivist creed. We can predict in the natural sciences—why should we not be able to predict with regard to social phenomena? "The only basis for our faith in the natural sciences is the idea that the general laws, known or unknown, which rule the phenomena in the universe, are necessary and constant; by what reason should this principle be less true for the development of the intellectual and moral faculties of man than for the other operations of nature?"[26] On this argument rests the idea of directing the destiny of mankind. The naiveté is breath-taking. To the question by what reason history is not a field of prediction in the same manner as inorganic nature, the historian is tempted to answer on the same intellectual level: because it ain't so. It is worth noting that the idea of directing history on the basis of a foreknowledge of its course is fully developed in Condorcet. The Marxist idea of direction has only changed the basis from the natural laws to the laws of dialectical materialism.

After this brilliant foundation, Condorcet begins to develop his program. It consists of three points: (1) the destruction of inequality between the nations, (2) the progress of equality within each nation,

26. Ibid., pp. 309f.

(3) the substantial perfection of man (*le perfectionnement réel de l'homme*).[27]

Condorcet's exposition of the first point, the destruction of inequality among the nations, is one of the most illuminating contributions to the problem of equality. By equality between the nations Condorcet does not mean that the nations should respect each other and treat each other on a footing of equality, and by the destruction of inequality he does not mean that the stronger ones should leave the others alone. Inequality means the differences of wealth and enlightenment between the various nations as well as between the classes in each nation. And the destruction of inequality means the raising of the backward peoples to the level of the progressive ones, whether they like it or not. "Will all the nations some day approach the state of civilization which has been reached by the peoples who are most enlightened, most free, and most liberated from prejudice, such as the French and the Anglo-Americans? Will the immense distance disappear which separates these peoples from the servitude of nations under kings, from the barbarism of African tribes, from the ignorance of the savages? Should there really be on the globe countries whose inhabitants nature has condemned never to enjoy freedom, never to use their reason?"[28] No, says Condorcet, we have no reason to entertain this distressing view. Spaniards, Germans and Swedes, Bantus, Patagonians and Eskimos—they all will rise some day to the Anglo-French level. We can discern already hopeful signs. The principles of the French revolutionary constitution are accepted by enlightened persons all over Europe and no efforts of tyrants and priests can prevent their realization on a European scale.[29] Moreover, we can hope that soon all the European colonies in the New World will be independent; and "then, as the European population in these immense territories increases rapidly, will it not civilize or cause the disappearance, without conquest, of the savage nations which still occupy vast stretches of land?"[30] And, finally, we can hope for a happy solution in Africa and Asia. The present oppressive regime of the rapacious trading companies will disappear, the Europeans will confine themselves to free commerce; "they will be too enlightened concerning their own rights to make light of those of other peoples; they will respect their independence which hitherto they have violated audaciously." The establishments will be maintained but "the offices of

27. Ibid., p. 310.
28. Ibid., pp. 310f.
29. Ibid., p. 313.
30. Ibid., p. 314.

brigands will become colonies of citizens who will spread throughout
Africa and Asia the principles and the example of the freedom, the
light and the reason of Europe." The natives will find brothers in the
Europeans and become their friends and pupils. Of course, occasional
friction may develop with savages and nomads; progress will be slower
in these cases and accompanied by some trouble. "Perhaps such natives
will be reduced to a small number; and, by and by, when they see
themselves pushed back by the civilized nations, they will end by disap-
pearing insensibly, or they will lose themselves in their midst." This
will be the inevitable consequence of progress in Europe and of the
freedom of commerce which the French and North American republics
have the interest and power to establish.[31]

This program of Condorcet seems to be the first systematic project
elaborated by a Western totalitarian for the radical destruction of all
civilizations of mankind, the high civilizations as well as the less differentiated native civilizations, and to transform the surface of the
globe into the habitat of a standardized mankind which is formed by
the ideology of a handful of megalomaniac intellectuals. There is
hardly any discernible difference on this point between the totalitarian
Progressivist and his Communist and National Socialist successors.
Who will not be reminded, in reading the exposition of equality, of
Mr. Orwell's quip: All animals are equal—but some animals are more
equal than others? Who will not recognize in the elevation of backward
mankind to the Anglo-French level the National Socialist *Gleichschal-
tung*, or Stalin's judicious solution given to the problem of nationalities:
"National in form, socialist in substance"? Who will not recognize in
the alternative, advanced with brutal equanimity, of civilize yourself
or perish, perceptibly or imperceptibly, the National Socialist slogan:
"*Wo gehobelt wird, da fliegen Spähne?*" And who would not recognize
in the colonies of "citizens" who replace the "brigands," the *Gauleiters*
and Commissars?

On the second point, the progress of equality within each nation,
we can be briefer. The reforms suggested by Condorcet do not touch
on the principles of a positivist philosophy of history and politics. They
belong rather to the general trend for the abolition of certain social
injustices, and they stem from the insight into the political instability
of a society having too deep a cleavage between the rich and the poor.
Condorcet distinguishes between the formal equality of citizens under
the constitution and the real equality of economic and educational status.
The disregard for this problem was the principal cause of the destruc-

31. Ibid., pp. 316–318.

tion of freedom in the ancient republics and for their surrender to foreign tyrants. The three points of attack are: (1) the inequality of wealth, (2) the inequality between the man who can operate with an inherited capital and the man who depends for his sustenance on his work alone, and (3) the inequality of instruction. Of the various suggestions for remedying these causes of social disturbance, we should mention especially the plans for compulsory life insurance, compulsory savings for the equipment of sons coming of age with a small capital, annuities for widows and children at the death of husband or father, and the creation of banks which extend loans to the small entrepreneurs. The basis for the operation of such institutions would be the calculus of probability. The institutions themselves could be founded *au nom de la puissance sociale*, but there is no reason why private capital should not engage in such enterprises, once the principles of operation are established and tested.[32]

The third point of the program, however, the substantial perfectioning of man, brings an important new development. A lengthy survey of the well-founded hopes for a general progress of mankind with regard to science, technology, health, the arts, welfare, security, virtue and happiness, is followed by a few concluding pages on the perfectibility of human nature itself. These reflections introduce a new element into the system of Positivist ideas and they change fundamentally the problem of history as it presented itself to Turgot. Turgot's speculation on progress ended, as we have seen, in the impasse of the tension between a progressing civilizational content and an unchanging problem of human existence. One solution to this problem would be the assumption that human nature does not remain unchanged but itself progresses indefinitely along with progress in the civilizational content. The assumption is absurd to the Christian humanist but it is bound to arise in the context of directing the destiny of mankind. If the intellectual is able to create in himself the model combination of reason and virtue, if he can destroy the civilization of mankind as it has grown historically, if he can create a new mankind in his image through propaganda and brutality and if he can direct the calculable course of mankind indefinitely on the path determined by his model qualities— why should his directive efforts not result in the creation of a substantially new man as the bearer of the perfect society? Up to this point Condorcet had assumed in his speculation that his direction would have to operate with the imperfect human raw material delivered to him by nature. Now he envisages the possibility of creating a new

32. Ibid., pp. 322–325; see also pp. 305, 307.

substance himself: the creation of man by God, which was eliminated as a superstition, now returns as the creation of the superman through Condorcet. The intramundane hubris of self-salvation culminates logically (by the *logique du coeur*) in the improvement on God through the creation of a man who does not need salvation. The Spirit has become reason, the Savior has become the enlightened director of mankind, the Father has become the creator of the superman—the Trinity has become intramundane in the intellectual.

The perfectibility of man is absolutely indefinite and can never be retrogressive. "If man can predict, almost with certainty, those appearances of which he understands the laws; if, even when the laws are unknown to him, experience of the past enables him to foresee, with considerable probability, future appearances: why," Condorcet asks, "should we suppose it a chimerical undertaking to delineate, with some degree of truth, the picture of the future destiny of mankind from the results of its history? The only foundation of faith in the natural sciences is the principle that the general laws, known or unknown, which regulate the phenomena of the universe, are regular and constant; and why should this principle, applicable to the other operations of nature, be less true when applied to the development of the intellectual and moral faculties of man?"[33] And as the human race marches inexorably towards the goal of perfection, it may not, Condorcet believes, be unreasonable to expect that death itself may be postponed indefinitely. Is it unreasonable, he asks, "to suppose that a period must one day arrive when death will be nothing more than the effect either of extraordinary accidents, or of the slow and gradual decay of the vital powers; and that the duration of the middle space, of the interval between the birth of man and his decay, will itself have no assignable limits?"[34]

It is this dream of mankind marching towards wisdom and immortality like gods, this picture of mankind liberated from all its chains, beyond the reach of accident and chance, beyond the reach of the enemies of progress, that consoles the philosopher for the errors, the crimes, the injustices that still disfigure the earth and of which he himself is often the victim.

> It is in the contemplation of this picture . . . that he finds his true recompense for virtue. The contemplation of this picture is an asylum in which the memory of his persecutors does not follow him, an asylum in which, living in imagination with mankind reestablished in its rights and in its true nature, he can forget

33. Ibid., p. 358.
34. Ibid., p. 361.

mankind corrupted and tormented by greed, fear, envy. It is in this asylum that he truly lives with his fellows, in a heaven which his reason has created, and which his love of humanity embellishes with the purest joys.[35]

A note of melancholy creeps into the idea of progress as the philosopher seeks the consolation of a vision that will obscure the reality of a "mankind corrupted and tormented by greed, fear, envy."

35. Ibid., pp. 369ff.

VI. THE APOCALYPSE OF MAN: COMTE

After a century of misunderstanding we are approaching today, on the basis of more recent experiences, a more adequate understanding of Comte both in his quality as an astute philosopher of history and in his more sinister quality as a spiritual dictator of mankind. The history of the misunderstanding of Comte and of the gradual dissolution of these misunderstandings is, at the same time, the history of our growing insight into the Western crisis. Auguste Comte (1798–1857) was well aware of the fact that Western civilization faced a crisis and while he misjudged the duration of the crisis he neither misjudged its scale nor its nature. While his attempt at a solution was as abortive as the contemporary ones, at least one important cause of the failure was the close relationship between Comte's ideas and the totalitarian practice of our times. We might say that our historical understanding is catching up today with the insight of Comte and our political practice with his projected solution.

The split in the life of Comte

If we set aside for a moment the important monographic studies on Comte which have been published in recent years, we may say that the picture of Comte is still determined by the incision in his life that was deep enough to make Comte himself speak of his "first" and "second" life. The crowning achievement of the "first" life is the *Cours de Philosophie Positive* (6 vols., 1830–42); in his "second" life Comte institutes the Religion of Humanity through his *Système de Politique Positive, ou Traité de Sociologie instituant la Religion de l'Humanité* (4 vols., 1851–54). Between the two periods lies the "incomparable year" of his relation with Clotilde de Vaux in 1845. In the first period he was the theorist of Positivism and the founder of the science to which he gave the name, sociology; in the second period he was the *Fondateur* and *Grand-Prêtre* of the new religion. Until quite recently, this articulation of Comte's life and work has remained the guiding principle for the critical interpretation of the thinker. Comte the positivist and founder of sociology was accepted while Comte the founder of the Religion of Humanity was rejected. For England in particular this pattern was set by John Stuart Mill's study on Comte, first published in the *Westminster Review*.[1] Part I of this study deals with the

1. John Stuart Mill, *Auguste Comte and Positivism, Reprinted from the Westminster Review* (London 1865).

Cours and, within the limits of Mill's abilities, gives a fair, critical appreciation of the work; Part II deals with "The Later Speculations of M. Comte" and gives a somewhat indignant account of the curiosities that are to be found in this later work and which, we agree, do not make sense to common sense. Mill concludes his account with the sentence: "Others may laugh, but we would far rather weep at this melancholy decadence of a great intellect."[2]

Mill's concluding sentence conveys two implications. First, it implies that there was a deep incision in the life and thought of Comte and that Comte's "two lives" self-interpretation should be accepted as correct; second, it implies that the incision has the nature of a "decadence," of something like a mental disturbance. Let us consider this second point first, for this assumption of a mental disturbance and decadence has been for more than one critic the reason which justified his rejection of the "second" Comte. The assumption of the mental disturbance originated in 1851 when Comte greeted with satisfaction the *coup d'état* of Louis Napoleon as a step toward the establishment of the Occidental Republic in which the Positivists would function as the *pouvoir spirituel*. A note, entitled *Essor empirique du républicanisme français* and dated June 17, 1852, gives a fairly clear idea of Comte's political conception at this time; it outlines the phases of development toward the final Republic:

(1) The French Government should be republican and not monarchial. (Crisis of February 1848).

(2) The French republic should be social and not political. (Crisis of June 1848).

(3) The social republic should be dictatorial and not parliamentary. (Crisis of December 1851).

(4) The dictatorial republic should be temporal and not spiritual, in the sense of a complete freedom of exposition, and even of discussion.

(5) Decisive arrival of the systematic triumvirate, characterizing the temporal dictatorship which Positivism has announced since 1847, as the preparatory government that will facilitate the organic transition.[3]

This conception of the *coup d'état* as the step that would lead to the dictatorial "systematic" republic, which in its turn would prepare the

2. Ibid., p. 199.
3. This note is embodied in the text of Comte's letter to Tsar Nicolas I, of December 20, 1852. The letter is reprinted in the preface to vol. 3 of the *Système* (1853).

final Occidental Republic of all Europe with Positivism as its state-religion and with Comte and his successors as the new High Priests—all that was too much for the liberals among Comte's followers. From this time dates the distinction between the unconditional Positivists and the others whom Comte styled the "intellectual Positivists." Among the liberals who left the *Société Positiviste* in December, 1851 was Emile Littré. It seems that to him is due more than to others the new attitude of loyally accepting the first part of Comte's work and of justifying the rejection of the second part by the charge of mental derangement. In his biography of Comte, Littré undertook to "split" his subject, and in a later work he suggested that "the absurdities (in Comte's late work) are more pathological than philosophical."[4] In support of the thesis, he recalled Comte's "*crise cérébrale*" of 1826, which incapacitated him for two years, and the charge received publicity when Mme. Comte demanded the annulment of the testament of the *Grand-Prêtre* "because of insanity of mind."

As a matter of fact, Comte was about as sane as anybody. The famous "*crise cérébrale*" of 1826, as far as one can determine on the basis of insufficient reports, seems to have been what today we would call a "nervous breakdown," caused by the unfortunate coincidence of ruthless overwork and domestic troubles; the recovery seems to have been complete. The seceding liberals did not find any insanity in Comte before the "incomparable year." Considering this situation, it will be worthwhile to examine the diagnosis and to see at precisely what point a man becomes insane in the eyes of a liberal, intellectual Positivist. We find the answer to this question in Littré's biography of Comte, in the chapter on "*Retour à l'état théologique.*" Littré first describes the "normal" state of mind which is the "positive" state. In this state the human mind conceives of phenomena as governed by immanent laws. There is no sense in addressing prayers to them or in adoring them. Man must approach them by intelligence; he must get acquainted with them and submit to them in order to achieve by these means an increasing dominion over nature and over himself, "*ce qui est le tout de la civilization.*"[5] This state of mind is the essential, mature state which is reached historically after the mind has passed through the nonessential, transitory, theological and metaphysical states. In his first period, Comte has developed this theory of the mind and Littré accepts it fully. In his

4. See the preface of Emile Littré, *Auguste Comte et la Pilosophie Positive* (Paris, 1863), as well as his *Auguste Comte et Stuart Mill*, published first in the *Revue des deux mondes* (1866); later in book form, together with Wyrouboff's *Stuart Mill et la philosophie positive* (Paris, 1867).
5. Littré, *Auguste Comte*, 2nd ed. (1864), p. 570.

second phase, however, Comte reverts to the theological type; he creates new divinities and, what is worse, he creates a trinity of supreme gods. This leads us to suspect the Catholic influences of his early youth, and we know that such influences, however quiescent they seem to have become, "sometimes will reawaken, not without force, at the decline of life."[6] Moreover, this relapse into theology, as into a kind of second childhood, is not an inconsequential weakness. The return to the theological state is a matter of principle for Comte. When the mind has reached the height of its evolution, when its attitude toward phenomena has become positive, then on Comte's view it must return to its fetishistic beginnings and superimpose on the universe of laws a world of "fictions" which give free expression to the affective and volitional part of the human soul. This part of Comte's philosophy is for the liberal Littré the great fall. The order of the mind can be preserved only if the affective part is under the guidance of reason, for the "heart" and "love" can generate heat but no light. And if it is accepted that the mind cannot do without the belief in divine entities, endowed with will and sentiments, then the whole system of positive philosophy comes crashing down. Positivism rests on the assumption that the theological and metaphysical phases of the mind are transitory and not necessary. If, however, the return to the theological state is considered the end of evolution and progress, if the mind is necessarily theological, then the struggle against this necessity would be as foolish as the struggle against the laws which govern the phenomena of the external world. If the end is the return to the theological state, then we might as well stay in the theological state in which we were before the advent of Positivism. Moreover, if that is the end, how can such dry fictions as those of Comte enter into competition "with the theology which emanates from the depth of history and is enhanced by the grandeur of its institutions and rituals?"[7]

The criterion of integral sanity is the acceptance of Positivism in its first stage. The criteria of decadence or decline are (1) a faith in transcendental reality, whether it expresses itself in the Christian form or in that of a substitute religion, (2) the assumption that all human faculties have a legitimate urge for public expression in a civilization, and (3) the assumption that love can be a legitimate guiding principle of action, taking precedence before reason. This diagnosis of mental deficiency is of an importance which can hardly be exaggerated. It is not the isolated diagnosis of Littré; it is rather the typical attitude

6. Ibid., p. 576.
7. Ibid., p. 578.

toward the values of Western civilization which has continued among "intellectual positivists" from the time of Mill and Littré down to the neo-Positivistic schools of the Viennese type. Moreover, it has not remained confined to the schools but has found popular acceptance to such a degree that this variant of Positivism is today one of the most important mass movements. It is impossible to understand the graveness of the Western crisis unless we realize that the cultivation of values beyond Littré's formula of civilization as the dominion of man over nature and himself by means of science is considered by broad sectors of Western society to be a kind of mental deficiency.

As far as the interpretation of Comte is concerned, it took a considerable time until the fable of his mental derangement was overcome outside the restricted circle of Comtean sectarians. The decisive publication is the monograph by George Dumas on the *Psychologie de Deux Messies*.[8] Dumas does not burden himself with the problem of the two lives of Comte; Saint-Simon has only one, but in this one life he is quite capable of developing the same messianic characteristics as Comte. Dumas, furthermore, dispells the atmosphere of strangeness, which disturbed Littré and Mill, by placing the two prophets into the spiritual situation of their time. The critique of the eighteenth century had ruined the prestige of Catholicism and monarchy; the Revolution had marked the end of a religious as well as of a political régime. The contemporaries were too near to the catastrophe to see how much was left standing of the old civilization in spite of the general destruction. They believed that nothing survived, that the future had to be made anew, and enthusiasts in great numbers felt the call to preach the moral and political gospel for the new age. Saint-Simon was only the first of them, through his *Lettres d'un habitant de Genève* of 1803, but he was soon followed by Fourier, Comte, d'Enfantin, Bazard and a host of minor Saint-Simonians. "They took themselves seriously for men of destiny, marked by a fatal sign on their forehead."[9] Saint-Simon entitles himself the scientific pope of humanity and vicar of God on earth; he acts as the successor to Moses, Socrates and Christ and he admonishes the princes to listen to the voice of God that speaks through his mouth. Enfantin divinizes Saint-Simon and sees himself in the role of the new Isaac, new Jesus and new Gregory VII. In a letter to Duveyrier he writes: "When you believe to speak to Moses, Jesus and Saint-Simon, Bazard and I shall receive your words. Have you well considered that Bazard and I have nobody above ourselves except Him

8. George Dumas, *Psychologie de Deux Messies Positivistes Saint-Simon et Auguste Comte* (Paris, 1905).
9. Dumas, p. 2.

who is always tranquil because He is eternal love." Comte released in 1851 the "decisive" Proclamation by which he "took over" the leadership of the Western world: "In the name of the past and the future, the theoretical servants and the practical servants of Humanity assume befittingly the general leadership of the affairs of the earth in order to construct, at last, the true providence, moral, intellectual and material; they irrevocably exclude from political supremacy all the various slaves of God, Catholics, Protestants, or Deists, since they are retrogrades as well as perturbators."[10] Dumas, finally, draws attention to the great model of the messianic figures on the historical scene as well as in contemporary literature, that is to Napoleon. His influence is visible, in various degrees, in most of the historical and literary figures of this type, and it is visible in particular in Comte. Not that Comte was his follower; on the contrary, he execrated him as the "retrograde genius." But Napoleon was nevertheless for Comte the concretization of the messiah, though of a rival messiah. The sentiment of rivalry was so intense that Comte considered it one of the foremost symbolic acts of the coming Occidental Republic to destroy the monument on the Place Vendôme and to replace it by a monument for the true founder of the Occident whose work Comte wanted to continue, that is of Charlemagne.[11] Saint-Simon and Comte, thus, were no more extravagant or strange than any number of their contemporaries. They were two instances of a species "that was rather widespread between 1800 and 1848 and of which one cannot say that it ever disappears completely, although in the great social revolutions it will without doubt find the occasion and the special reasons for its development."[12]

The work of Dumas has disposed of Comte's mental derangement. The disposal leads us back to the problem of Littré. If there was no decline in Comte's later years, if as a messiah he was a typical figure, one of many in his age, the question arises: What actually did happen? Did anything happen at all? Or did not perhaps the "second" life, in spite of the "incomparable year," quite intelligibly continue the "first" one? And is not the great break perhaps an invention of Littré's?

10. The text of the Comtean Proclamation is reprinted on the first page of the *Catéchisme Positiviste* (Paris, 1852), as well as in the *Système*, 4, pp. 532f. For the other sources see the preface of Dumas.

11. For Comte's evaluation of Napoleon see his long characteristic in the *Cours*, 6, pp. 315ff. (All page references to the *Cours* are to the third edition.) The passage on the destruction of Napoleon's monument is in *Système*, 4, pp. 397ff. The suggestion in Dumas, p. 5, that Comte wanted to replace the monument of Napoleon by his own, must be due to a misreading of Comte's text.

12. Dumas, p. 6. See also J. L. Talmon, *Political Messianism: The Romantic Phase* (New York, 1960).

We shall have to deal with the problem of continuity in Comte's life presently but for the moment we shall anticipate the result and state that there was no break in continuity. The messianism of Comte is not a second phase in his life; it is present from the beginning, that is from approximately 1820. The idea of the new *pouvoir spirituel* of which he will be the founder is fully developed by 1822. If anything is characteristic of Comte's life it is the peculiar "plan" which it follows from the mid-twenties to his death in 1857. Moreover, this "plan," as we shall see, was no secret, since several times in the course of its gradual realization it was published in print for everybody to read. The great theoretical work, the *Cours*, was never intended as anything but the basis for the later religious work, and anyone who cared to inform himself could know it.

If we realize this situation clearly, the withdrawal of Littré, as well as the indignation of Mill, appear in a new light. For the interpretation of this phenomenon, Dumas has given the clue. The contemporaries of the great revolutionary upheaval were too near to the catastrophe to see how much of the old structure of sentiments and institutions was left standing. Hence the crowding of the prophets and messiahs of the new age. By the middle of the century, in spite of unpleasant reminders that all might not be well (such as the revolutions of 1830 and 1848 and the *coup d'état* of Louis Napoléon), the structure of the liberal bourgeois society begins to emerge with the appearance of stability. Comte is a late comer. His messianism reaches in its origins into the unsettlement of the Revolution and it comes to its full flowering precisely at the opening of the temporary stabilization of the Western crisis in the second half of the nineteenth century.[13] That part of Comte's theoretical work that serves the destruction of the *ancien régime*, that attacks Christianity and establishes the scientistic creed, is acceptable to the generation of the mid-century; the part that serves the foundation of the new religion and the institutionalization of a new society is unacceptable to the liberals who feel comfortable precisely in the fragmentary civilization which Littré has so succinctly formulated as to its substance and which he calls "*le tout de la civilization.*" We have heard, furthermore, Littré's heart-felt complaint: for what purpose have we destroyed the unreasonable, nonpragmatic values of Western civilization, if now we must cultivate the same type of values again in a not so glorious imitation?

---

13. This is the thesis which Henri Gouhier develops in his *La Jeunesse d'Auguste Comte et la Formation du Positivisme*, in the introduction to vol. 1: *Sous le signe de la liberté* (Paris, 1933).

A diagnosis of Littré's liberalism

In this conflict between Comte and Littré, we can lay our finger on the principal structural problem of the Western crisis. Its structure is that of a gradual decomposition of civilizational values, consummated historically by repeated upheavals which destroy, or intend to destroy, the social bearers of the condemned values. Between the upheavals we find periods of stabilization at the respective levels of destruction. The attitudes toward this structure of the crisis may differ. In the case of Comte we see the great, intramundane eschatologist who underestimates the length of time which such a process of destruction needs, who anticipates its end, and who "plans" the new age. On the other side we see the liberal Littré who is satisfied by the amount of destruction worked up to this point and who is ready to settle down in the ruins. The two types are brothers under the skin though the virtues and vices are variously distributed among them. The Comtean type is vitiated by the megalomania that an individual man can grasp and "plan" the course of history and impose his "plan" on mankind. He is distinguished, however, from the other type by his profound insight into the nature and dimensions of the crisis. He knows that destruction is not an end in itself but the prelude to regeneration, and when he attacks the spiritual authority of the Church he does it in order to replace it by the church that lives by his own spiritual authority. Littré's type represents the peculiar mixture of destructiveness and conservatism that is an important component in the complex of sentiments and ideas which we call "liberal." He is willing to participate in revolution until civilization is destroyed to the point which corresponds to his own fragmentary personality. He is not literate enough to understand that Christianity is one thing, and the corruption of a Church quite another; hence, he is ready to eliminate Christianity from history because, quite understandably, he does not like the state of the Church. He is not intelligent enough to understand the problem of the institutionalization of the spirit. Since he lives in the illusion that one can ruin the prestige of a Church or abolish it, and that then matters will be settled, he is greatly surprised and frightened when a new variant of the spirit raises its head, one that he likes even less than Christianity, and clamors for institutionalization in place of the Church of which he has just got rid. He cannot understand these problems, because as a man he has not substance enough to be sensitive to spiritual problems and to cope with them adequately. On the other hand, he is only a mild megalomaniac; he certainly believes that this is the best of all worlds when it is ruined

enough to correspond to his limitations, but at least he does not believe
that he is a demiurge who can form men in his image. On the contrary,
there is left in him from the Christian and humanistic periods a certain
self-respect and respect for the personality of others, a sturdy sense of
independence which distinguishes French republicanism in its good
period, before it was finally broken by the mob hysterics during the
Dreyfus affair. By virtue of these qualities, the liberal of this type is
highly sensitive to movements which are apt to endanger his independence economically or politically. Since the process of decomposition
does not stop, he is pressed more and more into a conservative position,
until, in our time, the few surviving specimens of the genus are
labelled as reactionary. The break of Littré with Comte is due to his
fright in face of the dictatorial spectre, though he was blind to the inner
logic of Comte's movement from "intellectual Positivism" to its religious
form. In spite of our weighing of virtues and vices there is not much
to choose between them. The liberal Positivist reduces the meaning of
humanity to the dominion, by science, over nature and man, and
thereby deprives man of his spiritual life and freedom; the dictatorial
eschatologist collects the castrates and grafts his own spirit on them.
The one plays into the hands of the other and through their interplay
the crisis goes its accelerating course.

   We have stressed that Comte never made a secret of his plan. If a
contemporary did not have enough imagination to visualize the end
toward which theoretical Positivism must lead, he could inform himself
about the continuity of Comte's intention and about the aim toward
which it was moving from the ample expositions of Comte himself. The
enigmatic element in this situation receives some light from a passage
in Gouhier's treatise on Comte, where the author deals with the strange
blindness. As Gouhier points out: "It is easy for the independent historian to believe in the unity of Comte's thought; that does not oblige
him to anything. He must place himself, however, in the position of
Littré and Professor Ch. Robin, before he says that they have not
understood or, as certain positivists have suggested, that they were not
interested to understand. For them, let us not forget, it was a question
of conceding to a high priest the right to marry them and to baptize
their infants; they ran the risk of being appointed triumvirs and, on
occasion of their funeral, to be judged in public with an outspokenness
of which the unfortunate Blainville had experienced the severity, though
he was associated with Lamarck in the new calendar. That the 'intellectual positivists', as Comte said, have mutilated the authentic
doctrine, is certain; our historical reconstruction of the system, however
correct it may be, does not authorize us, however, to neglect the fact
that, beginning from a certain moment, eminent and sincere men have

no longer recognized the philosophy which study and their life had rendered them familiar."[14] Gouhier has touched the decisive point: the "eminent and sincere men" are willing to accept Positivism as long as it is an irresponsible intellectual attitude but they no longer recognize it when the necessity for order in their lives obliges them to practice its principles in every day life. Gouhier's book was published in 1933. A few years later, he might have recognized in the "eminent and sincere men" the forerunners of the good Germans who got emotionally drunk on the harangues of the savior as long as their intellectual stupor did not oblige them to anything, and who shrank back in horror when the program, about which they were perfectly well informed, was translated into political action. Littré and his contemporaries had the good fortune to live at a time when they could withdraw when the crucial moment came; their modern successors could barely murmur "*so haben wir es nicht gemeint*" before they were caught and silenced by the machinery of the new Golden Age.

The continuity in the life of Comte

The question of continuity in Comte's ideas, thus, has dissolved into the question of the split between integral Positivists and intellectual Positivists. A generation later, when the animosities among the living had died, agreement on the continuity is achieved. The work of Lévy-Bruhl on Comte is representative of the new atmosphere.[15] Nevertheless, with this agreement we have not reached the end of the affair. We remember that the seceding intellectuals could support their charges by Comte's own insistence on the great incision of 1845. Hence the love for Clotilde de Vaux and the bearing which it had on the development of Comte needs some clarification. Moreover, the word "continuity" raises a question rather than answering one. As a matter of fact, the question of what precisely the continuous element in the various phases of Comte's work consists turns out to be rather thorny. In endeavoring to answer this question we receive considerable help from the studies on Comte by Gouhier and Ducassé, but even these studies, masterful as they are, can hardly be the last word, for they are inclined to neglect what is most important, that is, the character of Comte as an intra-mundane eschatologist.[16]

14. Henri Gouhier, op. cit., 1, p. 26.
15. L. Lévy-Bruhl, *La Philosophie d'Auguste Comte* (Paris, 1900). For further literature that represents the new attitude see Gouhier, op. cit., 1, p. 20.
16. Henri Gouhier, *La Jeunesse d'Auguste Comte et la Formation du Positivisme*, 3 vols.: vol. 1, op. cit., vol. 2, *Saint-Simon jusqu'à la restauration* (Paris, 1936), vol 3, *Auguste Comte et Saint-Simon* (Paris, 1941). Pierre Ducassé,

We shall approach the problem through the intellectual autobiography which Comte has given, under the title *Préface Personnelle*, in the last volume of the *Cours*. The story is somewhat stylised but substantially correct. Comte came from a family of southern France, strongly Catholic and monarchical. He received his first education in one of the *lycées* which Napoleon had created for the restoration of the old "theologico-metaphysical" educational régime. At the age of fourteen he had already gone through the essential phases of the revolutionary spirit and had experienced the need for a "universal regeneration" that would be both philosophical and political. The later education at the *École Polytechnique* made him see the only intellectual path that would lead to this "great renovation": the methods of science which are used in mathematics and physics must be applied not only to inorganic phenomena but to organic and social phenomena as well. During the period in which he acquired a knowledge of biology and history, the idea of the true "encyclopedic hierarchy" of the sciences began to develop. And at the same time there was growing in him the instinct of a "final harmony" between his intellectual and political tendencies. These beginnings, which were influenced by Condorcet, were thrown into some confusion, on leaving the *École*, through his association with Saint-Simon. The older man had also understood the need for a "social regeneration" based on a "mental renovation" and this coincidence had a disturbing influence because it interrupted the philosophical work of Comte and turned his interests toward a regeneration through "futile attempts at direct political action." By 1822, however, he had recovered his equilibrium, and at the age of twenty-four he made the fundamental discovery of the law of the three phases which produced in him the "true mental and even social unity." Such a "philosophical harmony," however, could not be truly "constituted" before the actual elaboration of the new positive philosophy. In 1842, this task is finished and the reader now has in his hands the "final systematization" of this philosophy that had been in formation since Descartes and Bacon.

In the closing pages of the *Préface Personnelle*, Comte reveals some details of the technique which he employed in the conscious "operation" of producing his own "unity." He reflects that the philosophers of antiquity were in a more favorable position than the moderns because their "meditation" was not disturbed by reading vast quantities of literature; permanent irritation through reading affects the "originality"

Méthode et intuition chez Auguste Comte (Paris, 1939); *Essai sur les origines intuitives du positivisme* (Paris, 1939); *La méthode positive et l'intuition comtienne, Bibliographie* (Paris, 1939).

of a meditation as well as its "homogeneity." Comte protected himself against this disturbance in the following manner. In his early youth he amassed the materials which seemed to him necessary for his great plan of founding the final positive philosophy and "for the last twenty years" (this date would carry us back to the great discovery of 1822) he had imposed on himself a *hygiène cérébrale.* In order not to confuse the *"esprit fondamental"* of his work, he denied himself the reading of any literature which had a bearing on the subject-matter on which he was working. When he approached the second part of the *Cours*, that is the volumes on sociology, he went further and stopped reading any philosophical and political periodicals, dailies or monthlies. With regard to the sociological volumes, moreover, he reduced his preparatory reading and he prides himself on never having read Vico, Kant, Herder or Hegel in any language, though he is willing now to learn German in order to compare his "new mental unity" with the German systematic efforts. To this *hygiène* he attributes the "precision, energy and consistency" of his conceptions.

At the end of volume 6 of the *Cours*, finally, Comte views in retrospect what has happened during the "operation" of writing the six volumes. The *Cours* resumes "the philosophical impulse of Bacon and Descartes." This impulse was exhausted with the preliminaries of creating the inorganic sciences in the spirit of "rational positivity." Through the Revolution, the human mind was compelled to face the problem of "final renovation" in this spirit. At first this problem was only seen in a confused manner but now we know that a "situation without precedent" required "philosophical intervention" in order to dispel imminent anarchy and to transform the revolutionary agitation into organic activity. The *Cours* is this philosophic intervention in the troubles of the age. It is not, however, "direct action" in the Saint-Simonian sense; rather, it is the concrete process in which a man's intelligence reproduces "personally" the principal successive phases of modern mental evolution. As a consequence, the intelligence of Comte has disengaged itself at the end of this work completely from metaphysics and theology and arrived at the "full positive state." And by virtue of this substantial transformation it will now hopefully exert such a fascination on all energetic thinkers as will induce them to collaborate with him in the *systématisation finale de la raison moderne.* The "spontaneous reproduction," in the sense of Descartes, of modern evolution in the *Cours* which has elevated the reader and himself to the "positive state," must now be followed by the detailed elaboration of the various sciences in the spirit of the "new philosophical unity." This explanation is followed by the enumeration of the works through which he will participate in the systematization.

The most important of these works will be the *Philosophie Politique*, projected as a treatise of four volumes. Since the present *Cours* has culminated in the "universal mental preponderance" of the social point of view, conceived logically and scientifically, one cannot cooperate better toward the "final installation" of the new philosophy than by elaborating the "normal state" of the corresponding political science.[17]

The phases in Comte's work

The self-interpretation of 1842 can be corroborated by later utterances of Comte; we shall confine ourselves, however, to the present summary as the basis for further discussion because the autobiography of the *Cours* lies before the critical year 1845 and hence cannot be suspected of hindsight with regard to the problem of continuity. The foregoing passages cast light on several aspects of this problem. We shall consider them successively. The first will be the sequence of the phases of Comte's work that emerges from his own account.

The first phase is the period of the initial intuition, centering in the "great discovery" of 1822. The works of this period which in the opinion of Comte merited permanent attention were republished by him as the *Appendice Général* of Volume 4 of the *Système*. Besides two minor works, this appendix contains the *Plan de travaux scientifiques nécessaires pour réorganiser la société*. This is the work of 1822 in which Comte developed the law of the three phases. It was republished in 1824 under the title *Système de politique positive*. Comte appropriated this title later for his second main work, and assigned to the minor work the new title in the appendix. The *Plan* is followed by the *Considérations philosophiques sur les sciences et les savants* (1825) and the *Considérations sur le pouvoir spirituel* (1826). These three works together contain, indeed, as Comte maintained, the substance of his later elaboration. The second phase is the period in which Comte elaborates his positive theory, first orally, then in literary form. The result is the *Cours de Philosophie Positive*, published 1830–42. The third phase is that of the Occidental Republic and the writings which institute its religion and its spiritual power. The main work is the *Système de Politique Positive*, 1851–54. Other writings which are of specific importance for the history of political ideas are the *Discours sur l'ensemble du positivisme* (1848), later incorporated as *Discours Préliminaire* in Volume 1 of the *Système;* the *Appel au public occidental* (1848); the manifesto for the Positivist Society (1848): *Le*

17. *Cours*, 6, pp. 6–9, 34–35, 765–771.

THE APOCALYPSE OF MAN: COMTE

Fondateur de la Société positiviste, à quiconque désire s'y incorporer;[18] the *Calendrier positiviste* of 1849;[19] the *Catéchisme Positiviste, ou Sommaire exposition de la religion universelle en onze entretiens systématiques entre une femme et un prêtre de l'Humanité* (1852); and, finally, the *Appel au conservateurs* (1855), destined to fulfill for the Occidental statesmen the function which the *Cathéchisme* fulfills for "proletarians and women." The fourth and last phase we may call that of the Global Republic. The main work of this period is the *Synthèse Subjective, ou Système universel des conceptions propres à l'état normal de l'Humanité.* Of this work only the first volume, *Système de Logique Positive, ou Traité de philosophie mathématique* (1856), was published. In 1857 Comte died. This last work is written already within the new age and it is destined for use by the educational authorities of the new republic.[20] The work was planned in three parts. The first part, the only one published, contains the philosophy of mathematics, the second part was to contain the *Système de Morale Positive*, the last part was to be the *Système d'Industrie Positive.* We have designated this last phase as that of the Global Republic because in the 1850's Comte's imagination began to range beyond the Occidental Republic and to include the non-Western civilizations into his great plan. The documents for this final development are the letter *A Sa Majesté le tzar Nicolas* (December 20, 1852) and the letter *A Son Excellence Reschid-Pascha, ancien grand vizir de l'Empire Ottoman* (February 4, 1853), which must be considered as diplomatic approaches for a federation of Russia and the Islamic world with the Occidental Republic.[21] In the *Synthèse*, finally, we find indications that the religious system of the Republic was to be enlarged in such a manner that it could absorb African and Chinese forms of religiousness.

Meditation and personal renovation

The phases of Comte's work are no more than the skeleton of his mental development. Even the brief characterization of this skeleton,

18. Reprinted in Robinet, *Notice sur l'oeuvre et sur la vie d'Auguste Comte* (Paris, 1860), pp. 441–448.
19. The *Calendrier* experienced several editions and revisions; the final form published by Comte is to be found in vol. 4 of the *Système;* a last form, incorporating ms. corrections of Comte, is attached to the *Notice* of Robinet, p. 448.
20. *Synthèse,* "Préface du tome premier," p. vii: "Suivant cette destination, ce tome est directement ecrit pour des maîtres synthétiques dirigeant des élèves synthétiques dans les écoles positives normalement annexées aux temples de l'Humanité."
21. The texts of these letters are reprinted in the preface of vol. 3 of the *Système.*

however, confirms the interpretation which Comte himself has put on the process of his meditation. Let us turn now to this process itself. The works of Comte are not simply a series of treatises on various subject matters. They are connected with each other as the "elaboration" of an initial "intuition." Moreover, elaboration is not the systematic amplification of a "good idea," or the carrying out of a "project." While the term "elaboration" certainly contains the element of conscious direction or of a "plan," this "operation" is conceived as the "renovation" of a person, as its substantial transformation to the point where it has reached the state of "positive rationality." The initial intuition is the visionary anticipation of this final state and the meditative process (which precipitates in the literary work) is the means by which this state is reached. The insight into the character of the work as a precipitate of a meditation is the first requirement for understanding Comte's peculiar *modus operandi*. The encyclopedic survey of the sciences from mathematics to sociology in the *Cours* is not meant as an introduction to these sciences. It is meant, first, as the disengagement of the positive method from the actual state of the sciences in which it was previously employed, secondly, as the extension of this method to the science of man in society (which for this purpose had to be created) and thirdly, by means of this extension to clarify the true place of man in society in such a manner that in the thinker who has engaged in this meditation there will be created the disposition toward "a way of life" in conformity with this insight. Since the meditation is a spiritual practice, and not at all primarily a scientific exploration of the world, the question whether Comte's *Cours* renders faithfully the actual state of science, or the question of obsolescence, cannot legitimately be raised. Comte defends himself in the *Préface Personnelle* against criticisms of this kind precisely by the argument that the changing state of science has no bearing on the spirit which characterizes the positive method. The famous *hygiéne cérébrale*, which aroused Mill is therefore entirely appropriate to Comte's "operation": once the initial orientation and vision are given, the accumulation of new materials and the opinions of others can only disturb a process of which the end is known at the beginning.[22]

22. The problem is well formulated by Pierre Ducassé in his *Méthode et intuition chez Auguste Comte* (Paris, 1939), p. 21: "L'ascèse encyclopédique ne consiste pas à juxtaposer des faits ni même des procédés de raisonnement. C'est la contrôle, par la filière des contraintes rationnelles, d'une intuition directement unifiante. L'appel aux méthodes de la science ne saurait donc pas simuler, par leur appareil objectif, une unité fictive; cacher, sous l'impartialité apparente des attitudes abstraites, une determinante préoccupation subjective indifférente aux contradictions expérimentales. Car l'unité véritable, celle qui impose la loi de sa sincérité, est antérieure et d'un autre ordre. C'est essentiellement la volonté d'objectiver complèment un schéma de liason."

Intervention and social regeneration

Thus far we have considered the meditative process only in the solitary existence of the thinker. The Comtean operation, however, gains a further dimension through the relation between personal "renovation" and social "regeneration." We have seen that Comte characterized the state which the "great discovery" produced in him as a state of "mental and even social unity." The personal intuition has the consequence of integrating the thinker into society because the law of the three phases is a law of personal evolution as well as of social evolution. If we use a later biological terminology, we may say that the law is valid for the ontogenesis as well as for the phylogenesis. Comte passes from the early Catholicism of his home, through the revolutionary spirit of eighteenth century metaphysics, to the positive intuition, and correspondingly mankind passes from the theological, through the metaphysical, to the positivistic stage. The convergence of the two evolutions, however, is not automatic. Mankind does not pass from contemporary anarchy to the positive order without a personal effort. The social regeneration requires an active, personal intervention. A man of vision must come and realize the meaning of the critical epoch. He must produce in himself the transition to the positive state and through the fascination of his personal renovation inspire the regeneration of mankind. Correspondingly, his spiritual authority in this social operation will derive from the fact that the transformation which he produces in himself personally is the very transformation which it is the destiny of mankind to undergo at this crucial hour of its history. The man who initiates the social regeneration through his personal renovation thus becomes the chosen instrument by means of which the *esprit humain* operates its own progress to the new and final level of positive order.

The interlocking of the personal and the social processes in the one historical movement of mankind sometimes assumes curious forms in the routine of daily life. In the *Préface Personnelle*, Comte explains the reasons why volume 2 of the *Cours* appeared only in 1834, that is four years after the publication of the first volume, though it had been projected for a much earlier date. The reason was the upheaval of 1830 which compelled Comte to find a new publisher. The point is that the delay was not due to the fact that a finished manuscript could not go to press but that Comte would not even start to write the second volume before he had the guarantee that it would be printed as soon as he had finished the last sentence. "My nature and my habits," he tells us, made it impossible ever to write a book "unless it is written in view of im-

mediate publication." The personal meditative process has to stream
over immediately into the social process of regeneration. This is not
an accidental trait in Comte's character; it is a fundamental trait in his
style of communication. It accounts for the interminable length of
sentences, paragraphs, chapters and volumes which is not necessitated
by the requirement of clear presentation of the subject matter, but by
the desire for relentless communication of every intellectual shade of
the precious meditation. It accounts in particular for the monomanic
use of adjectives and adverbs which characterize and qualify nothing
but incessantly convey the sense of fatality of the urgent operation in
which the author is engaged and in which the reader through his
perusal is supposed to participate. These are *"les adverbes, les innom-
brables, les assonmants adverbes"*[23] such as *assurément, radicalement,
décisivement, spontanément, pleinement, directement, suffisament,
nécessairement, irrévocablement, certainement, exclusivement, princi-
palement, irresistiblement,* and so forth. These adverbs (of which we
have given the crop of two pages), a corresponding series of adjectives,
and the deadly host of adverbial appositions, swamp the nucleus of
meaning so effectively that only with a continuous effort can it be
disengaged from the steady stream of words. This does not mean that
Comte's writing is confused; on the contrary, the construction of the
sentences is logically and grammatically impeccable, and the organization of the subject matter is superbly clear. Comte's style is a phenomenon *sui generis* for which Ducassé has found the formula of a
complete explicitation of the meditative existence of the thinker. Nothing remains unsaid; every nook and corner of Comte's thought, every
swerve and every side path of this priceless operation must be communicated to the public.

    Comte seems to have been a man without privacy. His style is only
one symptom of the conscious and radical transformation of his personal
life into a part of the public, historical life of mankind. Nothing is too
intimate to escape this monumentalization. The details of his relation
with Clotilde de Vaux, the most intimate movements of his soul, have
been spread before the public in a manner that could not be called
anything but tactless and repulsive, unless this publicity is understood
as the eternal embodiment into the memory of mankind of a spiritual
event that is of greater importance than the birth of Christ. The
principle of *"Vivre au grand jour"* does not respect even the dignity of
death. Those who have entered into the body of positive mankind live

---

23. Alphonse Aulard, *Études et leçons sur la Revolution Francaise, Seconde
Série* (Paris, 1902), p. 11 in the study "Auguste Comte et la Révolution
française."

in it forever "subjectively" in commemoration. This memory of mankind must be both public and just; hence it is incumbent on the High Priest of Humanity to fix the just image of the deceased forever, and what occasion could be more fit for fixing this image than a speech at the grave? In fulfillment of this obligation, Comte delivered a most insulting appreciation of Blainville on the occasion of his funeral. He was not in the least abashed by the scandal which he created. He reprinted the speech in the appendix to volume 1 of the *Système* and he even added a postscript in which he reports how various public dignitaries left the ceremony when Comte disturbed it by his outrageous performance: "In order to understand this discourse better, one must note that its opening determined the brusque departure of all the official representatives of the various decadent classes, both theological and academic. That the field was left in this manner to the *esprits positifs* indicates sufficiently where the reputation of Blainville will find its permanent home."[24]

Let us, finally, record the monumentalization of troubles and trivialities of his personal life. A man of this character, as one can imagine, does not fit too well into social institutions and public functions. The professorship which he expected as his due never materialized and he was finally discharged even of his secondary functions. The details of this struggle with the educational authorities again were communicated to the public in long hagiographic accounts. And when Comte was ultimately without an income, he solved the problem by public subscriptions from Positivists sectarians. He issued annual "budget messages" to the subscribers in which he formulated his requirements for the coming year and accounted for the expenditures of the revenue received during the last year. These *Circulaires* were also communicated in print because they were public documents in which the High Priest, besides the budget of the sacerdotal power, also reported the progress which the Church had made in the spreading of membership and administration of sacraments during the past year as well as the projects for the future.[25] The monumentalizing, hagiographic obsession goes to such extremes that we are informed about the relation between the meditative progress of Comte and his consumption of stimulants. On the occasion of the crisis of 1826 he gave up tobacco, on the occasion of a minor crisis in 1838 he gave up coffee, and on the occasion of Clotilde

24. *Système*, 1, p. 746.
25. Some of the *Circulaires* can be found in the volumes of the *Système*. A complete collection is given by Robinet in his *Notice*, pp. 461–526. They are the principal source for the development of the Comtean cult to the death of its founder.

de Vaux he gave up wine—a sacrifice which reduced materially his personal expenditures, as he assured the subscribers in the *Circulaires*. If he had survived his death, he certainly would have informed mankind that now he had given up everything. As a matter of fact, even in death he did not give up everything for through his *Testament* he took care at least of his "subjective" survival. His apartment (10, rue Monsieur-le-Prince) will be the Holy See of the Religion of Humanity. It will belong to the successor in the pontificate on the same conditions as it belonged to Comte: that its content, and everything that will be added to it, will belong to the future pontiffs in the succession. Only one exception is made. The successor must respect all the reliques of Clotilde de Vaux as belonging to the sacred treasure of the universal Church. Particular veneration is due to "the red chair, enveloped in a green cover, and marked on its front board with my initials in red wax." This is the chair on which Clotilde de Vaux has sat during her sacred visits on Wednesdays. "I have erected it, even during her life-time, and still more so after her death, into a domestic altar; I have never sat on it except for religious ceremonies." It must serve no other function so long as it lasts.[26]

The divinization of woman

What influence did the relation with Clotilde de Vaux have on the development of Comte's ideas? While the relationship did not influence the theoretical content of Comte's philosophy it strongly affected Comte's *vie sentimentale*. The daily prayers which Comte offered to Clotilde are illustrative. In the *Prière du Matin* we find Comte saying: "It is only you, my saint Clotilde, to whom I am obliged that I do not leave this life without having experienced the best emotions of human nature. An incomparable year made spontaneously surge up the only love, pure and profound, that was destined for me. The excellence of the adored being allows me in my maturity, more favored than my youth, to glimpse in all its fullness true human felicity. *Vivre pour autrui*."[27] In the *Commémoration Générale*, which comprises a *Revue Chronologique de tous nos souvenirs essentiels d'après les passages correspondants de nos lettres*, we find, under the heading *Union définitive*, the quotation: "In order to become a perfect philosopher I needed a passion, profound and pure, that would make me appreciate the affective part of human nature." The letter from which this passage is taken continues: "Its explicit consideration, no more than implied in

26. *Testament d'Auguste Comte*, 2nd ed. (Paris, 1896), p. 19.
27. *Prières Quotidiennes*, reprinted in the *Testament*, 2nd ed., pp. 81ff.

my first great work, will now dominate my second one. This final evolution, even more indispensable for me today than eight or ten years ago, was the decisive upsurge of my aesthetic tastes."[28] The *Prière du Soir* continues this reflection: "By virtue of your powerful invocation, the most painful crisis of my intimate life has finally improved me in every respect, for I was able, though I was alone, to develop the sacred seeds of which the belated but decisive evolution I owe to you. The age of private passions had terminated for me. . . . From then on I surrendered myself exclusively to the eminent passion which, since my adolescence, has consecrated my life to the fundamental service of Humanity. . . . The systematic preponderance of universal love, gradually emanating from my philosophy, would not have become sufficiently familiar to me without you, in spite of the happy preparation which resulted from the spontaneous upsurge of my aesthetic tastes." "Under your various images, in spite of the catastrophe, you will always recall to me that my final situation surpasses everything I could have hoped for, or even dreamt of, before you. The more this harmony without example between my private and my public life develops (which I owe to you), the more you incorporate yourself, in the eyes of my true disciples, into every mode of my existence."

Without the transformation of the affective life of Comte through Clotilde there would have been a positive political theory which would have even postulated the preponderance of sentiment over intellect, but the faith would have lacked its existential concreteness. The religiousness of Comte that was released through the experience of 1845 has certain characteristics which merit attention. The concrete unity of Comte's existence is reached through the incorporation of Clotilde "into every mode of his existence." Comte's love, for which he has invented the term *altruism*, is not an *amor Dei* that would orient the soul toward transcendental reality. The place of God has been taken by social entities (by family, country and mankind) and more particularly by woman as the integrating, harmonizing principle. Woman in general and Clotilde concretely as the representative of the principle has become the unifying power for the soul of man; hence the cult of Clotilde is an essential part of the Comtean religious foundation. In the *Prières* we find a section *A genoux devant l'autel recouvert* (that is, the famous red chair), with the following litany:

> (A mon éternelle compagne)
> Amem te plus quam me, nec me nisi propter te!

28. Letter of March 11, 1846, *Testament*, p. 551.

(A l'Humanité dans son temple, devant son grand autel)
Amem te plus quam me, nec me nisi propter te!

(A ma noble patronne, comme personnifiant l'Humanité)
Vergine-madre, Figlia del tuo figlio,
Amem te plus quam me, nec me nisi propter te!

Tre dolci nome ha' in te raccolti
Sposa, madre, e figliuola!

(Petrarca)

To the new *vergine-madre* is transferred the Christian *Amem te plus quam me, nec me nisi propter te!*

The historicity of the mind

The pages of the *Discours Préliminaire* reveal Comte's conception of the historicity of the mind. The mind has a constant intellectual-affective structure. The possibility and necessity of historical evolution enters this structure because the two component factors can stand in various relations to each other. The history of the mind begins with an excessive preponderance of the affective and volitional life. This preponderant experience is projected into the environment and the events in nature are interpreted as actions which emanate from entities endowed with a will and affects. The evolution of the intellect is secondary. It has an "insurrectional" aspect because its function is to dissolve the false interpretation of the world that has been created by the affective component. Nevertheless, the volitional and affective interpretation is not altogether false. Once the domain of the intellect has been extended far enough to bring the order of the universe, and the place of man in it, into full view, the "insurrectional" function of the intellect must come to an end. The terminal point for the expansion of the intellect is reached when all sciences of the world content, that is the inorganic, organic and social sciences, are fully developed. The laws which govern this world are all that man can know and ought to know. Once he has become acquainted with this order, he must submit to it. He must fit his life into it and embrace it with affection. The advancement of science abolishes the excesses of the theological state but it does not abolish religiousness and the affective life. On the contrary, without the guidance of the affections the work of intellect would be aimless. The supreme affection of altruism must be the guiding principle of social life, providing the aims; the function of science can only be the increasing knowledge of the means by which the aims can be realized. Ducassé remarks rightly: "We must completely reverse the pejorative appreciation that is sometimes extended to the utilitarianism of Comte. If we charge the word 'utility' with its true affective, spiritualist and charitable intentions, we must say: Precisely because of the immediate connection which it institutes between the experience of mathematical invention and the exigencies of charity (that is of the desire of spiritual utility among men), is the Comtean form of inspiration new and superior."[29] Comte has compressed these principles of the constitution of the mind in the formula: *"L'Amour pour principe et l'Ordre pour base, le Progrès pour but."* In his last work, the *Synthèse,* he expresses the subordination of the intellect to the heart in the Christian formula: *"Omnis ratio, et naturalis investigatio fidem sequi debet, non precedere, nec infringere."*

Nevertheless, the Christian assonances, the magic of such words as "charity," "love," "spirituality" and "faith" must not deceive us. When Ducassé stresses the spirituality of Comte's utilitarianism, he certainly is right; but such spirituality is not at all reassuring. A consistent utilitarian who believes that the problems of life are solved when the standard of living is rising is a comparatively innocuous fellow. A spiritual utilitarian is a much more dangerous person for he speaks with the authority of spirit and for this reason his claims may gain a semblance of legitimacy. He does not merely insist that you make yourself "useful" (which would be bad enough in itself), he demands that you conform your personality to his faith—and the nature of his faith may not be to your liking. That there is such a thing as an evil spirit has never occurred to Comte, nor does it seem to have occurred to Ducassé, who is a convinced Comtean sectarian. Once such terms as "love" or "faith" can be used at all, no further problems of the spirit seem to exist. We also must beware of such formulations as Thomas Huxley's that Positivism is "Catholicism minus Christianity." The formula is brilliant but senseless. That the Comtean Religion of Humanity is not Christian, we may agree. That Comte has been inspired in his dogmatic formulations as well as in his ecclesiastical projects by Catholic forms, we may also agree. What Huxley's formula does not convey is the positive substance of Comte's religiousness which has to be expressed in such terms as the apocalypse of man, as intramundane eschatology, as divinization of world-immanent entities.

Hence Littré's complaint about Comte's *rétour à l'état théologique* must be taken with a grain of salt. Comte returns, indeed, to the *état théologique* of his conception but he does not return to the religiousness of Christianity as it has existed, and still does exist, historically. And he cannot return to a Christian religiousness because he never had an

29. Pierre Ducassé, *Méthode et intuition chez Auguste Comte* (Paris, 1939), p. 9.

adequate conception of it in the first place. Comte's conception of the mental constitution of man is monadic. To be sure, the mind evolves historically; but the historical evolution of the mind is immanent to its constitution; the component factors of the mind are the only forces which determine this evolution. The mind is a monad with an immanent history; at no point can this prison be broken. Religiousness, for Comte, is not a participation in transcendental reality, a communication in which the spirituality of man is constituted as the autonomous, organizing center of his personality; rather, religiousness is a movement of the *vie sentimentale* which results in a more or less true interpretation of the world. The fallacy of Comte's position can be put in one sentence; Religion is theology, and theology is an interpretation of the world in competition with science. This demonic closure of the monad is the basis of Comte's speculation. The historical world of Comte does not begin with an *état théologique;* it begins with Comte's "intuition." Insofar as this intuition has absorbed a certain amount of historical knowledge, this knowledge can be projected on a time scale and be called the evolution of the *esprit humain*, and since Comte's historical knowledge was considerable, the projection will even have a certain degree of empirical adequacy. Nevertheless, an adequate philosophy of history can never result from an "intuition" which is itself nothing but an event in history, for the problem of human history is precisely the tension between the historical existence of man and his transcendental destination. The speculation of Comte begins with a compact "intuition" and is followed by its "explication," "elaboration," and "concretization" quite legitimately supported by the *hygiène cérébrale*. The elaboration, therefore, can follow a "plan" and it can be directed from the beginning to the foreknown end. We should pay attention in particular to Comte's favorite word for this process, namely, the word "operation." The word awakens the association of the alchemystic *opus operatum*, of the successful liberation of the spirit from matter through a human agency.

The personal "renovation" of Comte merges with social "regeneration" into the one process of progressing mankind. The life of the *Grand Être*, of Divine Humanity, streams through the life of Comte. Every phase of this life is a divine manifestation since in this life is revealed the new, positivist phase of the *Grand Être*. This revelation is not a personal event but the public, historical coming of the new age, overflowing from the focal point of the revelation into ever-widening circles of humanity. The life of Comte is a true apocalypse in the religious sense of the word. Only if we recognize the apocalyptic character of Comte can we understand his actions in the political phase after 1845. The Third Realm of the positive spirit has come, its spiritual power institutionalized in the Pontifex Maximus who functions and administers sacraments. The Occidental Republic is founded in substance and in a few years it will have created institutions devised by the man who signs himself as *Fondateur de la Religion de l'Humanité*. By his authority as the High Priest of the Occidental Republic he sends diplomatic notes to the non-Western powers. And finally he sends an ambassador to the General of the Jesuit Order suggesting that he associate himself with Comte in a demand to the Pope that the ecclesiastic budgets be abolished. The abolition of state support for the Catholic Church would advance the free coming of the new spirituality, while the old spiritual power "would gain the independence and morality that is necessary for its positive transformation or its dignified extinction."[30]

In the present state of the crisis, we cannot know whether Comte is a forerunner of the apocalyptic founders of new realms whom we have witnessed in our time and of more formidable ones who will appear in the future, or whether the contemporary apocalyptic figures are the last ones of a breed of which Comte is by intellect and personal style the most grandiose specimen. Whatever the answer of the future will be, there can be no doubt even now that Comte belongs, with Marx, Lenin, and Hitler, to the series of men who would save mankind and themselves by divinizing their particular existence and imposing its law as the new order of society. The satanic Apocalypse of Man begins with Comte and has become the signature of the Western crisis.

30. Robinet, *Notice*, p. 276.

VII. THE RELIGION OF HUMANITY AND THE FRENCH REVOLUTION

Comte's intuition, which culminated in the foundation of the Religion of Humanity, was so strange and scandalous to the liberals of the mid-nineteenth century that it appeared to them as a mental derangement. One cause of this appearance of strangeness was the fact that by this time the continuum of politico-religious movements to which Comte's religion of humanity belongs had already been pressed below the level of social consciousness. This continuum, however, should not have been obscure, for Comte had been explicit about it in his intellectual biography.

We have seen that Comte derives his ancestry, as far as the positive method is concerned, from Bacon and Descartes, and that he mentions Condorcet repeatedly as the forerunner whose conception he is resuming and completing. Moreover, he has expressed himself literally in whole volumes on the problem of the positive era and of his place in it. The great event that marks the beginning of the epoch is the storming of the Bastille. With this event begins the "provisional" positivist era, the era of transition to the final, positive realm. The complete establishment of this realm Comte expects a century after the epochal events, i.e. in 1889. This *"siècle exceptionelle"* (in the history of mankind the equivalent to his personal *année sans pareille*) comprises three generations and the third of them is going to see the foundation of the new spiritual power and the transition to the final realm. The year of the foundation Comte has fixed at 1855, exactly two generations, of 33 years each, after 1789 (it is the year following the completion of his religious institutes, that is of the *Système*). Once the transition is completed, the government of the Occidental Republic will change the "provisional" era that Comte had let begin with 1789 into the "definite" era that will begin with the year 1855.[1]

Comte was never shy in fixing his true importance in the history of mankind. As the author of the *Cours* he saw himself in the role of the Aristotle of the new age, as the author of the *Système* he was the new Saint Paul, organizing the Church; and in his relations with Clotilde,

---

1. On the question of the era see the various editions of the *Calendrier Positiviste*, and the *Système*, vol. 4, chs. 2, 5.

inevitably he was Dante with his Beatrice.[2] The construction of the new era is his most unabashed stroke. The "provisional" era in itself would not be so surprising; it is simply a resumption of the French revolutionary era, shifting only its beginning, with some historical justification, from 1792 to 1789. What is breathtaking, however, is the articulation of the *siècle exceptionelle* and the fixation of the "definite" era with 1855. This is the first time in Western history that a man has arrogated to himself personally the place of Christ as the epochal figure which divides the ages. Comte goes even farther. His *Calendrier* commemorates the great men who belong to the *Préparation Humaine* that leads up to the positive age. The religious founders are accorded their places in it: Zoroaster, Buddha, Confucius, Moses, Abraham, Saint-Paul, Mohammed; only one name is omitted, that of Jesus. His name shall not be remembered in the age of Comte. The attitude is particularly curious because, at the same time, the *Calendrier* provides for an ample commemoration of Christianity through the Evangelists, Fathers and medieval Saints, and because in his catalogue of positivist books Comte has included such items as the *Bible*, the *Civitas Dei*, the *Divina Commedia* and the *Imitatio Christi*.[3] Christianity as a "sociological" phase in the history of mankind is not suppressed at all; on the contrary, Comte has an acute understanding of the civilizational and institutional achievements of medieval Christianity. The rejection of Jesus is a personal affair.

The Grand-Être *and the fiction of Christ*

The problem is fundamental for the understanding of Comte's politics as the culmination of a development which, quite correctly, he traces back to the French Revolution. In the person and work of Comte we find the first, considered creation of an immanent, sociological God and Comte was intelligent enough to understand the inevitable conflict with the God who has become flesh. Simple prophets, like Mohammed, are bearable for Comte; they speak in the name of God, and nothing is simpler than to interpret their symbolic language "sociologically" as an immature "hypothesis" concerning the world. The God that has become

2. Comte seems to have had no awareness at all of the possibility that Dante's symbolization of the *ecclesia spiritualis* through Beatrice is the opposite of his divinization of a woman.

3. See the *Bibliotèque Positiviste*, a list of 150 volumes for the education of the Positivist. The list is attached to vol. 4 of the *Système*. It is considered to be provisional; later it should be reduced to 100 volumes. This seems to be the origin of the fad of the one hundred great books.

flesh poses a problem of a different kind, for in this case the reality of God is historically present. The conflict between Comte's *Grand-Être* and Christ is a struggle between two historical Gods. A transcendental reality has to remain in its transcendence so that the faith can be interpreted as a human illusion; the transcendental God who walks personally on earth breaks the rules of the game.

Comte has dealt with this awkward affair on various occasions. In volume 1 of the *Système* he elaborates the dogma of the *Grand-Être*. He compares the new divinity with the Christian idea of God (or at least what he believes it to be). The Christian conception of God is "contradictory and consequently only temporary." The idea of an absolute, omnipotent God is incompatible with the attributes of infinite intelligence and infinite goodness. It is incompatible with the assumption of infinite intelligence because "our true meditations are no more than the prolongation of our observations." Only where observation is insufficient to supply the required information, do we start to think; thought supplies the insufficiency of observation. "If we could place ourselves always under the most favorable circumstances for research, we would have no use for intelligence, and we could appreciate things by simple inspection." "Hence omnipotence excludes omniscience." Still more obvious is the incompatibility with infinite goodness. All our sentiments and plans refer to obstacles, either in order to adapt ourselves to them or to remove them. The plans of an omnipotent being could, therefore, be nothing but pure caprices; they would not involve any true wisdom, which is always the submission to an external necessity in appropriating means to an end.[4] The *Grand-Être* as devised by Comte has none of these drawbacks, for the *Grand-Être* is mankind as it comes gradually into existence with every succeeding generation. The advantage of this conception is the coincidence of divinity with the real extent of our sociological knowledge. We are parts of this *Grand-Être* and insofar dependent on it, but its supremacy is strictly relative to our research and our needs. We could indulge, perhaps, in the fantasy that on some other planet an even more glorious *Grand-Être* than our mankind exists. "But, in view of the fact that we cannot know anything about it, this question will remain forever meaningless

4. *Système*, 1, pp. 408f. I should like to stress that the summary in the text is exhaustive. The argument is so insolently superficial and stupid that it is almost unbelievable. The reader is invited to verify it. Nevertheless, the argument contains formulations of the greatest importance for the understanding of certain puzzling phenomena in the intellectual life of our time. In particular the formula that "under the most favorable circumstances for research we would have no use for intelligence" has become an ideal to which reality is closely conforming.

and unapproachable, because such a being would in no way affect our destinies." We can be satisfied with the *Grand-Être* that is known to us, and only on its existence as it is known to us empirically do we feel our destinies dependent. This "restriction of power" is the true source of superiority of the rule of Humanity over the rule of God. The harmony of this supreme existence with the men over whom it rules does not require any explanation, for it results from its very composition. Moreover, its preponderance in this harmonious relation will reveal itself to the reflection of even the proudest subjects. Physically and morally man depends on the existence of this *Grand-Être*. Personal forces can prevail against it only within the narrowest limits. Still more impressive is its intellectual and moral superiority. For Humanity does not consist of the indifferent agglomeration of all individuals and groups who ever have lived, live and will live. A true whole can only result from associable elements. Hence the *Grand-Être* forms itself, in time and space, through those human existences which are assimilable, while it excludes those who would be nothing but a burden for the species. Hence in its vast majority it is composed of the dead who are the only ones who can be truly judged. The living are admitted on probation only and the whole of their lives will prove whether they will be permanently incorporated into it or rejected. Hence the Positivist dogma of a divine being provides "the indispensable combination of homogeneity and preponderance" which the Catholic dogma attempted clumsily through "the insufficient fiction of Christ."[5]

The topic of the "fiction of Christ" is continued in volume 2 of the *Système*. "*Ce divin médiateur*" was a symptom of the growing tendency of humanity to draw out of itself its supreme providence. This tendency has expressed itself in the following phases. The human type has furnished the basis even of fetishism, though on this level only the volitional and affective constitution of man was projected into the outside world, without personifying it. The type asserted itself more clearly in polytheism when imagination endowed the directing forces with the attributes of an idealized human nature. Catholicism goes still farther when it concentrates the attributes in one supreme unit in which the two natures are combined though not confused. Now we are approaching the final phase: "Such a progression must finally lead to the complete elimination of the fictitious being; in this state the real being will have acquired sufficient grandeur and consistence to replace entirely its necessary predecessor."[6]

5. Ibid., pp. 409–411.
6. Ibid., 2, p. 108.

We have assembled the essentials of the issue. The generous *ex-plicitation* of Comte reveals a good deal of his religious motivation. Above all, we get a glimpse of his profound anxiety as well as of his special fears. Comte is afraid of God—of his omnipotence, of his omniscience and of his goodness. The phrase "restriction of power" is a betrayal. He wants a God, if a God it has to be, who at least is not an "absolute unity" but rather "relative and composite." He grows historically and he consists of individuals with whom one can deal singly. Even so the aggregate of the *Grand-Être* has a growing and rather overpowering effect, but the effect of this power is reduced by the consciousness that the individual, to the extent of his personal existence, is part of this power and consubstantial with it. The result of these various reducing measures is a transformation of God into an open field of social relations, both intellectual and affective.

The second question would concern the means by which this reduction is achieved. An indication of the means is given in Comte's treatment of the possibility of other *Grand-Êtres* on other planets. The reaction to this problem is of admirable simplicity; Comte advises: don't ask idle questions! This brilliant handling of the questions which arise spontaneously in the soul of man with regard to the nature and meaning of the whole of existence is a principle with Comte. In the first lecture of the *Cours* Comte describes "the fundamental character of the positive philosophy." Its principle is: "to regard all phenomena as subject to invariable natural *laws*." The discovery of these laws and their reduction to the smallest possible number is its sole aim. "It considers it absolutely inaccessible and senseless for us to search for what is called the *causes*, be they primary or final causes." Man has passed through the theological and metaphysical phases in order to arrive at the present state in which he "considers nothing but the facts themselves" as well as "their normal relations of succession and similitude." The establishment of facts and laws is what we call the *explanation* of phenomena; questions with regard to causes do not belong in positive science. The key to this whole exposition is contained in the sentence: "Our intellectual activity is sufficiently excited by the hope of discovering the laws of phenomena, by the simple desire of confirming or invalidating a theory." In brief: the problems of the spirit and of the interpretation of the universe through a metaphysical system will disappear if you forget about them. Comte's positive philosophy is in its most intimate essence an invitation, and even a demand, to forget the life of the spirit and the *bios theoretikos*. And why should we forget such experiences as faith and grace, as contrition and penitence, as guilt and redemption? Why should we forget such questions as those of Leibniz: "Why is there something, why not nothing?" and "Why is this something as it is?" We should forget them because Comte is a man whose intellectual desires do not go beyond confirmation or invalidation of a theory, and more profoundly, because he is afraid of having desires beyond this restricted field. If he ventured beyond the small circle of a theory of phenomena, he would have to face the Why of existence and he could no longer hide himself before the mystery in the prison of his meditative operation. A deep-seated impotence compels him to enclose himself within the walls of phenomena and to deny himself the least curiosity with regard to the freedom beyond the walls of this prison.

If Comte had done nothing but lock himself up in his own existence as in a prison, he would not have become a figure of historical importance. His impotence, however, was accompanied by a tremendous will to power. He did not want to leave his prison, but he wanted to dominate the world outside. The two desires apparently cannot both be satisfied at the same time. Nevertheless, Comte found the solution: mankind itself must be locked up in the prison, too, and since a normal growth would not fit into such confinement, man must cripple himself in the same manner as Comte, and when he has acquired the impotence of Comte but not his will to power, he will be fit to enter the positive age as his follower. It is, on principle, the type of fantasy that began to raise its head in the middle of the eighteenth century and in this respect, the speculation of Comte lies on a line with the prison fantasies from Helvétius and Bentham to Lenin. We could observe the law of the three stages in its double function as the order in the biography of Comte and as the order of mankind in history. We have discussed the monadic character of Comte's meditation and the enlargement of the monadic process to reduce the history of mankind to an immanent evolution of the monad of Humanity. Once Humanity is caught in this prison, we see Comte further at work in judging mankind and determining who belongs truly in it and who has to be cast out into the limbo of eternal oblivion; and we see him creating the institutions that will for all time prevent religious and metaphysical miscreants from disturbing the anxieties and opposing the will to power of Comte and his clergy.

This boundless *ressentiment* culminates, finally, in the abolition of Christ. We can understand now the mechanism of the operation. The horizon of man is strictly walled in by the facts and laws of the phenomena; the course of history itself is the immanent evolution of the monadic mind. If gods exist, they certainly are not permitted to participate in history or society. The gods who seem to appear are figments of the mind and only the figments have reality and a history. Hence Christianity has existed, but not Jesus. Christianity is a system of figments which characterizes an important phase in the development of the mind and as such a system it has historical reality. Jesus, the incarnation of the spirit, however, cannot have existed; the Christ is a fiction of Christianity. Comte is therefore quite consistent when he excludes Jesus from the commemoration of the *Calendrier*. Only Saint Paul, the Fathers and the Saints can be included, for they are the men who have produced the fiction. Moreover, this fiction is the symptom of a trend; the mind is moving toward the complete elimination of the fictional elements until the one and exclusive reality, that is the mind of man, has become visible in its grandeur, and this great event—man visible in his fullness—has come to pass in 1855 in Comte.

On the surface, this operation is a consistent but nevertheless somewhat superficial theory. We must remember, however, the abyss underneath—the impotence, the *ressentiment*, the will to power. We would miss the demonic character of the construction if we forget that Comte *knows* that there is a reality outside the prison, a reality behind the "fictions." It is because he *knows* that there is such a reality that he so fervently prohibits the question of the Why. The whole theory of the fictions would be pointless if it did not serve the purpose of cutting off the quest for reality. Comte declares as illegitimate all questions that cannot be answered by the sciences of the phenomena. He can refuse the answers, but since he cannot abolish the questions he must let them fall flat against his wall of phenomena. If we consider this structure of the Comtean situation, we arrive at the core of his attempt: it is the murder of God. This is the great problem which in the next generation occupied Nietzsche. The Nietzschean formula "God is dead" is not a simple statement concerning the historical fact that in the age of crisis the Christian faith is suffering from social atrophy. It implies that God has lived and that now he is dead because he was murdered by man. Nietzsche, who was a thinker of a different stature, knew what happened; he probed the motivations and he suffered under the fate that made him participate in the assassination. But he neither planned it nor committed it. In the "operation" of Comte, we see the murderer himself committing the deed, and installing himself as the successor.

France and the Occidental Republic

The murder of God and the institution of the *sociolatrie* is for Comte the epochal event that opens the age of Positivism. At the same time, however, it is the culmination of a preparatory period which Comte dates from the "provisional" era of 1789. Through Charlemagne, France is the original founder of the Occidental Republic, comprising the five nations; after the disintegration of the medieval unit, France has again taken the lead, through the Revolution, in the spiritual and temporal unification of the West into the final, positivistic Occidental Republic. The degree to which the primacy of France, and in particular of Paris, was an obsession with Comte can be gleaned from his worries about the dangers which threatened it in the future. He observed that his Positivism found less recognition in France than in foreign countries, as for instance in England or Holland. There was the danger that other countries might press ahead in the Positivistic movement and impair the supremacy of Paris. He counselled restraint in the foreign movement in order to prevent this disaster. This concern of Comte is the direct continuation of an attitude which developed in the revolutionary and Napoleonic period. The Western world should be enlightened, all nations should be on an equal footing in the new age, but the spiritual and civilizational level on which they would all be equal would be determined by the spirit of the French Revolution. It is a principle which much later was to find expression in Stalin's formula "National in form, socialist in substance." We have seen the principle at work in Condorcet's project for the destruction of all historical civilizations and the standardization of mankind according to the pattern of the Paris intellectual. This element of destruction is inevitably inherent in the program of an imperialistic generalization of a local, historical development. It is, on the level of power politics, the locking up of the world in a prison, that we could observe, on the level of historical speculation, in Comte's imprisonment of the history of mankind in the pattern of his intuition. Comte has gone even further than Condorcet and has drawn the consequences of this program of destruction. Since the civilizational substance will be homogeneous throughout his Occidental Republic, the political form of the national state as the vessel of the historical nations becomes irrevelant. He proposes, therefore, quite consistently that the national states should be carved up into political units of an optimal economic and administrative size. For the former territory of France he projected 17 such new political units, and the principle of this reorganization should be extended "aux autres cas occidentaux."[7] It is the resumption and expansion of the revolutionary departmentalization of France which destroyed the historical

7. See his "Tableau des dix-sept Intendances françaises" in ibid., 4, pp. 421ff.

provinces. The revolutionary, so-called rationalism is deeply rooted in the eschatological furor of establishing the final realm on earth.[8]

Napoleon and the Occidental Republic

More specifically, the political program of Comte is related to the ideas of Napoleon. This is a question on which Comte is reticent, for Napoleon appears in his work only in order to be condemned as the *"génie rétrograde."* Nevertheless, the relation exists. In particular Comte's conception of the Occident is hardly conceivable before the consolidation of the Occidental idea through Napoleon's struggle with the new Orient, that is with Russia. Let us recall a few utterances of Napoleon: "There are only two nations in the world. The one lives in the Orient, the other occupies the Occident. The English, French, Germans, Italians, and so on, are governed by the same civil law, the same mores, the same habits and almost the same religion. They are all members of one family; and the men who want to start war among them, want a civil war."[9] The means for abolishing this state of Occidental civil war would be the political unification of the West. "There will be no peace in Europe except under a sole chief, under an emperor who has kings as his officers and distributes kingdoms to his lieutenants."[10] The political should be followed by the institutional and civilizational unification. "All the united countries must be like France; and if you unite them to the Pillars of Hercules and to Kamchatka, the laws of France must extend everywhere."[11] And in retrospect: "Why did my *Code Napoléon* not serve as the basis for a *Code européen*, and why my *Université imperiale* not as the model for an *Université européenne*. In this manner we would have formed in Europe one and the same family. Everybody, when travelling, would have found himself at home."[12] This Occident is a unit because of its internal history and coherence, but it is forced toward a still more intense unification because of its defensive position vis à vis Russia. Napoleon elaborates this problem on the occasion of the Russian plans with regard to Turkey. The ideas of the Tsar revolved around the conquest of Turkey.

8. The readiness to carve up the map of Europe, however, is not peculiar to Comte; we find the same inclination in Fichte and Mazzini.

9. This and the following quotations are taken from the collection Napoleon, *Vues Politiques, Avant-Propos de Adrien Dansette*, in the edition of Améric-Edit. (Rio de Janeiro, n.d.). The original edition is Paris, 1839. The passage quoted is from September, 1802, p. 340.

10. *A Miot de Mélito*, 1803, ibid., p. 340.

11. *Au Conseil d'Etat, Juillet 1805*, ibid., p. 341.

12. *A Las Cases, Sainte Hélène*, ibid.

"We discussed several times the possibility and eventuality of its partition, and the effect on Europe. At first sight the proposition attracted me. I considered that the partition would extend the progress of civilization. However, when I considered the consequences more coolly, when I saw the immense power that Russia would gain, the great number of Greeks in the provinces now subject to the Sultan who then would join a power which is already colossal, I refused roundly to have a part in it." The principal difficulty was Russia's design on Constantinople for "*Constantinople, c'est l'Empire du monde.*" It was obvious that France, "even if she possessed Egypt, Syria and India, would be nothing in comparison to what these new possessions would make of Russia. The barbarians of the North were already much too powerful; after this partition they could overrun all Europe. I believe this still."[13] In another mood he sees this danger present even now. "If Russia finds an Emperor who is courageous, impetuous, capable, in brief: a tsar who has beard on the chin, then Europe is his. He can begin his operations on German soil itself, at a hundred leagues from Berlin and Vienna whose sovereigns are the only obstacles. He enforces the alliance of the one, and with his help he will defeat the other. From this moment he is in the heart of Germany." At this junction, Napoleon puts himself in the place of the conqueror, and continues: "Certainly, if I were in this situation, I would arrive at Calais according to timetable in moderate marches; and there I would find myself master and arbiter of Europe." Then, in the conversation, the dream of the conquest of the Occident separates from the Russian problem. He is now himself the conqueror who is master and arbiter of Europe. And he addresses his interlocutor: "Perhaps, my friend, you are tempted to ask me, like the minister of Pyrrhus asked his master: And what is all this good for? I answer you: For founding a new society and for the prevention of great disasters. Europe waits for this relieving deed and solicits it: the old system is finished, and the new one is not yet established, and it will not be established without long and violent convulsions."[14] Let us, finally, recall that Napoleon also dreamed of making Paris the seat of the spiritual power of the Occident as well as of its temporal power. With the Pope in Paris, the city would have become "the capital of the Christian world, and I would have directed both the religious world and the political. . . . I would have had my religious sessions like my legislative sessions; my councils would have been the representation of Christianity; the popes would have been only

---

13. *A O'Meara, Sainte Hélène*, ibid., pp. 339f.
14. *A Las Cases, Saint Hélène*, ibid., pp. 337f.

its presidents; I would have opened and closed these assemblies, approved and published their decisions, as it had been done by Constantine and Charlemagne."[15]

The heritage of the French Revolution

In spite of Comte's emphasis on the continuity of his ideas with those of the Revolution and in spite of their obvious relation with those of Napoleon, the problem of this continuity has remained obscure until quite recently. The great treatise by Gouhier on the *Jeunesse d'Auguste Comte* is the first attempt to place this problem in its proper context: "Positivism is the religious answer to a religious problem that was posed by the Revolution."[16] Comte was well acquainted with the religious problems of the Revolution, he knew and distinguished clearly the various attempts at their solution, and he expressed his opinions on the *Culte de la Raison* and the cult of the *Être suprême*, as well as on Theophilanthropism and the Napoleonic solution of the Concordat. The *Culte de la Raison* held his particular attention. In the *Système* he writes: "It was necessary to found the true religion by rallying our sentiments, thoughts and actions toward a unique center, both public and private." Danton and his followers were the only group who had truly understood this need. Their attempt offers "a notable progress insofar as it ceases to adore the external world in order to make the *type humain* prevail." This substitution, however, was still too metaphysical. They "were incapable of elevating themselves to the spectacle of society, and were compelled to inaugurate the human attribute that is most individual (that is: reason)."[17] Positivism is a movement which renews the Dantonian problem but gives it a new social solution.[18] Comte has received the heritage of the Revolution as a living tradition through Saint-Simon. This transmission forms the second part of the thesis of Gouhier: "A son of the anticlerical and liberal Revolution, Auguste Comte has received, through the medium of Saint-Simon, an impulse which stems from the religious and Jacobin Revolution."[19]

What is the reason for the earlier suppression of this relation in historical consciousness and for its recent recognition? The reason is that in the era of secularistic historiography the history of the spirit

15. Ibid., pp. 181f.
16. Op. cit., 1, p. 10.
17. *Système*, 3, pp. 601f.
18. On the relation between Comte and Danton see also the essay by Aulard on *Auguste Comte et la Révolution française*.
19. Gouhier, op. cit., p. 18.

was taboo. In this period, the French Revolution was "antireligious." That "politics" and "religion" are not an antithesis, that the Revolution was more than a series of constitutions or of factional phases in a struggle for power, that it was not exhausted by such forms as constitutional monarchy, republic, directory, consulate and empire, that it was a movement which struggled with spiritual and intellectual problems in continuity with the preceding and successive periods and that precisely the spiritual and intellectual aspects of this politico-religious movement were the essential ones—all this could not be acknowledged as long as the religious aspects of the Revolution were considered irrelevant incidents in a process of secular politics. Only toward the end of the nineteenth century is a more serious study of the French Revolution undertaken and, as a consequence, our picture of the intellectual history of the Revolution has changed completely. The historians who have contributed most to this change are Aulard and Mathiez.[20]

The present context is not the place for a survey, however brief, of the religious history of the Revolution. The reader who is interested may refer to the monographs just cited. We must confine ourselves to a statement of the issues which emerge from these richly documented studies. In the first place, the misconception has been cleared up that the spirit of the French Revolution was antireligious in the sense that it inclined toward a separation of church and state. The secular state was not an ideal of the Revolution. The Revolution was anti-Christian and tended toward the establishment of a caesaro-papistic régime of a non-Christian religion. This tendency, moreover, did not arise within the Revolution itself but was present already in the works of the *philosophes* before 1789. Rousseau's idea of the *réligion civile* is perhaps the most famous expression of this tendency. Less famous but even more symptomatic of the trend is the attitude of Raynal. In the *Histoire philosophique des Deux-Indes*, the Abbé Raynal writes:

> The state is not made for religion, but religion is made for the state. First principle.
> The general interest is the rule governing everything that should exist in the state. Second principle.

20. F. -A. Aulard, *Le Culte de la Raison et le culte de l'Être suprême* (*1793–94*) (Paris, 1892). Aulard incorporated the results of his study in the *Histoire Politique de la Révolution française* (Paris, 1901). The principal studies by Albert Mathiez are *La Theophilanthropie et la Culte Décadaire 1796–1801* (Paris, 1903); *Les Origines des Cultes Révolutionnaires* (Paris, 1904); *Contributions à l'histoire religieuse de la Révolution française* (Paris, 1907); *La Révolution et l'église, Etudes critiques et documentaires* (Paris, 1910); *Autour de Robespierre* (Paris, 1925).

The people, or its representative authority, has the exclusive right of judging the conformance of any institution whatever with the general interest. Third principle.

This authority of the people has the right to examine the dogma and discipline of the churches. The dogma in particular must be examined with regard to its compatibility with common sense, for dangerous troubles might arise "if the ideas of a future felicity are complicated by the zeal for the glory of God and the submission to a truth which is regarded as revealed."

This authority, and this authority alone, can therefore proscribe an established cult, adopt a new one, or do without one if that is more convenient.

There is no other council than the assembly of the ministers of the sovereign. When the administrators of the state are assembled, the church is assembled. When the state has pronounced itself, the church has nothing more to say.

No other apostles than the legislator and his magistrates.

No other sacred books than those which they have recognized as such.

No divine right but that of the weal of the Republic."[21]

The idea of the state as a theocracy, with the legislators as the ecclesiastical authority, with the law as the divine manifestation, and with the commonweal as the substance, thus, is fully developed before the Revolution. The religious attempts of the Revolution pursued a tortuous path toward the realization of totalitarian theocracy. The transformation of the Catholic Church in France into a national church was the first attempt to bolster the events in the sphere of the struggle for power with a spiritual authority. When the attempt began to show unmistakable signs of failure, the non-Christian substitute attempts pressed to the fore. We have enumerated them already: the *Culte de la Raison* of the Dantonists, the cult of the *Être Suprême* of Robespierre, and finally the establishment of the *Culte décadaire*, that is of the state religion of the *Directoire*, under the pontificate of La Révellière. Of many such attempts the Theophilanthropy of Chemin-Dupontès was the only one successful at founding a new religious sect, which by its expansion seriously worried the Catholic Church and which rivalled with the *Culte décadaire* to become the state religion.

We can be briefer on the second point. The spiritual history of the

21. Raynal, *Histoire philosophique des Deux-Indes*, bk. 4, pp. 533ff. (Quoted in Aulard, *Le Culte de la Raison*, pp. 8–10.)

Revolution had been neglected for the further reason that the various movements and establishments which we have identified were considered ephemeral extravagancies of a few fanatics. Our contemporary experiences with political mass religions have shown us convincingly that the problem is of a different magnitude. The studies of Aulard and Mathiez have brought the rich documentary evidence that even at the time of the French Revolution one could not found state-religions by the decree of a few fanatics. The disposition to accept these state religions had to be present in the people. As a matter of fact, there was even more than a mere disposition to accept the religious ideas of the intellectuals. The studies of Mathiez show that in a spontaneous upsurge of the people a new state religion was created before any governmental authority started the first proddings in this direction. The establishments that were directed from the revolutionary upper-stratum could have the success which they had because they could harness the spontaneous emotions of the people toward a cult of the revolutionary-republican spirit. And this religious upsurge did not stop at the borders of France. The French Revolution, while starting with the chosen people, was considered the Revolution of Humanity. The religious sentiments originated in the experience of a national collectivity, but they were expanded immediately into the vision of a church of mankind. We find completely preformed the Comtean "operation" of expanding the particular existential upsurge universally over mankind and history by submitting mankind and history to the law of this upsurge. A symptom of this basic universalism are the decrees of the Legislative Assembly which extended French citizenship to foreigners in order to reward them for "having labored outside of France at the work of regeneration."[22] Recipients of this dignity were, among others, Paine, Joseph Priestly, Bentham, Washington, Klopstock, and Schiller.[23]

Revolution, restoration and crisis

We have traced the continuum between Comte's foundation of the Religion of Humanity and the religious foundations of the French Revolution. Important as the line of this continuum is, we must be aware that it is no more than one thread that runs through a rich

22. Albert Mathiez, *Les Origines des cultes révolutionnaires*, p. 25.
23. For the details of the popular movement we must refer the reader again to the monographs, in particular to Albert Mathiez, *Les Origines des cultes révolutionnaires*. In the first part of this study, Mathiez gives a careful account of the movement of the *Fédérations* in the single towns and of the ritual forms developed for the festivals, commemorations, and religious ceremonies before the "alters of the fatherland," etc.

historical fabric. The ideas of Comte certainly continue the ideas of the Revolution, in their liberal as well as in their Jacobin and Napoleonic aspects, but they certainly also go far beyond the Revolution and belong to the general movement of Restoration which intends to "terminate" the Revolution. The meaning of neither Revolution nor Restoration is exhausted by their functions as a movement and its counter movement, for both blend into each other in the enveloping movement of the Crisis. In 'approaching this larger context, into which the ideas of Comte must be placed, we encounter even greater difficulties than we met in the analysis of the preceding problem. The interpretation of the French Revolution is far from complete, but at least considerable advances have been made in recent years. The interpretation of the Restoration, however, is still at a stage where we cannot even be sure of the categories that have to be used in the undertaking. The situation is illuminated by the fact that Gouhier, the author of the *Jeunesse de Comte*, has seen his problem unfolding, in the course of the eight years that lie between the first and the third volumes of his great work, in a manner that he had probably not anticipated at the beginning; for the third volume is preceded by an introduction which deals precisely with the methodological problem of Revolution and Restoration, an introduction which might as well have preceded the first volume. Moreover, this introduction is entitled *Programme pour une étude historique de la Restauration comme problème philosophique*, a title which seems to indicate that the author intends to elaborate this program in further studies, independent of the specifically Comtean problems. Our remarks in this section are based on the *Programme* of Gouhier, in particular with regard to the selection of materials and their classification. With regard to the principles of interpretation we are following the suggestions of Gouhier, but we venture to go somewhat beyond his explicit propositions in an attempt to clarify further the relation between the problems of Revolution and Restoration on the one side, and of the Crisis on the other side.[24]

The relation between Revolution and Restoration becomes problematical as soon as we realize that this periodization refers conventionally to events on the level of pragmatic history but not necessarily to events on the level of the history of political ideas. By Revolution we mean primarily the period which extends from the convocation of the General Estates of France in 1789 to the abdication of Napoleon in 1814; by Restoration we mean correspondingly the period of the restored mon-

24. For Gouhier's *Programme* see his *Jeunesse d'Auguste Comte*, vol. 3: *Auguste Comte et Saint-Simon* (Paris, 1941), pp. 5–60.

archy from 1814 to the July Revolution of 1830. The meaning of
Restoration on this level is determined primarily by the reinstatement
of the Bourbon dynasty after the revolutionary interlude. Insofar as
the dynastic principle is through centuries one of the great factors in
Western political history, the periodization doubtless has its importance. Precisely, however, when we approach the period of the crisis
the importance diminishes, for one of the characteristic traits of the
crisis is the weakening and gradual elimination of the dynasties as a
factor in politics. The mere fact that the Revolution occurred and that
the Restoration was brief indicates that the great determinants of the
historical process have to be sought elsewhere. Hence, in a first approach to the problem, Gouhier shifts the meaning of Restoration from
the reinstitution of the Bourbons to the larger problem of terminating
the Revolution. The restoration of the monarchy is not the first attempt
at such a termination. The series of these attempts begins with the
Thermidor, and the sequence of Directory, Consulate, Empire, Constitutional Monarchy of 1814, and the liberal Bonapartism of the
Hundred Days marks so many abortive restorations. The return of
Louis XVIII in 1815 would be the sixth attempt in this series, and
Gouhier seems to be content that it is the last one. Whether it was the
last one, indeed, seems to us doubtful, but we shall defer the consideration of this question until we have reflected on another aspect of the
problem of Restoration.

When the meaning of Restoration has shifted from the restoration
of a dynasty to the termination of the Revolution, the question arises:
what does the Restoration restore? The answer would have to be that
it restores the order of the polity that has been disrupted by the
revolutionary events with their culmination in the Terror. Inevitably,
this answer raises the further question: what kind of an order should
be the object of restoration? Should it be the order of the *ancien régime*
before 1789, should it be the order of the liberal constitutional monarchy from 1789–1792, or should it be the republican order of 1792–
1793? The Restoration of 1814 and the following years contains all
three of the tendencies indicated by these questions. The *ultras*, with
their tendency to return to the prerevolutionary order, made themselves felt in the Restoration of 1814 to such a degree that they
wrecked the attempt and prepared the return of Napoleon from Elba,
and the *ultra* ministries of Charles X sealed the fate of the Bourbon
dynasty. The liberal tendency manifested itself in the policy of
Louis XVIII, in the *Charte constitutionnelle* of 1814, and in the timely
essay of Benjamin Constant on constitutional principles which maneu-
vered the interpretation of the *Charte* in the direction of English

constitutionalism.[25] The antiroyalist tendency revealed itself in the episode of the Hundred Days as well as in the abortive attempt at a republic under the presidency of Lafayette in 1830.

When we survey these tendencies, we see that Revolution and Restoration are not two periods which follow each other in time, but two processes which interlock and overlap chronologically. We may distinguish in the revolutionary process itself (1) the anticlerical and antifeudal liberal phase, (2) the antimonarchical, republican phase, and (3) the phase of the sectarian church-state culminating in the Terror. If we relate the restorative process to these phases, its various tendencies and attempts will appear as ambivalent—with the exception of the *ultra* tendencies. The plebiscitarian emperorship of Napoleon, for instance, belongs as much to the Restoration as it belongs to the Revolution. The constitutional liberalism of Louis XVIII resumes the Revolution approximately at its phase of 1791–92; hence it is as revolutionary with regard to the *ancien régime* as it is restorative with regard to the later phases of the Revolution. The Second and Third Republics resume the antimonarchical phase of the Revolution, but they are still restorative with regard to the revolutionary church-state; and so forth. This fundamental ambivalence which besets French history from the Thermidor to the present is due to the fact that the Revolution has run within four years the course from the *ancien régime* to the totalitarian church-state and terror. The meaning of the Revolution cannot be elicited by any partial political formula, such as the issues of feudalism and democracy, of monarchy and republic, of parliamentarism and dictatorship, of bourgeois society and proletarian movement. All these issues are contained in the Revolution and their periodical reappearance marks the oscillations of French politics between (1) radical populist revolution, (2) dictatorial order and (3) moderate republic, which have been so excellently analysed by Seignobos. All these partial issues, however, are overshadowed by the fundamental spiritual issue which the Revolution has revealed for the first time in full clearness, namely, that the apocalypse of man is driving, by the logic of sentiment, toward the deification of intramundane society. The Revolution has been carried by its momentum beyond the peripheral questions of governmental form to the very heart of the crisis, that is to the destruction of Western Christian civilization and to the tentative creation of a non-Christian society. And the restorative attempts consequently are affected by the necessity of grappling

---

25. Benjamin Constant, *Réflexions sur les Constitutions, la distribution des pouvoirs et les garanties dans une monarchie constitutionnelle* (Paris, 1814).

with the spiritual problem of the crisis that had been posed by the Revolution.

Hence Revolution and Restoration, in the French case, cannot be distinguished as a political and social upheaval which overshoots the aim that can be realized at the moment, and a counter movement which terminates the Revolution and stabilizes its results at a level that corresponds to the actual strength of the contending political forces. Such an interpretation would rather fit the English upheaval of the seventeenth century with its termination by the Glorious Revolution and the Act of Settlement. In the French case Revolution and Restoration are interlocked to the point of becoming indistinguishable because both movements penetrate to the spiritual core of the crisis. The situation is illuminated by the struggle between Robespierre and the Hébertists. On the level of power politics, it is a struggle between the Committee of Public Safety (represented by Robespierre) and the Commune of Paris (represented by Hébert); on the level of the spiritual crisis it is the struggle between Hébert's *Culte de la Raison* and Robespierre's cult of the *Être Suprême*. Here, in the very heart of the Revolution, we are faced by Robespierre's attempt to stabilize the Revolution spiritually somewhere near the Deism of the *philosophes* and his attack on the *Culte de la Raison* as an atheistic adventure that goes too far. Does this attempt of Robespierre, as some historians have suggested, already belong to the history of the Restoration? The question is of importance for the interpretation of Comte's position, for Comte, as we have seen, recognizes in the *Culte de la Raison* a step in the right direction, that is in the direction of his own cult of the *Grand-Être*. According to this self-interpretation, Comte's political religion would continue the Revolution and lead it to the logical conclusion that was forestalled by Robespierre; on the other hand, Comte is clear on the point that his Religion of Humanity will terminate the disorder of the Revolution, that it will be a restoration of order. Restoration becomes identical with completion of the Revolution.

The contradiction can be solved if we acknowledge that Revolution and Restoration meet in the problem of the Crisis. If we define the two concepts on the level of deposition and reinstitution of a dynasty, they will signify two successive periods in pragmatic history. If we define them as a movement of political forces and the reestablishment of order in accordance with a new balance of forces, then they will signify processes which overlap in time. If we extend their meaning to include the problem of spiritual order in society, then they will merge in the process of the Crisis. The question at which level we should fix the meaning is not one for arbitrary decision. The inclusion of the spiritual problem is a theoretical postulate, for man as a whole is engaged in the historical process, and we have no right to define our concepts on the basis of a fragmentary anthropology. If we neglect this postulate, the historical process becomes unintelligible and we are reduced to accepting the self-interpretations of the political movements at their face-value. Since the course of the crisis consists in the conflicts and spiritual failures of these movements, we could not overcome the disorder of the crisis through its interpretation by the order of the spirit but would permit the disorder to invade the historiographic attempt at finding its meaning. Our interpretation of Comte would have to sink, in this case, to the level of Littré and John Stuart Mill, while our interpretation of intellectual history would sink to the level of Comte's demonic monadism; our interpretation of Marx would sink to the level of those who see in him nothing but the threat of proletarian revolution and communism, while our conception of "ideology" would sink to the level of Marx. Our interpretation of constitutionalism and liberty would sink to the Fascist level, while our conception of National Socialism would sink to the level of progressive intellectuals who see in it nothing but a reactionary political movement.

The inclusion of the spiritual problem of the crisis into the concepts of Revolution and Restoration does not mean, however, that the concepts have become superfluous. Within the general process of the crisis, Revolution, Restoration and their international ramifications remain a distinguishable phase. The movement of 1789 with its rapid evolution into the terroristic church-state is still its well marked beginning, and the reassertion of the forces that survived the furor of this outburst still mark the Restoration. A problem of delimitation will arise only with regard to the formal end that should be assigned to the Restoration. As a matter of fact, the Restoration peters out with the generation of men who lived through the Revolution and tried to establish the post-Napoleonic order with the political forces and ideas that emerged from it. Whether one wishes to attribute a special symbolic significance to the year 1830 when the last brother of Louis XVI disappeared from the scene and Lafayette made his last appearance, or to the year 1832 which marks the end of the *ancien régime* in England, or to the year 1848 which removed Metternich—is a matter of choice and it will be decided differently by the historians of the various nations. Certain is that with the 1840's, that is with the generation of Bakunin and Marx, we have entered a new intellectual climate. The problem of the crisis has not changed, but the dimensions of the catastrophe have become clearer, the eschatological consciousness has sharpened, and the illusion has dissolved that after the Revolution a stable order had been restored by the arsenal of contemporary remedies.

Comte and his work have a peculiar place with regard to this periodization. The ultimate elaboration of Comte's ideas through the institution of the Religion of Humanity falls in the 1850's. His *Système* is written and published after the Communist Manifesto. The original intuition, on the other hand, occurs in the 1820's; it draws its inspiration from an intellectual environment that is determined by Condorcet and Saint-Simon, by Danton and Robespierre, by Napoleon and Louis XVIII, by Jean-Baptist Say and Lafitte, by Bonald and de Maistre. The elaboration and publication of his ideas coincides with Victorian liberalism and the opening decades of Communism and Anarchism; the intellectual means with which he meets the crisis belong to the Restoration. We shall now briefly survey the principal elements of the intellectual environment in which Comte formed his intuition.

The permanent revolution of the liberals

A first answer to the problem of the crisis is given by the liberals who wish to transform the violent rhythm of Revolution and Restoration into a gentle undulation of progressive reform. This idea was developed in the liberal periodical *Le Censeur* by its editors Charles Comte and Charles Dunoyer, in 1815. Revolution is recognized as a necessity insofar as it is required by the light of reason, but there are other revolutions which are motivated by pride and ambition. The revolution which resulted in the liberal monarchy of 1791 was commanded by reason while the Republic, the Consulate, as well as the movements which tend to restore the *ancien régime*, belonged to the second type. There are two states which are equally bad for a society: complete stagnation and prolonged, anarchical disorder. "The one clings too strongly even to its most puerile customs, and to its most superstitious practices; the other indulges in the disorderly movement of passions." Besides, the one state produces the other. Anarchical revolution is inevitable when a regime insists on its continuation against reason and history, while the reactionary despotism of a Bonaparte will rise fom anarchy. "There is only one means for nations to prevent the great revolutions; that is, to put themselves into a state of permanent and wisely regulated revolution." When a nation is guided intelligently it is protected against all revolution, or rather its revolution is "permanent, but slow and progressive, so that it follows without jolts the progress of reason."[26]

26. Charles Dunoyer, "Des révolutions en général et des révolutionnaires"; Charles Comte, "Du système répresentatif"; Charles Comte, "De l'autorité législatif." These articles were published in *Le Censeur*, vols. 3, 4. Quotations from Gouhier, op. cit., p. 17.

The articles of Charles Comte and Dunoyer have their importance because the *Censeur* represents the liberal restoration at its intellectual best. We see here developing an attitude toward the crisis which remains typical in later liberalism and we can observe in its origins the growth of an escapist cliché. The rhythm of Revolution and Restoration is considered a stupid exaggeration of the process of social reform, the violent swings of the pendulum ought to be toned down—under the title of "permanent revolution"—to the gentle process that today is called "peaceful change." The problem of the crisis itself disappears and is swallowed up by the category of progress under the guidance of reason. We have characterized this attitude as escapist because it skillfully dodges the real issues of the crisis. A society is by definition in a state of crisis when its remedial forces, while perhaps present, are socially ineffective. The social problems which urgently require a solution cannot be solved because the spiritual and moral strength for the task is lacking in the ruling group. In this situation, the counsel to do what is not done because it cannot be done is obviously vain. And the counsel is not only vain, it even adds to the gravity of the crisis because it detracts attention from a true alternative. The progressive counsel of Charles Comte and Dunoyer (and this has remained a constant factor in the aggravation of the Western crisis) poses the alternative of stagnation in the solution of social problems and intelligent gradual reform. This alternative does not exist concretely; the fact of the tardiness in the solution of explosive social problems is proof that on the level of pragmatic politics the alternative of intelligent gradualism does not exist. The true alternative would be the restoration of spiritual substance in the ruling groups of a society, with the consequent restoration of the moral strength in creating a just social order. The problem of the crisis must be stated in the Platonic terms of spirit and power. The pragmatic value of this alternative, as experience has shown, is not very high. The appearance of Plato did not change the course of the Hellenic crisis, the case of Nietzsche did not serve as a warning example for Germany nor did the appearance of Dostoievsky make a dent in the tsarist system. Nevertheless, this is the true alternative; and we must be clear on the point that a propaganda for gradualism which ignores and obscures the true issue has become a serious factor in the aggravation of the crisis.

The idea which emerges from the articles of the *Censeur* is so particularly grave in its consequences because it implies the further fallacy that the abolition of a social injustice will automatically result in a satisfactory stable order. The revolutionary abolition of a regime that is experienced as oppressive by a powerful stratum of society will certainly satisfy the successful revolutionary group, but it is not at all a guarantee that the new group will be more fit than the old one to discharge the obligations of rulership competently. Spiritual disorder is not the privilege of a ruling class; the revolutionary class which displaces it may be quite as deficient in this point, and even more so. The spiritual and moral incompetence of the bourgeoisie in handling problems posed by the industrial proletariat and the growing lower middle class was certainly a match for the incompetence of the prerevolutionary aristocracy in handling the problem posed by the rising bourgeoisie. The record of the German lower middle class in the National Socialist revolution is no more edifying. The worst problem in the dynamic of the Western crisis is the fact that the resistance of the ruling class of the moment against "peaceful change" can derive a degree of spiritual legitimacy from the qualities of the revolutionary groups. The liberal and progressive idea of the "permanent revolution" of the editors of the *Censeur* ignores this whole class of problems, and it must ignore them because the spiritual problem of the crisis is obscured for them by the enlightenment cliché of "reason." But the light of reason is a dubious guide in the night of the spirit.

Internationalism

The profounder problems of the crisis, however, did not escape the thinkers of the Restoration. They were forced upon them inevitably by the international aspects of the Revolution. The Napoleonic wars from Spain to Russia would bring home to everybody that the Revolution was more than a problem of French constitutional reform. And the Act of the Congress of Vienna, of 1815, was more than a simple peace treaty between former belligerents; it was a settlement of European order, comparable to the Treaties of Munster and Osnabruck which had concluded the international upheaval of the Thirty Years War. The events on the pragmatic level alone would make clear the European scale of the problem. The actual internationalism of the period, however, was nourished from a considerable number of other sources. We have already noted the international pathos of the Revolution itself, in the enlargement of the French upsurge into the idea of a Western civilization in conformance with the French spirit, as well as in the ideas of Napoleon. This revolutionary pathos even appears in America; in a letter to Lafayette, Washington writes: "We have sown a seed of Liberty and Union that will germinate by and by over the whole earth. Some day the United States of Europe will be constituted, modelled after the United States of America. The United States will be the legislator of all nations."[27] And this pathos is no more than the culmination of the internationalism of the eighteenth century which crystallized in the projects for perpetual peace of the Abbé Saint-Pierre, of Rousseau and of Kant, and which crystallized in such formulations as the "European Republic" (Rousseau) or the "*Assemblée des nations*" (Volnay).

The internationalism of the enlightened, humanitarian type precedes the Revolution and becomes only intensified in its early years. With the Revolution itself new sources of internationalism are opened by the course of events. The French emigration played an important role. The court society, like every closed group of this type, had a comparatively narrow horizon; the emigration was the discovery of the world, through the acquaintance with foreign national civilizations, and in particular through the discovery of the living medieval tradition of the European culture.[28] The horizon is enlarged beyond the period of the absolute national state and the common foundation of Western Christian civilization through Charlemagne comes into view. The experience of the Revolution had a similar effect on the French clergy. In the struggle with the revolutionary government, Gallicanism receives a blow from which it has never recovered, the international, European character of Catholicism gains a new weight, and the importance of the spiritual power which must not be too closely allied with a national government is rediscovered. Beyond these concrete occasions for remembering the temporal and spiritual sources of Western unity, the general lesson of this second conflagration following the first one of the religious wars was not lost on the contemporaries. The Revolution was understood as the second act in the drama of Western decomposition of which the Reformation had been the first act. And the quest for unity inevitably turned toward Christianity as the spiritual force which had produced the unity that now was visibly going to pieces. This awareness of the Christian unity of the past, and of the spiritual problem which it poses for the present, finds expression in a considerable literature. Let us mention only the works of de Bonald: the *Théorie du pouvoir politique dans la société civile* (1796), and the subsequent *Essai analytique sur les lois naturelles de l'ordre social* (1800) and *Législation primitive considérée dans les dernier temps par les seules lumières de la raison* (1802); Novalis's *Christenheit oder Europa* (1799); and the works of de Maistre: *Considérations sur la France* (1796), the *Essai sur le principe générateur des constitutions poli-*

27. Quoted by Gouhier, op. cit., p. 22.
28. Fernand Baldensperger, *Le mouvement des idées dans l'émigration française (1789–1815)* (Paris, 1924), vol. 2, pp. 151–152. Gouhier, op. cit., p. 24.

tiques (1809), the systematic main work *Du Pape* (1819), and the work which he left incomplete at the time of his death in 1821, *Les Soirées de Saint-Pétersbourg*.

De Maistre

A few formulations taken from these works will illuminate the intellectual climate in which Comte grew up. According to de Bonald, Europe could be considered a "single family" up to the sixteenth century; its foundation goes back to Charlemagne, "*le fondateur et le héros de la société civile*"; this happy family was troubled on occasion by the passions of its members, but always reunited "*par la même religion publique*"; the Reformation has torn apart this Christian Europe and by this blow has also "divided the political Europe."[29] In his *Considérations sur la France*, de Maistre resumes this problem on principle. "All imaginable institutions rest on a religious idea. . . . They are strong and durable in the measure in which they are divinized. . . . Human reason (or what one calls philosophy without knowing what one does) is no substitute for this basis (which one has called superstitious, again without knowing what one does); philosophy, on the contrary is an essentially disorganizing force."[30] This sentence could have been written by Comte, as well as the following: "It seems to me that every true philosopher should make his choice between two hypotheses: either a new religion is about to be formed, or Christianity will rejuvenate itself in an extraordinary manner. We have to make our choice between these two suppositions, according to our stand on the truth of Christianity."[31] De Maistre decides for Christianity, Comte for the new religion, but on the principle they are in agreement.

The area of agreement between de Maistre and Comte is even larger than their alternative choices of Christianity and the Religion of Humanity would suggest, for the Christian solution of de Maistre strongly partakes of the organizational, projective character which is peculiar to Comte. Let us consider, for instance, a passage from a letter of de Maistre to Blacas (1814): "Recall frequently this chain of reasoning: No public morality or national character without religion, no European religion without Christianity, no Christianity without Catholicism, no Catholicism without the Pope, no Pope without the supremacy that is due to him."[32] This type of argumentation which leads de Maistre

29. The passages are from the *Théorie du pouvoir;* Gouhier, op. cit., p. 26.
30. De Maistre, *Considérations sur la France* (1855), p. 67.
31. Ibid., p. 73.
32. Quoted by Gouhier, op. cit., p. 25.

to the supremacy of the Pope, is the same type which leads Comte to create himself the High Pontiff of the new religion of the Occidental Republic. Both thinkers are right insofar as they have diagnosed the problem of spiritual unity in Western civilization, and both are right insofar as they take the problem of an institutionalization of the spirit seriously. Both in common are astonishingly blind to the magnitude of the problem. If we assume that de Maistre did not consider his literary work a vain exercise, we must also assume that he seriously believed he could change the course of Western history by a clear analysis of the problem of the crisis and by suggesting the only organizational solution that seemed to make sense. That the critical situation of a whole civilization, which had been in the making for centuries, cannot be transformed into a harmonious order over night by an act of insight and by an agreement between intelligent people, or that something might be profoundly wrong not only outside Catholicism but within the Church itself, was not sufficiently clear to him, just as it was inconceivable to Comte that he could not restore the order of a civilization by his personal renovation or that anything could be wrong with his Religion of Humanity. In de Maistre as in Comte we sense the touch of enlightened reason that blinds the working of the spirit. Moreover this impression is strengthened when we see de Maistre, in *Du Pape*, indulging in the same far-reaching projections as Comte and including Russia and the orthodox Church in his reflections on a restored Europe under Papal supremacy.[33]

In the last work of de Maistre, the *Soirées de Saint-Pétersbourg*, a strong apocalyptic tone makes itself felt that is even closer to the temper of Comte. "We must keep prepared for an immense event in the divine order toward which we are marching with an accelerating speed that should strike every observer. There is no longer any religion on earth: mankind cannot remain in this state." Catholic as well as Protestant writers find in the *Revelation* of Saint John the announcement of the impending event. Some even believe that it has begun already "and that the French nation will be the great instrument of the greatest of revolutions." "There is perhaps not one truly religious man in Europe (I am speaking of the educated class) who does not, at this moment, expect something extraordinary. And, do you believe that this agreement of all men can be mistaken?" For evidence observe the march of science and see where it leads us. From Newton the way goes to Pythagoras. Once the natural affinity between religion and

33. See in *Du Pape*, in bk. 3, the chapters on Russia; and the whole of bk. 4: "Du Pape son rapport avec les églises nommées schismatiques."

science will have become concrete "in the head of one single man of genius," then the eighteenth century will truly have come to its end. The apparition of this man is not far off; "perhaps he lives already." De Maistre concludes these reflections with a speculation on the function of the mystical number Three in history. "God has spoken the first time to man on Mount Sinai; and this revelation was restricted for reasons, which we do not know, to the narrow limits of a single people and a single country." "After fifteen centuries, a second revelation addressed itself to all men without distinction . . . ; but still the universality of its action was infinitely restricted by circumstances of time and space." Fifteen centuries again have lapsed and America was discovered; the whole earth and all mankind now is drawn into a unity and we must expect "a third explosion of the omnipotent goodness in favor of mankind." "Everything announces . . . I do not know what great unity toward which we are marching rapidly."[34]

The vision of a third revelation, the expectation of a new messianic figure, the unity of science and religion—all this is so close to Comte that further elaboration is unnecessary. How close it is can be gathered from the fact that the rival movement to Comte's Positivism, that is the Saint-Simonism of Enfantin and Bazard, appropriated the prophetic expectation of de Maistre as an announcement of the Savior who had come in Saint-Simon: "Let us keep prepared, as says de Maistre, for an immense event in the divine order toward which we march with an accelerating speed that ought to strike all observers; there is no longer any religion on earth, mankind cannot remain in this state; but, happier than de Maistre, we no longer wait for the *man of genius* whom he announced and who, according to him, should imminently reveal to the world *the natural affinity of religion and science:* SAINT-SIMON has appeared."[35]

The Holy Alliance

"It is impossible that mundane forces balance each other; only a third element, which is mundane and transmundane at the same time, can solve this task."[36] This sentiment—that the postrevolutionary order cannot be achieved as a balance of secular powers—pervades the Resto-

34. De Maistre, *Les Soirées de Saint-Pétersbourg*, 11th ed. (1854), pp. 270–285.

35. *Doctrine de Saint-Simon, Exposition, Première année,* 1829, edition by Bouglé and Halévy (Paris, 1924), pp. 418f.

36. Novalis, *Die Christenheit oder Europa* (1799), *Schriften,* ed. J. Minor (Jena, 1923), 3, p. 42.

ration; it has found its public, political expression in the document that sprang from the curious relationship between Tsar Alexander I and the Baroness von Kruedener, that is the *Holy Alliance* of September 26, 1815. The popular misunderstandings concerning this document have been dispelled by now; nevertheless it may be worthwhile repeating that the *Holy Alliance* must not be confused with the Quadruple Alliance and that its intentions must not be identified with the reactionary policies of the era Metternich. The *Holy Alliance* seems to have had its origin in the more or less accidental intersection of the two life-lines of Mme. de Kruedener and the Tsar. The Livonian Baroness (1764–1824) experienced a conversion in 1804 and from then on her life was a colorful series of associations with the various pietistic groups of the age: with the Moravians at Herrenhut, with the circle of Heinrich Jung-Stilling at Karlsruhe, with Fontaines in the Alsace, with Wegelin in Strassburg, and with Jean Frédéric Oberlin (after whom Oberlin College is named) in Waldbach. Of special interest for us is the association with Jung-Stilling and the Court of Baden because the Empress Elizabeth of Russia, as well as the wife of Gustavus Adolphus IV of Sweden, were Princesses of Baden, belonging to this pietistic group; here we touch on the international social basis for the pietistic element in the Restoration in Russia and Germany, as well as for the fact that Mme. de Kruedener could find access to the Tsar. Through the medium of parsons and other mystical personalities, Pietism had created a community of sentiments and ideas which linked, socially, the peasantry with the courts and, geographically, West Germany with Russia. Politically this community was strongly imbued with chiliastic ideas in which Napoleon figured as the Anti-Christ and the hopes were directed toward a savior from the North, on the basis of the prophecy of Isaiah 41:25: "Here is one I have raised from the north, I have called him by name from the east; he shall trample rulers down like mortar, like a potter treading clay."[37] Alexander I, who seemed most eminently a

37. Cf. E. Muhlenbeck, *Étude sur les origines de la Sainte-Alliance* (Paris, 1909). The full weight of these chiliastic expectations, however, can be understood only if we separate the chiliastic symbolism from its accidental historical content. That Napoleon and Alexander I would seem to fill these symbols is historically accidental to the first decades of the nineteenth century. The chiliastic movement itself goes back to the period of the Reformation. It is based on the Biblical prophecies of the Isaiah passage quoted in the text, as well as on Daniel 11 (the king of the north), Jeremiah 4:5 (the lion from the north), Jeremiah 50:9, 41–44 (the people from the north). This complex of Biblical suggestions crystallized into a firm symbolism in the so-called Prophecy of Paracelsus, probably to be dated 1541. The Prophecy announces the *"Loewen von Mitternacht"* who after a great struggle will remove the claws of the eagle from the Empire. In the seventeenth century this Prophecy had a great career

savior from the north, was a soul in anguish, burdened with the guilt of patricide; his search for the peace of his soul, which induced his contacts with representatives of various sectarian movements, did not come to an end before his strange disappearance from the throne in 1825 and (which seems at present the most probable assumption) his withdrawal to Siberia. In 1815 he had used the opportunity of the campaign for seeking this peace in an interview with Jung-Stilling in Karlsruhe; the attempt failed. In June, 1815 he had his headquarters at Heilbronn, not far from a village where Mme. de Kruedener was engaged in persuading some peasants to sell their property and to flee from the impending eschatological catastrophe. This was the chance of her lifetime for the lady; she obtained an interview with the Tsar, and in several hours of preaching she broke the sobbing man to the point that he "found peace"—at least for a while. At his request she followed the Tsar to Paris and they were in daily contact at prayer-meetings. Overnight the lady had become a political force of European importance, and at her religious *séances* assembled such persons as Chateaubriand, Benjamin Constant and Mme. Récamier. From this association emerged, in September 1815, the *Holy Alliance.*

The *Holy Alliance* was published in the names of the sovereigns of Austria, Prussia and Russia.[38] The three monarchs confess to being impressed by the events of the last three years. Divine Providence has showered its blessings on the states which have placed their confidence on it alone. And the monarchs are convinced that the mutual relations of the powers must be based on the sublime truths which are taught by the eternal religion of the Savior God. Hence they declare now, "*à la face de l'Univers,*" that they will adopt as their rule of conduct the principles of Justice, Charity and Peace, in domestic as well as in foreign relations. These principles are not applicable to private life only, but must exert a direct influence on the actions of princes. Only when these principles guide all their steps will human institutions be consolidated and their imperfections remedied. Scripture commands all men to consider each other as brethren. The three monarchs will remain

---

when it was applied to Gustavus Adolphus, as the "Lion from the North," in his struggle against the Emperor. The consciousness of this symbolism never died, but was continued in a rich mystical, Rosicrucian and alchemystic literature. The history of this symbolism is finely treated in Johan Nordström, *Lejonet fran norden* (Upsala, 1934). The Prophecy of Paracelsus is reprinted in the appendix to Nordström's study. A reprint in modern German is found in Hans Kayser's edition of *Schriften Theophrast's von Hohenheim* (Leipzig, 1924), no. 297.

38. The text of the *Holy Alliance* is to be found in *Recueil Martens*, 2 (Goettingen, 1818), no. 60, pp. 630ff.

united by the bond of a true and indissoluble fraternity. They will consider each other as compatriots. They will consider themselves and their peoples as members of one Christian nation; the three princes regard themselves as delegated by Providence to govern three branches of one and the same family and they recognize as their common Sovereign no other than Him, to Whom all power truly belongs, that is God, our divine Savior Jesus Christ, the Word of the Most High, the Word of Life. In relation to their subjects and armies they will regard themselves as fathers of families and will guide them, in the spirit of brotherhood, to protect Religion, Peace and Justice. Force between them will be used only for the purpose of rendering reciprocal service. The monarchs recommend to their peoples that they fortify themselves daily more and more in the principles and duties which the Savior has taught, for this will be the only means to enjoy the durable peace that arises from good conscience. And the other Powers are invited to join in this agreement for the happiness of nations who have been agitated too long, so that from now on these truths will exercise their due influence over the destinies of men.

The interpretation of this document has been obscured by the fact that it is couched in the form of an international treaty. If it is taken at the face value of its legal form, then it can be discarded as "innocuous" or "irrelevant," as is done by pragmatic historians. The contemporaries who were invited to sign it, and actually did sign it out of deference for the Tsar, were under no illusion about its irrelevance. The monarchs of Austria and Prussia did not sign it willingly. Francis I remarked that, when it came to its implementation, he would have to consult with his chancellor with regard to temporal matters and with his confessor with regard to spiritual matters. The prince regent of England assured the monarchs that he would always endeavor to regulate his conduct by these sacred maxims, but refused to sign because his signature was without value without the countersignature of a minister. Metternich spoke of it contemptuously as a loud-sounding nothing. Nevertheless, in the history of ideas one cannot dispose of such documents with Castlereagh's dictum: "a piece of sublime mysticism and nonsense." We have experienced in our own time two statesmen, who were otherwise quite intelligent, promising "freedom from want and fear" to the world at large, also in the form of an international agreement. In spite of its legal irrelevance the phenomenon requires attention.

Once we have discounted the legal form, and have reduced the document to its proper status by referring it to the encounter between Mme. de Kruedener and the Tsar, we have no difficulty in its characteriza-

THE RELIGION OF HUMANITY

tion. We have to see in it the protestant-chiliastic response to the problem of the crisis, just as we have to see in de Maistre's work a catholic-
chiliastic response. In the pietistic program of spiritual restoration we
must, of course, not expect projects for an institutional organization of
the spiritual power with a de Maistrean Pope or a Comtean High Priest
at its apex; we must expect the transfer of the spirit of brotherhood that
animated the pietist communities to the international scale, and that is
precisely what we do find. All men are brethren, and the monarchs will
be brethren, too. The nations in their separate political existence will
be abolished and transformed into members of the one Christian nation.
The rulers themselves will cease to be sovereigns and be transformed
into family heads under the sovereignty of Christ, and so forth. Over
night we have entered the millennium of Peace, Charity and Justice
under Divine Providence. Such force as may still be necessary will
serve only purposes of reciprocal assistance against miscreants; and,
quite consistently, the document is not submitted to such unbrotherly
infidels as the Sultan and the Pope. In this projection of the pietistic
community on the European scale, we recognize the same procedure as
in the enlargement of the French revolutionary humanitarianism into
the new order of mankind, or in Comte's enlargement of his personal
intuition into the order of the Occidental Republic. Under this aspect
the legal form of an international agreement finds its place in the pattern: the public formalization partakes of the magic operation by which
Comte brings salvation to a society in crisis through the publication of
a book. It is a type of magic that survives today in certain intellectual
circles where political problems are approached by "high resolves"
and declarations of "lofty principles." For the rest, the *Holy Alliance*
was not without pragmatic consequences in the environment in which
it originated. The intervention of Nicholas I, in 1849, in breaking the
Hungarian revolution, was inspired by the idea of "reciprocal assistance" to the Austrian "brother," and the rescript of Nicholas II, in
1898, which initiated the First Hague Peace Conference, drew part
of its inspiration from this source—though another part has to be
sought rather in the financial difficulties of keeping up the armament
race.

Saint-Simon

The intellectual climate of the Restoration exerted its influence on
Comte most strongly through the medium of Saint-Simon (1760–
1825), during the years of association between the two men, that is
in the years 1817–24. For the details of this relationship the reader

should refer to the monographic literature, in particular the volumes of Gouhier. The association was so close that even now it is difficult to decide concretely what belongs to Comte and what to Saint-Simon in a complex of ideas that was formed in the years of collaboration. Fortunately, the question is not as important as the task of separation is delicate and complicated. Neither Saint-Simon nor Comte have their place in history because of the originality of their ideas or the profoundness of their systematic thought; their ideas were a common possession of the age, and their achievement in systematic penetration is at best dilettantic. They hold their distinguished place because of their keen sensitivity to the critical character of the epoch and because of their ability for embodying the apocalyptic atmosphere in blazing symbols of doom and salvation. While it is certain that Saint-Simon was for Comte a most important mediator of ideas, it would be difficult to say with precision what ideas Comte has received from Saint-Simon that he could not have received from elsewhere. Once the details of this relationship have been cleared up completely and the debate has settled down, we shall probably arrive at the conclusion that most important in the relationship between the two men was the fact that there were two of them. The assurance which springs from the mutual confirmation of minds which move in the same direction was perhaps the most precious gift of Saint-Simon to Comte. Nevertheless, the very likemindedness of their intellectual movement permits us to name at least two great complexes in which the mutual confirmation or influence must have been strongest, that is (1) the scientistic creed, and (2) the insight into the social consequences of the Industrial Revolution. In the following remarks on Saint-Simon, we shall concentrate on these aspects of his ideas.[39]

A few months before his death, in a conversation with Olinde Rodrigues, Saint-Simon summarized the intentions of his profuse work: "Like all the world, I wanted to systematize the philosophy of God. I wanted to descend successively from the phenomena of the universe to the phenomena of the solar system, further on to the terrestrial phenomena, and finally to the study of the species considered as a subdivision of sublunar phenomena; from this study I wanted to derive the laws of social organization, the original and essential object of my enquiry." Saint-Simon confesses a dream that was inspired by Newtonian physics, the dream of expanding the type of science that had

39. For the materials of this section we rely mostly on the presentation of Saint-Simon in vols. 2 and 3 of Gouhier. For tracing the line of the scientistic creed we draw mostly on the study of F. A. von Hayek, "The Counter-Revolution of Science," *Economica* (February, May, August, 1941).

evolved in mathematical physics to embrace systematically the whole world, including human society. It is the dream that also inspired Comte's *Cours de Philosophie Positive*. The dream came to nought because it proved impossible to extend Newton's fundamental law to the other fields of enquiry and thus to realize the aim which today goes by the name of "unified science." Saint-Simon continues his summary, as reported by Rodrigues: "But I became aware, in due course, of the impossibility of ever establishing the positive and coordinating law of this philosophy." He abandoned the idea about 1813. But the law of gravitation still haunts the first lecture of Comte's *Cours*, and Comte exchanged the name of *physique sociale* for the name of *sociologie* only at the beginning of volume 4 of the *Cours*—not without a nasty remark about Quetelet who had appropriated the name *physique sociale* for his statistical work. Comte's solution for Saint-Simon's problem was the substitution of the positive *method* as the unifying agency for the unifying *substantive principle* of gravitation.

The failure in realizing a unified Newtonian science of society induced Saint-Simon to change his approach. In his remarks to Rodrigues he continues: "I turned toward the *general science of man;* here one does not consider the sciences directly, but rather the scientists; not philosophy, but rather the philosophers, under the positive aspect of their functions in human society." Saint-Simon has not abandoned the "original and essential aim" of his inquiry—his aim is still the exploration of the *"organization sociale."* But he will no longer pursue this aim by searching for a social law of gravitation, rather, he will pursue it by the development of blueprints for a society in the age of Newtonian science, technology and industry. Scientists and philosophers have the "positive" function of developing the systematic body of knowledge that will guarantee human domination over nature. The social organization will abolish the old domination of man over man and replace it by a government of scientists, engineers and industrialists who secure and increase the domination of man over nature for the benefit of society at large. Politically, the advancement of science turns into the "counter-revolution of science" (as Bonald has called this development), with the vision of a totalitarian society dominated by theoretical and practical technocrats. It is important to isolate this factor in the thought of Saint-Simon, as von Hayek has done it in the above quoted study, because this factor can amalgamate with widely differing political ideas and movements. Indeed, it has remained one of the great constants in political thinking to this day. We find it as a component in the managerial "industrialism" of Saint-Simon and Comte, in the conception of the *crédit mobilier* banking institutes for the purpose of financing industrial expansion, in the socialism of Marx and Engels, in the modern conceptions of government by management, as well as in the progressive interventionism of the welfare state.[40]

We cannot enter here into the details of the voluminous work of Saint-Simon. We shall restrict ourselves to the bare enumeration of the principal political symbols that emerged in its course and remained effective in the work of Comte as well as in later history. The earliest work is the *Lettres d'un habitant de Genève à ses contemporains* (1802). We may characterize its atmosphere as transitional from the eighteenth to the nineteenth century. From the eighteenth century it retains in full vigor the Voltairian cult of Newton; to the nineteenth century belongs the project of a totalitarian organization of society. Saint-Simon, in the *Lettres*, is in search of financial backers for the project of a Council of Newton for which the subscribers will nominate the members from the mathematicians, physicists, chemists, physiologists, writers, painters and musicians of the age. The Council of twenty-one, elected thus by "mankind," will meet under the chairmanship of the mathematician who has received the highest number of votes. It will represent God on earth; it will abolish the Papacy which has not understood the divine science that one day will create the terrestrial paradise. It will subdivide the world into regions with local Councils of Newton, with worship, research and instruction centered in the Temples of Newton. The revelation comes from the Lord Himself, who has Newton by His side as the *logos* that will enlighten the world and Saint-Simon is his prophet. In brief: here we have the third type of apocalyptic vision, that is the scientistic by the side of the Catholic and the Pietistic.

The project contains certain details which unfold fully only in the later works of Saint-Simon. The social structure which he implies at this stage involves a stratification into scientists (and liberal intellectuals generally), property-owning industrialists and propertyless workers. His project has for its purpose, among other things, the avoidance of a class struggle that otherwise would be inevitable. The new society will be permeated by the ethos of work. All men will work; "the arms of the poor will continue to sustain the rich, but the rich will be ordered to let their brain work; and if their brains are not fit to work, they will soon be obliged to work with their arms; for Newton will certainly not leave on this planet (which is so close to the sun) workers who are voluntarily useless in the shops." All men will regard themselves as

---

40. The summary of Saint-Simon is to be found in Olinde Rodrigues, *De Henri Saint-Simon* (*Le Producteur*, vol. 3), 1826; quoted in Gouhier, 3, p. 61.

laborers attached to one workshop, and their work will be directed by the Council of Newton. It is hardly necessary to expatiate on the importance of this concentrate of ideas. Here we can lay our finger on the point where the enlightened utilitarianism and scientism of d'Alembert and Condorcet acquires the industrial society as its institutional body and blossoms out into the vision of the totalitarian workshop without escape. Even the ferociousness of branding and treating the dissenters as subhumans is already developed, for anybody who does not obey orders "will be treated by the others as a quadruped."[41]

The *Lettres* contains in germinal form the substance of Saint-Simon's later thought, as far as it is of interest in this context. Let us mention only a few variants and developments. In the *Introduction aux travaux scientifiques du XIXe siècle* (1807–8) he envisages, in place of the former Council of Newton, an editorial committee for a new *Encyclopédie* that will unify all science from the point of view of physicism. This physicism is a new phase of human religiousness, following the earlier phases of polytheism and monotheism. The new encyclopedic work is necessary because the work of the eighteenth-century intellectuals was merely destructive and not yet positive. We can discern in these reflections the germ of Comte's later characterization of the "metaphysical" stage as merely transitory and critical, as well as the development of physicism into the new religion with a "physicist clergy." We find in the *Introduction*, furthermore, the typical categories of Restoration politics: the "*société européenne*" founded by Charlemagne, broken in its spiritual unity by "*le défroqué Luther*," but nevertheless still forming a civilizational unit of the five nations, lacking today nothing but a federative religious bond. This stock of conceptions of the Restoration, however, is now combined with the idea that the solution will come through the formation of a new temporal power, consisting of the proprietary class, and a new spiritual power, consisting of scientists and intellectuals.[42] The *Memoire sur la science de l'homme* (1813) again stresses the necessity of a unified, positive

41. For the *Lettres* see Gouhier, *Jeunesse*, vol. 2, and von Hayek, op. cit., pp. 26ff.

42. See von Hayek, op. cit., pp. 29ff.; Gouhier, 3, pp. 67ff. The conceptions of Saint-Simon were at this time strongly influenced by Napoleon's corporative constitution for the Kingdom of Italy. In this constitution the electorate was divided into the three groups of landowners, merchants and scientists, and clerics. Saint-Simon expected a reconstruction of Europe through a reorganization of all nations along these lines, and a union under the Emperor. The working class did not receive any representation; this feature has remained constant in the work of Saint-Simon; his conception of the industrial society was that of a welfare state with industrialists and scientists as the temporal and spiritual ruling class.

science of society, and brings, in this connection, a new variant of the three phases: the first or preliminary epoch ended with Socrates, the second or conjectural lasts to the present, and the third and positive is about to begin.

Let us, finally, select two ideas from the late work of Saint-Simon which indicate the transition to the post-Restoration phase of the crisis. In the *Système Industriel* (1820–22), Saint-Simon gives a new precision to the class structure of society. The new society will not only have to dispose of the old feudal and clerical aristocracy, it also will have to eliminate the "second class," consisting of people living on their rents, of the military, the magistrates and all persons occupied in useless work. In the *Catéchisme Industriel* (1823–24) he assigns to this class the name *"bourgeois"* and includes in it all property owners who are not industrialists; the temporal ruling class thus is circumscribed precisely as consisting of persons who combine ownership with managerial work. The French Revolution is the work of the *bourgeois*, not of the industrialists. The second idea, also contained in the *Catéchisme Industriel*, is that of the new freedom: the exploitation of man by man will be succeeded by the exploitation of nature by man, the military or governmental regime will be replaced by the industrial or administrative regime. At this point, we may say, occurs the split between the Restoration proper and the later revolutionary socialism. In the *Doctrine de Saint-Simon*, Bazard and Enfantin still follow their master in this point.[43] In the Saint-Simonian *Globe* of 1831, however the position is already reversed: "It is not a question only of administering things, but of governing men, a difficult, immense and saintly task." The revolutionary idea of Saint-Simon that government will disappear, and the administration of things will take its place, on the other hand, is resumed by Engels in the *Anti-Dühring* (1877): "The government over persons is replaced by the administration of things. The state will not be abolished, it withers away." The Saint-Simonians and Comte still have an appreciation of the historical governmental order; with the generation of Bakunin and Marx the eschatological fever has corroded this element of the tradition, too.[44]

---

43. *Doctrine de Saint-Simon*, p. 162.

44. On the formula of the "administration of things," its origin and fate, see the illuminating note of Bouglé and Halévy in ibid., pp. 162ff,

VIII. REVOLUTIONARY EXISTENCE: BAKUNIN

In the life of Michael Bakunin (1814–76) depths of Satanism and nihilism become visible which in the life and work of other great figures of the Western crisis are covered over by remnants of traditional order and by veils of futuristic planning. Comte wanted to extirpate Christianity and metaphysics from Western civilization but his will to destruction was buried under the program of scientism and the dream of the Occidental Republic. In the case of Bakunin all traditional and futuristic scaffolds are consumed by the lust of destruction: in the present the past must be destroyed to its very roots and the future must not even be imagined by men who are still tainted by the past. In Bakunin the destructive existence of the revolutionary appears in its nakedness.

Reaction and revolution

We gain some access to the operations of the revolutionary mind through Bakunin's early article on "Reaction in Germany," a study on the nature of freedom and democracy and on the obstacles to their realization in history.[1]

The great enemy of the principles of democratic revolution is for Bakunin the reactionary party which began to form in the period of Restoration all over Europe. He sees it manifesting itself in conservatism in politics, in the historical school in law, and in the positive philosophy in speculation. This reactionary party he does not consider a historical accident. History is not a field of contingencies; it is a free and, therefore, necessary evolution of the spirit. The democratic creed, founded as it is in the freedom of the spirit, would be served badly if the assumption of contingencies were admitted in explaining the course of history. The democratic party can be victorious only, if and when it transforms its enthusiasm and the vagueness of its fantasies into an existential insight into the process of history. Its difficulties are not

---

1. "Die Reaktion in Deutschland: Ein Fragment von einem Franzosen." Published in Arnold Ruge's *Deutsche Jahrbuecher für Wissenschaft und Kunst*, nos. 247–251 (Dresden, October 17–21, 1842), pp. 986–1001. Pseudonym: Jules Elysard. We quote from the reprint in *Michael Bakunin, Zwei Schriften aus den 40er Jahren des XIX Jahrhunderts* (*Internationale Bibliothek für Philosophie*, vol. 2, no. 11/12 [Prague, 1936]). The *Bibliothek* and these two publications of Bakunin are edited, with valuable notes, by Boris Jakowenko.

caused by the opposition of obscurantism but arise "from the fullness
of the totality of human nature which cannot be exhausted by abstract,
theoretical propositions." There will be no hope of victory until democracy emerges from its present difficulties through the understanding
that the enemy is not outside but within, and that first it has to conquer
the internal enemy. The revolutionaries will first have to understand
that democracy does not consist only in opposing the government of
the hour, nor in a particular constitutional reorganization, nor in a
politico-economic change, "but that it announces a total reversal of the
state of the world," that it is an "original, new life that has not existed
in history before." They will have to understand that "democracy is a
religion," and by this knowledge they will have to become religious
themselves; they will have to be *penetrated* by their principles, so that
they express them not in thought and reasoning only "but truthfully in
their concrete life, into its minutest manifestations."[2]

Bakunin, thus, is concerned with the *metanoia* of the person: intellectual propositions concerning democracy are meaningless unless they
are rooted in the truly transformed personality of the revolutionary. We
are moving in the tension between a phenomenal realm of political
theorizing and acting and a substantial "truth" in the ground of existence. Hence the contest between reaction and revolution is not primarily
concerned with forms of government. As a matter of fact, revolutionary
democracy, as we shall see later, will have to resort to dictatorial means
of government, while a bourgeois republic cannot be considered a
democracy simply because it has universal suffrage. If democracy is
to be realized truly, it must be born from true existence. The principle
of democracy is historically still at the stage of opposition to the existing
political state. As a mere negation "it necessarily has the whole fullness
of life outside itself"; it exists *only* as a party which, as a party, presupposes the existence of its reaction; it does not yet exist affirmatively.
In this "bad form" it will have to perish together with the reaction in
order to be reborn "from its free ground." And this change of the
democratic party will not occur as a quantitative increase of its present
"bad existence," but as a qualitative transformation, as "a new, living
and vivifying revelation, a new heaven and a new earth." "A mere
expansion would mean a flattening out of the whole world, and the
result of the whole story would be absolute worthlessness (*Nichtig-
keit*)."[3]

It is not necessary to dwell at length on the fact that Bakunin's idea
of revolutionary, democratic existence clearly bears the traces of the

2. Ibid., p. 5.
3. Ibid., p. 6.

Christian past from which it emerges. The "total reversal of the state of the world" stems from the Old Testament "turning of the tables"; the "living and vivifying revelation which brings a new heaven and a new earth" belongs to the complex of messianic annunciations; the distinction between intellectual lip-service to an idea and its truthful realization in "concrete life" reflects the Christian change of heart; the "original, new life" we know as the *renovatio Evangelica*. The whole atmosphere of an impending new dispensation is strongly reminiscent of English sectarian expectations that "God will come skipping over the mountains" and establish His kingdom on earth.

Beyond this formal structure of Christian eschatology, however, there is noticeable in Bakunin's ideas a continuity with the Christian past. The "freedom of the spirit" which he evokes is supposed to be an ultimate realization of Christian spirit. Bakunin sees the struggle for freedom inherent in Catholic Christianity from its beginnings. The principle of freedom is "the source of all heresies"; without it, Catholicism would have been immovable and, hence, "it was the principle of its aliveness as long as it was contained as a mere moment in its totality." Freedom is the source of the victorious heresy of Protestantism which also was inherent in Catholicism from its Pauline beginnings until it became an independent principle.[4] And, in general, liberation of the essentially free spirit from its fetters of unfreedom is the meaning of history. At present we have arrived at a new, critical epoch that opens a future beyond Catholicism and Protestantism. "The opposition of freedom and unfreedom has been driven to its last and highest culmination in our present which is so similar to the periods of dissolution of the pagan world." "The mysterious and terrible words" *Liberté*, *Egalité* and *Fraternité* suggest "the complete annihilation" of the existing political and social world. Has not Napoleon, this supposed tamer of democracy, spread the levelling principles victoriously through Europe? Do not Kant, Fichte, Schelling and Hegel represent the same levelling, revolutionary principle in the intellectual world? The autonomy of the spirit is the new principle of order, and it stands in highest opposition to all past religions and churches.[5]

If his opponents should answer that the conflicts have been solved and appeased politically in the France of Louis Philippe, and intellectually through Schelling, he would have to refer them to the spectacle of the present. What is still living of the old Catholic and Protestant worlds? And where is intellectual harmony in the face of the works of

4. Ibid., pp. 17f.
5. Ibid., pp. 18f.

Strauss, Feuerbach and Bruno Bauer? There is a state of utter confusion
and disharmony and such a state cannot last. "You know," Bakunin addresses the reader, "that mankind in accordance with its ultimate destiny
can only find peace and quiet in a universal-practical principle which
powerfully forces together the thousandfold manifestations of spiritual
life—and where is this principle?" Is it to be found in Protestantism?
But the world of Protestantism is a prey to the anarchy of its sects.
Schelling had said that without a great enthusiasm only sects can
exist, no public opinion. And the Protestant world is not penetrated by
a great enthusiasm, it is the soberest world one can imagine. And
Catholicism? Its old glory is gone; from its rule over the world it has
sunk to the level of an instrument for a foreign, immoral policy. And
the State? The state is involved in the profoundest internal contradictions
because a state without religion, without a strong public sentiment
(*allgemeine Gesinnung*) is impossible. "Look into yourself and tell me
truthfully: are you satisfied with yourself and can you be satisfied?—
are you not all sad and bedraggled manifestations of a sad and bedraggled time?—are you not full of contradictions?—are you whole
men?—do you believe in anything really?—do you know what you
want, and can you want anything at all?—has modern reflection, the
epidemic of our time, left a single living part in you; and are you not
penetrated by reflection through and through, paralyzed and broken?
Indeed you will have to confess that ours is a sad age, and that we all
are its still sadder children." "All peoples, all men, are filled with a
certain premonition, and everybody whose vital organs are not completely paralysed looks with shuddering apprehension into the approaching future that will speak the word of salvation." "That is why we call
to our blinded brethren: Repent! Repent! The Kingdom of the Lord is
near!" "Let us trust the eternal spirit which destroys and annihilates
only because it is the unfathomable and eternally creative source of all
life. The joyful passion (*Lust*) of destruction is a creative passion."[6]

Bakunin's historical perspective leaves no doubt about his role as a
new St. John the Baptist who announces, after Catholicism and
Protestantism, the Third Realm of the ultimately free spirit. As far
as the dialectical technique of the perspective is concerned, there is
hardly a difference between Bakunin's speculation and Hegel's dialectical unfolding of freedom in history, or Schelling's speculation on the
three Christianities. Under this aspect, his eschatology appears as a
late derivation of Christian experiences, mediated through the German
metaphysic of freedom and reason, and by virtue of this mediation con-

6. Ibid., pp. 20–21.

nected with European mystical tradition. At this point, however, a break occurs between the derivative Christianity of Hegel and Schelling on the one side, and the revolutionary speculation of Bakunin. Hegel's and Schelling's interpretations of history were contemplative in the sense that the understanding of history was for them the most important cathartic exercise in clarifying and solidifying their own existence. However far their ideas diverged from orthodox, dogmatic Christianity, however far they went in the direction of Gnosis, they still remained substantially Christian thinkers and were concerned about the order of their souls. Bakunin's *pronunciamento* breathes an entirely different spirit. The consciousness of crisis is strongly alive in him, and he uses the historical perspective sensibly, though not impeccably, for its expression. Nevertheless, history is now more than the cathartic means for clarifying a man's position in his world; under the influence of Feuerbach, it has become the legitimating basis for action. The consciousness of crisis moved Schelling to his "inner return," toward the ground in the soul in which the identity of freedom and necessity is to be found. The same consciousness moves Bakunin toward revolutionary action, an action which like Schelling's inner return is supposed to produce the identity of freedom and necessity—but freedom understood as political and economic freedom, and necessity understood as the inexorable revolutionary pressure of the masses.

Bakunin, indeed, admonishes us to direct our attention to "the poor class which, without doubt, is the vast majority of mankind" in order to identify, if possible, our freedom with their necessity. At present, this poor class is condemned to factual slavery through its ignorance and lack of property. This class "which is the real people" becomes menacing and begins to demand the enjoyment of the rights which everybody grants them theoretically.[7] The social preconditions are growing for the realization of the new realm through "direct action" in which human freedom does not find its identity with God's necessity, but with the material power that can be supplied by an enraged mass of people. Such action cannot form the soul, but will be directed against the present political institutions as the vessels of the old spirit. No compromise is possible with them. "The revolutionary propaganda is in its deepest nature the negation of the existing conditions of government; for in its innermost nature it has no other program than the destruction of what exists."[8] "And how could possibly that of which the

7. Ibid., p. 20.
8. Ibid., p. 6. This sentence seems to be a quotation from *Die europäische Pentarchie* (Leipzig, 1839), published anonymously, attributed to Goldmann (1798–1863). On this point see n. 2 by Jakowenko, ibid., p. 46.

whole life is destruction come to an external compromise with that which, according to its innermost nature, it must destroy?"[9]

We have assembled the elements from Bakunin's article that will permit us now to appraise the new phase which the Western crisis has reached in him. His revolutionary politics is eschatological in nature; it belongs to the type of speculations on the Third Realm that we find established in the medieval sectarian movements. Within this general type, it belongs to the variety of activist mysticism which produces Paracletes as the founders of the Realm of the Spirit. Within the activist type, it must be distinguished from the genuine, Christian Paracletic type (as instanced by Jan van Leyden) through the humanization and immanentization of the spirit. Bakunin is not a Paraclete in whom the *logos* has become flesh—all traces of Christian transcendentalism are gone. His spirit is immanent to history and to man who makes history; in this respect, Bakunin's ideas are founded on Feuerbach's anthropology. Not the spirit of God, but the spirit of man, and quite specifically the spirit of Bakunin, will bring salvation in immanent historical action. In this respect, the eschatological politics of Bakunin is closely related to the Apocalypse of Man which we noted in the case of Comte. These determinations enable us, finally, to isolate the elements in Bakunin's complex of ideas which are specifically his own; we find them (1) in the radical absence of a positive idea of order, (2) in the identification of freedom with the "joyful passion of destruction"—which in Bakunin's existence seems to be as much the cause for the absence of an idea of order, as its consequence—and (3) in the discovery of the "masses" as the historical agent that will provide the brute force for the work of destruction.

The isolation of these three elements which we may consider specifically Bakunin's will permit us to clarify the relationship between him and Marx. The publication in 1932 of Marx's manuscript on *Nationalökonomie und Philosophie* (1844) has put it practically beyond doubt that the formation of Marx's ideas was strongly influenced by Bakunin's article on *Die Reaktion in Deutschland* (1842). We may formulate the relation between the ideas of the two men in the following terms: the fundamental position of Marx is the same as Bakunin's. We find the same consciousness of crisis, as well as the same background of Feuerbachian anthropology and immanentization of the spirit. Moreover, we find Marx in agreement with Bakunin on the *metanoia* as the essence of revolution, and consequently in agreement concerning the externality of mere political and economic revolution. For Marx,

9. Ibid., p. 6.

no more than for Bakunin, would the abolition of capitalism and the establishment of a communist property order without a change of heart result in the creation of a free society. And, finally, we find Marx in agreement with Bakunin in the discovery of the "masses" as the massive, historical force that will lead to a successful revolution which otherwise would be confined to the ineffectual rantings of intellectuals.

Again, the determination of this area of agreement will permit us to fix the point at which Marx departs from Bakunin. Marx does not share the primordial lust of destruction with his rival, nor the absence of any idea of order. He is willing to guide the revolution by providing it with a "scientific" system of social theory and a "philosophy" of history. In this respect, the organizing will of Marx, his dictatorial intellectualism, is related to that of Comte. Bakunin, on the other hand, heartily detests both Marx and Comte because their "authoritarianism" would limit his lusty passion for destruction by visions of responsible, ordering action. Moreover, Marx goes beyond Bakunin in defining the "proletariat" as the specific agent of the revolution instead of the vague "poor classes," "masses" and "real people." In the 1860's, when Marx is engaged in laying the groundwork for an international organization of the proletariat, Bakunin still indulges in romantic pamphlets glorifying the Russian robber. Nevertheless, while at the end of their lives the scientistic, authoritarian socialism of Marx and the anarchistic revolutionary existence of Bakunin have moved far apart, we should be aware of the common beginnings. The Marxian line of revolution was successful because of the elements that were missing in Bakunin, but the system of Marx would never have been written and never exerted its influence unless it had originated in the genuine pathos of revolutionary existence that we find in its purity in Bakunin.

Bakunin's Confession

In 1849 Bakunin was arrested and tried by the Saxon authorities for his participation in the uprising of Dresden and in 1850 he was sentenced to death. The sentence, however, was not executed because the Saxon authorities agreed to surrender him to the Austrians, who sought him for his participation in the Czech revolt of 1848. Again he was tried, and in 1851 sentenced to death. This time the sentence was commuted to imprisonment for life. The commutation was a formality for it had been decided in advance that on the day of the sentence he would be transported to the Russian border and handed over to the Russian authorities. In Russia, in 1844, Bakunin had already been sentenced *in absentia* to loss of the privileges of nobility and to hard labor for life in Siberia when he refused to obey an order to return to Russia. Hence in 1851 Bakunin was not tried by the Russian authorities but simply imprisoned in the Peter-Paul's fortress in execution of the earlier sentence.

In the fortress at first nothing happened and Bakunin waited in vain for his deportation to Siberia. After two months the door of his cell opened to admit Count Orlov, aide-de-camp to the Tsar and chief of the Third Section. The caller informed Bakunin that he was sent by the Tsar personally, and was ordered to invite him to write a confession of his sins to the Tsar. "Tell him," the Tsar had ordered, "that he shall write to me like a spiritual son to his spiritual father." Bakunin accepted the invitation and the result is the Confession.[10]

To write a confession of one's sins to the Tsar is not considered good form among revolutionaries. The biographers of Bakunin, who are either revolutionaries themselves or at least have sufficient sympathy for the revolutionary *code d'honneur* to feel apologetic about their hero, have worked hard to minimize the horror. Some of their arguments point quite aptly to the circumstances of the confession. Bakunin was a pioneer and the code of conduct for revolutionaries had not yet become standardized. Moreover, Bakunin was a nobleman and an officer, and for a man in his social position it was not extravagant to communicate with men of his own class. Beyond this point, however, there is not much to go on. What some of the biographers have to say about the psychological motivations of Bakunin and the still more fascinating occurrences in the soul of Nicholas I is mostly literary fancy.[11]

Besides the Confession itself, there are only two immediate sources which could be of help in understanding it. The first source is the letter to Herzen quoted above. Bakunin tells in this letter that in an ordinary trial he would have pursued the same course as in his Saxon and Austrian hearings where he confessed to his principles but did not reveal any information whatsoever. "But within four walls, in the power

10. The source for the visit of Count Orlov is a letter from Bakunin to Herzen, in *Michail Bakunin's sozial-politischer Briefwechsel mit Alexander Iw. Herzen und Ogariow,* ed. Dragomanov (Stuttgart, 1895), p. 35. The confession was published from the Archives of the Third Section by V. A. Polonsky in vol. 1 of his *Materiali dlya biografii M. A. Bakunina* (Moscow, 1923). The text used is *Michael Bakunins Beichte aus der Peter-Pauls-Festung an Zar Nikolaus I,* ed. Kurt Kersten, with a preface by W. Polonski (Berlin, 1926).
11. On Bakunin's Confession see Polonski in the preface to *Michael Bakunin's Beichte;* Hélène Iswolski, *La vie de Bakounine* (Paris, 1930); E. Yaroslavski, *History of Anarchism in Russia* (New York, 1937); and Guy A. Aldred, *Bakunin* (Glasgow, 1940). The excellent work by E. H. Carr, *Michael Bakunin* (London, 1937), is adequate, but brief in its account.

of the bear," he might relax and write a sort of confession, in the manner of *Dichtung und Wahrheit*. Besides, his actions had been quite open anyway and he had nothing to hide. He only took care not to mention any names of persons who might be compromised by him. "In the consciousness of my apparently helpless situation and considering the energetic character of Nicholas, my letter was very decided and bold—and that is why he liked it."[12]

The other source is a secret letter which he smuggled into the hands of members of his family when they were permitted to visit him. Here he details his physical decay as well as his fear of approaching mental deterioration brought on by solitary confinement for a period of two years. He assures his relatives that his former convictions have not changed but have become more burning and unconditioned. All that is left to him is comprised in the one word "Freedom!" This is not a desire for freedom from imprisonment only, but the desire to act again as a revolutionary. "Give me the possibility to act. It seems to me that I have never had so many ideas, never sensed such a burning urge for movement and action. I am not yet quite dead; and precisely this life of the soul which has through concentration become profounder and more powerful, now demands more than ever to express itself, now has become for me the inexhaustible source of sufferings which I do not even attempt to describe. You will never understand what it means to be buried alive, to say to oneself every minute of the day and night: I am a slave, I am annihilated, I have become helpless the body still living." To hear the echo of the great struggle, and to be condemned to silence! Rich in ideas, and unable to realize a single one! "To feel love in the heart, yes, love in spite of the walls around, and not to be able to give it away for something or somebody. To feel oneself full of self-denial, and even heroism, to serve a thousandfold holy idea—and to see all this striving broken by the four naked walls, my only witnesses, my only confidants."[13]

The two sources, together with a few other indications which we shall introduce presently, provide an understanding for Bakunin's situation which makes all speculation superfluous. There is, first of all, the plain, vital horror of physical and mental decay; any step that would bring relief in this respect, such as the hard labor requested as an act of grace by Bakunin, would seem justified as long as other per-

12. Letter to Herzen from Irkutsk, December 8, 1860; in *Sozial-politischer Briefwechsel*, pp. 35f. In weighing the value of this letter one will have to consider that it was written almost ten years after the Confession.

13. Text of the letter in *Michael Bakunins Beichte*, "Introduction" by Kurt Kersten, pp. xiiif. This letter is approximately contemporary with the Confession.

sons are not endangered by the Confession. On the spiritual level, however, the situation is more complex. There seems to be a contradiction
between the secret letter and certain formulations of the Confession.
In the secret letter Bakunin admits freely that still there is firm in his
heart the hope "to begin anew where I had to stop the work that brought
me here, only with greater tenacity, perhaps with greater circumspec-
tion." The Confession, on the other hand, concludes with the formula:
"the sincerely repentant sinner M. B."

The contradiction is obvious but not simple, for the formula is not
a straight lie. The formula of repentance in its turn is contradicted by
the whole content of the Confession itself in which Bakunin frequently
expresses his repentance in such terms that his nonrepentance is clear.
Towards the beginning Bakunin begs the Tsar not to ask of him to
become a traitor and to confess the sins of others. "Even in your own
eyes, Emperor, I would rather appear as a political criminal deserving
the severest punishment than as a rascal."[14] The Tsar, who was of the
stuff of which inquisitors are made, noted on the margin: "By these
words already he destroys all confidence; if he feels the full weight of
his sins, only a *complete* confession, not a *conditioned* one can be
considered a confession." A few pages later Bakunin speaks of his
philosophical and political disease which has brought him into his
present condition, "and I do not know even now whether I am completely healed." Note of the Tsar: "N.B.!"[15] Further on Bakunin addresses the Tsar: "Emperor, I shall not talk to you of my late repentance: Repentance in my situation is as useless as the repentance of a
sinner after death." The Tsar did not fall for the trick; he noted:
"Wrong; repentance of every sinner can bring salvation if only it comes
from a pure heart."[16] The Confession thus is not an attempt at deceiving
the Tsar. What then do the assurances of repentance mean, if by their
very formulation they defeat the purpose of moving the Tsar by a sincere repentance? There seems to be only one answer to the question:
the moods of Bakunin are complex, and while the secret letter shows the
rebellious mood, in the Confession Bakunin worked himself into such
a state of sincerity and repentance as is revealed in his words that he
could stand before the Tsar to a degree at least as a repentant sinner.

How was that possible? A key is perhaps offered by certain reflections of Bakunin in his early article on *Reaction in Germany.* In 1842
Bakunin distinguished between two types of reactionaries: the consistent and the mediating. The mediating type has his full contempt,

14. *Michael Bakunins Beichte,* pp. 2ff.
15. Ibid., p. 5.
16. Ibid., p. 16.

but not so the consistent. "In our bad and conscienceless age, when so many try to hide before themselves the strict consequences of their own principles out of sheer cowardice, in order to escape the danger of being disturbed in the artificial and weak shell of their supposed convictions, we are greatly obliged to these men. They are sincere and honest; they want to be whole men. . . . They are honest and whole men, or rather they want to be honest and whole men; and they hate every halfheartedness, just as we do, because they know that only a whole man can be good and that halfheartedness is the foul source of all wickedness."[17] "The source of their striving is almost always honest."[18] There is more in common between Bakunin and a consistent reactionary than between him and a man who wants to compromise between traditions and the necessities of reform. The Tsar was a consistent reactionary in this sense, and the letter to Herzen referring to the energetic character of Nicholas I seems to indicate a genuine respect for the enemy. Imponderables may have intensified this attitude, such as the fact that the Tsar was not the secular ruler only, but indeed Bakunin's spiritual head, as well as memories of the officer school and the enthusiasm of the young cadet for the Tsar on which the Confession dwells at length. To measure himself with this intimate and respected enemy was certainly a temptation.

A further stratum of the soul is touched in the passages of the secret letter in which Bakunin expresses his despair that his self-denying and heroic love breaks in vain against the walls of the prison. This love of Bakunin, his political eros, does not only embrace the "holy idea" of the revolution in a partisan fashion. It embraces also the opposing actors in the drama of freedom. The article of 1842 is again revealing. Bakunin asks himself whether the revolutionary should return in kind the hatred of the reactionaries. His answer: "No, that would not be worthy of the good cause of which we are the organs." By its very existence a partisan onesidedness presupposes the existence of another onesidedness. The revolutionary as a human being will be filled in the struggle with "evil passions," he will be partial and hateful. But that cannot be the last word, for in this case the revolution would not be any better than the reaction. To be a revolutionary partisan in politics can be justified only if "the onesided, merely political existence is perpetually overcome (*aufgehoben*) in the religion of the comprehensive and allsided principle." The revolutionary has to recognize in his reactionary opponent that his opponent really wills the good and that only "by an incompre-

---

17. Bakunin, *Die Reaktion in Deutschland*, p. 7.
18. Ibid., p. 9.

hensible misfortune" has he been distracted from his true destiny. "To us alone, who are called the enemies of the Christian religion, is it reserved and even made our highest duty to practice love concretely even in the hottest struggle, this highest command of Christ and this only essence of true Christianity."[19] The love that recognizes in the enemy a brother who also wills the good, and is perhaps even a secret partner in the common struggle, is a strong trait running throughout Bakunin's life. In the Russian legend Christ kisses Judas for his betrayal: before the face of God both have their roles in the drama of salvation; the one has to betray so that the other can redeem as the victim of the betrayal. That kiss is given again by Christ to the Great Inquisitor in the *Brothers Karamazov*.

Finally, we have to consider another "confession" of Bakunin, made a few years earlier in a letter to Annenkov.[20] Bakunin tells his friend that his life had been determined by almost involuntary turns, independent of his own plans. "God knows where it will lead me. I only feel that I shall never retrace my steps and never shall be disloyal to my convictions. In this lies the whole strength and dignity; in this lies the whole reality and the whole truth of my life; in this lies my faith and my duty; for the rest I care little. This is my confession." If this should sound like mysticism, he continues—well, who is not a mystic? Is there any life without mysticism? "Life is only where there is a severe, unlimited and therefore somewhat mystical horizon. Indeed we know almost nothing; we live in a living sphere, surrounded by miracles and vital forces; and everyone of our steps can bring them to light without our knowledge and frequently even without our will." The "severe and unlimited horizon" is the perfect symbol of a force that feels direction but sees no aim. The most unexpected contingencies in the sense of the *fortuna secunda et adversa* may arise to a force which can acknowledge no other standard but loyalty to its demonic urge. And who could say what *might* happen when the Tsar reads the Confession? The demonic adventure of throwing the Confession into time, as a potential crystallizing point for unknowable happenings, has to be taken into account in understanding Bakunin's act of confession.

The Confession itself is one of the best literary pieces written by Bakunin. It surveys his life from his youth in the officer school, and dwells at length on his revolutionary activities in the forties in France, Prussia, Saxony and Austria. Because of this content it is, together with his other writings of the late forties, an important source for under-

19. Ibid., p. 8.
20. Letter to Annenkov, Brussels, December 28, 1847; in *Sozial-politischer Briefwechsel*, p. 7.

standing the revolutionary events of 1848 and 1849. The problems of political history, however, are not our primary concern. We have to explore rather the elements of the Confession which contribute to the understanding of Bakunin's revolutionary existence in the amplitude of crime and repentance. We have to ask, therefore, of what precisely did Bakunin repent and what were the motives of his repentance?

Disillusionment and repentance

Bakunin did not repent for a moment his revolutionary existence as such. He repented its futility. And he repented because his observation of the revolutionary events in Paris and Berlin, in Frankfurt, Baden, Dresden and Prague had filled him with a disgust for the freedom-loving republicans who betrayed their revolution as soon as they felt their property interests at stake and were only too glad to return to the fold of conservative power. His revolutionary experiences produced in Bakunin a profound contempt for the West, especially of Germany. Correspondingly his Russian national sentiments became warmer than they were before, and, while he was not at all blind to the Russian evils, he discovered that Russia was not quite so bad as the West. He recognized the consistently reactionary Tsar as a figure of quality compared with the European monarchs who trembled abjectly in the face of the revolts of 1848. "In spite of my democratic convictions, I have worshipped you profoundly in the last year, as it were against my will. Not I alone but many others, Poles and Europeans in general, have understood like myself that you are the only one among the ruling heads of the time who has preserved his faith in his imperial calling."[21]

The disillusionment and repentance of Bakunin are closely connected with his attitude towards communism and the communist sects and secret societies of the forties. From the point of view of his revolutionary existence, Bakunin does not envisage a communist property order as the direct aim of a revolution determined to abolish the evils of society. A mere change of property order without a "real," democratic revolution would not interest him. Communism would inevitably be incidental to the revolution but it would not be its purpose. Hence the communist movement is a symptom of social decay; it does not open a road to salvation. Bakunin insists in the Confession that he never was a communist, though he followed the movement with great interest because he saw in it "the natural, necessary and inevitable result of the economic and political development of Western Europe." The social order of the West is

21. *Michael Bakunins Beichte*, p. 25.

corrupt and can be maintained only with the greatest effort. This state is the only explanation for "the panic terror" which in 1848 gripped the Western countries with the exception of England. "Wherever one turns in Western Europe one sees decadence, unbelief and corruption, a corruption which has its roots in unbelief. From the uppermost social levels down, no person, no privileged class, has the faith in its calling and right." Privileges are maintained by egoism and habit only. "This is in my opinion the essence and the strength of communism . . . : communism had and has its starting point at least as much from the top as from below; below in the masses it grows and lives as an unclear but energetic demand, as the instinct of revolt; in the upper classes it appears as the instinct of a threatening and deserved disaster, as an indeterminate and helpless anxiety caused by their own weakness and bad conscience." This anxiety has contributed more to its spreading than the propaganda of the communists. "I believe that this indeterminate, invisible, intangible, but omnipresent communism, which under various forms but without exception is alive everywhere, is a thousand times more dangerous than the exact, systematized variety which is preached only in a few secret and public societies." In 1848, these societies have revealed their impotence in England, France and Belgium; moreover, their program is so impractical that they could not survive three days of success. For once Bakunin and the Tsar are in hearty agreement, and the analysis of a Western society that is plagued by its bad conscience is annotated by Nicholas I with such remarks as "Right" and "A pertinent truth."[22]

The change of the economic order would interest Bakunin only as the inevitable accompaniment of a genuine Western revolution. But for a real revolution the West is not ripe, as the events of 1848 have shown. With this disillusionment and with the despair caused by a futile life, we touch the core of Bakunin's revolutionary attitude, and not of Bakunin's only but generally of the Russian revolutionaries of the nineteenth century. Bakunin was forced into revolutionary existence because only in a revolutionized Russia could a man of his energy and quality find an adequate field of action. The revolution in the West was of vital importance for him because he hoped that it would be the signal for the revolution in Russia, and the Russian revolution would enable him to go home and play an active role in the politics of his country. The Russian intelligentsia of the nineteenth century grows into a class outside the classes because the social and political order (in which even praise of the government was considered a subversive insolence) does not leave room for constructive action within the order to men of intel-

22. Ibid., pp. 7f.

ligence, temperament, education, mature personality and the moral will to reform. It has become a commonplace in the analysis of revolution that a government is in danger when the intellectuals are in opposition to it. As a surface description the commonplace contains a truth. But it does not bring out the underlying problem that intellectuals oppose the government because in their society they can find nothing better and more dignified to do. A social order reaches its critical phase when men of intellectual and moral integrity have to debase themselves if they want to participate in public life. The gravest insult to human personality is the denial of opportunity to let qualities of high value become an active force in society. When a society has reached the stage of corruption where its most valuable members are simply shoved aside the consequence will be, according to personality types, the withdrawal into contemplation or the active resistance to the point of revolutionary destruction and criminality.

The Russian social order of the time of Bakunin had developed a degree of repression which produced as its counterpart the extreme forms of nihilism. In his time, an educated Russian in his social position had the choice of sitting on his property and exploiting serfs, or of entering an administrative service in which he would have to submit to the rules of conduct of a depraved bureaucracy, or of becoming an officer in the army with a life of dull routine in out-of-the world places in the company of uninspiring comrades.[23] In the generation after Bakunin when the problem of an intellectually mature and active life had spread to the middle class, the situation became aggravated because the lower-class intellectuals did not even have the career chances of a Bakunin. In a country without a public life of the people, wedged in between the governmental organization of an upper class which they despised and a peasant people with whom they had no contact, the intellectuals stood

---

23. A forceful outbreak of the sentiment of repression is to be found in Bakunin's speech on the anniversary of the Polish revolution in 1847: "Nous aussi nous sommes gouvernés par une main étrangère, par un souverain d'origine allemande qui ne comprendra jamais ni les besoins ni le caractère du peuple russe, et dont le gouvernement, mélange singulier de brutalité mongole et de pédantisme prussien, exclut complètement l'élement national. De sorte que, privés de tous droits politiques, nous n'avons pas même cette liberté, patriarcale, pour ainsi dire, dont jouissent les peuples les moins civilisés et qui permet du moins à l'homme de reposer son coeur dans un milieu indigène et de s'abandonner pleinement aux instincts de sa race. Nous n'avons rien de tout cela: aucun geste naturel, aucun mouvement libre ne nous est permis. Il nous est presque défendu de vivre, car toute vie implique une certaine indépendance, et nous ne sommes que les rouages inanimés de cette monstrueuse machine d'oppression et de conquête qu'on appelle l'empire russe." (The speech was published in *La Réforme*, December 14, 1847; we quote from the reprint in *Sozial-politischer Briefwechsel*, pp. 279f.)

before a blank wall of nothingness and nihilism to the point where terroristic murder became a sensible means of expression because for some of them it was the only one at their disposal. The prison walls against which the love of Bakunin broke were only the ultimate physical embodiment of the prison walls of society against which an active intelligence hammered until it was exhausted and broken. In this light we have to read the touching confession of Bakunin: "I would have subordinated myself to anybody if I had recognized in him the ability, the means and the firm will to serve the principles which I held as absolute truths. I would have followed him joyfully and would have subordinated myself to him with pleasure, *because I have always respected and loved discipline that rests on conviction and faith.*" And then he turns his great problem even into a personal vice: "My nature had always a deep-rooted vice: my love for phantastical, for unusual, unheard-of adventures which open unlimited horizons. In an everyday and quiet circle I felt I had to suffocate. Usually men are in search of quiet and see in it the highest good. But to me quiet brought despair; my soul was in incessant excitement; it demanded action, movement and life. I should have been born somewhere among western colonists in the American woods, where civilization is only about to blossom forth, where life is still an incessant struggle against wild men and against a wild nature, not in a well-ordered bourgeois society."[24]

Faith under will

The purpose of Bakunin's revolutionary activity is the hope of returning to Russia, to a Russia that will have room for him in public life. "To my life in Russia I could return only on a revolutionary, criminal path."[25] But how could such a revolution be effected? The answer of the Confession goes in its implications far beyond the immediate occasion: it reveals a characteristic of Bakunin's life that breaks through again and again in the enterprises of his later years; it goes far to explain the personal fascination which Bakunin had for everybody who met him and it goes even beyond Bakunin's personal existence and reveals a source of strength which carries the revolution to success. The answer: "I had only one confederate: Faith! I told myself that faith moves mountains, overcomes obstacles, defeats the invincible and makes possible the impossible; faith alone is one half of victory, one half of success; complemented by powerful will it creates circumstances, makes men ripe, collects and unites them. . . . In one word: I wanted to believe, I

24. *Beichte*, pp. 47f.
25. Ibid., p. 14.

wanted others to believe." This is perhaps the most perfect description ever given of the magic of evil, of creating a reality out of nothing. It is the opposition of the demonic faith under will to the Christian will under faith. This "faith under will" manifests itself later in Bakunin in the prodigious invention of nonexisting revolutionary societies and the injection of such figments of imagination into reality with quite tangible results. The faith and imagination of an isolated will break into the course of history, create indeed the circumstances, and produce the most incredible effects among bewildered contemporaries who cannot believe that such things can happen. It is the first appearance of the black magic of the isolated will which later recurs in Nietzsche's "magic of the extreme," in Lenin's persistence through hopeless years until he grasped his kairos, and in Hitler's staying power and "Victory of Faith." In the mood of the Confession, however, Bakunin is sensitive to the forced character of the "faith under will." He admits that it was not without great effort that he "achieved this hypocritical, artificial, violent faith," that he was tormented by doubts "about the morality and possibility of his enterprise" and that he "heard voices of inner reproach," etc.[26] The experiential source of the doubt seems to have been Bakunin's revolutionary activity itself. In political practice a man is likely to encounter *ananke*, the fate of being caught in a network of obligations and necessities which determine the course of action so narrowly that not much room is left for choice. Bakunin confesses that he has understood "one truth fully and thoroughly": that the business of ruling is difficult and requires experience, "that in the life of states and peoples there are higher conditions and laws, not to be measured by everyday standards, and that in politics much is determined by a necessity that in private life seems unjust, oppressive and cruel." "History has its own, secret course," and rarely has a private individual, "however sincere, honest and sacred his convictions may be," the vocation "to raise his rebellious thought and his impotent hand against the inscrutable forces of destiny."[27]

The tension between faith and repentance in the Confession is only the strongest manifestation of a tension which is permanently present in Bakunin's existence. We have noted the earlier manifestation in the respect for the consistent reactionary and the love of the enemy. Even in his most destructive moods Bakunin always preserves the awareness of mystery in the historical drama and of an inscrutable fate that has assigned their roles to the actors. We never find in Bakunin the Marxian

26. Ibid., p. 38.
27. Ibid., p. 43.

confusion of attributing to the individual enemy as a personal guilt the role which is determined by biographical accidents and social and economic circumstances. There is evil in Bakunin, and in his later years criminality and open Satanism, but there is at no time in him the mean streak of the little beast that coops itself up in righteousness and spits poison at the enemy. We have to stress this trait in Bakunin's existence because in contrast with it we gain a clearer understanding of the forces which determine the politically successful line of Western revolution and crisis: of the forces of spite, hatred and defamation. In this main line we have to observe the crescendo in the moral decomposition of the West: from the Voltairean vulgarities of enlightenment through the hatred, moral hypocrisy and technique of defamation of the middle-class intellectual Marx (which becomes a force in history through the movement of Marxism) to the final decomposition of Western society in the twentieth century with the mutual defamations of the Western middle classes. The most important factor shaping the political and civilizational destiny of the West in this period is hatred of the middle classes.

Pan-Slavic imperialism

Bakunin envisages the Russian revolution as part of a pan-Slavic revolution. The first aim is the destruction of tsaristic power. The abolition of the monarchical form of government, however, should not be more than the opening of the great Slavic liberation. A free Russia should take the lead of the Slavic peoples in wars against Austria, Prussia and Turkey, and if necessary against Germany and Hungary, for the liberation of the Slavs from foreign domination. "Half of Prussian Silesia, the greatest part of West and East Prussia, that is all Slavic and Polish speaking territories, should be separated from Germany." In a further sweep also Hungary, the Moldavians, Rumanians and Greeks should be induced to join the Slavic Federation so that a united, free, Eastern Empire would emerge, as a new Eastern world power against the West, with the capital in Constantinople.[28] The revolutionary re-

28. Ibid., p. 45. For details of the Slavic Federation, with autonomy of the member nations and a common military and foreign policy, see Bakunin's *Statuten der neuen slavischen Politik*, and the *Grundzüge der slavischen Föderation*, of 1848, in *Sozial-politischer Briefwechsel*, pp. 285–289. For an even further extension of the revolution see the *Appel aux peuples slaves par un patriote russe:* "En déclarant la guerre aux oppresseurs, la révolution proclamait donc le remaniement, le bouleversement de tout le Nord, de tout la partie Oriental de l'Europe, l'emancipation de l'Italie, et, comme but final: la féderation universelle des républiques Européenes!" The *Appel* was published for the first time in Josef Pfitzner, *Bakuninstudien* (Prague, 1932). The *Appel* is the first draft, considerably more radical in content, of the *Aufruf an die Slawen. Von einem*

public would not be built upon the foundations of Western liberalism. It would not be representative, constitutional, or parliamentarian and it would have no balance of powers. Democracy cannot be realized through parliamentary representation in a country where the vast mass of the people is not politically articulate and cannot form its own representation. A parliament of aristocrats and bourgeoisie, however, would only continue the oppression. "For Russia, there is necessary a strong dictatorial power which concerns itself exclusively with the elevation and enlightenment of the masses; a power which is free in tendency and spirit but without parliamentary form; a power which prints books of a free content without introducing the freedom of the press; a power which is surrounded, advised, supported by the free cooperation of likeminded men but which is not limited by anybody or anything." The only difference between dictatorial and monarchical power would be the tendency of the former to make itself superfluous as rapidly as possible through education of the people, while the monarchical tries to perpetuate its existence by keeping the people in unchanged childhood.[29]

Revolt of the soul versus Marxian necessity

It is unnecessary to elaborate the significance of Bakunin's program in the light of the twentieth century. The development that leads from Bakunin to Lenin and Stalin is clear. It is more important to accentuate the difference between his conception of revolution and that of Marx. The difference becomes acute over the question: how should such a revolution be made and by whom? On this point Bakunin reveals the absence of concrete ideas. He assures the Tsar that he certainly had no personal ambition to become the dictator of Russia. On the contrary, he is convinced that he would perish in the struggle. His generation is called to destroy, not to build; "the building will be done by others who

---

russischen Patrioten. Published in December, 1848, by E. K. Keil in Leipzig, bearing on the title page the designation, "Koethen, Selbstverlag des Verfassers." The *Aufruf* is reprinted and annotated by Boris Jakowenko in *Michael Bakunin, Zwei Schriften aus den 40er Jahren des XIX Jahrhunderts* (*Internationale Bibliothek für Philosophie,* vol. 2, no. 11/12, Prague, 1936).

29. *Ibid.,* p. 46. The idea of the benevolent, "provisional, iron dictatorship" recurs in Bakunin's Siberian years. Bakunin formed a close friendship with the governor of East Siberia, a cousin on his mother's side, the General Muraviov-Amurski. The empire-builder and the revolutionary apparently found much common ground, for in the letter to Herzen from Irkutsk, November 17, 1860, Bakunin praises at length the merits of Muraviov, the true democrat and "unconditionally one of us." He seems to have contemplated with some seriousness the possibilities of a Russian revolution and a pan-Slavic liberation under the leadership of a liberal dictator like Muraviov. (The letter to Herzen in *Sozial-politischer Briefwechsel,* pp. 11–29.)

are better, cleverer and fresher than we are."[30] And if one should ask how he could plan the horror of a Russian revolution without having a clear idea of what should become of the enterprise, he would have to admit that he himself was trembling when he envisaged the consequences. Revolutionary Russian peasants are bestial in their cruelty, and he remembered Pushkin's word: "Deliver us, oh Lord, from the Russian revolt which knows no sense nor mercy!" Partly he had hoped that the drunken wildness of the masses could be restrained, partly he comforted himself with the thought that at certain times a terrible disaster is necessary.[31]

This attitude towards the process of revolution is not a passing mood with Bakunin. The willingness to start the revolt, in the hope that out of terror wholesome forces will emerge and build the new society, remains throughout his lifetime. In a pamphlet of 1871, Bakunin formulates the question on principle. He insists that human dignity in nations and peoples manifests itself only in "the instinct of freedom, in the hatred of oppression, and by the force of revolting against everything that has the character of exploitation and domination in the world."[32] With this "firm conviction" that the instinct of freedom is the source of revolt and the essence of human dignity, that the revolt of the soul is the primary moving factor of history, and that the realm of freedom somehow will emerge, without bothering too much about techniques, once the revolt has started, Bakunin puts himself into opposition to the Marxian idea of revolution. The school of "German authoritarian communists," he continues, has developed the materialistic principle that human history "even in the ideal manifestations of the collective and individual life of mankind, in its intellectual and moral, religious, metaphysical, scientific, artistic, political, juridical and social developments" is nothing but the reflex of economic facts. "This principle is profoundly true if considered from a relative point of view; but if it is taken absolutely, as the only basis and first source of all other principles, it becomes completely wrong."[33] The materialistic conception of history contains for Bakunin a relative truth insofar as he too assumes that the social world, and the specifically human manifestations of the spirit, rest on the animal basis of man, and the animal basis in its turn on matter. Spirit is the culmination of the evolution of matter. But it can be the culmination

30. Ibid., p. 48.
31. Ibid., p. 49.
32. Bakunin, *L'Empire Knouto-Germanique et la Revolution sociale*, in Michel Bakounine, *Oeuvres*, ed. James Guillaume (Paris, 1907), 2, p. 455.
33. *Sophismes historiques de l'École doctrinaire des communistes allemands, Oeuvres* (Paris, 1908), 3, pp. 9–18.

of matter only because matter is not inorganic but contains spirit. The rise of matter to humanity means the release from matter of the independent principles of thought and revolt. The negation of mere animality, the blossoming out of matter into the revolt of the soul, is the new independent factor forming history.[34] The opposition between the principles of the free, independent soul in revolt and of the determination of thought through the economic situation, as well as the ensuing opposition between the two revolutionary tactics, has remained the issue between Bakuninists and Marxists to this day. On the one side there is the faith in personality and the ability of free men to produce order out of revolutionary likemindedness without authoritarian leadership, on the other side the belief in the necessary march of history that progresses through the action of not too revolutionary souls under the authoritarian leadership of the executors of the historical will.[35]

The revolutionary will, untrammeled by doctrinaire conceptions of historical necessity, allowed Bakunin a considerable latitude of political imagination. In the Confession he reveals that at one time, in 1848, when the pan-Slavic hatred against everything German was roused to its height by the Frankfurt Parliament, he had thought of appealing to the Tsar himself to assume the leadership of the pan-Slavic liberation. Not only the Poles, but all the Slavs of Prussia and Austria would have followed at this time, in Bakunin's opinion, a call of the Tsar to a war against Germany and all Western Europe. He had drafted the appeal but destroyed it because he considered the attempt futile. The Tsar, indeed, was not enthusiastic about the idea. Bakunin's assurance that all Slavs would have followed his call for liberation, he annotated on the margin: "I do not doubt it; and I would have stood at the head of a revolution of a Slavic Masaniello; no, thank you!"[36]

As far as Bakunin's fate was concerned, the immediate effect of the Confession was nil. He remained in the Peter-Paul's fortress. Over his later life, the Confession seems to have hung like a shadow. During the Polish resurrection of 1863, Bakunin was in Stockholm participating in the movement. The Third Section prepared at this time a pamphlet containing the Confession and a few other documents. This pamphlet was never printed. Bakunin, however, suddenly broke his relations with the Poles and left Stockholm. In 1870 Bakunin participated in the uprising of Lyons; again a similar pamphlet was prepared and again

34. Bakunin, *Dieu et l'État, Oeuvres*, 3, pp. 18ff.
35. For a good comparison of the two positions see a modern Bakuninist, Erwin Rholfs, in the preface to vol. 1 of Bakunin, *Gesammelte Werke* (Berlin, 1921).
36. *Beichte*, p. 53.

Bakunin withdrew from the scene. Authors who wish to pile all nefariousness on the tsarist regime assume a connection between the threatened publication and Bakunin's withdrawals. There is, however, no proof of such pressure and there were other reasons sufficient to justify a withdrawal.[37] Whatever went on behind the scenes, the Russian government never made public use of the Confession although its publication would have discredited Bakunin in revolutionary circles.

37. On these events in Bakunin's life see Kurt Kersten in the introduction to ibid., p. xvi.

IX. BAKUNIN: THE ANARCHIST

In 1861 Bakunin escaped from Siberia and came, by way of America, to England. The years between his escape and his death in 1876 are filled with a maze of events of such complication that even a short account cannot be attempted here. For the biographical details the reader should refer to the excellent presentation of Bakunin's life by E. H. Carr.[1] In the present context we shall confine ourselves to an analysis of the transformation which Bakunin's revolutionary existence underwent in his later years.

The revolutionary existence of Bakunin crystallized, in his later years, into what is commonly called his anarchism. Today, unfortunately, the term anarchism is obscured by its application to a variety of subphenomena. Before turning to an analysis of Bakunin's anarchism, therefore, it may be helpful to clarify the meaning of the term.

Closely associated with anarchism in the popular usage of the term is the use of terroristic tactics such as bomb-throwing and assasination, that is the so-called propaganda of deed. But the use of violence is not specifically anarchistic. Some anarchists have used violent acts for the promotion of revolutionary ends and some have not. Some anarchists have condemned such tactics and such methods have been used by revolutionary groups who were not anarchists. On a deeper level than the pragmatic, however, the problem of terrorism is of relevance because it reveals a dimension of revolutionary existence which is found in Bakunin although he never himself resorted to acts of terror.

The reader will recall our earlier discussion concerning the impasse in which an active intelligence finds itself in a social order when legitimate channels for constructive action are barred. The experience of guilt for the misery and evil in a society, coupled with the will to reforming action and with the experience of impotence, can issue in a person of high moral sensitivity the desire for self-sacrifice. The terroristic act offers the opportunity for sacrifice in a double sense: first, the terrorist risks his life physically for he will be executed when he is caught; second, and more important, in committing murder the terrorist sacrifices his moral personality. To overcome the profound abhorrence of murder and to annihilate oneself morally in committing murder, perhaps of innocent people, is the supreme sacrifice. To the man who breaks under the consciousness of social guilt because he is frustrated in action, this sacrifice remains the only proof that he is indeed capable

1. E. H. Carr, *Michael Bakunin* (London, 1937).

of "doing" something; it is his ultimate justification. This supreme act, however, reveals the pneumapathological state of the person who commits it. It is not an act of love but rather an act of self-assertion by which the man who brings the sacrifice claims for himself an exceptional status in comparison with other men and the men to whom he brings the sacrifice are misused as the audience for his own justification.[2] Moreover the sacrifice is spiritually vain because the sacrificial act, if understood as a model of conduct, would implicitly deny moral personality to the men for whom it is brought. A man has no right to suggest the sacrifice of moral personality to others, nor has he a right to place them in a position where his own sacrifice of moral personality would appear as requested by them for their benefit. The terroristic act as a moralistic model is a symptom of the disease in which evil assumes the form of spirituality.[3]

Kropotkin

A second aspect of anarchism appears in the work of Prince Peter Kropotkin (1842–1921). The general pattern of a revolution, followed by a realm of freedom, is shared by Kropotkin with Bakunin. The present institutions, economic as well as political and ecclesiastical, have to be destroyed in order to release the inherent forces of cooperativeness in man for the building of a new society that will be free of evil. Political and economic institutions have created the dependence of man and thereby have become the source of evil; only their destruction in a social upheaval will make possible the rebuilding of society through voluntary activity. While the general pattern of the course of events is similar to Bakunin's, the sentiments underlying the ideas are very different. There is much more of Rousseau's critique of civilization in Kropotkin than of Bakunin's dialectic of reaction and revolution. The revolutionary conception shows the impact of Bakunin as well as of the Marxist analysis of economic institutions, but there is nothing left in Kropotkin of the mysticism of freedom in history. The "leap" into the new realm is not conditioned by an internal renovation of man, he does not have to be penetrated by a new "principle," all that will happen is the external smashing of existing institutions and by this act the good nature of man

2. The pneumapathology of the "exceptional man" returns as a fundamental problem in Nietzsche.

3. In the analysis of terrorism we follow the excellent presentation by Karl Nötzel in his treatise on *Die soziale Bewegung in Russland. Ein Einführungsversuch auf Grund der russischen Gesellschaftslehre* (Stuttgart, 1923), pp. 214ff., and passim.

which is present even now will have the opportunity of unfolding, un-warped by the evil of compulsion. This also is a theology of history, though not Bakunin's; it is rather the reversal of the Christian idea of the necessity of institutions. In the Christian idea the Fall has corrupted the nature of man and in the corrupt state he is unfit to govern himself and to live with others at peace without external control. In Kropotkin's idea the institutions are the Fall and with the elimination of the Fall the life without sin will be restored. In the Christian idea the necessity of institutions is explained by the Fall; in Kropotkin's idea the Fall is ex-plained by the institutions. Both ideas are concerned with evil in society and the necessity of institutions but in the Christian interpretation a realistic anthropology is used which recognizes the reality of evil in man, while Kropotkin, in the phrase of Schelling, "is not sufficiently ac-quainted with man in himself and outside himself" and operates with an anthropology which commits the cardinal mistake of projecting the evil in man into his environment. In spite of the relation to Bakunin, we have to understand, therefore, Kropotkin's anarchism as the extreme consequence of ideas which are to be found as a pervasive tendency in the age of enlightenment and crisis, of the anti-Christian idea of the fundamental goodness of man and of the denial of radical evil. It is a trend of ideas which manifests itself in such variegated phenomena as Rousseau's return to nature, the praise of the innocent savage who has preserved his natural goodness untainted by civilization, in the liberal Protestant theology of the nineteenth century which abolishes original sin and therewith Christ as the Redeemer, and in that strain in the idea of democracy which assumes that what the people wills is always good. In Kropotkin's anarchism this idea has been radically isolated and made the basis of an interpretation of politics. If the goodness of man is taken seriously, evil must have a source external to man and with the revolutionary removal of the external source mankind can enter the paradise of its own good nature.

Tolstoi

A third perspective on anarchism is found in the work of Count Leo Tolstoi (1828–1910). What Tolstoi has in common with Bakunin and Kropotkin is the assumption that the state and property are the sources of evil in society. What separates him from both is the condemnation of force as the instrument for removing the present state of evil and creating the good society. He founded his anarchism on an evangelical Christian ethics, and he was clear on the point that salvation cannot come from a change of institutions. For Tolstoi the devising of new institutions is no substitute for the *metanoia*, for the change of heart. Reform cannot be brought about by conspiratorial activities and by revolts; it has to be effected by enlightenment and persuasion, by arousing the conscience, by a model conduct of life, and if necessary by passive resistance to un-Christian commands of the state. On the surface, his attitude strongly resembles the Christian call to repentance and inner return and Tolstoi understood his position as a return to Christian ethics based directly on the Gospel. His followers understand him in the same sense and his interpreters are frequently inclined to accept the thesis and to classify his ideas as Christian anarchism. But substantially Tolstoi's attitude is quite as anti-Christian as that of Bakunin or Kropotkin and as a phenomenon in the history of the Western crisis it is an anarchistic form of the pneumatic disease. The anti-Christianity of Tolstoi consists precisely in what he considers his Christianity, that is in the acceptance of a Christian code of ethics. The problem of Tolstoi in this respect is similar to that of Kropotkin. Accepting the ethics of Christianity and rejecting the spiritual substance is a trend that has become increasingly marked since the Age of Enlightenment. Tolstoi does no more than radicalize and isolate an idea which is present as an ingredient in previous attempts at establishing an autonomous system of ethics without founding it on the spiritual experience that is its source. For Kropotkin we stressed the ancestry of Rousseau's critique of civilization; for Tolstoi we now must stress the roots of his idea in the ethics of enlightenment and particularly in the commonsense morality of Voltaire. The conception of Christ as a "progressive" moral thinker, the secularization of Christianity and its reduction to a code of ethics, is a general Western movement that has deeply corroded Christian sectarian life. The typical consequences of such despiritualization are to be found in Tolstoi. Christian ethics without Christian love is prone to produce righteousness and critique of the sinner. We have to recall that the *Sermon on the Mount* is not a code for the life in the "world"; it is addressed to men who live between the worlds in eschatological expectation. In historical existence, entangled in the network of social obligations, man has to pay his debt to nature and is obliged to commit acts in violation of the *Sermon*. If he is struck on the right cheek, he will not turn his left, but hit back in defense of his life, his family and his community. But in hitting back, he will do good, as a Christian, to remember the *Sermon*, and to be aware that in defense he is involved in guilt and that the man who struck him may have had quite as excellent "worldly" reasons for the attack as he has for the defense. Both are involved in a common guilt, both are engulfed in the inscrutable mystery of evil in the world, and in their enmity both have to respect in each other the secret of the heart that is known only to God.

This Christian attitude is not the attitude of Tolstoi. He falls into the series of fallacies which a revolutionary of the nineteenth century does not seem able to avoid: (1) the concrete evil in social relations and institutions is not accepted as emanating from the nature of man, to be remedied as far as possible in concrete instances but not to be abolished on principle, (2) the concrete evil is generalized, in a next step, into an abstract evil that attaches to institutions, not to man, and, in a last step, (3) the abstract evil attaching to institutions is attributed as a personal guilt to those men who by biographical circumstance happen to be the bearers of the institutions. In his political tracts Tolstoi points his accusing finger at the evil of governmental institutions and at the men who are responsible for it and he presents the evils so vividly that his accusations could be taken over by the radical, violent anarchist groups for their propaganda-pamphlets inciting to revolt. Tolstoi's admonitions to practice "pardoning love" are in vain in face of the unpardoning, critical content of his writings, and in vain are his assertions that the use of his writings for revolutionary purposes would be like setting a village on fire by means of a gospel-book. As Nötzel in his fine analysis remarks aptly: the difference between the gospel-book and Tolstoi's writings is that the gospel-book contains nothing that would justify incendiary action.[4]

His Christianity is in substance an extreme form of enlightened Puritanism. Tolstoi occupies a most conveniently situated island of righteousness: it is close enough to the "world" to hurl his accusations of guilt at it, but far enough from the "world" to deny responsibility for his acts as acts in the "world." He is no St. Francis who conformed with Christ and left the institutions alone, rather he despiritualizes the *Sermon* by transforming it into a code of Christian ethics governing human conduct in the world and creates for himself an "exceptional" position, like the terrorists, that permits him to indulge in action in the world without the responsibility of the world. If we compare his position with Bakunin's, we would have to say that the latter, in his spiritual striving, has deeply penetrated the mystery of evil in spite of the fact that his diseased existence ended in the willing recognition of its Satanic character, while Tolstoi, though not less diseased, escaped the consequences of Bakunin by virtue of his enlightened superficiality.

Gandhi

A word has to be added on certain phenomena which are closely related with the anarchism of the nineteenth century, that is on the non-

4. Karl Nötzel, op. cit., pp. 180ff.

resistance trends in English politics. Towards the end of the century the spreading of Russian anarchistic literature, particularly of the works of Tolstoi, had created in the West an atmosphere of general knowledge of civil disobedience and passive resistance as political weapons in the struggle against governmental authorities. Out of this atmosphere emerge at the beginning of the twentieth century the suffragette incidents in England with their civil disobedience and their hunger strikes, and in their wake the fateful incorporation of these weapons into the political arsenal of Gandhi (1869–1948).[5] The technique of passive resistance was practiced by Gandhi first in the Transvaal in 1907 in protest against the Asiatic registration bill of the Transvaal government, and after the general war it was continued in India beginning with the noncooperation campaign of 1920. In the course of this campaign the same problems arose for Gandhi that had worried Tolstoi. Gandhi insisted on nonviolent action, and the result was the terroristic outbreaks and peasant uprisings of 1921. Faced with such incendiary violence as a consequence of his nonviolent propaganda, Gandhi resorted to vigorous denunciation of violence towards the end of 1921 and the result was the Chauri Chaura affair of 1922, where a mob of insurgent peasants stormed the police station and killed the policemen. The affair compelled him to order the immediate suspension of civil disobedience and noncooperation. The experience of violent outbreaks was repeated in the second civil disobedience campaign of 1930. The position of Gandhi is on principle the same as that of Tolstoi: an eschatological ethic is introduced as a political weapon into the struggle of the world. The not so important difference is that Tolstoi could rest his anarchism on the prestige of the Gospel, while Gandhi successfully developed a halo of Eastern saintliness.

Founding the new realm

If we compare the later period of Bakunin's revolutionary existence with his earlier one, before his imprisonment, we might say that in the 1840's he participated in various revolts as the opportunity offered itself, while after Siberia he embarked on his own work of revolutionary organization. In the earlier years he was drawn into revolutions, in the later years he was active in preparing the revolutionary situation that ultimately would issue in the foundation of a new realm. In these years he organized and influenced groups of revolutionary workers in Switzerland, Italy and Spain, and in these years he engaged in the struggle

5. On the personal relations between Tolstoi and Gandhi see Ernest J. Simmons, *Leo Tolstoy* (Boston, 1946), pp. 722f.

with Marx for the International Workingmen's Association (the First International). His organizational activities left their imprint on the workers' movement in Italy and Spain until they were obliterated, at least for the time being, by the Fascist and Falangist revolutions of the twentieth century. To a minor degree his influence extended over all of Europe and into anarchist circles in America. His struggle with Marx for the control of the International was not successful but it compelled Marx, after the Congress in The Hague, of 1872, to transfer the General Council from London to New York in order to withdraw it from Bakuninist influence, and it ended in the demise of the First International.

The activity of Bakunin expressed itself in the prodigious creation of revolutionary societies. To what extent these organizations existed in social reality or only in Bakunin's imagination cannot always be clearly determined. This point, however, is of less importance for us than the principle on which they were conceived. An insight into Bakunin's organizational ideas is offered by the most effective of his creations, the International Social-Democratic Alliance of 1868.

The International Social-Democratic Alliance

Bakunin founded the Alliance as an instrument for wedging his way into a leading position in Marx's International Workingmen's Association and it existed after a fashion. But the question might be asked, for what purpose should an organization be founded which seemed merely to duplicate Marx's organization with unlikely revolutionary success? In his *Rapport sur l'Alliance*, of 1871, Bakunin revealed part of his answer to this question.[6] It should be the policy of the Alliance to form a smaller nucleus of ardent revolutionaries within the International of Marx. The operation through the general assemblies of the sections seemed to defeat the purpose of the International and Bakunin preferred smaller meetings of 20 to 40 members selected from the various sections with an eye to their devotion to the principles of the International. The Alliance should not develop principles and programs but rather "character, unity, solidary action and mutual confidence among serious wills; in brief, it wanted to form propagandists, apostles and ultimately organizers."[7] The general assemblies were to be used for formal occasions and for representative support but preparation for the public meetings would be the responsibility of the smaller meetings; the select members would have to influence the majorities of the assemblies and

6. Bakunin, *Rapport sur l'Alliance*, *Oeuvres*, vol. 6 (Paris, 1913).
7. Ibid., pp. 245f.

make them understand the meaning of the questions submitted for their decision.[8] The larger assemblies would be restricted in their discussion since many questions cannot be aired in public and more serious-minded members cannot participate in debates which are conducted on a low level. Hence the assemblies are not sufficient for the triumph of revolutionary principles and for a serious organization of the International.[9]

Up to a certain point there is nothing extraordinary in Bakunin's idea. One cannot operate an organization through general assemblies. Democracy needs the gradation by which the will of the people, for the purpose of action, is filtered down to a small executive by means of parties, conventions, caucuses, steering committees, etc. The problems arise rather from the nature of revolutionary foundation. Above all there was the conflict with the International: Bakunin wanted the Alliance to become, under his leadership, the general staff of the International. Naturally Marx and his friends of the General Council in London were of the opinion that they were quite capable of being the general staff themselves. Beyond this conflict opens the genuine revolutionary problem which Bakunin had in common with Marx. It is one thing to filter down the will of an existing people, as for instance the English, from the millions to a Cabinet through the processes of elections, caucuses, party seniority, etc.; it is quite another thing to perform this filtering operation in a vacuum. The workers are not a people, and to organize an international workers' revolution implies the creation of a people outside the Western nations. We have to distinguish between the problem of political articulation for the vast infra-bourgeois masses for the purpose of integration into the national body politic and of participation in constitutional government—a purpose which is served by the self-organization of workers in trade unions, syndicates, labor parties, etc.—and the idea of an international revolution which envisages the destruction of the nations as determining forces in history and the creation of a new, supra-national community. Neither Bakunin nor Marx wanted to form national labor parties. They wanted rather to inspire a revolutionary movement for men without a country and by means of revolutionary organization they wanted to create a country for these homeless people.

The man without a country

The creation of a new community through a movement, however, raises delicate problems. The leadership cannot rise from the people be-

8. Ibid., p. 246.
9. Ibid., p. 247.

cause the people does not exist, and the human raw material that could be molded into a new community has some difficulty in molding itself in the absence of an articulated existence which produces natural leaders. In this peculiar situation are rooted the traits of the international revolution which beset it into the period of its contemporary successes. The idea of the man without a country who finds his fatherland in the revolution does not arise among the workers, it is rather a projection into the workers of the attitude of the homeless intellectual who becomes the leader of masses which for various reasons are ready to be formed.[10] As a matter of fact, workers are not quite as much without a country as the homeless intellectuals who try to persuade them that they are. The discrepancy between the intellectuals' idea of an international revolution and the social reality of the workers—and still more of the peasants—results in various "surprises," such as the national alignment of the workers of the Second International in 1914 and the drift into nationalism of the Russian revolution of 1917. The second feature originating in this situation is the impossibility of organizing the revolution democratically. An international revolution is not a party in which an existing community organizes itself for action; it is a movement in which a nonexisting community is created from the top. It requires inevitably a concentration of leadership in the hands of a few revolutionary activists who rarely are workers themselves. As a social form, the movement is centralized in a nucleus of leadership from which emanate the founding influences in their two modes of apostolate and institutionalization. The insight into this problem is common to all the great figures of the revolution but the accents shift with personal abilities and inclinations and with the requirements of the unfolding revolutionary drama. The historic function of Marx was the creation of a formidable system of doctrine that could serve as the Sacred Writing for the apos-

10. On the situation of Central European intellectuals at the time of Marx see the survey in Karl Löwith's *Von Hegel bis Nietzsche* (Zurich, New York, 1941), pp. 91–98. Most of the men who led the critique of society were socially "derailed" in one way or another: Feuerbach, Ruge, Bruno Bauer, Stirner, Dühring, Marx, Schopenhauer, Kierkegaard, Nietzsche. The self-expatriation of the Russian intellectuals of the period is well known. On the revolution as the new fatherland see Bakunin's *Programme et objet de l'Organisation Révolutionnaire des Frères Internationaux*, sec. 8: "La révolution devant se faire partout par le peuple, et la supreme direction devant en rester toujours dans le peuple organisé en fédération libre d'associations agricoles et industrielles—l'Etat révolutionnaire et nouveau s'organisant de bas en haut par voie de délégation révolutionnaire et embrassant tous les pays insurgés au nom des mêmes principes sans égard pour les vieilles frontières et pour les différences de nationalités, aura pour objet l'administration de services publics et non le gouvernement des peuples. Il constituera *la nouvelle patrie, l'Alliance de la Révolution Universelle* contre l'Alliance de toutes les Réactions."

tolate and this function overshadows by far his performances as an organizer. Lenin was able to evolve the doctrine still further, but his peculiar achievement is the ruthlessness of centralizing organization, leading to the uncompromising breaks with former associates. Moreover he is the great statesman who saw his moment and used it decisively, though in order to use it he had to graft the international workers' revolution onto the strength of a Russian peasant rebellion. With Stalin emerges the General Secretary of the movement as the organizer who builds the international revolution into the body of a people—a process which is sometimes interpreted in a mistaken analogy as the "Thermidor" of the Russian revolution. As an international movement this branch of the revolution has come to its end and the Communist parties in the Western countries are no longer the ferments of an international revolution but instruments of Russian state politics. What has survived in Russia is the apostolic and organizational centralism of the original movement, now built into the Soviet Constitution. The line of political success from Marx to Stalin is the line away from the original revolutionary impulse towards a dictatorial organization of power with an inflexible doctrine. The movement began as a revolt against the nation, against the state, against the church and bourgeois ideologies; it ended in Russian imperialism, in the power of the Soviet state and in the monopoly of indoctrination. This end was sensed by Bakunin even in Marx. Beyond the conflict of personal ambitions lies the profound antagonism between the authoritarianism of Marx and Bakunin's truly revolutionary existence. The importance of Bakunin for the understanding of the revolution lies precisely in those elements of his existence which prevented a durable political success. The insight into the necessities of apostolate and organization is present, but in the execution Bakunin relies primarily on the contagiousness of the charisma which he possessed in the highest degree. His action, even when in conception it is dictatorial and centralistic, operates always through arousing revolutionary sentiments in his fellowmen, through the intended transformation of personality. Moreover the organizations conceived by him are never envisaged as a "state within the state" destined to become the nucleus of state power after a successful coup; they are strictly meant as instruments for the destruction of existing institutions and would have to give way when success is obtained to the free federal life that is supposed to rise from the new revolutionary people.

In the absence of a will to create permanent institutions, the activities of Bakunin move in an atmosphere of the fantastic. This has sometimes aroused the sense of humor of his biographers, sometimes their scorn at his political naiveté, and it has led to the characterization of Bakunin as the Poet of the Revolution. Such sentiments and phraseology, pardonable as they are considering the facts, do not contribute much to understanding.

The element of the fantastic is rooted deeply in the disease of the spirit which constitutes the revolutionary crisis and it is related to the earlier discussed "magic of the extreme." In healthy spiritual existence the action on others receives its limits and its style through the spiritual substance that is to be communicated and, by such communication, to be transformed from a potentially to an actually common substance. In Plato's *Republic* the idea of the polis rests on assumptions with regard to the receptiveness of men for a mystical insight and in Plato's attempts at actual foundation the limits of action dwindle rapidly from the unsuccessful search for a philosopher-king to the narrow confines of the Academy. In Bakunin's state of pneumatic disease the style is determined by the striving of the radical, particular will to exist *as if* it were spiritual. Since, however, the communicable, limiting substance is missing, the attempts of the *as if* existence can be piled up without responsibility into a fantastic pyramid of foundations without substance.

The Alliance of 1868 was such an attempt, piling a further organization on top of the International without its distinctive purpose ever becoming particularly clear. But this excrescence was not all. In the fall of 1868 Bakunin invited the French socialist Charles Perron, whom he scarcely knew, to join the Alliance, and when Perron agreed he told him that even the Alliance might be contaminated by men who were not genuine revolutionaries and that there should be formed back of the Alliance a more restricted circle, the International Brothers. Perron was willing to become an International Brother if it had to be. But a few days later Bakunin suggested to him that even the International Brothers were too large a group and that back of them should be formed a Directorate of Three, of whom Perron should be one. And, of course, back of the Directorate there would rise into the revolutionary stratosphere the person of Bakunin himself.[11] The style of fantastic pyramiding is most clearly visible in Bakunin because there is lacking in him the limiting effect of the striving for a stable power organization which characterizes the revolutionary line from Marx to Stalin. Nevertheless the element of piling is a component in the successful line, too, stemming from the initial revolutionary situation. We can recognize it still in the pyramid of: (1) the mass of reactionary mankind which is good for nothing; (2) the select part of mankind, the "toilers," who are the salt of the earth; (3) the industrial workers who are the most advanced group of the toilers; (4) the Communist Party which is the vanguard of the proletariat; (5) the inner circle of leaders within the party, cul-

11. E. H. Carr, *Michael Bakunin*, pp. 348f.

minating in the Polit Bureau; (6) the stratosphere of the fathers and founders, that is of Marx and Lenin. The fantastic element deserves serious attention because the categories of the phantasma have on the one hand become the great obstacle to an adequate understanding of the real process of the revolution, particularly in Russia, while on the other hand their style is a formative force in the course of events.

The Nechaiev affair

The phantasma of foundation reached its climax in the Nechaiev affair.[12] Sergei Nechaiev was a Russian student who came to Geneva in 1869, at the age of 21. He presented himself to Bakunin as the leader and delegate of a revolutionary movement of students, with a Central Committee in Petersburg and affiliations throughout the country. The movement was imaginary. Bakunin took an immediate liking to the young man. Here was the young generation of Russia, represented by a man who resembled himself much in type, with an ardent revolutionary will and with the iron resolve to perform the work of destruction.[13] Bakunin matched Nechaiev's imaginary movement by creating for his benefit the World Revolutionary Alliance, consisting of a seal, and issued to Nechaiev a membership card for the Russian section, bearing the No. 2771, while Bakunin himself acted as the Central Committee of the European Revolutionary Alliance. Having thus established and allied their respective movements, the two men proceeded to produce some literature for them. The results were *Some Words to the Young Brethren in Russia, How the Revolutionary Question Presents Itself*, the *Principles of Revolution, An Appeal to the Officers of the Russian Army*, an *Appeal to the Russian Nobility*, and the *Catechism of the Revolutionary*.[14]

The Principles of Revolution

Of special importance for us are the *Principles of Revolution*. In the *Principles* the authors advance the thesis that revolution means the

12. Concerning the Nechaiev affair, see ibid., ch. 28.
13. Bakunin characterized Nechaiev in a letter of April 13, 1869, to James Guillaume in the following terms: "J'ai maintenant ici un spécimen de ces jeunes fanatiques qui ne doutent de rien et qui ne craignent rien, et qui ont posé pour principe qu'il en doit périr sous la main du gouvernement beaucoup, beaucoup, mais qu'on ne se reposera pas un instant jusqu'à ce que le peuple se soit soulevé"; James Guillaume, *L'Internationale, Documents et Souvenirs* (1864–78) (Paris, 1905), 1, p. 147.
14. *Michael Bakunin's Sozial-politischer Briefwechsel* (Stuttgart, 1895), pp. 344, 349, 358, 364, 369, 371.

radical substitution of new forms for all contemporary forms of European life. Only from complete "amorphism" can healthy forms arise. If elements of old forms are retained, they would poison the new life; a partial revolution is no revolution at all, as the events of 1848 have shown. "No genuine revolution has happened as yet; and if it happens it can only start in one state, but then it will have to spread to all countries." The personnel of the revolution is not to be found among those who are in leading positions in the present institutions. The new men have to live among the people and they have to be the mediating link between the masses so that the movement is given uniform direction, spirit and character. "This is the one and only meaning of leading a secret, preparatory organization." The leaders of a real popular revolution show themselves in action as soon as life has prepared them and they close their ranks in the course of the revolution itself. The long, subterranean work, devoid of real action, has brought an infiltration of men who fall back under the pressure of circumstances, but when the real popular movement comes nearer "the schism between thought and action becomes rarer." As the critical time approaches some revolutionaries will not be able to restrain their destructive rage and resort to individual action. High-placed persons who are representative of the governmental and economic corruption will be "annihilated." "This is the natural way": from individual action to an epidemic of violence, and finally to the great revolt. "We have to finish with that idealism which prevents action according to deserts; it has to be replaced by cruel, cold, ruthless consistency."

The revolution has a beginning and an end, that is it unfolds in the two phases of destruction and reconstruction. The true revolutionary has no plans for reconstruction. "All noble and holy men who were animated by the idea of a new life and who attempted to give the existing institutions a better form in a peaceful way, were persecuted and banned." Now the time for the cold, embittered fight has come; "our aim is the complete destruction of all fettering bonds." Since the present generation is itself under the influence of the abominable conditions which it has to destroy, reconstruction is not its task; this task is reserved for purer forces which will rise in the days of renovation. "The abominations of contemporary civilization in which we have grown up have deprived us of the ability to erect the paradisical structure of future life; of this future life we can form only nebulous ideas by imagining the opposite of the existing, revolting stuff." To the revolutionary, all contemplation of the nebulous future is criminal; it would only put obstacles in the course of destruction, and thereby make the future more remote. "In a practical cause this would be a useless desecration of the spirit." We have to submit to necessity and justice, and to dedicate ourselves to permanent, relentless destruction up to a *crescendo* in which no existing social form is left to be destroyed. Conspiracy is not the task of the present generation but actual fight from the first step. "They will call it terrorism!— But we must remain indifferent to all this howling and not enter into compromises with those who are destined to perish!"

These pages of the *Principles* are perhaps the most important document for understanding the explosiveness of a pneumatically diseased existence. They are revealing because the description is sufficiently close to traditional philosophical language to make the cause of the explosiveness intelligible. The contraction of existence into an explosive shell of destruction is due to the diminution and ultimate disappearance of the tension between contemplation and action. The *bios theoretikos*, as well as the life of the spirit, have vanished to the point that the planning of action and its ultimate orientation by the order of spirit become impossible. The particular will without orientation cannot express itself in purposeful action; it can express itself only in the negation of order without positive imagination of new order. The contraction of existence moreover is linked historically with the decadence of civilization, its destructiveness results from the concrete experience of the negative civilization against which it directs its action and it is not a negativism for its own sake. It is clearly understood as a crippled type of existence, which, nevertheless, has its historic function in producing the transition from the old world to the future paradise. Again the conscious sacrifice of personality appears that we noted earlier as an ingredient in terrorism. Hence the man who submits to the contraction is not a criminal but a "noble and holy man," the contraction is a feat of the spirit, and any expansion towards contemplation would in its turn be criminal and a desecration of the spiritual act. This consistency and clearness about the structure of revolutionary existence is peculiar to Bakunin and Nechaiev and it constitutes their genuine superiority over other revolutionaries—for even in evil there are degrees of profoundness.

Self-annihilation—the mystical "leap"

Bakunin has sounded the depth of negative existence and understood the mystical leap from the world into paradise. The total destruction to the point of amorphism is the intramundane counterpart to the spiritual "death to the world" and to the sanctification of life in preparation for the redeeming grace in death. The intramundane annihilation, however, does not do away only with the world that is to be destroyed; it also engulfs the personality of the revolutionary himself. For the revolutionary his action means his death to the life in the old world, but, unlike the Christian, he will not see the paradise of the future. Hence the question imposes itself: to what purpose does the revolutionary bring the sacrifice of his existence, if it does not serve, like the Christian sanctification, the catharsis and salvation of the soul? The answer will have to be: that in the revolutionary contraction we must recognize the self-defeating climax of the intramundane search for immortality through survival in posterity. The radical revolutionary does not simply live in posterity through his fame like a Renaissance statesman or man of letters; he rather moves into the role of the Savior who reverses the Fall and redeems of evil. And he does not assume the role of the Son only but even that of the Father. For Bakunin does not promise the Kingdom of God in the beyond, he promises the earthly paradise: God has driven man from paradise, Bakunin through his action will lead him back.

The mysticism of the contracted existence reappears in diluted form in revolutionary movements generally. Bakunin's prohibition, for instance, to contemplate the future life follows consistently from the insight into the nature of the "leap." But we find it also, in the Marxist movement, in the prohibition of discussion concerning the postrevolutionary society, although neither Marx nor Lenin envisaged their revolutionary action as the sacrifice of their personality. And we find the same hesitation to describe the future state in the National Socialist movement with its concentration on the "seizure of power," although the "seizure of power" contradicts the nihilism of a radical revolutionary existence. In both movements the hesitation with regard to a program stems from the initial mystical impulse; but this impulse is diluted by the compromise with the exigencies of establishing a permanent power structure. The intersection of the mystical with the worldly plane results, in Russia, in the conflict between a social reality that is bound to go the way of all institutionalization, and the idea of a classless and stateless society, an idea which inevitably has to evaporate; in National Socialism there resulted from the same interaction the catastrophic conflict between the unlimited expansiveness of the mystical will and the opposing power-reality of the surrounding world.

Bakunin the mystic has understood clearly that the revolutionary belongs to the world which he intends to destroy and that he will not see the paradise; he cannot even imagine it, and the place of such imagination is taken by the indulgence in opposites to the existing institutions. This insight into the character of radical revolutionary imagination is again peculiar to Bakunin. If the mysticism of imagining opposites is misunderstood, and if the attempt is made to elaborate positively the nature of future man and society, the results are grotesque. This attempt was made by Nietzsche. The sector is Nietzsche's work which projects the mysticism of the will to power into the symbool of the superman corresponds functionally to the "nebulous future" of Bakunin. The symbol of the superman is the opposite of the despiritualized middle-class society which Nietzsche despised; it is the *as if* creation of a new order without spiritual substance. In this respect—but not in others—Bakunin is superior to Nietzsche; the self-sacrifice in destructive action is evil but it is profound; the rivalry with God in negative contemplation is merely absurd.

The mystery of evil in historical existence

Finally, these pages open a general insight into the nature and function of destructiveness in society. The life of mankind in historical existence is not a life of sweet reason and sensible adjustment. In the lives of nations and civilizations, situations arise in which through delay of adjustment to changed circumstances the ruling groups become evil to the point that the accumulated hatreds of the victims break the impasse through violence. We are faced by the mystery of evil in history: by the mystery that evil sometimes can be remedied only by opposing evil; that destructive outbreak of evil supplies the force for breaking an unjust order and substituting an order of superior justice. It is with an awareness of this mystery that we have to read Bakunin's praise of criminality and of the Russian "robberdom."[15] The Russian robber is a peasant who escapes governmental oppression by taking to "the life of the woods." "The robberdom is one of the most honorable forms of Russian political life." It is the desperate protest of the people against the social order. Who does not sympathize with robberdom has no heart for the immeasurable suffering of the people. Robberdom is cruel and merciless, "but it is not more merciless and cruel than the governmental power which by its nefariousness has produced robberdom." The end of robberdom in Russia would mean either the final death of the people or its total liberation. "The robber is the only genuine revolutionary in Russia." When the robber and the peasant unite, the result will be the people's revolution. And Bakunin concludes with the appeal: "Let us throw ourselves into the people, into the movement of the people, into the revolt of the robbers and peasants. Let us unite the

15. *How the Revolutionary Question Presents Itself*, pp. 349ff.

isolated explosions of the peasants into a well-considered, but merciless revolution!"

With the progress of civilization the revolutionary symbolism changes and the industrial worker takes the place of the robber as the vanguard of the suffering people, but the principle of mobilizing the hatreds of the oppressed for the establishment of the new order remains a constant in the dynamics of revolution. In order to gain an adequate perspective of the problem we have to distinguish between the permanent problem of evil in revolution and the new factor that has entered the situation through Bakunin. Ignoble sentiments and interests are the firm cement of every order of man in the world, even of the most sublime; and a revolution which has to break the ignoble cement of an established order and supply new cement for the establishment of its own order needs a particularly strong dose of this ingredient. Man cannot escape nature, and one can discern the component of cruelty in the spiritual hardness even of Jesus and St. Francis. The storm of revolution, with its horrors and moral confusion, is by an inscrutable fate the darkness through which man has to wander in order to find the light of a new justice. We have to face the problem that on the level of historical existence on which the life of mankind in community is enacted, the man who assumes consciously the responsibility for releasing the storm is perhaps moved deeper by the sense of justice than the man who resists it because he wishes to preserve the values of the existing order; and that even the rascal who uses the upheaval for his personal profit, and who is dull to its moral and spiritual issues, may have a positive function in the establishment of the new order which is denied to the man who has to stand aside because he cannot sacrifice his integrity. The new factor that becomes manifest in Bakunin is the contraction of existence into a spiritual will to destroy, without the guidance of a spiritual will to order. This new absoluteness of evil, however, is not introduced into the situation by the revolutionary; it is the reflex of the actual despiritualization of the society from which the revolutionary emerges. The revolutionary crisis of our age is distinguished from earlier revolutions by the fact that the spiritual substance of Western society has diminished to the vanishing point, and that the vacuum does not show any signs of refilling from new sources. Bakunin understood his own situation thoroughly; in his anarchism he consciously realized one half of the revolution, the half which he called the "beginning"; he knew that with success the other half would claim its rights. This other half has not been forthcoming yet in the successful line of the revolution, and the crisis of the spirit which manifested itself in Bakunin's mysticism of evil lingers on. It lingers on in Russia in spite of the fact that an element of Western enlightened humanism is preserved in the Marxian conception of the worker as the true man.

The late work of Bakunin

In the decade of 1863–73, Bakunin produced a considerable body of written work which in one way or another contributes to the clarification of his late anarchistic ideas.[16] The fraction of the *corpus* that is of systematic relevance is suprisingly small, however. The discrepancy between quantity and substance is due partly to the occasional character of the writings, partly to certain peculiarities of exposition. We have to indicate, therefore, the principles of elimination rather than of selection which will permit us to isolate the relevant nucleus.

A first section of the work of this period can be eliminated because its consists of memoranda and lectures for congresses and workers' audiences; the author is restricted in these pieces to a dogmatic statement of his position and cannot enter into a critical elaboration of his ideas. Other pieces of this section have the form of polemics against political opponents and again do not lend themselves to systematic exposition. And the more voluminous writings of this class have the disconcerting habit of starting as a letter to a friend, then growing into an article on some question which arrested Bakunin's attention, and expanding finally into a volume of which the unit is created rather by a chain of associations than by the organization of problems. This circumstantial and associational character of Bakunin's writing produces a vast amount of repetition without an increase of penetration. A second section of the work can be eliminated because Bakunin had acquired the stylistic idiosyncrasies of a positivistic dogmatist. He was in possession of the truth and did not have to worry too much about the critical foundation of his problems. As in the case of Comte, a large proportion of Bakunin's writing is elaboration of detail which stands or falls with the validity of the fundamental assumptions. The foundations of a social science were laid for Bakunin by Auguste Comte and his *philosophie positive;* all Bakunin had to do was to draw the consequences, or at best to expunge some of the obscurantist elements of the great thinker.[17] This profuse application again can be neglected.

Not entirely to be eliminated are the references to the future state of

---

16. Michel Bakounine, *Oeuvres*, 6 vols. (Paris, 1907–13).
17. *L'Antithéologisme*, *Oeuvres*, 1, p. 71.

society, though we can dispose of them briefly. Bakunin knew, as we have seen, about the "nebulousness" of perspectives into the future, and he understood that a futuristic imagination would have to proceed by the creation of opposites to the present state. Nevertheless, he indulged occasionally in the enunciation of such negations—much to the fright of a not too large bourgeois public. Religion is an instrument of degradation—therefore away with religion; private property is the instrument of exploitation—therefore away with private property in the instruments of production; bureaucracy is an instrument of oppression —therefore away with the *salariat;* the state is the source of evil compulsion—therefore away with the state; all authority in general is a restraint on liberty—therefore away with theology, with institutionalized science (against Comte), and with any form of institutionalized political leadership (against Mazzini).

In these futuristic indulgences there appear only a few points which merit attention because they are related to concrete experiences of the present state. One of them is Bakunin's insistence on federalization from the bottom to the top as the structural law of future society. Federalization is again an opposite to the centralized state, but it is not a mere negation; it has a positive content insofar as this pair of opposites is modelled on the contrast between American federalism and French revolutionary centralism: "It should be clear to all who really wish the emancipation of Europe that we have to reject the politics of the French revolution (while preserving our sympathies for its great socialist and humanitarian ideas) and to adopt resolutely the politics of freedom of the North Americans."[18] It may be doubted that Bakunin's insight into the nature and problems of American federalism was profound; nevertheless, the image of the American federal democracy has exerted a vague guiding influence not only on Bakunin, but generally on the federalistic visions of anti-state revolutionaries.

A second touch of reality makes itself felt in a passage which reveals what is perhaps the profoundest experiential reason for Bakunin's anti-statism. In the course of his polemic against Mazzini, Bakunin reflects on the nature of man: if you give man the possibility of doing evil, that is if you nourish his vanity, his ambition, his cupidity at the expense of others, he will do evil. "We certainly are sincere socialists and revolutionaries, *but:* if we would be given power and could preserve it only a few months, we would not be what we are today. As socialists we are

---

18. *Proposition Motivée au Comité Central de la Ligue de la Paix et de la Liberté, Oeuvres,* 1, p. 13.

convinced, you and I, that the social environment, the position, the conditions of existence are stronger than the will and the intelligence of the strongest and most energetic individual. And precisely for this reason we do not demand natural but social equality of all men as the condition of justice and the basis of morality. And that is why we detest power, all power, as the people detests it."[19] This passage is of importance for the understanding of the revolutionary mind because it shows in operation the fallacy which assumes the "social environment" as an independent factor and neglects the interaction between environment and man. Bakunin is aware that the opportunities of the environment can be a temptation; he seems not to be aware that the fundamental structure of any social environment has something to do with the nature of man which creates it. In this passage, if we take it in isolation, Bakunin gives the appearance of having never thought of the possibility that on the morning of the revolution human nature will set to work to create a new environment with opportunities for doing evil, which perhaps will not be precisely the same as the ones just abolished but still will be a comparable substitute. For many revolutionaries this fallacy is, indeed, the fundamental dogma which inspires and justifies their attack on the shortcomings of society. As far as Bakunin is concerned, the impasse is broken in the main line of his thought by the faith in a mystically renovated human nature which produces the cataclysm of destruction. Nevertheless, the passage itself is not qualified in the context by a reminder of the mystical *renovatio;* and it therefore shows instructively the transition from a mystical revolutionary existence as represented by Bakunin in his clearer moments to the vulgar revolutionary dogma that the nature of man changes automatically with a change of institutions. In the total evolution of the dogma we can distinguish, therefore, the following three phases: (1) at the mystical center is the radical eschatological sentiment which expresses itself consistently in the demand of the *renovatio* as the primary condition for a perfect state of society; (2) a transitional phase is marked by Bakunin's assumption in the passage under discussion: that the nature of man will not change and that, therefore, compulsory institutions with their temptations have to be abolished; (3) the final form is the vulgarian dogma which animates the successful line of revolution: that with the deposing of a ruling group the new rulers will have a changed nature so that with the successful "seizure of power" the new society can move towards perfection without a radical revolution involving the eschatological change of heart.

19. *Circulaire à mes amis d'Italie, Oeuvres,* 6, pp. 343ff.

Satanism and materialism

What remains after these eliminations and corollaries are a few systematic ideas, best formulated in the study on *Dieu et l'État* and in the appendix on the *Fantôme Divin*.[20]

The first idea to be disengaged from this body of writing is the Satanic inversion of the Fall. Bakunin narrates the story of *Genesis* with the prohibition to eat from the Tree of Knowledge: "God wanted to deprive man of the consciousness of self; He wanted him eternally to remain an animal, on its four paws before the eternal God, his Creator and Master. But then comes Satan, the eternally revolted, the first *libre penseur* and emancipator of the world. He shames man for his ignorance and his bestial obedience; he emancipates him and presses on his forehead the seal of freedom and humanity by persuading him to disobey and to eat from the fruit of knowledge (*science*)."[21] Bakunin then continues to explain what he considers to be the true meaning of the myth: "Man is emancipated, he has left his animality and has constituted himself as man. He has begun his history; the specifically human development started from disobedience and knowledge (*science*), that is from *revolt* and *thought*."[22] In this act of emancipation originates the historical nature of man with its three strata of animality, thought and revolt; and the three strata of human nature manifest themselves socially in the creation of the three realms of social and private economy, of science, and of freedom.

Having used the myth as a starting point, Bakunin drops its symbolism and proceeds to give to his conception of the nature of man a basis of materialistic metaphysic. The materialism of Bakunin is "genuine" in the sense of Lucretian materialism as opposed to a phenomenalist materialism. In its development Bakunin displays considerable critical acumen. He is careful not to deny the autonomy of moral and intellectual phenomena; he does not attempt to explain them as epiphenomena of matter. He distinguishes between the *vile matière* of the idealists who project the most important content of matter into God so that nothing remains but a *caput mortuum* deprived of its spiritual content, and the matter of the materialist who conceives matter as

20. The study on *Dieu et l'État* forms part of the long manuscript which bears the title *L'Empire Knouto-Germanique et la Révolution sociale;* it was published separately by Elisee Reclus and Cafiero in 1882; the appendix has the title *Considérations philosophiques sur le Fantôme Divin, sur le Monde réel et sur l'Homme.* Both manuscripts are unfinished. *Oeuvres*, vol. 2.

21. Ibid., pp. 20ff.

22. Ibid., p. 23.

containing the forces of life and intelligence, to be manifested in the course of progressive evolution. Bakunin's matter is not matter in opposition to mind; it is not the matter of inorganic nature; it is rather the fundamental force of the universe which manifests itself in the differentiated realms of being—in the inorganic as well as in the organic and in the moral and intellectual realms. As a consequence of these assumptions, the materialism of Bakunin would appear to be rather close to the metaphysical conceptions of Nietzsche, of Valéry and Santayana.

The genuine materialistic construction in Bakunin is broken, however, by a line of thought which announces itself in the designation of the specifically human element as "revolt." Existence in the mode of revolt precludes existence in the inner dimension in which the soul opens itself towards its own ground. Freedom cannot be for Bakunin, as it is for Schelling, the identity with inner necessity. Freedom is "domination over external things, founded on the respectful observation of the laws of nature."[23] The science of phenomena, not the *cognitio fidei*, is the road to freedom. There is submission in Bakunin, too, but a submission to the experience of the senses, not of the soul. "Wherein consists everybody's experience? In the experience of his senses, directed by his intelligence. I, for my part, do not accept anything that I have not encountered materially, that I have not seen, heard and, if necessary, touched with my fingers. For me personally that is the only means of assuring myself of a thing."[24] Experience of phenomena alone, however, does supply knowledge of means; it does not supply guidance for action. What then is the source of guiding principles? Quite consistently, Bakunin again appeals to the laws of nature. Freedom is domination over nature, founded on submission to nature. It is domination over nature insofar as the knowledge of nature's laws provides us with the knowledge of means for the realization of ends; it is submission to nature insofar as the ends themselves are to be found in nature. But where in nature do we find the ends?

At this point the problem of freedom merges for Bakunin with the problem of social organization. Even if we know the ends of nature and are willing to submit to them, the submission becomes impossible if conflicting ends are imposed on man by social authority. The will to submit to nature has to be secured in its freedom against social intervention. Bakunin proclaims, therefore, as the negative criterion of freedom, "the independence from pretentious and despotic acts of other

23. Ibid., p. 246.
24. Ibid., pp. 318ff.

men." But how do we know whether an act is pretentious and despotic or not? This question has to be decided ultimately by the authority of "political revolt." What arouses revolt is despotism. Freedom can be secured only by the creation of a social environment which does not incite to revolt, and such an environment can be created only by the organization or society in conformity with the laws of nature "which are inherent in all soicety."[25] This seems to be a circle insofar as society, in order to provide the conditions of freedom, will have to be organized in accordance with the laws of nature which are inherent in all society anyway. And setting aside the problem that society should be organized in accordance with its own laws, we still do not know what precisely these inherent laws are. As a solution for both problems, Bakunin offers the practical advice "to model one's spirit and heart as often as possible after the spirit and the real interests of the masses."[26] To the end, Bakunin shrinks back from an articulated idea of society; the laws are never defined. The right order is determined dynamically through a permanently renewed accordance of the individual soul in revolt with the sentiments of the masses. Freedom remains an existential tension between revolt against authority and immersion into the people. In the late work, Bakunin frequently has recourse to the flux of nature as the image most adequately expressing his existential feelings: mankind in history is a sea in movement, and man is a wave crest, curling up for a moment, to be dissolved forever. In the mysticism of the flux, in this ultimate balance of revolt by immersion in the natural stream of humanity, it is perhaps permitted to recognize the specifically Russian component in Bakunin—though one should always be cautious with such surmises. This last word of Bakunin, assuming the form of systematic materialism, is substantially the same as his first in 1842: the inner return is to be replaced by the political revolt; the spiritual orientation by the orientation towards the "real interests" of the masses; and the renovation of the soul by the immersion into the revolution of the people.

25. Ibid., p. 246.
26. *Réponse à l'Unità Italiana, Oeuvres*, 6, p. 299.

X. MARX: INVERTED DIALECTICS

In discussing Comte we reflected on the difficulties that beset the interpretation of a thinker whose ideas form part of the contemporary crisis. A good deal of what we had to say there is also valid in the case of Karl Marx (1818–83). All major works of Comte were published during his lifetime and in the struggle between integral and intellectual Positivists it was at least possible to appeal to Comte himself. In the case of Marx, however, the struggle of the partisans has even affected the accessibility of his work. Since the Marxists considered them unimportant, a considerable body of manuscripts remained unpublished until the volumes of the *Marx-Engels Gesamtausgabe* began to appear in the years 1927–32. Within the Marxist movement of the first generation there had arisen the legend of an early, philosophical Marx who, circa 1845,[1] broke through to his true insights in economics, sociology and philosophy of history. Hence, according to this legend the early work was not worth reading. As a consequence, for the wider public Marx became the author of the *Communist Manifesto* and *Das Kapital*, the founder of the First International and, in a wider sense, of the Communist movement; he became the Marx of the Marxists and the Father of the Russian Revolution. Practically in his lifetime the historical Marx disappeared behind the mythical ancestor of the movement that bears his name. The transfiguration was so thorough that the question of the "real" Marx became the question whether he was the Marx of Bernstein and Karl Kautsky, or the Marx of Rosa Luxemburg and Lenin. The question whether the claims of diadochi and epigoni were not altogether doubtful was never raised seriously.[2] This impasse opened only when, after the First World War and the Russian Revolution, the Marx-Engels-Lenin Institute in Moscow began publishing the works of the *patres* as a matter of ecclesiastical duty, and when, at the same time, German Social Democrats began to take some interest in the manuscript treasures in their party archives. As a consequence of this

1. I am giving 1845 as the approximate legendary date because Lenin (in his encyclopedia article of 1914 on "The Teachings of Karl Marx") assumes that by this time the "materialism" of Marx had found its definite shape.
2. Even today the situation is so heated and confused that it will not be quite unnecessary to stress that we do not raise this question in order to establish a "real" or "true" Marx in our turn. It is a question that arises as a matter of historical analysis. Our attempt at presenting the ideas of Marx does neither intend to save him from the Marxists, nor to create a "true" Marx in rivalry with others; our analysis has the purpose of establishing a critically tenable picture of Marx's ideas and, at the same time, of explaining how Marxism could develop out of them.

curious development, a serious interpretation of Marxian ideas got under way only after 1932.[3]

Behind this story of misinterpretation and rediscovery lies the tragedy of an activist mystic. In the fundamental structure of his activist mysticism, Marx conforms to the well-known pattern. He was aware of the crisis of his age and his awareness was intense to the degree of an acute consciousness of epoch. He experienced the age as "a parting asunder of the times," the old world of corruption and iniquity to be followed by a new world of freedom. The contemporary bourgeois society "closed the prehistory of human society" and after an epochal upheaval the real history of society will begin.[4] The transition from the old to the new world will not be achieved by a simple change of institutions, but like Bakunin, Marx assumes a *metanoia*, a change of heart, as the decisive event that will inaugurate the new epoch. For its production, Marx relies on the experience of the revolution itself. "For the mass creation of communist consciousness, as well as for the achievement of the object itself, a mass change of man is necessary which can occur only during a practical movement, that is during a *revolution*. Hence, the revolution is necessary not only because the *ruling* class cannot be overthrown in any other way, but also because only through a revolution can the *overthrowing* class reach the point where it gets rid of the old filth (*Dreck*) and becomes capable of a new foundation of society."[5] The revolution, thus, is conceived as an intramundane process with two main functions: (1) the function of an institutional overthrow, and (2) the function of purification.

The fundamental structure is conventional and the tragedy of the idea is foreknown: if the predicted revolution should ever take place, the heart of man will not change and the new world will be exactly as prehistorical and iniquitous as the old world. Nevertheless, even on this level of general structure the idea contains a peculiarity that was apt

3. One of the best, though brief, analyses of the early thought of Marx is the introduction by S. Landshut and J. P. Mayer to their edition of Karl Marx, *Der Historische Materialismus. Die Fruehschriften*, 2 vols. (Leipzig, 1932). Of great value are the sections on Marx in Karl Loewith, *Von Hegel bis Nietzsche* (Zurich, New York, 1941). Of special interest for the philosophical anthropology of Marx is the section "Feuerbach et l'illusion religeuse" in Henri de Lubac, S.J., *Le Drame de l'Humanisme Athée*, 3rd ed. (Paris, 1945). The English reader will find a report on the content of Marx's writings up to 1847 in H. P. Adams, *Karl Marx in his Earlier Writings* (London, 1940). Unfortunately the author, while reporting the contents, has refrained from analysing the problems of Marx.

4. Karl Marx, *Zur Kritik der Politischen Oekonomie* (1959), ed. Karl Kautsky, 2nd, enlarged ed. (Stuttgart, 1907), p. lvi.

5. *Deutsche Ideologie* (1845–46), 5, p. 60. (All references, unless marked otherwise, are to the respective volumes of the *Marx-Engels-Gesamtausgabe. Erste Abteilung*.)

to have, and actually did have, far-reaching political consequences before the misery had run its course. We are speaking of the double function of the revolution. Marx did not, like earlier sectarians, first create a "People of God" with changed hearts and then lead the People into a revolution. He wanted the revolution to happen first and then let the "People of God" spring from the experience of the revolution. While for Marx personally the overthrow of the bourgeoisie was senseless unless the revolution produced the change of heart, the historical proof that the overthrow was not the proper method for producing such a change would only come after the revolution had occurred. The pneumapathological nonsense of the idea could not break on the rock of reality before the damage had been done. In the meantime a tremendous amount of disturbance and destruction could be engineered, animated by the pathos of eschatological heroism and inspired by the vision of a terrestial paradise.

Even this peculiarity of the Marxian idea, however, might not have had the historical consequences which we already know unless a further factor had entered the structure of the idea. The Marxian double function of the revolution in itself does not differ substantially from Bakunin's idea. Nevertheless, Bakunin's conception of a total destruction out of which mysteriously a young and beautiful world would be born was a bit too vague for the average man, who wants to have at least *some* idea where the revolution will lead him. The factor that makes the Marxian idea effective to a degree which Bakunin's ineffectual anarchism could never have achieved is the content which Marx gives to his vision of the new world. We must therefore examine the background and nature of Marx's vision.

The vision—the realms of necessity and freedom

Marx is distinguished among the revolutionaries of his generation by his superior intellectual powers. As a mystic he could evoke a new world, but as a shrewd thinker he would not fall into the various traps which beset the path of eschatological speculation. From his insight into the evils of the industrial system he would not jump to the conclusion that the industrial system ought to be abolished nor would he indulge in the type of socialist fantasies which he stigmatized as "utopian." In particular, he would never countenance the idea that the remedy for industrialized society could be found in a return to more primitive forms of production. Whatever the new world would bring, it certainly would have an industrialized society like the old world, only more so. Moreover, not for a moment would he entertain the Comtean metamorphosis of French-Catholic traditions with its priesthood of positivistic intellectuals and its temporal power consisting of the managerial class. Through Hegel and the young Hegelians he was steeped in the traditions of intellectualized Lutheran Protestantism, hence his new world would have to be a "true democracy," that is a society in which the new spirit would be realized in the concrete existence of every single man. Marx, thus, envisages a new world in which mankind operates an elaborate industrial apparatus for the satisfaction of its wants, while spiritually men have entered a new realm of freedom through the "emancipating" experience of the revolution.

We have drawn the general outline of his vision and we shall now turn to the account that Marx himself gives of it. For this purpose we shall not use the formulations of the early works but rather the last account in order to put it beyond doubt that the vision of Marx was not a peculiarity of his "philosophical" youth, but was the motivation of his thought to the end of his life.

In volume 3 of the *Kapital*, Marx reflects on the advantages of the capitalist system of production. As compared with more primitive forms of production, the capitalist system permits a more rapid expansion of productivity so that, with a minimum of sacrifice, an increasing population can be provided with an increasing amount of goods. This excellent system must be maintained after the revolution for it alone makes possible the reduction of the workday and the corresponding creation of leisure time for the broad masses of mankind. "The shortening of the working-day is the fundamental condition." "The realm of freedom begins only where work that is determined by need and external aims ends; in the nature of the case, it lies beyond the sphere of material production in the strict sense." Civilized man, just as primitive man, must struggle with nature in order to satisfy his wants; no form of production and no revolution can abolish the human condition. This "realm of natural necessity" will even expand with advancing civilization for wants will multiply and increase. As far as there is any freedom in this realm at all, it will consist in the "rational regulation of this metabolism with nature." "Socialized man" (*der vergesellschaftete Mensch*), that is "the associated producers" will bring the metabolism under their "communal control" instead of being dominated by it as by a blind power; they will dispose of it with a minimum of effort and under conditions that will satisfy the dignity of human nature. In spite of all such improvements, it "still will be a realm of necessity." Only beyond such necessity "begins the unfolding of human forces that can be considered an end in itself"; only here "begins the true realm of freedom—which however can only blossom out of the realm of necessity as its basis."[6]

These passages are probably the clearest formulation which Marx has ever given of his vision. He distinguishes between the realms of natural necessity and human freedom. The realm of necessity comprises the system of economic production in which the dependence of human existence on nature manifests itself. The precise extent of this realm is essential for the understanding of Marx's vision. The realm of economic production does not cease to be the realm of natural necessity when it has undergone the revolutionary change from private property to "communal control." The abolition of private property is not an end in itself and communal control is of interest only insofar as it will reduce drudgery and working hours for the broad masses and leave them with more leisure time. These newly gained hours, free of necessity, are the soil in which the "true realm of freedom" will grow and hence it would be of interest to know *what* Marx envisaged as growing in these hours of leisure. On this point, however, little is to be found in his whole work. In the pages which we analyse at present we find only the remark that capitalist society is characterized "by pure loafing of one part of society." This may be a clue. Most probably Marx did not plan an epochal revolution in order to democratize the art of loafing; and most probably he would have considered as bourgeois loafing most of the "entertainment," "amusement," "recreation," and "play," in which our working contemporaries indulge in their leisure hours. If "loafing" is ruled out, what then did he mean by the realm of freedom? We only know for certain that he meant some kind of action which he defined as "an unfolding of human forces that can be considered an end in itself." Considering his background of classical scholarship, he may have thought of something like an Aristotelian *bios theoretikos* and *schole*. But we should not press this point too far. Let us stress only that communal control of the industrial instruments of production is *not* the ultimate purpose of the revolution; the ultimate purpose is the realm of freedom. Communal control will only furnish the material basis and the freedom that will blossom out into a realm does *not* stem from the material basis but from the experience of the revolution. Let us emphasize again that this was the idea of Marx not only in his early years, but in his last period when he was working on the third volume of *Kapital*.

6. *Das Kapital. Kritik der politischen Oekonomie*, Herausgegeben von Friedrich Engels (Hamburg, 1894), pp. 354ff.

The analysis of Marx's vision will enable us now to understand the interlocking of the following problems: (1) the derailment of Marx in his later yers; (2) the derailment of his ideas in the Marxist movement that followed from it; (3) the legend of a "philosophical" early Marx; (4) the miscarriage of Marxism as far as the realization of Marx's vision is concerned; and (5) the political success of Marxism in a form that would cause Marx, if he could see it, to pronounce his favorite four-letter word.

The derailment

Marx devoted the work of his early years, that is roughly of the decade from 1837 to 1847, to the elaboration of the idea of which we have studied a late expression. A good deal of this early work was never published, and was not even cast into form for publication, because it had served its purpose in clarifying his thought. And once the vision was clear, revolutionary action would have been in order, not further writing or talking. As a matter of fact, not much writing or talking about the vision was done by Marx in his later years. The concoction of utopian programs was ruled out. The realm of necessity would be an industrial society minus the bourgeoisie. Organizational details were not so important since administrative control in the new world would have no political implications because of the change of heart. And the realm of freedom had to grow; it could not be planned. At this point, when Marx seemed to be faced with the alternative of sinking into revolutionary existence in the manner of Bakunin or of lapsing into silence, the grandiose possibility for writing and acting opened that filled the rest of his life: it was the preparation of the revolution.

This possibility was rooted in the structure of his idea. If Marx had been obliged by his idea to create the realm of freedom as to its substance, if he had been obliged to produce a revolutionary *renovatio* in his fellowmen through his spiritual authority, not much would have followed except his personal tragedy. But no such obligation was imposed on him. Freedom would be the result of the revolution and the revolution itself would be enacted within the realm of necessity. In order to engineer the revolution, Marx did not have to appeal to the spirit; it was sufficient to move the Acheronta in man. In his idea Marx wanted to save and ultimately secure the dignity of man; in his action he could indulge in his contempt of man. Moreover, the revolution in the realm of necessity had a clearly circumscribed content, that is the overthrow of the bourgeoisie. Hence preparing the revolution meant the well circumscribed task of (1) critically analysing the factors in capitalist society that of necessity would disintegrate the system to the point where the proletarian revolution would be both inevitable and successful, and (2) forging the proletarian organization that in the decisive hour would strike the blow. In brief: the maieutic work within the realm of necessity could, and did, become for Marx an occupation in itself. He did not become the leader of a revolution; instead he wrote the *Communist Manifesto*—the call, not for a revolution, but for the organization of the forces that would execute the inevitable revolution. He did not write a treatise on the future communist society, instead he wrote the *Kapital*, the analysis of the moribund society. In the first half of the 1840's, we may say, the mood of Marx was still close to the mood of Bakunin's revolutionary existence; from then on, the emphasis of his life and work shifts increasingly to the midwifery of the revolution. This shift from making to preparing a revolution is what we call the derailment of Marx. The immenseness of the preparatory work in the realm of necessity completely overshadowed the eschatological experience which had motivated the revolutionary vision as well as the ultimate purpose of the revolution, that is the realization of the realm of freedom.

The Marxist movement—Revisionism

In the life of Marx, the derailment into maieutic operations overshadowed experience and idea but it never broke the revolutionary tension. However deeply Marx was immersed in his intellectual and organizational preparations, he never lost his eschatological vision. When it descended to the level of the movement, the derailment had far-reaching consequences. The penchant for preparing the revolution could be followed by men who never had the experience in which the Marxian ideas originated. Marx had actually experienced the death of the spirit through Hegel, and his existence moved in the tension between this experience and the hope for renovation of the spirit in a new world after the revolution. The Marxists of the movement for the most part were men who could not experience the death of the spirit because they were dead souls themselves and consequently the Marxian vision of freedom meant little, if anything, to them. Nevertheless, while they could not experience the tension of spiritual death and freedom, they still could experience the tension between the present, grievous state of the working class and a future state with a shorter workday and a higher standard of living. If the revolution could not bring the change of heart and the realm of freedom, it still could bring a vastly improved realm of necessity and the overthrow of the bourgeoisie.

With increasing distance from the original Marxian tension, the immanent logic of the derailment asserted itself more strongly. Preparing the revolution intellectually through the writing of articles and books and preparing it organizationally through party work and parliamentary representation became an occupation in which one could live and die without ever coming near a revolution. Famous dicta became possible, like Bernstein's "What is commonly called the ultimate end of socialism is nothing to me, the movement is everything," or Karl Kautsky's "The socialist party is a revolutionary party, it is not a revolution-making party." Such dicta indicate that with the lengthening of the preparatory period, the revolution itself was being transformed into an evolutionary process. This trend was inevitable if the purpose of the revolution could be exhausted by occurrences in the realm of necessity. If the aims of the shorter workday, of higher wages and of communal control of the industrial apparatus could be achieved within a reasonable time "by means of economic, legislative and moral pressure" (K. Kautsky) there was no point in making a revolution. In the derailment, the existential change of heart had flattened out into a gradual improvement of the workers' lot through an appeal to social morality. The Revisionist wing of the derailment had become in substance a movement for social reform.

In the realm of ideas Marxist problems are of a rather petty nature. Since in actual history, however, Marxism is of immense importance (at least for the time being) it is excusable if we add a note on the context from which the dictum of Karl Kautsky is taken. The sentence quoted above occurs in an article by Kautsky in the *Neue Zeit* of 1893 (it is reprinted in Karl Kautsky, *Der Weg zur Macht* [Berlin, 1910]).

We quoted the sentence in order to show the evolutionary trend in the process of derailment but Kautsky, on the contrary, advances his dictum in order to show that he is an ardent revolutionary. As he explains it: "We know that our aims can be accomplished only through a revolution but we also know that it is no more in our power to make this revolution than it is in the power of our opponents to prevent it. Hence we do not even think of instigating a revolution or of preparing it."[7] This apparent nonsense finds its solution through Kautsky's conviction that because the revolution must occur as a matter of historical necessity (as proven by Marx), all the revolutionary has to do is to wait until bourgeois society has sufficiently disintegrated (which is inevitable) and then take over. As long as disintegration has not proceeded far enough, revolutions are doomed to failure. The "true revolutionary" will keep his discipline and wait; it is only the utopian

7. *Der Weg zur Macht* (Berlin, 1910), p. 52.

who will rush into adventures before the time is ripe. Thus, by definition, a revolutionary is one who knows that the proletarian revolution is inevitable and who lives in pleasant anticipation of that event, hastening it, perhaps, with a bit of "pressure" of the indicated kind. The interesting point about Kautsky's position is the fact that he can support it by quoting from the sacred texts of Marx and Engels.

The derailment which in Kautsky assumed somewhat comic proportions originated in the period 1848–50. Up to the February revolution of 1848, we might say, Marx lived in eschatological tension in the sense that he expected the epochal revolution to occur in the very near future, he expected the realm of freedom to be established in a matter of a few years. The *Communist Manifesto* (section 4) still breathes this spirit: "The communists turn their attention chiefly to Germany, because that country is on the eve of a bourgeois revolution that is bound to be carried out under more advanced conditions of European civilization, and with a much more developed proletariat, than that of England was in the seventeenth and of France in the eighteenth century, and because the bourgeois revolution in Germany will be but the prelude to an immediately following proletarian revolution." When the revolution, however, miscarried, a lot of explaining was necessary. Marx explained the first phase of the miscarriage in *Die Klassenkämpfe in Frankreich* (1850), the second phase (after the *coup d'état* of Napoleon) in *Der Achtzehnte Brumaire des Louis Napoleon* (1852). But theoretical explanations were not enough; members of the League of Communists had to be told what would happen next. This duty Marx discharged in his *Ansprache der Zentralbehörde an den Bund* (1850). In this tract Marx developed for the first time what later came to be called the "tactic" of the class struggle while waiting for the actual revolution, and it was here that he coined the new slogan: *Die Revolution in Permanenz.* The permanence lasted for quite a long time. On the next major occasion, after the miscarriage of the Paris Commune, an explanation was due again and it appeared in the form of an address on *Der Bürgerkrieg in Frankreich* (1871). After the death of Marx, Engels took over. In a study *Zur Geschichte des Bundes der Kommunisten* (1885) he still saw the revolution just around the corner. He based his prediction on the "rule" that revolutions throughout the nineteenth century had occurred at intervals of fifteen to eighteen years.[8] Since the last revolution had occurred in 1870, the next, according to Engels, was due in about three years. The last utterance of

8. Engels's *Geschichte* is reprinted in Karl Marx, *Enthüllungen über den Kommunistenprozess zu Köln*, ed. Mehring (Berlin, 1914). The prediction is found on p. 45.

Engels on the subject, which occurs shortly before his death, appears in his introduction to the reissue of the *Klassenkämpfe in Frankreich* of 1895. Engels dwells on the irony that revolutionaries thrive much better on legal than on illegal methods. In the expansion of Social Democracy, measured in terms of electoral support, he sees an undermining of society comparable to that of the undermining of the Roman Empire by the Christians. He stresses with gusto the fact that within a generation of Diocletian's great persecution of the Christians in 303, Constantine made Christianity the official religion of the Empire. He expects a similar happy solution within a generation of the persecutions of the socialists by the German Diocletian, Bismarck. Karl Kautsky could claim, in view of all this, that he was carrying on the torch of permanence which was lighted by Marx after the eschatological expectations had been discouraged by the events of 1848. Tracing this continuity permits us to fix the beginning of Marx's derailment at about 1850.

The Marxist movement—Communism

The derailment which led to the Communist revolution seems at first sight to be what it claims to be, that is a return to the "true" Marx. And the claim is justified, indeed, insofar as the radicals who began to stir in the 1890's did not accept evolutionary reformism as a substitute for revolution. Lenin's attitude toward the Kautsky wing of Social Democracy resembles very closely that of Marx toward the English trade-union movement. The rejection of democratic cooperation, the rejection of sluggish socialist mass parties, the shaping of an élite, disciplined organization of professional revolutionaries in the form of the Bolshevik (later Communist) Party, the concentration on the seizure of power, the deep distrust of, and contempt for, the broad masses who can be "bribed" by immediate advantages into the betrayal of the revolution—all this certainly indicates the return to a genuine revolutionary tension. When we compare Lenin's Geneva speech (1908) on *Lessons of the Commune* with Engel's *Introduction*, of 1895, to the *Class Struggles in France*, we feel a new breeze. Engels, fascinated by the two million German Social Democratic voters, accentuates the possibilities of peaceful advance toward the hour of decision. He considers the German bloc the "shock troops" of the international proletarian army, a force not to be frittered away in preliminary skirmishes. Nothing could halt the development of this force except a bloodbath like that of the Paris Commune of 1871, hence he urged the avoidance of imprudent revolts as the first duty of the movement. Lenin, still fresh with memories of the Russian Revolution of 1905, stresses the violent aspects of the Commune as its most valuable lesson. The Commune failed because it was still encumbered with dreams of establishing justice and did not ruthlessly expropriate the expropriators, because it indulged in magnanimity toward its enemies and tried to influence them morally instead of killing them, and because it did not fully grasp the importance of purely military action in civil war and through its hesitations gave the enemy time to rally. Nevertheless, the Commune did fight, it demonstrated the value of civil war and thereby taught the proletariat "how to handle concretely" the problems of revolution. The Russian insurrection of December, 1905 showed that the lesson had been learned. The "Soviets of workers' and soldiers' deputies" symbolize the double aspect of the revolution. There is a time for using peaceful weapons in preparing the revolution, but there comes a time when the proletariat must destroy its enemies in open battle. An insurrection that fails is worth the sacrifice because it keeps alive the consciousness that revolution means imminent civil war and violence.

The revolutionary tension, thus, is regained at least on the level of action in the realm of necessity. Whether the Marxian vision of the realm of freedom, however, was seriously recaptured at any time is doubtful. Certainly a shadow of that vision appears in the work of Lenin, and this is prolonged into the very formulations of the Soviet Constitution of 1936 in the recognition that the successful socialist revolution has so far not produced the genuine communist realm in which the state will wither away and men will work to the best of their ability without the incentive of compensation according to performance. The distinction between socialist and communist society entered into the style of the Soviet Union as a union of *socialist* soviet republics that would be guided to the perfect state by a *communist* party.[9] It must be doubted, however, that even before the Revolution of

9. The distinction goes back to Karl Marx, *Zur Kritik des sozialdemokratischen Parteiprogramms 1875*. This critique of the Gotha Program was reprinted by Hermann Duncker in his edition of Marx-Engels, *Kritiken der Sozialdemokratischen Programm-Entwürfe von 1875 und 1891* (Berlin, 1928). As the editor indicates in his foreword this republication from the Communist side served the special purpose of reminding again of the revolutionary nucleus of Marxism in opposition to the reformism of the Social Democratic Party. In the foreword to the second edition of 1930, the editor recommends Lenin's article on Marx as an "excellent supplement" to the *Kritik*. We shall turn to Lenin's article presently in the text. In the *Kritik*, Marx distinguishes between a communist society as it emerges from the revolution still tainted by marks of its origin, and a "higher phase of communist society." The worst mark of the lower phase is compensation of work according to quantity and quality of performance. In the higher phase work no longer will be a "means for life, but rather the foremost want in life (*Lebensbedürfnis*)." When this stage is reached, incentives for work will no

1917 too much importance attached to this strand in Lenin's ideas. Lenin resumed it because he found it in Marx's critical notes on the Gotha Program and it was an excellent weapon for distinguishing orthodox Marxism from the reformist type of derailment. Nevertheless, precisely this "tactical" context of Marx's distinction should remind us that the *ultimate* end of communism was characterized in this manner in order to make it clear that the more *immediate* phase of communism was something vastly different. The ultimate phase is remote (Marx counted its distance in decades, Lenin in centuries); the immediate phase will be the reality following a successful revolution. Hence we should consider the distinction less a recapture of the original vision than one of the famous "explanations" of Marx by which he proved to the Marxists' satisfaction that the miscarriage of the millenium was an inevitable tactical step toward its realization.[10]

That even Lenin did not regain the original vision is made most probable by his previously mentioned encyclopedia article, *Karl Marx* (1914). The article opens with a brief biographical introduction. Then it explains the doctrine of "Philosophic Materialism," mostly based on the crude naturalism of Engels's *Anti-Dühring*, the doctrine of "Dialectic," again based on Engels and Feurerbach, avoiding Marx, and the "Materialist Conception of History," based on the famous page in *Kritik der Politischen Oekonomie*, avoiding the voluminous early writings of Marx on the subject. The article then proceeds to "Class Struggle" and "Economic Doctrine." The subsequent section on "Socialism" dwells on the inevitability of socialism as evolving out of capitalism, based on passages from Marx, while for the vision of the future Lenin relies again on Engels.[11] The article comes to a close with a section on

---

longer be necessary, and the principle of society will be: "From each according to his ability, to each according to his needs." Duncker's footnote (p. 27) indicates that the formula originated with Enfantin in 1831, and received the wording which Marx uses through Louis Blanc in 1839. The distinction of the two phases was resumed by Lenin in his *State and Revolution* (1917) and from then on remained one of the semantic icons in Russian communism.

10. After the First World War the "explanations" and "tactics" of the Marxist movement became a joke to non-Marxists. On the occasion of repeated wrong predictions and masterful explanations of the tactician Otto Bauer, Karl Kraus, the Austrian satirist, coined the term "tic-tac-tic."

11. Lenin quotes the famous passage from Engels, *Herrn Eugen Dührings Umwälzung der Wissenschraft* (1878), 19th ed. (Stuttgart, 1919), p. 302: "The Proletariat seizes state power and at first transforms the instruments of production into state property. In this act, however, it abolishes itself as proletariat, abolishes all class differences and class conflicts, and thereby also abolishes the state as state. . . . The first act, wherein the state appears as the real representative of the whole society—the taking over of the instruments of production in the name of society—is at the same time its last independent act as state.

"Tactics." Nowhere in the whole essay do we find a single word on the realm of freedom and the precariousness of its realization.

With regard to the radical wing of the derailment we come, therefore, to the conclusion that the revolutionary tension was regained on the level of necessity but not on the level of freedom. Through the mere lapse of time, the derailment made it necessary to cover more and more historical events with the categories of tactics. This extension of tactical explanations, finally, had to cover the revolution itself, and not only the revolution but also the historical events following the revolution. Into this latter class belong the Marxist debates on the question whether the Russian Revolution of 1917 was really *the* Revolution or only its beginning; whether the Revolution in Russia had to be expanded, through the Communist International, into a world revolution; whether the Russian Revolution was safe so long as *the* Revolution had not occurred throughout the world, or whether one could settle down, for the time being, with socialism in one country; how long it would take for the state to wither away, how long the dictatorship of the proletariat would have to last; what the dictatorship of the proletariat could mean when there were no nonproletarians left to whom one could dictate; whether this dictatorship would have to last as a defense precaution until the revolution had engulfed the rest of the world, etc.

This game of tactics, however, ran into an interesting difficulty, again through the mere lapse of time. Once the revolution had been successful in Russia, and the Pentecostal miracle of freedom through revolutionary experience did not occur, the people began to get restive. The game of tactics can sustain in tension those who are actively engaged in it in a leading role but apparently the average man is not willing to live by tactics alone. The Revolution had happened, the world-shaking importance of the event was being hammered into everybody, but ten, fifteen, twenty years elapsed, the state did not wither away, the revolution still went on. At this juncture, a substitute of a more tangible nature had to be found for the receding millenium, and it was found in the "fatherland," the revival of Russian traditions and a "Soviet patriotism."

The intervention of state power in social relations will become superfluous in one field after the other and will gradually cease (*schläft ein*). The government over persons will be replaced by the administration of things and the management of processes of production. The state will not be 'abolished,' *it dies off* (*er stirbt ab*)." Engels removes from the original idea precisely the point that had worried the younger Marx most, before the derailment, the point that the mechanics of expropriation might not produce the realm of freedom at all but an even more hideous rendition of the corrupt society which this measure intends to overcome.

If we interpret the injection of a new patriotism into Russian communism as determined by the logic of the original vision, if we understand it as a substitute apocalypse for masses who cannot live permanently in eschatological tension, we shall at the same time be rather hesitant about seeing in it a fundamental change in the history of the Marxist derailment. The tactics of the derailment have not been abandoned because a tactical sop has been thrown to the people. Up to this time, there is no shadow of an indication that in the ruling stratum of the Marxist movement the revolutionary tension has relaxed. We do not think, therefore, that the Marxist derailment has come to its historical end, to which indeed it would have come if the revolutionary tension had dissolved into a "conservative" national policy, however imperialistic. The sources show no more than a tactical inclusion of the forces of Soviet nationalism into the revolutionary drive that is carried on by the leaders in the upper stratum of the Marxist movement. A retarding effect becomes visible only insofar as the success of the revolution in a very powerful country inevitably imparts an intense color of national imperialism to the tactics of world revolution and thereby may arouse national resistance even among those groups on which the tacticians of the movements count for their support.[12]

We have followed the problem of the movement to its systematic, though not to its historical end and we can now summarize the results.

The Marxist movement is connected in continuity with the Marxian idea through the derailment that has occurred in Marx at the latest after the experience of the February Revolution of 1848. The derailment we have defined as the shift of emphasis from the ultimate end of the revolution to the tactics of its preparation. This shift of emphasis was possible because the end of the revolution, that is the establishment of the realm of freedom, was conceived as resulting from the experience of the revolution itself. The ultimate end of the Revolution was, therefore, beyond preparation. What could be prepared was the revolution in the realm of necessity; for this purpose no change of heart is necessary. The appeal is made to such sentiments as moral indignation, idealism, pity, compassion, the "humanitarian" calculus that minor sufferings will be compensated by great bliss for the greatest number, *ressentiment*, envy, hatred, the moderate desire to improve one's position, greed, lust of destruction, lust of terrorism and domination, and plain lust of killing. The combination of this appeal with the premium of morality, fight for freedom, eschatological heroism and historical destiny is a psychologically appealing mixture. The only serious draw-

12. A serious case of this kind, even within the Panslavic area, has occurred in the Yugoslav resistance against Russian domination, begun in 1948.

back which the recipe could have from the Marxist point of view is the possibility that it can be imitated and used by others—as the Marxists (but unfortunately not only the Marxists) found to their grief when the National Socialists used it and improved upon it.

In the derailment we can hitherto distinguish the following historical phases:

(1) The derailment in Marx himself, as it becomes manifest after the February Revolution of 1848.

(2) The derailment on the level of German Revisionism. The threat to overthrow the bourgeoisie became the *épater le bourgeois* of revolutionary language, while the actual policy became that of a progressive reform party. Without the First World War and the Russian Revolution, this might have been the end of Marxism through transformation of the movement into labor parties within the national polities. The radical revolutionaries would have become an innocuous sectarian group.

(3) The derailment on the level of Russian Communism. The Russian Revolution of 1917 has reversed the trend toward an euthanasia of Marxism. With the Communist seizure of power in a major country (more by way of a coup d'état than of an actual revolutionary development), the revolution was put to the test of fulfillment. Since no fulfillment in terms of a realm of freedom was forthcoming, the distinction of the two phases of communism (of which the first, actual one could run indefinitely into the future), as well as the substitute apocalypse of Soviet patriotism, had to be incorporated into the tactics of the movement.

(4) The derailment on the level of Russian imperialism. With the end of the Second World War, the problem that had already plagued the comintern between the wars became intensified with the increasing identification of the Communist movement with Russian imperialism. Just as the failure of the revolution within Russia could be partially overcome through Soviet patriotism, this difficulty could be overcome in the Eastern- and Central-European area, at least in part, through mobilizing Panslavic sentiments which, after a fashion, cover up the absence of freedom after "liberation." For the expansion farther West no new tactical cover-devices have yet appeared, with the exception of the symbol "fascism" for the designation of all governments and political groups which resist Soviet imperialism.

From the survey of the phases it appears that the derailment draws its continued strength from wars and revolutions that are not of its making. While the movement does not in itself seem to have any serious revolutionary power, it is excellently equipped (through its "tactics" and highly developed technique of political struggle) with the ability of grasping opportunities that are offered by the paralysis and disintegration of Western society. Hitherto the movement could revitalize its revolutionary tension, and avoid facing the problem of the receding millenium, through events which originated outside the movement itself. Since this source for revitalization is still richly flowing, the further course of the derailment is unpredictable.

That the derailment was made possible through the logic of the idea, however, is not a sufficient explanation for the persistent appeal of the idea in the crucial moments of Western disintegration. In order to secure its success the idea not only had to rest on a substantially sound analysis of the actual state of Western society; it also had to be a part of the crisis itself. Only because the idea was the manifestation of a profound spiritual disease, only because it carried the disease to a new extreme, could it fascinate the masses of a diseased society. We shall now turn to the genesis of the idea and the nature of the disease which produced it.

Inverted dialectics

We can best arrive at an understanding of the Marxian disease through an analysis of its central symptom, which goes by the name of "dialectical materialism." The dialectics of matter is a conscious inversion of the Hegelian dialectics of the idea. We have dealt with the problem of inversion several times in the course of this study. It is a mode of thought which occurs in the last sophistic periods of a disintegrating civilization. We encounter it for the first time in Hellenic, sophistic politics, and it reappears in a decisive manner in the Enlightenment as we saw in the case of Helvétius. We noticed it again in the chapter on Bakunin.

The case of Marx is very similar in its structure to that of Bakunin, and in itself it would hardly merit an analysis. If we give extensive attention to it nevertheless, this is admittedly a concession to the political importance of the Marxist movement. It is also a concession to the present deplorable state of political science and of political discussion in general. Dialectical materialism has found wide social acceptance under the more conventional name of "historical materialism," and even more so under the distinctly respectable label of the "economic interpretation" of politics and history, and it has found such acceptance not only with Marxists but generally in the environment of up-to-date intellectuals who have absorbed psychoanalysis. We have reached the situation where every day we encounter the assertion that nobody has a right to talk about politics who has not understood, and is able to apply, the profound insights stemming from Marx. The philosophical dilettantism, and sometimes the plain silliness, of the theories involved, has proved no obstacle to their mass influence. In view of this situation, the present analysis of Marxian dialectics may be excused.

The term "dialectical materialism" poses a problem insofar as it is a *contradictio in adjecto*. Dialectics, whatever other qualifications one may introduce into the definition, is an intelligible movement of ideas. The concept may be applied not only to a process in the mind but also to other realms of being, and in the extreme case dialectics may be used as a principle of gnostic interpretation for the whole of the universe, under the assumption that reality is intelligible because it is the manifestation of an idea. Hegel could interpret history dialectically because he assumed the *logos* to be incarnate in history. When reality is not conceived as the incarnation of the *logos*, the talk of a dialectic of reality becomes senseless. While the term in question, thus, contains a *contradictio in adjecto*, the train of thought which has led to the senseless formula may still be intelligible. We cannot dismiss the problem out of hand but must inquire into its origin. Nevertheless, as a point of sociological interest, we should be aware that the senselessness of the formula has never disturbed a Marxist, and in the Russian abbreviation of *diamat* it has become one of the sacred symbols of Communist doctrine.

Marx himself has given the most mature formulation of his theory of dialectics in the Foreword to the second edition of the *Kapital*, in 1873. There he says: "In its foundations my dialectical method does not only differ from the Hegelian, but is its direct opposite." When in the first edition he declared himself a disciple of the great thinker, he did so rather out of spite against mediocrities who treated Hegel as a "dead dog." In opposition to such epigoni he wanted to stress that Hegel after all was the first thinker who presented the movement of dialectics in a comprehensive and conscious manner. Nevertheless, "for Hegel the thought-process (which even he transforms into an autonomous subject under the name of Idea) is the demiurge of the real which is only its external garment. With me, on the contrary, the ideal is nothing but the material transformed and translated in the head of man." He then distinguishes between the "mystified" and the "rational" forms of dialectics. In its mystified, Hegelian form it glorified whatever exists. In its rational, Marxian form it is obnoxious to the bourgeoisie "because in understanding the existing positively, it also implies the understanding of its negation, that is of its inevitable perishing." Rational dialectics understands "every form of becoming in the flux of movement"; it is "not impressed by anything; it is essentially critical and revolutionary."[13]

The passage is brief, but rich in implications. Above all, we can see that the Marxian intention of "turning Hegel upside down" (*umstülpen*) in order to put dialectics on its feet, is rooted in a fundamental misunderstanding of Hegel's metaphysics. The Idea is for Hegel, of course, not the demiurge of the "real" in the sense in which Marx understands the term, that is in the sense of empirical reality. Rather, it is the demiurge of the "real" only insofar as reality is the revelation of the Idea. Empirical reality contains for Hegel a good deal that is not the unfolding of the Idea. It is precisely because empirical reality and the reality of the Idea are *not* identical that the problem of the Idea arises, or, to formulate it more fundamentally: Hegel was a philosopher and in this capacity he was concerned with the most basic philosophical problem, namely, with the nature of reality. Empirical reality could either be a disorderly flux of events (which it is not) or it could have a discernible order; in the latter case, this peculiar structure of reality inevitably becomes a problem for the philosopher and he must distinguish between the source of order and the source of the elements which do not fit into that order. Hence, when Marx says that his rational dialectics stands Hegelian dialectics on its feet, he does not correctly describe what he is doing. Before the actual inversion begins, he has done something much more fatal: he has abolished Hegel's problem of reality. And since only the answer to this problem (the dialectic of the Idea) is specifically Hegelian, while the problem itself is a general philosophical one, he has by this act abolished the philosophical approach to the problem of reality on principle. The Marxian position is not anti-Hegelian, it is antiphilosophical; Marx does not put Hegel's dialectics on its feet, he refuses to theorize.

Inevitably at this point certain questions arise, such as: Did Marx know what he was doing? How can one theorize, as Marx seems to do in voluminous works, without theorizing? The questions are thorny, and the answers will require lengthy exposition. Let us approach the first question concerning the sincerity of Marx and the self-consciousness of his undertaking.

In the previously quoted Foreword Marx refers to his critical study of Hegelian dialectics which he had given "almost thirty years ago." If we turn to this early work, we find that Marx had an excellent under-

13. Karl Marx, *Das Kapital*, 4th ed., ed. Friedrich Engels (Hamburg, 1890), 1, pp. xviif.

standing of Hegel's problem of reality but preferred to ignore it.[14] He criticized Hegel's concepts of idea and reality not by showing that they were uncritically formed or inconsistently used, but by measuring them against his own concept of reality and by condemning them because they did not conform with it. Since the reality of Marx was not the reality of Hegel, we cannot be surprised when Marx shows convincingly that, indeed, on every single point Hegel's theory of political reality is in conflict with his own. What must surprise us is that Marx should consider this demonstration a refutation of Hegel's philosophy. It would have been a refutation if Marx had given a critical foundation to his own concept of reality, for in that case the demonstration of non-agreement would have shown that Hegel's concepts were untenable in terms of Marxian critical standards. Marx, however, never attempted such a critical foundation for his theory of reality. As the editors of Marx's early writings have formulated it: "He tacitly argues from a position that is unphilosophical on principle" and the justification of this position "is simply assumed." "The position from which Marx undertakes his critique is a plain, not explicitly discussed negation of the philosophical position as such. By simply referring to what in common parlance is called reality, the philosophical question concerning the nature of reality is cut off."[15]

14. Of the study on Hegel's dialectics only a small part had been published under the title *Zur Kritik der Hegelschen Rechtsphilosophie. Einleitung* (1843). The main body, the *Kritik des Hegelschen Staatsrechts*, remained in manuscript. Both the *Einleitung* and the *Kritik* are now published in *Gesamtausgabe*.

15. S. Landshut and J. P. Mayer, introduction (Karl Marx, *Der Historische Materialismus* [Leipzig, 1932], vol. 1), p. xxii. The key passage which puts Marx's position beyond doubt is to be found in the *Kritik*, in the notes on sec. 262 of Hegel's *Rechtsphilosophie*: "Das *wirkliche* Verhältnis ist: 'dass die Zuteilung des Staatsmaterials am Einzelnen durch die Umstände, die Willkür und die eigene Wahl seiner Bestimmung vermittelt ist.' Diese Tatsache, dies *wirkliche Verhältnis* wird von der Spekulation als *Erscheinung*, als *Phänomen* ausgesprochen. Diese Umstände, diese Willkür, diese Wahl der Bestimmung, diese *wirkliche Vermittlung* sind bloss die *Erscheinung einer Vermittlung*, welche die wirkliche Idee mit sich selbst vornimmt, und welche hinter der Gardine vorgeht. Die Wirklichkeit wird nicht als sie selbst, sondern als eine andere Wirklichkeit ausgesprochen. Die gewöhnliche Empirie hat nicht ihren eigenen Geist, sondern einen fremden zum Gesetz, wogegen die wirkliche Idee nicht eine aus ihr selbst entwickelte Wirklichkeit, sondern die gewöhnliche Empirie zum Dasein hat. Die Idee wird versubjektiviert. Das *wirkliche* Verhältnis von Familie und bürgerlicher Gesellschaft zum Staat wird als ihre *innere imaginäre* Tätigkeit gefasst. Familie und bürgerliche Gesellschaft sind die Voraussetzungen des Staats; sie sind die eigentlich Tätigen, aber in der Spekulation wird es umgekehrt. Wenn aber die Idee versubjektiviert wird, werden hier die wirklichen Subjekte, bürgerliche Gesellschaft, Familie, 'Umstände, Willkür, etc.', zu *unwirklichen*, anderes bedeutenden, objektiven Momenten der Idee" (vol. 1, p. 406). This method of criticism did not appear in Marx for the first time in his discussion of Hegel. In his studies for his dissertation *Ueber die Differenz der demokritischen und*

Logophobia or the Fragesverbot

The procedure is disconcerting. The question whether Marx was unable to understand Hegel's problem must definitely be answered in the negative; Marx understood Hegel perfectly well. What purpose, then, did he pursue in writing an elaborate commentary on Hegel's *Rechtsphilosophie* which proved nothing but that the world view of a critical philosopher is not identical with the precritical, prephilosophical world view of the average man? In performing this feat, with the implied understanding that it demolished the Hegelian system, was Marx being intellectually dishonest? When he measured Hegel's concept of reality against his own, did he deliberately misrepresent Hegel's intention? To this last question the answer cannot be unhesitating. The dilemma becomes manifest in the sentence in which Marx's editors grapple with the question: "Marx—if we may express ourselves in this manner—misunderstood Hegel as-it-were deliberately."[16] They do not dare outrightly call Marx an intellectual faker, but they are not so sure that the solution of the puzzle is not found in this direction.

Tempting as the suggestion is, we cannot follow it. The affair certainly suggests intellectual dishonesty but, after all, Marx was not a common swindler. Nevertheless, in interpreting his procedure we are in a real difficulty. On the level of rational discourse we come to the dead end of the question just raised. Unless we want to give up at this point, we must transfer the problem to the level of pneumapathology. Marx was spiritually diseased and we have localized the most glaring symptom of his disease, that is, his fear of critical concepts and of philosophy in general. Marx refuses to express himself in any other terms than precritical, unanalysed concepts. The deeper causes of this fear we shall discuss later. For the present we have to characterize the symptom and since a pneumapathological terminology is hardly developed, we shall coin the term "logophobia" for this symptom.

We can even go a bit beyond the narrow definition of logophobia as fear of critical concepts, for Engels, in his *Anti-Dühring*, has fortu-

---

epikuräischen Naturphilosophie (1840), Marx had expressed his grievance against philosophy on principle in the sentence: "Alle Philosophen haben die Prädikate selbst zu Subjekten gemacht" (vol. 1, p. 119). Marx has correctly observed that *all* philosophers are given to the vice of tampering with reality. They just will not leave it alone and accept order as an agreeable, unproblematical byproduct of the mess of reality as it appears to the common man; instead of leaving essence in its homely place as a predicate of reality, they have the nasty habit of pulling it out and making it a subject. We may say, therefore, that Marx was quite conscious, when he attacked Hegel, that he was attacking philosophy.

16. Loc. cit.

nately supplied us with the larger context of the symptom when he elaborated the antiphilosophical position of Marx. Engels reflects on the new, materialistic science of the nineteenth century. "Modern materialism" recognizes history as the evolutionary process of mankind and tries to discover the laws of its movement. Moreover, it has abandoned the static concept of nature that was still held by Newton and Linné, and also recognizes nature as process and evolution under discoverable laws. With regard to history as well as nature, "modern materialism" is "essentially dialectic and no longer needs a philosophy above the other sciences." This is for Engels the decisive point: when science is occupied with the discovery of the laws of process and evolution, philosophy becomes superfluous. Why this curious result should follow does not become quite clear. Engels insists: "As soon as each particular science is approached with the demand to become clear about its position in the total context (*Gesamtzusammenhang*) of things and of knowledge of things, a particular science of the total context becomes superfluous." All that remains of philosophy as we know it is the "science of thinking and its laws—that is formal logic and dialectics." "Everything else is dissolved in the positive science of nature and history."[17]

An interminable series of questions could be raised with regard to these sentences. Why does philosophy become superfluous when the sciences of history and nature recognize the evolutionary character of reality? Why, for instance, is philosophy less necessary in the age of Darwin than in that of Linné? Is it perhaps because a new philosophy of reality has superseded the old one? But in this case, would we not have a new philosophy rather than none at all? Or is it the philosopher who becomes superfluous when every scientist does his own philosophizing? Is it not strange to call such a sociological shift an abolition of philosophy? Has Engels perhaps subsumed philosophy under the name of science?

But it is useless to subject this hash of uncritical language to critical questioning. We can make no sense of these sentences of Engels unless we consider them as symptoms of a spiritual disease. As a disease, however, they make excellent sense for, with great intensity, they display the symptoms of logophobia, now quite outspokenly as a desperate fear and hatred of philosophy. We even find named the specific object of fear and hatred: it is "the total context of things and of knowledge of things." Engels, like Marx, is afraid that the recogni-

17. Friedrich Engels, *Herrn Eugen Dührings Umwälzung der Wissenschaft* (1878), 19th ed. (Stuttgart, 1919), pp. 10f.

tion of critical conceptual analysis might lead to the recognition of a "total context," of an order of being and perhaps even of cosmic order, to which their particular existences would be subordinate. If we may use the language of Marx: a total context must not exist as an autonomous subject of which Marx and Engels are insignificant predicates; if it exists at all, it must exist only as a predicate of the autonomous subjects Marx and Engels. Our analysis has carried us closer to the deeper stratum of the Marxian disease, that is the revolt against God.[18] In the surface stratum of theory that we are analysing at present, the meaning of logophobia now comes more clearly into view. It is not the fear of a particular critical concept, like Hegel's Idea, it is rather the fear of critical analysis in general. Submission to critical argument at any point might lead to the recognition of an order of the *logos*, of a constitution of being, and the recognition of such an order might reveal the revolutionary idea of Marx, the idea of establishing a realm of freedom and of changing the nature of man through revolution, as the blasphemous and futile nonsense which it is.

Since Marx refuses to move in a universe of rational discourse, since critical concepts are barred from his argument, we must first gain some understanding of the language symbols which he actually uses in his writings. Only after we have established the nature of the symbols can we arrive at conclusions with regard to the content of Marxian dialectics itself.

Marx, and Engels, have created a specific medium of expression for themselves: whenever a critical point arrives at which ultimate clarification would be required, their discourse blossoms out into metaphorical language which forces relations between undefined terms. Take as an example the previously quoted sentence from Marx's Foreword: "With me the Ideal is nothing but the Material transformed and translated in the head of man."[19] The sentence sounds excellent and carries a vivid impression; it would have to be considered brilliant if it were an occasional, rhetorical flourish that metaphorically expresses what has been set forth with critical thoroughness in another context. The trouble is that the other context in which this metaphor would receive

18. The connection is formulated in so many words by Lenin (encyclopedia article on Marx) when he says: "Marx decidedly rejected idealism, always connected in some way with religion." The sentence follows a quotation from Engels's *Feuerbach*, where the author characterized idealists as persons who declare that spirit exists before nature and therefore assume that the world was created, while materialists are persons who regard nature as primary. Lenin adds that any other philosophical usage of the terms idealism and materialism would be "only confusing."

19. "Bei mir ist umgekehrt das Ideelle nichts andres als das im Menschenkopf umgesetzte und übersetzte Materielle" ("Vorwort," p. xvii).

its critical meaning does not exist in the collected works of Marx. The metaphorical sentence is all that we have. We are faced with an "Ideal" and a "Material" without knowing what these terms signify. We are told that the Ideal is the same as the Material but "transformed and translated" and we are left to ponder what the terms "transform" and "translate" in this relation might conceivably mean. And, finally, we learn that the locale of this mysterious process is the "head of man" and we wonder whether Marx means a miracle of brain physiology or a mental activity, whether he thinks of cognitive acts of some specific man or of a cosmic process under the collective skull of mankind. Nevertheless, to the kind of reader who swallows that sentence hook, line and sinker, it conveys an awe-inspiring picture of an intellectual giant who performs such wonderful metaphorical feats as "turning dialectics upside down," and putting it "on its feet" while formerly "it stood on its head."

The nature of this technique of expression will become even clearer when we consider not a single sentence, but a series of sentences in which the thought of Marx moves from more concrete problems to an ultimate general formulation. As an example we shall use the famous passage from the *Kritik der Politischen Oekonomie* which is considered Marx's authoritative formulation of his materialistic interpretation of history. The passage begins: "In the social production of their means of existence men enter into definite, necessary relations which are independent of their will, productive relationships which correspond to a definite stage of development of their material productive forces." With this sentence we are, on the whole, on safe ground. All necessary explanations of terms are given by Marx in other contexts.[20] The beginning of the next sentence is a definition: "The aggregate of these productive relationships constitutes the economic structure of society." We are still on safe ground. Then Marx goes on: "The economic structure of society is the real basis on which a juridical and political superstructure arises and to which definite forms of social consciousness correspond."[21] Here we may begin to question: Why is the economic structure the "real basis" and why are other structures in society, such as the political, a superstructure? What is a "social form of consciousness" and what does it do when it "corresponds" to the "real basis"? In part these questions are answered by the next sentence: "The mode of production

<hr/>

20. *Kapital*, 1, p. 45.
21. "Die Gesamtheit dieser Produktionsverhältnisse bildet die ökonomische Struktur der Gesellschaft, die reale Basis, worauf sich ein juristischer und politischer Ueberbau erhebt, und welcher bestimmte gesellschaftliche Bewusstseinsformen entsprechen" (*Kritik der Politischen Oekonomie*, p. lv).

of the material means of existence conditions the whole process of social, political, and intellectual life."[22] But this answer shows that we are already running off into intangible metaphors. That economic structure is basic and all other structures are superstructures is now justified, indeed, insofar as the basic structure "conditions" the other ones. But what does "conditioning" mean? The term is hardly clarified by an earlier formulation that political forms are "rooted" in material relations.[23] Now, when critical clarification is urgently required, comes the typical Marxian climax: "It is not the consciousness of men that determines their being; it is, on the contrary, their social being that determines their consciousness."[24] We have arrived at terms like "being," "social being" and "consciousness" at large and the relation between them is no longer one of "conditioning" but of "determining."

This classical passage of Marx admirably illustrates the sweep from concrete problems of economics and sociology to grandiose ranting with uncritical symbols. Again, let us emphasize that the climactic sentence, while devoid of theoretical meaning, is brimming with revolutionary pathos and certainly apt to make the unwary and uncritical reader believe that now a solution has been found for all social problems. But again let us stress that the collected works of Marx contain nothing that would be of any help in establishing the precise meaning of such terms as "being" and "consciousness." The great formula is not the beginning of a discussion, it is the dictatorial instrument which cuts off all discussion on principle. The reader will now understand more clearly why a critical analysis of Marxian doctrine is impossible. To put it bluntly: A Marxian *theory* of historical materialism does not exist.

Pseudological speculation

Even if there is no theoretical content in the so-called theory of historical materialism, obviously there is something in it. What Marx has to say is not theory, but it is not unintelligible nonsense. We must return to our paradoxical question: How can one theorize without theorizing? We encounter again certain terminological difficulties since spiritual disease has never been made the object of systematic inquiry and no suitable vocabulary has been developed for its description. In

22. "Die Produktionsweise des materiellen Lebens bedingt den sozialen, politischen und geistigen Lebensprozess überhaupt" (ibid.).
23. "*Rechtsverhältnisse wie Staatsformen . . . wurzeln, etc.*" (ibid., p. liv).
24. "Es ist nicht das Bewusstsein der Menschen, das ihr Sein, sondern umgekehrt ihr gesellschaftliches Sein, das ihr Bewusstsein bestimmt" (ibid., p. lv).

order to speak with convenience of theorizing in the nontheoretical medium that we have just analyzed, we shall coin the term "pseudo-logical speculation." Into the meaning of this term will enter the following elements: (1) that speculation of this kind is theory in appearance only, not in reality; (2) that in the intention of the thinker who indulges in it, it is meant as genuine theoretical speculation; (3) that historically it presupposes the existence of a genuine philosophy of the *logos* which furnishes the subject matter that can be translated into the pseudological form.

Equipped with this new term, we can now approach the next step in the Marxian inversion, that is the pseudological transformation of Hegel's speculation. The importance of this step will easily be overlooked by those who rely blindly on such Marxian metaphors as the "turning of dialectics upside down" and "putting dialectics on its feet." Even when it is turned upside down the Hegelian gnosis of history is still present in the fullness of its amplitude, including the movement of the idea. Marx, like Hegel, develops a philosophy of the idea. One cannot even say that he has inverted the dynamics between idea and reality, for neither is his "material" Hegel's reality, nor is his "ideal" Hegel's idea. This erroneous impression certainly has been fostered by the Marxian metaphors but it would nevertheless be unfair to adopt the vulgarian misunderstanding of historical materialism as the profound insight that human beings are endowed with the gift of finding good reasons for advancing their material (economic and political) interests. If we assumed that such wisdom is the substance of Marxism and its denial the substance of Hegelian dialectics, the excitement aroused by Marxism and its revolutionary effectiveness would become enigmatic. Marx is not as simple minded as that. And Hegel was not unacquainted with such elementary psychological mechanisms, nor did he ever deny them. The Hegelian gnosis is retained by Marx and history is still the realization of the realm of freedom.

The pseudological transformation of Hegel's gnosis can best be studied in certain passages of the more discursive Engels. In order to transform this gnosis, Engels must first accept its problem. He praises Hegel because he has occupied himself with the intelligible order of history. In his system, history was no longer a senseless series of deeds of violence best forgotten, rather it was the evolutionary process of mankind, and it became the task of thinking to demonstrate an order behind the apparent accidents. Although Hegel failed to solve this task, he still has the "epochal merit" of having set it. His system failed because it suffered from an internal contradiction. On the one hand, it viewed history as an evolutionary process "which by its nature cannot find its intellectual conclusion through the discovery of a so-called absolute truth." On the other hand, it insisted "that it was the total (*Inbegriff*) of this absolute truth." "An all-comprehensive, once and for all conclusive system of knowledge of nature and history is in contradiction with the fundamental law of dialectical thinking; this, however, does not exclude, but on the contrary implies, that the systematic knowledge of our whole external world can advance with giant strides from generation to generation."[25]

The passage is a fine example of the intellectual confusion in which pseudological speculation alone can thrive. Engels rightly attacks Hegel for his attempt to interpret history as the unfolding of an Idea that has reached its conclusion in the present. The total meaning of history can be construed only as a transcendental drama, not as a mundane drama that comes to its close within empirical time. This is the fallacy of historical gnosis which inevitably comes to grief through the fact that history continues. From both the theoretical fallacy and the empirical failure of gnostic interpretation, one should properly advance to the insight that the empirical course of history must not be interpreted as the unfolding of an Idea.

This, however, is not the argument of Engels. First of all, he misinterprets Hegel when he argues that the process of history, by its nature, cannot find its intellectual conclusion through the discovery of an absolute truth. On the contrary, this is the only way in which it can find its intellectual conclusion but because (1) this is the only way, and (2) the empirical stream of history is not closed, "absolute truth" must remain transcendental. The fallacy of gnosis consists in the immanentization of transcendental truth. Correctly, Engels would have had to say that the immanentist intellectual conclusion does not stop the stream of history and, hence, must not be used for its interpretation. What, then, does Engels gain by his misformulation? The second part of his argument shows the gain: it is an empirical reality which has meaning *as if* it were the unfolding of an idea but it is not burdened with the conclusion of the unfolding. Theoretically, of course, this is nonsense, for meaning is not meaning unless it is concluded, at least in imaginative anticipation. Nevertheless, this is the purpose of the argument: Hegel's reality of the unfolding Idea is abolished and empirical reality has become meaningful as if it were an Idea. With this result we also touch on the deeper motive of the "as-it-were deliberate" misunderstanding of Hegel's problem of reality in the early Marx: by substituting empirical reality for the reality of the Idea,

25. Engels, *Herrn Eugen Dührings* . . . , pp. 9f.

Marx and Engels can draw the meaning of the Idea into reality without encountering the problem of a metaphysic of the Idea.

The summarizing masterpiece of this confusion is the proposition that a conclusive, all-comprehensive system of knowledge is in contradiction with the fundamental law of dialectical thinking. By means of the confusion between empirical reality and the Hegelian reality of the Idea, the dialectics of the idea has now been drawn into empirical reality. Since empirical reality is an open stream, dialectics must be open, too. The philosopher is left standing like a schoolboy who indulges in the amusing idea that systems of dialectical meaning must be closed. We have at last arrived at the bottom of the confusion which has produced the *contradictio in adjecto* of "dialectical materialism." At the same time, this confusion misrepresents a system of metaphysics as a system of empirical knowledge. And Engels, quite consistent in his confusion, concludes his argument with the assurance that the abolition of metaphysical conclusiveness does not make an advancing systematic knowledge in the empirical sense impossible. On the contrary, this system will advance with giant strides in the future.

At this juncture, the reader might well ask whether Engels has not proved too much, whether his argument does not defeat its purpose. He certainly has got rid of Hegel and metaphysics, but he also seems to have arrived at the simple idea of a progressing science which in due course will make the Marxian system obsolete. Certainly, this could not be Engel's intention. But the reader need not worry. In the confusion in which Engels moves, difficulties of this kind can be overcome by simply forgetting about them. When Engels takes up his train of thought again (about a hundred pages later), we are in the middle of a pseudological speculation on the dialectics of empirical reality. The course of history is the realization of freedom. Hegel was the first to understand the relation between freedom and necessity correctly. He knew that freedom is insight into necessity. "Necessity is blind only as long as it is not conceptually understood (*begriffen*)." Should history after all be the realization of the *logos* in the Hegelian sense? But Engels does not return to metaphysics. His *logos* is the knowledge of the laws of nature and the possibility, based on such knowledge, of "letting them operate according to plan for definite aims." By laws of nature are not meant only those of external nature but also those "of the bodily and mental existence of man." "Hence freedom of the will means nothing but the ability of making decisions based on expert knowledge (*Sachkenntnis*)." This formula would reduce the *logos* to the rationality of the means-end relation and it would leave open the question of substantive reason, of the ends themselves.

This problem of ends is solved by a theory of the convergence of freedom and necessity. "The *freer* the judgment of a man is with regard to a certain question, the greater will be the *necessity* which determines the content of the judgment." Insecurity of decision has its source in lack of knowledge; freedom of choice is truly unfreedom because in such indecision man is dominated by the object which he ought to dominate in his turn. "Freedom, thus, consists in the domination of man over himself and external nature that is based on his knowledge of natural necessity."[26] The freedom of man advances with technological discoveries. At the beginning of human history there stands the discovery of the production of fire through friction; at the end of evolution there stands the steam engine, the great representative symbol of the productive forces that alone will make possible a state of society without classes and without concern about the means of subsistence. The steam engine is the promise of "true human freedom, of an existence in harmony with the known laws of nature." The incarnation of the *logos* has become the advancement of pragmatic knowledge to the point where it has absorbed into its system, and dissolved, the mystery of human existence. Christ the Redeemer is replaced by the steam engine as the promise of the realm to come.

The speculation of Engels is of particular interest because the author's utter lack of intellectual discipline allows him associatively to weave various trends of Western disintegration into it, thus revealing their inner connection.

(1) Let us first clarify the line of pseudological speculation. The attack on the conclusiveness of the Hegelian system proved, after all, to be an attack on philosophy as such. As soon as Engels had submerged his dialectics in empirical reality, he embarked on an intellectual conclusion of his own. The empirical stream of history does not move indefinitely toward an uncertain future, it moves toward its end in the convergence of freedom and necessity. As far as the factor of "intellectual conclusion" is concerned, the Marx-Engels gnosis differs from the Hegelian only by shoving the intellectual end of the world a bit farther into the future in order to make room for their revolutionary upheaval.

(2) Since, however, only the form of "intellectual conclusion" is taken from Hegel and not its substance (that is, the movement of the *logos*), pragmatic intellect becomes the carrier of the movement. In the execution of his pseudological speculation, Engels shows an admirable consistency. Marx solves the problem of freedom through his

26. Ibid., pp. 112f.

idea of a revolutionary "leap" into the changed nature of man. This Marxian strain, as we shall see, is not quite absent from the meanderings of Engels either, but in Engels it is tucked away in another context. In the present context, Engels undertakes quite seriously to solve the problem of human existence on the pragmatic level. In this respect he brings certain tendencies that we observed in d'Alembert's and Diderot's *Discours* to their logical conclusion. The life of the spirit and the *bios theoretikos* are not merely pushed into the background by Engels, they are definitely eliminated. Man will be free when he has achieved perfect knowledge of the external world and with perfect knowledge the problem of purpose, which causes indecision, will have disappeared. Again quite consistently, Engels achieves this position by subsuming all knowledge of man under knowledge of the external world (p. 112f). Spiritual experience is abolished as an autonomous source of order; it is absorbed into "external," empirical knowledge. Lenin (who relies frequently on Engels rather than Marx) has seen the importance of this point and in the encyclopedia article on Marx he praises Engels for this transformation of the unknown but knowable Kantian *Ding-an-sich*, of the "thing-in-itself," into a "thing-for-us," of the substance of things into "phenomena." The destruction of the substance of man becomes the declared program as a last consequence of the scandal of the *Encyclopédistes*.

(3) In spite of the intellectual conclusion which Engels gives to his pseudological speculation, he does not renounce the pleasures of anticipating the wide-open spaces of progress. Though the end is foreknown, we have an advancement of science in giant strides from generation to generation. We also can locate the specific origin of Engels's indulgence. In the formula that freedom consists in the domination of man over himself and nature, the reader will have recognized the formula by which Littré defines *le tout de la civilization*. There is a strong dose of Saint-Simon and Comte in the complex of Marx-Engels, and more specifically we find in Engels a penchant for the liberal-intellectual type of Positivism that is represented by Mill and Littré. Just as the *encyclopédiste* background (which emerges strongly not only in Engels but also in Lenin's *Materialism and Empirio-Criticism*) must not be neglected in the understanding of the Marxist movement, so the liberal and positivist sources deserve attention. As we explained at length in discussing the internal development of Positivism, an avalanche of destruction cannot be stopped at will by those who have released it when enough destruction is worked to make them happy; the avalanche rolls on.

Again the reader may find that Engels, in spite of his pseudological gnosis, has watered down the "intellectual conclusion" too much by empirical progress. We know the end, but before it arrives an indefinite period of nonrevolutionary progress seems to intervene. And again the reader need not worry, for there is enough space between the covers of a book written by Engels to take care of such problems. In spite of the fact that in his main line of pseudological speculation he has dissolved the existence of man into a system of pragmatic knowledge, on another occasion Engels is concerned about the problems of ethics. He speaks of various moral systems which have arisen on the basis of different economic systems. We have a Christian-feudal system of morality, a modern bourgeois system, and the proletarian morality of the future. At least these three theories of morals coexist in contemporary society and their existence proves that no absolute ethics is possible. "We reject the suggestion that any moral dogma be imposed on us as an eternal, ultimate, immovable moral law, under the pretext that the moral world has permanent principles which are higher than history and the differences of nations."[27]

This blast seems to dispose of moral truth altogether. Nevertheless, while Engels cannot see an ultimate moral truth, he has criteria of preference between moral systems. He can gain such criteria because he understands the "ultimacy" (Endgültigkeit) of a moral system as its historical survival in the end. The system which contains more elements with "the promise of duration" is preferable and that system is the proletarian because in the present it represents the revolution of the present into the future. Even proletarian morality, however, is imperfect because it reflects the class situation of the proletariat. Only after the revolution, when the classes, and with them the proletariat, have disappeared will "a truly human morality" be possible, beyond class antagonism and beyond even the memory of it. We are "on the eve of this social revolution" and in this situation it is particularly foolish to advocate one or the other systems of class morality for they are all destined to be swept away tomorrow by the truly human morality to be ushered in by the revolution. Thus, while enjoying the immense perspectives of progress, we are nevertheless on the eve of the revolution that will put an end to progress by realizing its aim. In this phase of his thought, Engels has recaptured the revolutionary fervor of his gnosis. He also has pleasantly slipped in a morality which seemed superfluous in the pseudological speculation proper. The only factor

27. The discussion of good and evil is to be found in Engels, ibid., pp. 88–90.

that is missing (and we never find it in Engels) is the fear of Marx that, perhaps, on the morrow of the revolution the change of heart will not have occurred.

Inversion

We can be brief on the problem of inversion proper. Our analysis has shown that the so-called inversion of Hegelian dialectics through Marx is a complicated operation. We have, first, isolated the anti-philosophical attack which results in the establishment of an empirical pragmatic reality as the object of further investigation as well as of a special linguistic medium for its expression. This first phase of the operation is not an inversion of dialectics but the logophobic destruction of philosophical problems in general. Within the new medium of expression, nothing is inverted; the Hegelian gnosis is translated as a whole into pseudological speculation. The inversion in the technical sense occurs in a third phase in which the result of the first two operations is construed as an interpretation of the realms of being from the bottom of the ontological hierarchy. On this third phase, however, we can be brief, because Marx has said next to nothing about it beyond assuring us that this was indeed his intention.

The execution of his plan would have involved a philosophy of culture. First, he would have had to explain the nature of cultural phenomena; secondly, it would have been necessary for him to show that these phenomena could be interpreted from whatever he would consider the bottom of existence, as for instance, matter; and, finally, it would have been necessary to explain what this bottom of existence is. Of this whole plan, as far as principles are concerned, nothing exists but the previously analysed formula of the consciousness that is conditioned by existence.

Beyond this formulation of the principle, we have a few meagre passages concerning the sphere of culture which he designates by the term "ideology." The most important of these passages appears in the context of the *Kritik der Politischen Oekonomie* (pp. lvf.). Marx speaks of social revolutions which begin in the economic sphere and draw after them the corresponding revolution in the sphere of the "superstructure." "In observing such revolutions we must always distinguish between the material revolution in the economic conditions of production (which can be observed truly scientifically) and the juridical, political, religious, artistic or philosophical, in brief ideological forms, in which men become conscious of the conflict and fight it out." As far as one can extract anything from this sentence, it seems to imply that the content of culture is nothing but a fight over conflicts which arise in the economic sphere. To this proposition one can answer nothing but: it is not so.[28]

With regard to the bottom of existence, the most interesting passage is a footnote in the *Kapital*, on the problem of technology.[29] Marx regrets that no critical history of technology exists. The history of the productive organs of man in society would deserve at least the attention which Darwin devoted to the history of plant and animal organisms, because these human organs are "the material basis of all specific organization of society." Besides, it would be much easier to write than the corresponding history for plants and animals since, "as Vico says," the history of man is distinguished from the history of nature insofar as we have made the one and not the other. Technology "reveals the active behavior of man toward nature, the immediate production process of his life, and therewith of the social relations of his life as well as of the mental conceptions (*geistigen Vorstellungen*) springing from them." Up to this point, the note is mainly a different wording of the being-consciousness principle; only the curious appearance of Vico in the ancestry of historical materialism is of some interest. Beyond this point the note becomes polemical. "Even a history of religions which abstracts from this material basis, is uncritical. It is much easier through analysis to find the earthly core of the nebulous figments of religion, than to go the opposite way and to develop the celestified forms (*verhimmelten Formen*) out of the respective real relations of life. The latter way is the truly materialistic and therefore scientific method. The defects of an abstract naturalistic materialism (*naturwissenschaftlichen Materialismus*) that excludes the historical process can be recognized even in the abstract and ideological conceptions of its protagonists as soon as they dare extend themselves beyond their narrow specialty." What Marx seems to criticize is a psychologizing history which explains religions by revealing their "earthly" motives. From such abstract materialism he distinguishes his historical materialism, the only truly scientific method, that would make religions intelligible as arising out of economic conditions. The formulation is of interest as a clarification of intentions but no step is taken toward an execution of the program.

28. In Engels, *Anti-Dühring*, p. 83, we find the phrase: "the social relations, the legal and political forms with their ideal superstructure of philosophy, religion, art, etc." Engels seems to include legal and political forms with economic relations in the "structure" and to confine the "superstructure" to philosophy, art, religion, "etc." Whether he seriously meant to differ from Marx on this point is doubtful. In view of the general mess, however, it is hardly worth while to investigate such refinements of inaccuracy.

29. *Das Kapital*, 1, pp. 335f., n. 89.

Let us, finally, quote a passage from Engels which makes at least a gesture toward a metaphysical formulation of the inversion. In the *Anti-Dühring* Engels says: "The unity of the world does not consist in its being. . . . The real unity of the world consists in its materiality; and this materiality is proven . . . through a long and arduous development of philosophy and science" (p. 31). With some goodwill one might extract from this sentence the insight that historical materialism, in order to become a system, would need a theoretical foundation in a principle.

These are the ideas that shake the world.

XI. MARX: THE GENESIS OF GNOSTIC SOCIALISM

The starting point for the independent movement of Marx's thought seems to be a gnostic position which he inherited from Hegel. Specifically, the Marxian gnosis expresses itself in the conviction that the movement of the intellect in the consciousness of the empirical self is the ultimate source of knowledge for the understanding of the universe. Faith and the life of the spirit are expressly excluded as an independent source of order in the soul. Moreover, this conviction is from the beginning accompanied by an attitude of revolt against "religion" as a sphere which recognizes the existence of a *realissimum* beyond human consciousness. This is the Marxian position as it appears in his doctoral dissertation of 1840–41.[1]

In the preface to the dissertation Marx attacks the "theologizing intellect" of Plutarch who dares to criticize a philosopher like Epicurus. Against such presumption, Marx defends the "sovereignty" of philosophy. "Philosophy does not make a secret of it. The confession of Prometheus: 'In one word, I hate all the gods,' is its very own confession, its own sentence against all heavenly and earthly gods who refuse to recognize human self-consciousness (*das menschliche Selbstbewusstsein*) as the supreme divinity. And none shall be held by its side." Human self-consciousness is the god for the philosopher and "Prometheus is the foremost saint and martyr in the philosophical calendar."[2]

The subject is elaborated in a note on the existence of God.[3] Demonstrations of the existence of God are logically worthless and besides, they miss the point. All Gods, whether Greek or Christian, have really existed insofar as they were "a real force" in the life of man. If Gods are imagined as real they will be effective, indeed, in the minds of the believers. Nevertheless, they are subjective ideas, and they are ineffective where the subjective idea is not entertained. "Bring paper-money into a country where the use of paper is unknown, and everybody will laugh about your subjective idea. Come with your Gods in a country

1. Karl Marx, *Über die Differenz der demokritischen und epikureischen Naturphilosophie, Gesamtausgabe*, vol. 1.
2. Ibid., p. 10.
3. This is a note to the appendix of the dissertation, entitled "Kritik der plutarchischen Polemik gegen Epikurs Theologie." The appendix itself is lost. The note in op. cit., pp. 80f.

where other Gods are believed, and people will demonstrate to you that you are suffering from imaginations and abstractions." "What a particular country is for particular Gods from abroad, the country of reason is for God on principle; it is a region where He ceases to exist." The implications of this ultimacy of reasonable self-consciousness become clearer through the use to which, in the opinion of Marx, demonstrations of the existence of God can be put. If they cannot demonstrate the existence of God, at least they will demonstrate the existence of human self-consciousness. In fact they are "logical explications" of consciousness. In the ontological proof, for instance, the being that is given in its immediacy as the source of the idea of God is not God but the very self-consciousness. In this sense, all proofs for the existence of God are in fact proofs of his nonexistence. Correctly such demonstrations would have to be formulated: "Because nature is badly organized, God must exist," or "Because the world is unreasonable, God must exist." But what can be the meaning of such formulations unless they mean that "God exists for a man for whom the world is unreasonable, and who therefore himself is unreasonable?" Marx summarizes the result of these reflections in the sentence: "Un-reason is the existence of God."[4]

The sovereignty of consciousness and the antitheistic revolt are present in his thought from the very beginning. They enter as motives into the reflections of Marx on the philosophical situation that had been created by the system of Hegel. There are systems like the Hegelian and Aristotelian in which philosophy "closes itself into a completed, total world"; they are "nodal points" in philosophy which interrupt advancement in a straight line. A further perfection of the system is impossible in contemplation and the successors will turn toward a philosophical practice and critique of the age. "It is a psychological law that the theoretical mind, when it has become free in itself, is transformed into practical energy, and as *will* turns against the mundane reality which exists independent of it."[5] The spectacle of such half-contemplation and half-action is not edifying in either the post-Aristotelian or the post-Hegelian "*curriculum vitae*" of philosophy. But while the performance of the epigoni is depressing, the situation as such is inescapable.[6] Once human self-consciousness has become completely "concretized" in

4. Ibid., p. 81.
5. Ibid., pp. 64, 131.
6. The choice of the subject for the dissertation was determined by this insight. Marx was interested in post-Aristotelian philosophy because of the parallel with his own post-Hegelian situation. The point is expressly mentioned, ibid., p. 131.

a system of this kind, one cannot go back to the unreason of faith.[7] One can only advance, beyond the half-hearted epigonic compromise between philosophy and world, toward a complete surrender of philosophy and a radical "critique" of the world. "When Athens was threatened by devastation, Themistocles induced the Athenians to leave the city entirely, and to found a new Athens on the sea, as on a new element."[8] The precise nature of this step apparently had been clear to Marx even earlier than at the time of the dissertation. At least, in the letter to his father of November 10th, 1837, we find indications that an old faith had been shattered and that "new gods" had to be placed on the altar. From idealistic philosophy, Marx had turned (at the age of nineteen) toward "searching the idea in reality itself." Formerly the Gods had lived above the earth, now they have become its center.[9]

The attitude of revolt becomes historically effective through the fascinating program of incarnating the *logos* in the world by means of revolutionary human action. For Hegel, the *logos* (reason) was incarnating itself in reality, and because reason was in reality its manifestation could be discovered through the reflection of the philosopher. His philosophy of history was a contemplation of the actual unfolding of the Idea in reality. Never could the unfolding of the Idea be made the intention of human action. We should be aware in particular that Hegel's definition of the great historical figure as a person whose actions are in conformance with the movement of the Idea is not a recipe for becoming a great historical figure by producing this conformance at will. Nevertheless, this is precisely the perversion in which Marx indulged. Hegel's gnosis was contemplative. Instead of abandoning gnosis and restoring true contemplation, Marx abandoned contemplation and translated gnosis into action.

We have encountered this spiritual disease before in the late-medieval and Renaissance Paracletes, and in its full modern development in the Comtean Apocalypse of Man. Neither the fact that the *logos* in the Christian sense had been thinned out in Hegel to the Idea nor the ver-

7. Marx characterizes the religious culture of the Middle Ages as "the age of realized unreason" (ibid., p. 9). In this argument lies the fallacy of Marx's thought. When philosophical speculation has become completely "concretized," that is when it has reached the impasse of a radically gnostic interpretation of the universe like Hegel's, the *only* thing a spiritual realist can do is to drop gnosis and return to the original sources of order in the soul, that is to the experiences of faith. The "necessity" under which Marx considered himself to be burdened does not stem from the philosophical situation, but from the fact that he was in demonic revolt against God.
8. Ibid., p. 132.
9. Edition of Landshut and Mayer, 1, p. 7.

bose antireligiousness of Marx should obscure the fact that Marx was a Paraclete in the best medieval, sectarian style, a man in whom the *logos* had become incarnate and through whose action in the world mankind at large would become the vessel of the *logos*.

This characterization must be qualified, however, insofar as Marx does not conceive the *logos* as a transcendental spirit descending into man, but as a true essence of man which comes into its own through the process of history. Man, that is the true man, must be "emancipated" from historical encumbrances which still hold him in fetters in order to achieve his completely free existence in society. The true essence of man, his divine self-consciousness, is present in the world as the ferment which drives history forward in a meaningful manner. At some point, this essence will break through—first in one man, then in a few, until the great revolution will bring the full social realization of true man. The conception of this breakthrough is substantially the same as in Comte's realization of the positive mind in one individual through the process of his meditation and the expansion of this personal renovation into social regeneration. The Marxian spiritual disease, thus, like the Comtean, consists in the self-divinization and self-salvation of man; an intramundane *logos* of human consciousness is substituted for the transcendental *logos*. What appeared on the level of symptoms as antiphilosophism and logophobia, must etiologically be understood as the revolt of immanent consciousness against the spiritual order of the world.[10]

The Theses on Feuerbach—*the new materialism*

This is the core of the Marxian idea. This core itself has been elaborated frequently and voluminously by Marx, and beyond this core stretch the even more voluminous ramifications of detail. We shall restrict ourselves to the presentation of a few documents in which the formulations are most strongly concentrated. Let us first consider the *Theses on Feuerbach.*[11]

The *Theses on Feuerbach* are important for us principally as a concise dictionary that permits us to relate the Marxian terminology to traditional philosophical terms. On the fundamental problem of the conflict between philosophy and the new nonphilosophy, *Thesis 11* informs us:

10. Incidentally, this should make it clear why "discussion" with a Marxist or Positivist is senseless. One cannot enter into rational discourse with a "case" whose disease consists in the denial of the order of the *logos.*

11. Under this name go two pages of a notebook of Marx, containing eleven theses "*ad Feuerbach.*" They are published in *Gesamtausgabe,* 5, pp. 533–535.

"the philosophers have only *interpreted* the world in their various ways; the point, however, is to *change* it." This sentence is the key to the understanding of the aggregate of theses. If the opposition of "interpretation" and "change" were related to the traditional Aristotelian division of theory and practice, there would be no point in the antithesis. Philosophers, of course, interpret the world, for that precisely is the function of the *bios theoretikos;* to deprecate this function by pointing to the relevance (*es kömmt darauf an*) of changing the world would be senseless, for nobody maintains that contemplation is a substitute for practice, or vice versa. Moreover, one cannot "change the world" as one can "interpret the world"; one can only act *within* the world. This curious terminology, however, reveals the intention of Marx of embodying into "practice" the attitude toward the world that is possible only as contemplation. The "practice" of Marx can change the "world," because the world is understood as a stream of existence within which the idea, or reason, moves concretely. The *logos* is not an unchangeable order of the soul and the world, to be discovered in contemplative detachment from the world, it is instead a dialectically moving idea within the world, and we can come to grips with this moving idea only by embedding ourselves through practice into its historically concrete motion. The Marxian "practice," we may say, is a pseudological practice, corresponding to the pseudological speculation that we discussed previously.

The "world" is the concrete stream of history. The life of man is essentially social, a part of the life of mankind in history. Man has no destiny of the soul in the religious sense, apart from the destiny of the social, historical world of mankind. From this position, Marx criticizes Feuerbach because the latter has dissolved religion psychologically as an illusionary construction of man but still has left standing the nature of individual man as the originator of the illusion. According to Feuerbach, God is an imaginary subject, projected by the mind of man, to which are attributed the highest human values. "The absolute being, the God of man, is the being of man itself." God is the "mirror of man"; into God man has projected "his highest thoughts and his purest feelings," God, therefore, is "the essence of man." The great turning point of history will come when "man becomes conscious that the only God of man is man himself." "*Homo homini Deus!*" "The spectre of God must be laid, and man must take back what he has thrown away by projecting it into a divine, supernatural existence."[12] With all this, Marx is in hearty agreement. He is not satisfied, however, with what he calls

12. On the views of Feuerbach see Henri de Lubac, *Le Drame de l'Humanisme Athée*, pp. 23ff.

Feuerbach's dissolution of "the religious essence into *human* essence" (*Thesis 6*). Such human essence, the "religious mind" of the individual, is a nonexisting abstract (*6* and *7*). Feuerbach assumes an "isolated" individual as the creator of the religious illusion. The individual, however, has no "human essence"; in its reality it is "the whole of social relationships" (*6*). The "religious mind" in itself is a social product and an individual feels religiously because it "belongs to a specific social form" (*7*). Feuerbach has correctly seen the "fact of religious self-alienation" in the creation of a supernatural divine existence, and, in its wake, "the duplication of the world into a religious and a mundane world." He has, indeed, "reduced the religious world to its mundane basis." But he has not seen the most important problem: that there must be a reason why "the mundane basis distinguishes itself from itself, and fixes for itself an independent realm in the clouds." This peculiar process can be explained only through "a schism and self-contradiction within the mundane basis." Feuerbach's analysis does not go far enough. The contradiction in the mundane basis itself must be "theoretically understood and practically revolutionized" (*Thesis 4*).

We must read a summarizing sentence like, "Social life is essentially *practical*" (*Thesis 8*), with these clarifications of the meaning of practice in mind. We should not misunderstand the practice of social life as a basis for a life of meditation in solitude. The attributes mean that all life is social, that it has no dimension of solitude, and that all life is practical, that it has no legitimate dimension of contemplation in the Aristotelian sense. Hence, "all mysteries that might induce mysticism in theory, will find their rational solution in human practice and in understanding this practice" (*8*). In his zeal for closing the stream of existential practice hermetically against all deviations into contemplation, Marx expressly condemns any attempt at producing social change through education. Such an attempt would overlook the fact that the educators must be educated themselves; it would split society into two parts of which one is superior to the rest in a miraculous manner. Circumstances can be changed only through human action and this change and action coincide so that in fact a change of circumstances is a self-transformation. This self-transformation is the very process that must be understood as "*revolutionary practice*" (*Thesis 3*). The idea of a subject of cognition and morals as distinguished from objects of cognitive and moral action must be abolished and the subject itself must be conceived as "objectional" (*gegenständlich*) and human activity as "objectional activity." Reality, on the other hand, must not be conceived as object for a subject, but as "sensuously human activity" (*sinnlich menschliche Tätigkeit*) (*Thesis 1*). In terms of philosophical tradition, revolutionary practice is thus defined as an existential stream in which the subject is objectified and the object subjectified. This is the position which Marx calls his "new materialism." It is the position of "human society or social humanity" as distinguished from the position which recognizes individual man and bourgeois (*bürgerliche*) society (*Theses 9* and *10*).[13]

Critique of heaven and critique of the earth

The Marxian critical practice starts with the critique of religion and it proceeds to the critique of politics and economics. The problem of this systematically second phase has been formulated by Marx in the *Kritik der Hegelschen Rechtsphilosophie*.[14] "The critique of religion ends with the insight that man is the highest being for man; this implies the categorical imperative to overthrow all relationships in which man is a humiliated, oppressed, neglected, despised being."[15] "The critique of religion is the presupposition of all critique." In the illusionary reality of heaven, man "has looked for the superman"; instead he found the reflection of himself. Now he realizes that he himself is the superman and he will no longer be satisfied with recognizing himself as the "non-man (*Unmensch*)" that he formerly believed himself to be. "Man makes religion, not religion man." "Religion is the self-consciousness and self-feeling of a man who either has not yet found himself, or who has lost himself again." This man, however (directed against Feuerbach!), is not an abstract being outside the world. "Man is the world of man," that is state and society. This social world produces religion "as a perverted consciousness of the world because it is a perverted (*verkehrte*) world." Religion is the "general theory" of a perverted world. It gives "imaginary reality to human essence (*Wesen*) because human essence has no true reality." "The struggle against religion is the struggle against that world of which religion is the spiritual aroma." Religious misery is the manifestation of real misery, and at the same time a protest against it. Religion is the cry of oppressed creatures—"it is the opium of the people."[16]

The destruction of religion is the beginning of the revolution, not its end. The "illusionary happiness of the people" must now be replaced by

13. For an entirely different interpretation of the *Theses on Feuerbach*, the reader should refer to Sidney Hook, *From Hegel to Marx* (London, 1936), pp. 272–307.

14. Karl Marx, *Kritik der Hegelschen Rechtsphilosophie*, "Einleitung" (1843), *Gesamtausgabe*, 1, p. 607ff.

15. Ibid., pp. 614f.

16. Ibid., p. 607.

"its real happiness." The "imaginary flowers on the chain" have not been torn off in order that mankind would have to wear an "unimaginative chain without consolation"; on the contrary, man should now throw away the chain and break the living flower.[17] Disillusioned man should now regain his reason, and "move around himself as around his real sun." Now that the "beyond of truth" has disappeared, it is "the task of history" to establish "the truth of this world." "The critique of heaven changes into a critique of the earth," the critique of religion and theology into the "critique of law and politics."[18]

When Marx embarks on his critique of law and politics, however, he does not criticize actual institutions; instead, he criticizes Hegel's *Philosophy of Law*. In justifying this procedure, he has made a contribution to the understanding of German politics and of its conflict with Western political culture that even today is well worth reading as a whole. In the present context, however, we must confine ourselves to his principle of interpretation. Marx has observed the time lag in political development between Germany and the West. The English and French revolutions have abolished the *ancien régime* in their areas and established the modern national state as the expression and instrument of bourgeois society (*bürgerliche Gesellschaft*). The revolutions were carried to success by a class but they were experienced as representative revolutions of the nation. A revolution of this kind cannot always be made with success since certain conditions must be fulfilled. That "a *part* of society emancipates itself and obtains *general* rule" is possible only if the revolutionary class can undertake "the general emancipation of society from its particular position." The political emancipation from the feudal regime can be experienced as generally valid only when the new values of economic and educational privileges become accessible to everybody—at least on principle. In fact, this will hardly ever be the case. Hence, "no class of society can play this role without evoking a moment (*ein Moment*) of enthusiasm in itself and in the masses, a moment in which it fraternizes and flows together with society at large, in which it can be taken for society and be experienced and recognized as its *general representative*." "Only in the name of universal rights of society can a particular class vindicate general rule for itself." "Revolutionary energy and spiritual pathos (*Selbstgefühl*)" are not sufficient for obtaining this emancipatory position. In order to achieve this "coincidence of a national revolution with the emancipation of a particular class," another class must exist which is experienced as the "social sphere of the notorious crime against the whole of society," so that the

17. Ibid., pp. 607f. The simile of the "imaginary flowers on the chain," etc., is probably the last transformation of the Rosicrucian symbolism of Hegel.
18. Ibid., p. 608.

liberation from this class can appear as the general liberation. The "negative-general" importance of the French nobility and clergy conditioned the "positive-general" importance of the French bourgeoisie as the emancipating class.

In all these respects, German political development is behind the times. No revolutions have occurred and an anachronistic *ancien régime* continues to exist. And there is no prospect of a revolution in the Western sense, for neither has Germany a class of such "courage and ruthlessness" that it could appear as the "negative representative" of society, nor does it have an estate of sufficient "breadth of the soul" and "revolutionary audacity" that even the momentary identification with the "soul of the people" would be possible. "In Germany the relation between the various spheres of society is not dramatic, it is epic." As a consequence, every sphere of German society "experiences its defeat, before it can celebrate a victory," develops its narrowness before it can unfold its generosity, is involved in its struggle with the next lower class when it begins its struggle against the higher class. "The princes are engaged in a struggle against kingship, the bureaucrats against the nobility, the bourgeoisie against them all, while the proletarians already enter into their struggle against the bourgeoisie."[19]

The difference of political development in the Western national states and in Germany has important consequences. The Western revolutions are not the end of history. The modern state in its perfection has liberated man insofar as differences of religion and property no longer determine differences of political status for the individual. "The perfect political state is by its nature the generic life of man in opposition to his material life." The whole structure of "egoistic life," however, is retained as social life outside the sphere of the state. In the perfect political state, man leads a double life: in political community he lives with his generic being, in society he lives as a private individual. The complete liberation through complete socialization of man is not yet achieved. "Political emancipation is a great progress"; nevertheless "it is not the last form of human emancipation" but only "the last form of human emancipation *within* the present world order."[20] In Germany, on the other hand, not even political emancipation has been achieved. But precisely because the German political situation is anachronistic, German political speculation could abstract from this reality and instead, through Hegel, develop "the idea of the modern state" into its last consequences. "The Germans have *thought* in politics, what the other nations have *done*. Germany was their theoretical *conscience*." The in-

19. Ibid., pp. 617ff.
20. Karl Marx, *Bruno Bauer: Die Judenfrage* (1843), op. cit., 1, pp. 584ff.

completeness of human emancipation through the political state has come to consciousness in German political thought. The question is: can Germany achieve a practice, that is a revolution, *à la hauteur des principles*, lifting it not only "to the *official level* of modern nations, but to the *human height* that will be the next future of these nations?"[21]

In this opposition of Germany and the Western nations, and in particular in the question just raised, Marx is closest to being a German national thinker. He was seriously concerned about the place of Germany among the nations. He saw the political misery that seemed to cut off all hope for a historical role of importance but he also saw the splendid intellectual achievement. He regarded himself as a thinker who could draw the practical consequences of the Hegelian philosophy of the state but he was in doubt as to whether the German people could become the carrier of the ultimate revolution for the liberation of mankind. Germany has not scaled "the middle steps of political emancipation together with the modern nations." It has not reached in practice the steps which in theory it has passed. How should the *"salto mortale"* of the "radical revolution" be possible? Much more probable seems to be another end: "One morning, Germany will find herself on the level of European decadence (*Verfall*), before she has ever reached the level of European emancipation."[22] This prophetic vision, however, is rejected by Marx. He does not consider a political revolution in the Western sense a possibility for Germany, but he still believes in the possibility of the revolution. "Not the radical revolution is a utopian dream for Germany, not the general human emancipation, but rather the partial revolution that is only political."[23] The German emancipation will never be achieved piecemeal by particular classes of society, as in the West, but it can be achieved at one stroke by a class which is part of the bourgeois society and at the same time not part of it, that is by the proletariat.[24]

The proletariat is "an estate which is the dissolution of all estates," "a social sphere which has universal character through its universal suffering"; it has no particular claim because no particular injustice, but injustice as such is committed against it; it has no historical title, it has nothing but the human title; it is a social sphere "which cannot emancipate itself without emancipating all other spheres of society"; it is "the complete loss of man, and, therefore, cannot regain itself without regaining man completely." "The proletariat is the dissolution of society in form of a particular estate." "When the proletariat announces the dissolution of the present order of the world, it only reveals the secret of

21. "Einleitung," pp. 613f.
22. Ibid., p. 616.
23. Ibid., p. 617.
24. Ibid., pp. 619f.

its existence, for it is in fact the dissolution of this order of the world."
The proletariat, thus, will be the material weapon of philosophy, while
in philosophy it finds its spiritual weapons. When the lightning of
thought has struck into this soil of the people, the emancipation of the
German into Man will be accomplished. "The head of this emancipation
is philosophy, its heart is the proletariat. Philosophy cannot become
reality without abolishing the proletariat, the proletariat cannot abolish
itself without realizing philosophy."[25]

This faith in the translation of philosophy into reality through the
German proletariat is supported by a historical reflection on the German Reformation. The faith in a revolution that starts with speculation
makes sense in the light of the German past. "Germany's revolutionary
past is theoretical, it is the Reformation. At that time it was the *monk*,
now it is the *philosopher*, in whose brain the revolution begins." Luther's Reformation was the first step of a German revolution. He broke
the faith in authority, but he put in its place the authority of faith. He
liberated man from external religiousness but he made religiousness the
substance of man. Protestantism, thus, has not brought the true solution, but it has revealed the true task, that is: the struggle against the
priest. The struggle of the layman with the priest outside himself had
been won; now the struggle has to be continued against the priest
within man, against the priestly substance of man. "The most radical
fact of German history," the Peasant War, broke against the wall of
the new Protestant theology. Today, when this theology itself has broken down, the anachronistic, political state will be broken by the new
philosophy.[26] These passages show that Marx was perfectly aware of
the connection between his own thought and German Protestantism.
There is, indeed, an intelligible line of meaning running from Luther's
destruction of ecclesiastical authority, through the destruction of dogmatic symbols in the generation of Strauss, Bruno Bauer, and Feuerbach, to the destruction of "all the gods," that is of all authoritative
order, in Marx. While it would be incorrect to say that the way of Protestantism leads with any inner necessity from Luther to Hegel and
Marx, it is true that Marxism is the final product of disintegration in
one branch of German, liberal Protestantism.

Emancipation and alienation

Emancipation is the general category under which Marx conceives
the advancement of man to his complete freedom. "*All* emancipation is
reduction of the human world, of relationships, to *man himself*." Re-

25. Ibid., pp. 619–621.
26. Ibid., p. 615.

ligious emancipation is the reduction of religion to the religion-making consciousness of man, as accomplished by Feuerbach. "Political emancipation is the reduction of man, on the one hand to a member of bourgeois society, that is to the *egoistic, independent* individual, on the other hand to the *citizen*, that is to the moral person." This schism of man must be overcome through the next and last step in emancipation. Only when "the real, individual man takes back the abstract citizen," only when as individual man he has become *generic being* (*Gattungswesen*) "in his empirical life, in his individual work, in his individual relationships," only when man "has recognized his '*forces propres*' as *social* forces and organized as such," only when, as a consequence, he "no longer separates social force from himself in form of *political* force," is human emancipation completed.[27] The overcoming of the state is a historical problem which resembles in its structure the overcoming of religion. "The political constitution was hitherto the *religious sphere*, the *religion* of a people's life, it was the heaven of its generality in opposition to the *earthly existence* of its reality. . . . *Political life* in the modern sense is the *scholasticism* of a people's life."[28]

The course of past history has been the "alienation" of man, the task of future history is his "emancipation." In alienation, or self-alienation, man loses himself to the beyond of religion and social institutions, through emancipation he draws these objectified sectors of his essence back into his existence. We have arrived at the core of the Marxian philosophy of history. The history of emancipation (from religious, through political, to ultimate social emancipation) is the reversal of the process of alienation. In order to arrive at the critical solution, the revolutionary thinker must have a critical understanding of the genesis of the evil. The contemporary evil has its origin in the relation between man and nature; it can be overcome only through bringing nature under the control of man so that freedom beyond nature can unfold. The vicissitudes of man's relation with nature are the subject matter of history. We must trace the history of man from its most primitive beginnings, when man emerges from his animal condition. We must follow it through the various phases in which man becomes ever more deeply involved in the process of production, to the point of complete self-alienation. We must, further, study the possibilities of emancipation which grow parallel with increasing alienation and we must, finally, conceive the idea of the revolutionary overthrow of the order of alienation and its replacement by the order of freedom.

27. *Zur Judenfrage*, op. cit., p. 599.
28. *Kritik der Hegelschen Rechtsphilosophie, ad* sec. 279, op. cit., p. 436.

Substance and process of history

All critical history must start with certain "presuppositions." They must, however, not be of a dogmatic nature; they must be "real presuppositions." They are "the real individuals, their actions and material conditions of life." The first presupposition is "the existence of living human individuals" with a bodily organization and the relation to the rest of nature which is conditioned by this organization.[29] Man distinguishes himself from animal as soon as he starts *producing* his means of life; in such production men indirectly produce their material life. Their way of production becomes their way of life (*Lebensweise*). From this starting point, Marx traces the differentiation of production from sexual reproduction and division of labor on the level of the family, through further differentiation on the tribal and other local levels, to the system of production and division of labor under the conditions of modern national societies and their interrelation in a world market. Parallel with this differentiation of production goes the development of ideas in politics, law, morals, religion and metaphysics in close correlation with the process of material production of life. "Consciousness can never be anything but conscious being (*Bewusstsein, bewusstes Sein*), and the being of man is his real life-process." "Ideologies" have no history of their own; they are a by-product of the material process. "Not consciousness determines life; it is life that determines consciousness." With the development of critical history, "philosophy loses its medium of existence." It can be replaced, at best, "by a summary of general results that can be abstracted from the study of the historical development of mankind." Such abstractions, however, are worthless if they are separated from real history. They can only facilitate the ordering of historical materials—in the manner in which Marx is doing it.[30]

The "material process of production" and its differentiation through division of labor are established as the irreducible substance of history. This process of differentiation contains an inevitable conflict of increasing acerbity, that is the conflict between the interest of the working individual and the interest of the larger group of individuals who are engaged in production through division of labor and exchange of products. "As soon as labor is divided, a definite, exclusive range of activity is assigned to everybody; this range is imposed on him, he cannot escape it; he is hunter, fisher or herdsman, or critical critic, and he must re-

29. *Deutsche Ideologie* (1844–45), *Gesamtausgabe*, 5, p. 10,
30. Ibid., pp. 10–17.

main it unless he wants to lose his means of life."[31] While under more primitive technological conditions such dependence on specialized activity is still bearable because even specialization on this level leaves a broad field for diversified human work, the situation becomes disastrous under conditions of industrial production for a world market. "The fixation of social activity, the consolidation of our own product into an objective power (*sachliche Gewalt*) dominating us, growing out of control, crossing our expectations, destroying our calculations, is one of the principal factors in historical evolution."[32] "The more wealth he produces, and the more his production gains in power and volume, the poorer becomes the worker." "Work does not produce commodities only; it produces itself and the worker as a *commodity*." "The realization of work is its objectification." "The worker puts his life into the object; but then his life is no longer his but the object's." "What the product of his work is, he is not." "The life that he has given to the object, opposes him as inimical and alien." "The worker becomes the serf of his object." "His work is external to his being." "He does not affirm, he negates himself in his work." "Only outside his work the worker is with himself, in his work he is outside himself." "He is at home when he does not work, and when he works he is not at home." "Hence his work is not voluntary but compulsory, it is *compulsory labor*. It is not a satisfaction of his wants, but only a means for satisfying wants outside his work." "The result is that the working man can feel himself free only in his animal functions of eating, drinking and procreating, and perhaps in his housing, ornaments, etc., while in his specifically human functions he is only an animal." "Eating, drinking and procreating certainly are genuine human functions, too. But in the abstraction which separates them from the wider range of human activity and makes them ultimate and sole aims, they are beastly (*tierisch*)." Man is distinguished from animal through the universality of his relation with nature; he does not produce for necessity alone, but can give form to his material existence through science and beauty. This whole range of productive activity which distinguishes human life is degraded to the level of a means of life. The productive, free existence of man "becomes a means for his physical existence." This "alienation" of human productivity is inherent in the division of labor; it has nothing to do with higher or lower wages. A rise in wages would be nothing "but a better salary for slaves; it would not for the worker and his work recover their human destiny and dignity." "Even an equality of income, as demanded

31. Ibid., p. 22.
32. Ibid., pp. 22f.

by Proudhon, changes only the relation of the worker to his work into that of all men to their work. Society would then become the Capitalist in the abstract."[33] The conditions of existence in modern society have become an accident for the worker over which he has no control and "over which no *social* organization can give him control."[34]

The last sentences should destroy the assumption (which is frequently made) that Marx was impressed by the actual misery of the worker in his time, and that with the material improvement of the worker's lot the causes of the revolution would disappear. Social reform is *not* a remedy for the evil which Marx has in mind. This evil is the growth of the economic structure of modern society into an "objective power" to which man must submit by threat of starvation. The principal characteristic features which appear on and off in the descriptions of Marx can now be summarized:

(1) The separation of the worker from his tools. This characteristic is determined by industrial technology. No man can individually own and operate the tools of modern industrial production. The "factory" or, generally, the "place of work," cannot be the "home."

(2) Job dependence. This characteristic has the same determining cause. No man can earn a living in an industrial system unless he finds a job in some "enterprise" which assembles the tools for production and markets the product.

(3) Division of labor. No man can produce any whole product. The process of production must be centrally planned, and the single worker is confined to the phase in the process assigned to him. Marx was very much aware of the supreme insult to human dignity which lies in the fact that at the end of his life, when a man summarizes what he has accomplished, he may have to say: all my life I have spent in cooperating in the production of a certain type of Grand Rapids furniture and thereby degraded humanity in myself and others.

(4) Specialization. This characteristic is intimately connected with the preceding one. Even if the total product is not an insult to human dignity, the productivity of man has no appreciable range for unfolding if his work is confined to a small sector of production on which as a whole he has no influence.

(5) Economic interdependence. No man can live a whole life if his existence is permanently threatened, not by natural catastrophies as in the case of a peasant, but by social actions beyond his control—be they new inventions, or the closing of a market through a tariff, or miscal-

33. *Oekonomisch-philosophische Manuskripte* (1844), *Gesamtausgabe*, 3, pp. 82–93.
34. *Deutsche Ideologie*, op. cit., p. 66.

culation of management, or change in customers' taste, or a general economic crisis.

Socialistic man

All of these characteristics are connected with the industrial system of production. Since Marx does not wish to abolish the industrial system, and in particular since he is fully aware that no change in social organization, as for instance public ownership of the instruments of production, can abolish these evils, the question arises: what precisely does he want to achieve by a Communist revolution? This is the crucial point of the Marxian system of thought and it is the point which ordinarily is neglected. Marx has not said much about it, but he has said enough to make his intentions clear beyond a doubt. Wild as it may sound, he wanted to retain the industrial system of production with its inevitable technological differentiation of work, but he wanted to abolish human specialization. Man was supposed to emerge from the revolution as an integrally productive being that at his will would work one day at a machine, the next day in an office, and the third day as a *litterateur*. A primitive, but unmistakable formulation of the idea occurs on the occasion of his complaints that division of labor produces such occupational fixations as hunter, fisher, etc. This evil will be overcome in "Communist society, where nobody has an exclusive range of activity, but everybody can train himself in every branch; where society regulates general production and thereby makes it possible for me to do one thing today and another thing tomorrow, to hunt in the morning, to fish in the afternoon, to be a husbandman in the evening, and to indulge in critical work after supper, as it pleases me, without any necessity for me ever to become a hunter, fisherman, husbandman or critic."[35]

Again, incredible as it may sound, this is the vision which Marx transfers to the situation of the modern industrial system. The revolution in face of "alienation" is necessary in order that men can regain their "self-activity" (*Selbstbetätigung*) as well as in order to secure their existence. It will assume the form of "an appropriation of the existing totality of productive forces." Under international division of labor, these forces exist in the form of a universal, world-wide system of interdependence. "The appropriation, therefore, must have a universal character which corresponds to the universality of productive forces and commerce. The appropriation of these forces is in itself nothing but the development of individual faculties in correspondence with the material

35. Ibid., p. 22.

instruments of production. Hence, the appropriation of a totality of instruments of production is the development of a totality of faculties in the individuals." In order to achieve a human revolution of this kind, a certain type of individual is needed. Only the proletarians are capable of performing the feat because their individual existence is no longer bound up with a special type of property that would limit the interest of their activity. All former revolutions were limited (*borniert*), because the self-activity of the revolutionary class was limited by its specific kind of private property. The proletarian without property is the fit agent to bring a mass of productive instruments "under each individual," and to "subsume property under all." Moreover, the method of the revolution is determined by the universal character of the industrial system. Only a universal association of proletarians on a world scale can break the power of the present economic and social structure and only such a universal revolution will develop the universal character and the energy that are necessary to execute the appropriation. Only after this revolution will "self-activity coincide with material life." Only then "are individuals developed into total individuals," "work will have changed into self-activity," and the "hitherto conditioned commerce will have changed into the commerce of individuals as such." The division of labor cannot be abolished by forgetting about it; the "individuals must subsume the objective forces under themselves and thereby abolish (*aufheben*) division of labor. This is impossible without community. Only in community with others does the individual have the means at his disposition to develop his faculties in all directions."[36]

The "total individual" or (in other contexts) "socialistic man" is the aim of history. Man must regain himself completely from his alienation in order to become the perfectly free and independent being which in essence he is. The "liberation from property" is the last act of this drama. Let us now turn to a passage in which Marx has concisely formulated the connection between his idea of social revolution and his original revolt against God. "A being is independent only when it stands on its own feet; and it stands on its own feet only when it owes its existence to nobody but itself." A man who lives by grace of somebody else, is dependent; and I live most completely by the grace of somebody else when he "has created my life," when the source of my life lies outside

36. Ibid., pp. 57f., 63f. The reader should also compare *Kapital*, 1, pp. 42–46. The thought is substantially the same as that in the *Deutsche Ideologie*. There occur, however, such famous formulations as the "*Fetischcharakter der Warenwelt*" (p. 39), the very revealing comparison of the postrevolutionary industrial society with the situation of the all-sided Robinson (p. 45), and the reflection on Christianity as the ideological environment in which the idea of the limited individual thrives (pp. 45f.).

myself. Creation, Marx reflects sadly, is an idea that is rather deeply rooted in the consciousness of man. The being-through-itself of nature and man is inconceivable to him because it contradicts all tangible experiences (*Handgreiflichkeiten*) of practical life. Man knows himself as a link in the chain of being, and of necessity he will ask: where is this chain suspended? And what can we answer to the inopportune questioner? Marx gives the same answer as Comte: don't ask such questions; they are "abstractions"; they make "no sense"; stick to the reality of being and becoming![37] As in the case of Comte, at the critical moment we are faced by the demand not to ask idle questions. The man who does not ask such questions is, by definition, "socialistic man."[38]

Crude communism and true communism

For socialistic man the "whole so-called history of the world" is nothing but the production of man through the work of man. In this process he has under his eyes "the irresistible proof of his *birth:* Through himself, of his genetic process." The essentiality (*Wesenhaftigkeit*) of man in nature is given to sensual intuition and in the face of this experience the quest for an *alien* being beyond nature and man becomes a practical impossibility. "Atheism, as the denial of this nonessentiality (*Unwesentlichkeit*), no longer makes sense, for atheism is a *negation of God* and through this negation posits the *existence of man.*" Socialism needs no such mediation. It starts immediately with the sensuous consciousness of man in nature as true essence. It is positive self-consciousness of man, not mediated through the denial of religion. And in the same manner, "true life" is the positive reality of man, not mediated through abolition of private property, that is through communism. For the next phase in history, communism is positive as "negation of the negation," "but communism as such is not the aim of human development,—it is not the form of human society."[39] Communism, like atheism, is a counter idea to a historical state that must be overcome. Marx, like Bakunin, is aware of the danger that lies in facile attempts to give content to the vision of the future by elaborating a catalogue of concrete demands which can be nothing but negatives of present evils. Communism is not an institutional reform; it is, rather, a change in the nature of man.

With this danger in view, Marx has distinguished carefully between "crude communism" (*roher Kommunismus*) and "true communism" or socialism. Crude communism is the "positive expression" of abolished private property; it establishes "general private property" which is only

37. *Oekonomisch-philosophische Manuskripte* (1844), 3, pp. 124f.
38. Ibid., p. 125, ll. 18ff.
39. Ibid., pp. 125f.

a "generalization and perfection of private property." The domination of the property in things is so enormous that crude communism wants to annihilate everything that cannot be owned as private property by everybody. It considers physical, immediate ownership the only purpose of life. The worker's existence is not abolished, but extended to everybody; it wants to destroy all distinguishing talent by violence, etc. The nature of this type of communism becomes particularly clear in its idea of a communalization of women. "We may say that the idea of a community of women reveals the secret of this crude and thoughtless communism": woman leaves marriage and enters into general prostitution; the world of wealth leaves private property and enters into general prostitution with the community. Such communism, "in its radical negation of the *personality* of man," is a continuation of the former private property. "The general *envy* which constitutes itself as power is only a hidden form in which *avarice* restores itself and satsifies itself under a different form." Competition under conditions of private property is envy and desire of levelling, turned against greater private property. The crude communist manifests the perfection of this desire for levelling from the position of an imagined minimum. Such abolition of private property is not its true appropriation; it negates civilization in its return to an unnatural simplicity of poor people who are not beyond private property but have not yet arrived at it. Hence, the community of crude communism is nothing but a community of work and of equality of income paid out by the community as the general capitalist. "Crude communism, thus, is only a manifestation of the rascality (*Niedertracht*) of private property that wants to establish itself as a positive community."[40]

The nature of true communism we have discussed already. Let us, in conclusion, add a few formulations from the present passage. True communism is the return of man to himself as social man "within the whole wealth of human development up to this point." It is a completed humanistic naturalism, "the true solution of the conflict between man and nature." "It is the solved riddle of history and knows itself as the solution." Communist society "is the true resurrection of nature, the realized naturalism of man and the realized humanism of nature."[41]

The Manifesto

The genesis of the idea is substantially completed with its appearance on the world scene in the form of the *Communist Manifesto* (De-

40. Ibid., pp. 111–113.
41. Ibid., pp. 114, 116.

cember 1847–January 1848).[42] As far as the ideas of history, revolution and communism are concerned, the *Manifesto* contains nothing that is new; on the contrary it contains considerably less than the result of our preceding analysis, as is inevitable in a document which does not pursue theoretical intentions but serves a propaganda purpose. Nevertheless, we must briefly dwell on the formulations. The *Manifesto* is a masterpiece of political rhetoric. After a century, its formulae have lost nothing of their revolutionary pathos and their effectiveness on the political scene.

In the Preamble the authors fix the scale of importance for their pronunciamento. Communism is recognized as a force by all European powers. It is a spectre that haunts Europe. The pope and the tsar, Metternich and Guizot, French radicals and German policemen have allied themselves in a "holy alliance" to exorcise this spectre. Such recognition by the old powers creates an obligation for the Communists to clarify their views and to submit them to the public. The new world force enters the lists against the powers of the old world.

The first section of the *Manifesto* develops the historical perspective of Communism. "The history of all society up to the present is the history of class struggles." There have always been classes and estates, oppressors and oppressed. Modern society, however, is distinguished from all earlier periods through the simplicity of the pattern. "Our whole society is splitting more and more into two great hostile camps, into two great classes facing each other—Bourgeoisie and Proletariat." The appealing pattern of Manichaean simplicity is set; there are only two forces, good and evil, and anyone who is not on the good side is inevitably on the bad side. The *Manifesto*, then, follows this pattern and deals, first, with the rise of the bourgeoisie and second, with the proletariat.

The bourgeoisie has risen from the serfs of the Middle Ages to become the operator of modern industry and commerce, spanning the globe. As its political instrument it has created the modern representative state. "The bourgeoisie has a most revolutionary role in history." The description of the revolutionary role begins with such remarks as: the bourgeoisie "has destroyed all feudal, patriarchal, idyllic relationships." But the derogatory beginnings soon change into a praise of the achievements of the bourgeoisie as no enlightened progressivist has ever written. The bourgeoisie "has accomplished much greater miracles than Egyptian pyramids, Roman aqueducts and Gothic cathedrals." It has made "production and consumption of all countries cosmopolitan," it has

42. *Manifest der Kommunistischen Partei, Gesamtausgabe,* 6, pp. 523ff.

"drawn away the national soil from under the feet of industry." The old "local and national self-sufficiency and exclusiveness" has been replaced by a general interdependence of all nations. And what it has done for material it has done for intellectual production. "National onesidedness and limitation becomes more and more impossible, and from the many national and local literatures, there rises a world literature." Through improvement of communications "even the most barbaric nations are drawn into civilization." All nations must adopt bourgeois methods of production, unless they want to perish. "In one word, it has created a world in its own image." It has created our great cities, and "torn an appreciable part of the population from the idiocy of rural life." "It has made the countryside dependent on the city, the barbaric or half-barbaric countries on the civilized ones, the peasant nations on the bourgeois nations, the Orient on the Occident." "In its class rule of barely a century the bourgeoisie has created more massive and colossal forces of production than all preceding generations together." In brief: we hear the authentic tones of a Condorcet, with the massive pride in the expected complete destruction of all historical civilizations and the transformation of all mankind into a universal bourgeois society.

The splendor of the bourgeoisie, however, is transitory like everything in the world except Communism. The bourgeoisie must go and its achievements will be inherited by the successor that has grown under its rule, by the proletariat, i.e. "the class of modern workers who live only as long as they can find work." The characterization of proletarian existence contains nothing new. Of interest, however, is the description of the phases in the struggle. "Its struggle against the bourgeoisie begins with its existence." At the beginning we have no more than individual and local struggles against individual and local oppression. With the expansion of industry, the masses of proletarians grow and their common situation becomes more visible to them. Coalitions and associations are formed and local revolts break out. Momentary victories are followed by defeats; the real result is nation-wide coalition and the centralization of the class struggle. The proletariat is on its way toward organization as a class and party. The progressive proletarization of ever larger groups in society throws educated people into the proletariat. And the disintegration of the old society induces small groups of the ruling class to become renegade and to join the revolutionary class which has the future in its hands. "As formerly a part of the nobility went over to the bourgeoisie, so now a part of the bourgeoisie goes over to the proletariat, and in particular a part of the bourgeois-ideologists who have worked themselves through to an understanding of the historical movement." Thus, we have finally arrived at Marx and Engels themselves, the bourgeois-ideologists who can tell the proletarians what the historical process is all about and provide intellectual leadership in their capacity as organizers of the Communist party.

The second section of the *Manifesto* deals with the relation between proletarians and Communists. Here we find a new set of ideas concerning the function of Communist leadership in the proletarian struggle against the bourgeoisie. The opening sentences are of particular importance because they contain the principles which later were developed into the idea of Communism as the universal church of the proletariat. The section begins humbly enough: "The Communists are not a separate party in opposition (*gegenüber*) to other workers' parties." But the next sentence turns this rejection of rivalry into a universalist claim: "They have no interests separate from those of the proletariat as a whole." The implications are far-reaching, for this sentence is neither a statement of fact that would be open to verification, nor is it a program; it is the fundamental dogma which declares the spirit of the proletariat as a whole to be residing in the Communist party. Any programmatic intention is explicitly rejected by the following sentence: "They do not set up principles of their own by which they want to shape the proletarian movement." The Communists are not distinguished from other proletarian groups by principles and programs but by the universal level of their practice. "In the various national struggles of proletarians, they emphasize, and put to the fore, the common interests of the proletariat as a whole, independent of nationality"; and: "In the various successive stages through which the struggle between proletariat and bourgeoisie must pass, they always represent the interests of the movement as a whole." Beyond regional and temporal diversification of the struggle, there looms the central leadership of the Communists. And, indeed, the next paragraph formulates the vanguard principle: "In their practice, the Communists are the most resolute, ever forward pushing, section in the workers' parties of all countries; in their theory, they have the advantage over the great mass of the proletariat through their insight into conditions, course, and general results of the proletarian movement." In their immediate aims, for the rest, the Communists do not differ from other proletarian parties; these aims are: "Formation of the proletariat into a class, overthrow of bourgeois rule, conquest of political power through the proletariat."

The remainder of the second section deals with exposition and defense of the ultimate aims of Communism.

The authors stress the nonprogrammatic character of these aims. "The theoretical theses of Communists are in no way based on ideas or principles that have been invented or discovered by this or that world-reformer (*Weltverbesserer*)." "They are no more than general expressions of actual relationships in a real class struggle, in a historical movement that goes on under our very eyes." Communist theses, thus, must not be misunderstood as programmatic demands for changing an actual state of things; on the contrary, they reveal the actual state of things and suggest that the tendencies, actually inherent in the historical process, are carried to their full realization. Hence, the accusations levelled against Communism are unfounded. The opponents charge the Communists with the intention of abolishing private property. The *Manifesto* agrees that this is the substance of Communist theory. But what does this abolition mean in face of the fact that the socially relevant private property is capitalist property and the great mass of the people has no such property anyway? And if it is taken from those who already have it, is that really expropriation? No, for "Capital is a collective product and can be set into motion only through the common activity of many members of society, and in last resort only through the common activity of all members of society. Capital, therefore, is not a personal, it is a social power"; and to be a capitalist means "to hold not a purely personal, but a social position in production." "If, therefore, capital is converted into communal property, belonging to all members of society, such conversion does not transform personal property into social property. Only the social character of property is transformed. It loses its class character." The so-called expropriation, thus, only transforms an actual situation into a principle of public order. The same type of argument is, then, applied to the charges against abolition of bourgeois marriage, of nationality, of religion and of "eternal truths, like freedom, justice, etc."

The theses of Communism lift the march of history into consciousness. They are not a program for interference with an established order; they are an insight into an order that is coming into being, that is growing under the disintegrating order of the old society. The Communists and their followers can feel themselves the executors of the law of history. Again we must note the strong touch of Condorcet in this conception of the Communists as the directorate of mankind on its march toward the realm of freedom. (We cannot stress often enough that there is no fundamental conflict between enlightened progressivism and Communism.) Nevertheless, history does not march all by itself; the directorate must lend a helping hand. The raw material for the realization of the aim is present, that is: the proletarians as a class outside society, without property and without nationality ("The workers have no country"). But this material must be shaped through the awakening of class-consciousness, and then the revolution itself must be undertaken.

The conquest of power will be a prolonged process; between bourgeois rule and free society there will be interposed the transitional period of the dictatorship of the proletariat.[43] The first step will be the elevation of the proletariat to the place of the ruling class in democracy. The political domination will then be used "gradually to wrest all capital from the bourgeoisie, to centralize all instruments of production in the hands of the state, i.e., the proletariat organized as ruling class, and as rapidly as possible to increase the total of productive forces." This can be done only "through despotic interventions in the right of property and bourgeois conditions of production"; such measures may appear as indefensible by economic standards but they are inevitable for the purpose of revolutionizing the whole method of production. In the course of this development, class differences will disappear, production will be concentrated in the hands of the associated individuals, public power will lose its political character because it is no longer an instrument of class rule and, finally, the old society will be replaced by "an association in which everybody's free development is the condition for the free development of all." The *Manifesto* ends with the famous call to revolutionary association: "The proletarians have nothing to lose in it but their chains. They have a world to win. Working men of all countries, unite!"

Tactics

The *Manifesto* was published in February 1848. In the same month the revolution in Paris broke out. In 1850, when it was clear that the time for a proletarian world-revolution had not yet come, the eschatological excitement of the *Manifesto* subsided and the problems of revolutionary tactics came to the fore. We may conclude this study of the genesis of the Marxian idea with a few passages on tactics from the *Address* to the *Bund der Kommunisten* of March 1850.

The immediate problem for Communists was no longer the seizure of power in a democratic revolution. The democrats who were capable of winning a revolution were not Communists. The immediate problem was the alliance with revolutionary democratic groups wherever they started moving, and the ruthless fight against the allies on the morning after the common victory. It was already substantially the situation that we experienced in the Popular Front politics of the 1930's and the resumption of the fight against democracy after the Second World War. Marx informs his listeners that "the democratic petty-bourgeoisie want to

43. The term is not yet used in the *Manifesto*, though the subject matter is discussed.

conclude the revolution as fast as possible" as soon as they have taken care of their own interests. But "it is our interest and our task to make the revolution permanent until all more or less propertied classes are removed from power, until state power is conquered by the proletariat and until the association of proletarians has advanced not only in one country but in all important countries of the world to the point where rivalry between proletarians in different countries has ceased and at least the decisive productive forces are concentrated in their hands. We are not interested in a change in private property but only in its annihilation, not in conciliation of class antagonisms but in the abolition of classes, not in reforms of present society but in the foundation of a new one."[44] In order to carry on the fight, as far as possible a stabilization of the political situation must be prevented. During the conflict as well as immediately afterward, the proletarians must counteract all attempts at calming down the revolutionary excitement. The democratic parties must be held to their most radical promises and their most terroristic threats. Mob violence should not be prevented or even only tolerated, it should be fostered and organized by the Communists in order to compromise the democrats.[45] In the special German case, the Communists must oppose any attempt at a federative construction of the constitution. "Under no circumstances must it be tolerated that every village, city and province can oppose revolutionary activity which must proceed from a center in order to be most effective."[46] When a constitutional settlement is reached at last, the Communists must top every legislative reform measure proposed by the democrats by a more revolutionary demand of their own. "When the petty-bourgeois propose the purchase of railroads and factories, the workers must demand that these railroads and factories should be confiscated by the government without compensation because they are property of reactionaries. When the democrats propose a proportional tax, the workers demand a progressive one; when the democrats propose a moderately progressive one, the workers insist on a tax which rises so fast in the upper brackets that big capital will be ruined. When the democrats propose a regulation of the public debt, the workers demand a declaration of public bankruptcy. Hence, the demands of the workers must always be guided by the concessions and measures of the democrats."[47]

The details of the advice will change with the situation. The pattern

44. *Ansprache der Zentralbehörde an den Bund*, reprinted in Karl Marx, *Enthüllungen über den Kommunistenprozess zu Köln* (Berlin, 1914), p. 130.
45. Ibid., p. 132.
46. Ibid., p. 135.
47. Ibid., p. 137.

is clear and well-known to all of us: it is the systematic disruption of society in the hope of creating such disorder that the Communist minority can rise to victory.

Conclusion

While presenting the genesis of the Marxian idea, we have refrained as much as possible from critical commentary. In conclusion, a few evaluating remarks will be useful in order to balance the parts of the system against each other, as well as to estimate their historical relevance—which, of course, is not identical with the relevance attributed to them by Marx.

At the root of the Marxian idea we find the spiritual disease, the gnostic revolt. Not much need be said about it. The disease shows the characteristics that we have observed in the case of Comte and the Comtean characteristics, in their turn, belong to the larger pattern of the scientistic, antireligious disease that preceded him. The soul of Marx is demonically closed against transcendental reality. In the critical, post-Hegelian situation he cannot extricate himself from the difficulties by returning to the freedom of the spirit. His spiritual impotence leaves no way open but derailment into gnostic activism. Again we see the characteristic combination of spiritual impotence with the mundane lust for power, resulting in a grandiose mysticism of Paracletic existence. And again we see the conflict with reason, almost literally in the same form as in Comte, in the dictatorial prohibition of metaphysical questions concerning the ground of being, questions that might disturb the magic creation of a new world behind the prison walls of the revolt. Marx, like Comte, does not permit a rational discussion of his principles —you have to be a Marxist or shut up. We see again confirmed the correlation between spiritual impotence and antirationalism; one cannot deny God and retain reason.

Spiritual impotence destroys the order of the soul. Man is locked up in the prison of his particular existence. It does not, however, destroy the vitality of intellectual operations within the prison. The *Theses on Feuerbach*, whatever we may think of them in other respects, are an unsurpassed masterpiece of mystical speculation on the level of a demonically closed existence. Marx knew that he was a god creating a world. He did not want to be a creature. He did not want to see the world in the perspective of creaturely existence—though he admitted that man has difficulties in getting out of the rut. He rejected the great diremptions of being that are given in experience, the diremptions of man and world, of immanent being and transcendental reality, of man and God, subject and object, action and contemplation, the diremptions which point to the mystery of creation. He wanted to see the world from the point of the *coincidentia oppositorum*, that is from the position of God. He achieved this view in the *Theses* through the construction of the hermetically sealed stream of existence in which the opposites are transformed into each other. He created the symbol of the closed world in which subjects are objects and objects a subjective activity; where things are what they are, and at the same time are their opposites. In brief: in describing his stream of existence he used the methods of speculation which mystics use in translating the experience of God into world-immanent language. By standards of mystical speculation, the construction is impeccable. It is probably the best world fetish ever constructed by a man who wanted to be God.

We must realize the full seriousness of this undertaking. The spectacle of a man who indulges in such demonic extravagances may be loathsome, but the loathsome and perhaps comic aspects of the performance make it no less socially dangerous. There are a good number of men who want to be gods. While Marx was quite justified in his pessimism with regard to the abilities of the average man for pulling himself up to divinity by his own boot straps, the average man is quite able to run after a self-created superman who promises to make him a superman, too, at low cost.

The effectiveness of the Marxian idea, however, does not rest in the strength and intellectual consistency of his antitheistic revolt alone. Marx has laid his finger on the sore spot of modern industrial society, on the cause of serious trouble (even if the trouble should not take the form of a general communist revolution), that is the growth of economic institutions into a power of such overwhelming influence on the life of every single man, that in the face of such power all talk about human freedom becomes futile. With socially irrelevant exceptions, in an industrialized society man is not the master of his economic existence. Marx has treated the problem under the title of "alienation" and we have quoted at length from his inexhaustible variations of the theme. His model case was the fate of the industrial worker, but it is a fate which is engulfing practically our whole society. How far the disease has advanced we know through the dire experience of the National Socialist revolution in which the carriers of the movement were not the industrial workers but the lower middle class—very much to the dismay of orthodox Marxists who believe that industrial workers have a monopoly on the misery of economic insecurity and of threatening unemployment, and consequently a monopoly on revolution.

Though Marx has erred with regard to the extent of the evil, he has not erred with regard to its nature. Marx is the only thinker of stature in the nineteenth century (and none has followed him) who attempted a philosophy of human labor as well as a critical analysis of the institutions of industrial society from his philosophical position. His main work, *Das Kapital*, is not an economic theory like that of Adam Smith, or Ricardo, or John Stuart Mill and one cannot dispose of it by showing the defects of the Marxian theories of value, of interest, of the accumulation of capital, etc., all of which are certainly defective. It is, as its subtitle states, a critique of political economy; it is an attempt to reveal the social myth that is contained in the concepts of economic theory, and to penetrate to the core of the matter, that is to the relation of man to nature and to a philosophy of this relation, that is of labor. That no economic theorist after Marx was sufficiently interested in the philosophical foundations of his science to explore this problem further, that no modern school of economic theory exists that would understand and develop the very important beginnings of Marx, casts a significant light on this whole branch of science.

The result of the Marxian attempt, as we have seen, is dubious. The idea of the "total individual" that will "appropriate" the working range of an industrial system into its "self-activity" like a Robinson Crusoe who does his chores, is empirically unrealizable; and the eschatological part of the solution, the change in the nature of man through the experience of the revolution that will make the feat possible, is a piece of derailed intramundane mysticism. Nevertheless, the diagnosis of the evil is on the whole sound. The industrial system in present society looks empirically like a human impasse, threatened by a communist revolution whenever the stop-gap remedy of buying off the revolution through "prosperity" and the "rising standard of living" should fail for any appreciable length of time. And what this communism most probably would look like Marx has described in his impressive characterization of "crude communism."

While "crude communism" in its most horrible form is an unmistakable ingredient in the social revolution spreading westward from Russia, and while we must consider it a possibility that it will generally mark the next phase in the decadence of Western society, this course is not an historical necessity. In his construction of history, Marx has conceived the development of economic forms as occurring in an abstract mankind with an appendix of ideologies. In fact, the development occurs in historical societies and the ideological appendix is nothing less than the spiritual life and the civilization of these societies. The formidable economic problem has a noneconomic setting, considered by

Marx as a *quantité négligeable*, and the existence of this noneconomic environment makes it impossible to predict what means may be found to alleviate the worst consequences of "alienation" and generally to grapple with the problems of industrialized society.

Let us, finally, consider the most interesting practical question that is raised by the antirationalism of the Marxian idea. We have seen that Marx can maintain his philosophizing on the level of spiritual revolt only by prohibiting unpleasant questions. What havoc the perversion of theory into pseudological speculation must work in the life of the intellect we could observe in the burlesque of Engels and the low comedy of the German, Revisionist Social Democrats. A climax of grotesque nonsense is Lenin's idea that the dialectics of history is concerned with transforming the Kantian *Ding an sich* into phenomena. When the Marxian idea becomes a public creed, obviously such dilettantism and downright stupidity can be protected against ridicule only by a radical prohibition of philosophy. What consequences a prohibition of philosophy will have for a society on the industrial level of production, which for its survival depends on strict standards of rationality in the sciences, only the future can show. Incidents which are reported from Russia, such as the Lysenko affair, seem to indicate that irrationalism to the degree of mountebankery has made inroads even in the natural sciences. Russian "philosophical" articles which have been published in American journals live up to our worst expectations. We cannot exclude it as a possibility that a society in which Marxism is enforced as the official creed will commit suicide through intellectual dishonesty.

Epilogue

The expansion of the will to power from the realm of phenomena to that of substance or the attempt to operate in the realm of substance pragmatically as if it were the realm of phenomena—that is the definition of magic. The interrelation of science and power and the consequent cancerous growth of the utilitarian segment of existence have injected a strong element of magic culture into modern civilization. The tendency to narrow the field of human experience to the area of reason, science and pragmatic action, the tendency to overvalue this area in relation to the *bios theoretikos* and the life of the spirit, the tendency to make it the exclusive preoccupation of man, the tendency to make it socially preponderant through economic pressure in the so-called free societies and through violence in totalitarian states—all these tendencies are part of a cultural process that is dominated by the idea of operating on the substance of man through the instrumentality of pragmatically planning will. The climax of this is the magic dream of creating the Superman, the man-made Being that will succeed the sorry creature of God's making. This is the great dream that first appeared imaginatively in the works of Condorcet, Comte, Marx and Nietzsche and later pragmatically in the Communist and National Socialist movements.

INDEX